# GARDENS AND HISTORIC PLANTS
## OF THE ANTEBELLUM SOUTH

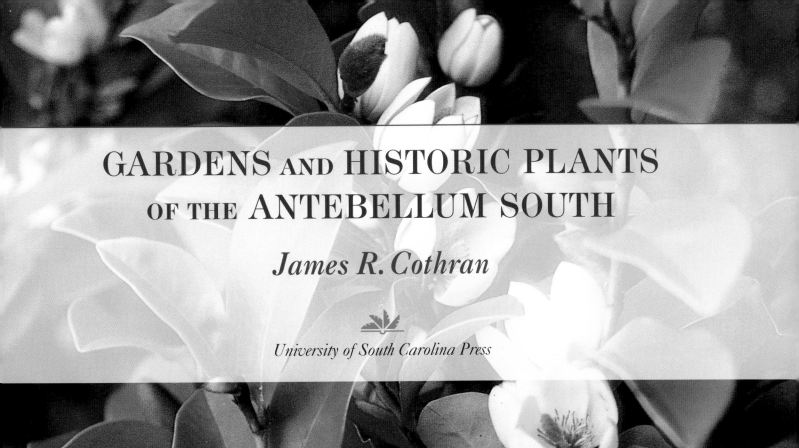

# GARDENS AND HISTORIC PLANTS
## OF THE ANTEBELLUM SOUTH

### *James R. Cothran*

*University of South Carolina Press*

Published in Columbia, South Carolina, by the
University of South Carolina Press

Manufactured in China

07 06 05 04 03  5 4 3 2 1

Library of Congress Cataloging-in-Publication Data

Cothran, James R., 1940–
    Gardens and historic plants of the antebellum South / James R. Cothran.
        p. cm.
    Includes bibliographical references (p.   ).
    ISBN 1-57003-501-6 (cloth : alk. paper)
    1. Gardens—Southern States—History. 2. Historic gardens—Southern States. 3. Plants,
Ornamental—Southern States—History. I. Title.
SB466.U6 C58 2003
712'.6'0975—dc21                                                                         2003000799

*To*
*Frances Walton Cothran*
*and*
*Mary Stafford Walton*

# ⇥ CONTENTS ⇤

LIST OF ILLUSTRATIONS  *ix*
PREFACE  *xiii*
ACKNOWLEDGMENTS  *xv*

## [1]
### HISTORICAL OVERVIEW  *1*
Agriculture  *2*
Planters and Plantations  *4*
Architecture  *6*
Gardens  *8*
The Civil War and Its Consequences  *10*

## [2]
### TRAVEL ACCOUNTS OF ANTEBELLUM GARDENS AND LANDSCAPES  *12*
South Carolina  *13*
Georgia  *20*
Alabama  *27*
Mississippi  *30*
Louisiana  *35*

## [3]
### FORMS AND FEATURES OF ANTEBELLUM GARDENS AND LANDSCAPES  *46*
Garden Design  *47*
Garden Plans  *52*
Avenues  *55*
Groves  *62*
Fences  *65*
Hedges  *69*
Lawns  *74*

## [4]
### ANTEBELLUM GARDENS  *81*
City Gardens  *82*
Town Gardens  *96*
Plantation Gardens  *112*

[5]

SUMMARY OF ANTEBELLUM GARDENS
AND LANDSCAPE TRADITIONS *122*


[6]

GARDEN BOOKS, AGRICULTURAL JOURNALS,
AND NURSERY CATALOGUES *126*

Garden Books *126*

Agricultural Journals *132*

Nursery Catalogues *133*


[7]

SOURCES OF GARDEN SEEDS AND ORNAMENTAL PLANTS
FOR SOUTHERN GARDENS BEFORE 1861 *135*


[8]

HISTORIC PLANTS OF THE ANTEBELLUM SOUTH
AND DATES OF INTRODUCTION *146*

Plant Profiles and Dates of Introduction *151*

Trees, Shrubs, and Vines Available to
Southern Gardeners before 1861 *266*

Flowers for the South *270*

Roses for Southern Gardens *273*


APPENDIXES

A. Biographical Sketches *285*

B. Historical Resources for Documenting the Past *293*

C. Composite List of Pre-1861 American Nursery Catalogues *297*

SELECTED BIBLIOGRAPHY *301*

INDEX *307*

ILLUSTRATION CREDITS *319*

# ILLUSTRATIONS

Cotton (*Gossypium vitifolium*) by George Ehret    *2*

The Rise of King Cotton    *4*

*Ile Copal* by Marie Adrien Persac    *5*

Melrose—Natchez, Mississippi    *7*

Kolb-Pou-Newton Place (1851)—Madison, Georgia    *8*

An Antebellum Garden    *9*

Huntsville, Alabama. As Seen from General Logan's Headquarters    *10*

View of Charleston: Drawing by M. Duraad-Brager    *14*

A Garden in Charleston    *15*

*Camellia japonica*    *17*

A View of Savannah    *21*

The Pride-of-India (*Melia azedarach*)    *22*

Monterey Square (1855)—Savannah, Georgia    *24*

Bull Street—Savannah, Georgia    *26*

View from the River (circa 1830)—Mobile, Alabama    *28*

Gathering Magnolia Blossoms in the South    *29*

Dunleith—Natchez, Mississippi    *31*

A Southern Garden    *33*

New Orleans from the Lower Cotton Press (1852) by J. Hill and B. Smith    *36*

*The Orange* by Antoine Risso    *38*

A New Orleans Courtyard    *40*

The Place d' Armes—New Orleans, Louisiana    *41*

Oak Alley Plantation—Vacherie, Louisiana    *43*

Greenwood Plantation Garden Plan—West Feliciana Parish, Louisiana    *44*

The Batersby-Hartridge Garden—Savannah, Georgia    *48*

*The Compleat English Gardner: or, A Sure Guide to Young Planters and Gardners*, Eleventh
    Edition, 1710    *49*

The Battle-Friedman Garden Plan—Tuscaloosa, Alabama    *51*

San Francisco—St. John's Parish, Louisiana    *53*

The Low House Garden—Savannah, Georgia    *54*

A Live Oak Avenue at Chelsea Plantation—Beaufort, South Carolina    *55*

An Avenue of Live Oaks Leading to Boone Hall Plantation—Mount Pleasant,
    South Carolina    *56–57*

The Eastern Red Cedar (*Juniperus virginiana*)    *58*

The Southern Magnolia (*Magnolia grandiflora*) by George Ehret    *60*

Faye-Webster Plantation—St. Mary's Parish, Louisiana    *61*

The Reynolds House—Camden, South Carolina    *62*

The Stevens Thomas Place—Athens, Georgia    *63*

The American Beech (*Fagus grandiflora*)    *64*

View of Christiansburg by Edward Beyer    *66*

Catalpa Plantation—Coweta County, Georgia    *66*

The Worm Fence   67
The Wallace House—Onslow County, North Carolina   68
View from a Garden Overlooking Augusta, Georgia   70
The Cherokee Rose (*Rosa laevigata*)   72
The Osage Orange (*Maclura pomifera*)   73
Montgomery Place—Located along the Hudson River near Tarrytown, New York   75
English Parks   76
Lawns   78
A Charleston Single House—Charleston, South Carolina   83
The Jenkins Mikell House—Charleston, South Carolina   84
A Parterre Garden—Charleston, South Carolina   85
Fountain in Forsyth Park—Savannah, Georgia   87
Plans of Parterre Gardens—Savannah, Georgia   88
The Richardson-Owens-Thomas House—Savannah, Georgia   89
The Green-Meldrin House—Savannah, Georgia   90
House and Garden Plan—New Orleans, Louisiana   91
Hermann-Grima House Site Plan and Courtyard—New Orleans, Louisiana   92
The Bosworth House—New Orleans, Louisiana   94
A Garden in the Lower Garden District—New Orleans, Louisiana   96
Boxwood—Madison, Georgia   97
The Hampton-Preston Garden Plan—Columbia, South Carolina   99
The Hampton-Preston Property   100
The Caldwell-Boylston Garden Plan—Columbia, South Carolina   101
A View of the Caldwell Garden   102
The Thomas Grant House—Athens, Georgia   103
The Thomas Grant House and Garden Plan   104
Sarah Coleman Ferrell   105
Plan of Ferrell Gardens—LaGrange, Georgia   106
Hills and Dales—LaGrange, Georgia   107
View of the Battle-Friedman House and Garden—Tuscaloosa, Alabama   108
Rosalie—Natchez, Mississippi   110
A View of Brown's Garden—Natchez, Mississippi   110
Garden Plans of Natchez Town Gardens—Natchez, Mississippi   111
A Plan of Crowfield Plantation—Located outside Charleston, South Carolina   112
Casulon Plantation, High Shoals, Georgia   114
Eden Hall—McCormick County, South Carolina   115
Eden Hall House and Garden Plan   116
Valley View—Bartow County, Georgia   117
Valley View House and Garden Plan   117
View of Rosedown Garden—St. Francisville, Louisiana   119
Rosedown House and Garden Plan   119
Evergreen Plantation—Edgar, Louisiana   120
Evergreen House and Garden Plan   121
*Myrtle Land* by Father Joseph M. Paret   123
Rosemary—Newnan, Georgia   125
*Ladies' Southern Florist* by Mary C. Rion   128
Andrew Jackson Downing   129

*Nouveau Jardinier de la Louisiane* by J. F. Lelievre   *130*

*American Cotton Planter*   *132*

Pomaria Nurseries of Pomaria, South Carolina, and Fruitland Nurseries of Augusta,
    Georgia   *134*

*Camellia japonica*, "Reine des Fleurs"   *137*

The Tea Plant (*Camellia sinensis*)   *138*

Bois de Fléche—St. Martins Parish, Louisiana   *140*

The Rose   *141*

Home of Thomas Affleck—Washington, Mississippi   *142*

Louis A. Berckmans, Robert Craig Berckmans, P. J. Berckmans Jr., and P. J.
    Berckmans Sr.   *144*

Oak Lawn—Thomasville, Georgia   *147*

Center Hall—Darlington County, South Carolina   *148*

*Azalea indica* from Flore Des Serres (1856)   *150*

Plant profiles   *153–264*

The Dahlia   *271*

*Viola odorata*—Fragrant violet   *273*

*Rosa Noisettiana* by Pierre-Joseph Redouté   *274*

The Rose   *277*

# ✦ PREFACE ✦

A HISTORICAL ACCOUNT of the antebellum South is largely and foremost a story that is intrinsically tied to the land—a story filled with agrarian traditions, rapid expansion westward into the southern frontier, and above all an accumulation of great wealth made possible by the lucrative production of cotton and sugar cane. The availability of fertile and productive land facilitated the emergence of a small but elite planter class that greatly influenced southern culture during the antebellum period in regard to social values, fashion, travel, architecture, and the decorative arts. Perhaps the least documented aspect of southern history during the antebellum period is that associated with gardens and ornamental plants. To discover and unravel the myths and mystique associated with gardens and landscape history of the antebellum South, one must look for clues and tantalizing bits of evidence contained in old diaries, letters, garden plans, maps, paintings, photographs, travel accounts, advertisements, garden books, and agricultural journals, as well as evidence found in extant gardens that have survived the ravages of time. While not everyone had an ornamental garden, there is substantial evidence documenting the fact that many fine gardens existed in towns, cities, and plantations during the antebellum period—all made possible by a flourishing economy, an abundant labor supply, a consuming interest in new and exotic plants, and a passionate love of the sights, sounds, and scents of the seasons that have historically tied southerners to the joys and pleasures of the land.

While the primary objective of the following text is to provide the reader with an overview of ornamental gardens and historic plants of the antebellum South, its secondary goal is to stimulate and encourage greater interest in southern garden history. Little has been compiled or written on ornamental gardening and historic plants in the South prior to 1860, and even less is known about the region's gardening and landscape practices following the Civil War. Many facets of southern garden history await research, documentation, and interpretation as a means of obtaining a greater understanding of our gardening past. Relevant topics include: the influence of itinerant European gardeners in the design and layout of southern gardens; the importance of gardens as an artistic expression of women in the nineteenth century; historic garden furnishings and features popular in southern gardens; the role and influence of slave gardeners; the importance of high-style gardens as a status symbol in antebellum society; the layout, planting, and management of kitchen/vegetable gardens; changing themes and garden styles following the Civil War; growth and development of the southern nursery trade; important and influential gardeners, horticulturists, and nurserymen in the annals of southern garden history prior to 1900. These, along with a myriad of other topics, offer unlimited opportunities for research associated with southern garden history.

# ⇥ ACKNOWLEDGMENTS ⇤

SINCERE APPRECIATION IS extended to the staff of the U.S. Department of Agriculture's National Agricultural Library in Beltsville, Maryland, whose vast collection of American nursery catalogues proved invaluable in my research on historic plants. In addition to its extensive collection of American nursery catalogues, the National Agricultural Library also contains a vast array of archival materials relating to America's agricultural and horticultural history. Other institutions from which information on American nursery catalogues and historic plants was obtained include the libraries of Longwood Gardens, Kenneth Square, Pennsylvania; the Horticultural Branch of the Smithsonian Institution Libraries, Washington, D.C.; the University of Delaware, Newark, Delaware; Cornell University, Ithaca, New York; the University of South Carolina, Columbia, South Carolina; Clemson University, Clemson, South Carolina; the University of Georgia, Athens, Georgia; and Tulane University, New Orleans, Louisiana.

I am also deeply indebted to the Cherokee Garden Library of the Atlanta History Center for the use of its comprehensive collection of historic books, pamphlets, journals, magazines, and ephemera relating to southern horticulture and garden history. Founded in 1976 by the Cherokee Garden Club, this outstanding facility includes the collections of Elisabeth Woodburn, Virginia Hand Callaway, Elizabeth Lawrence, Larry Gulley, and Henry Hicks. Special appreciation goes to Blanch Farley, who served as librarian of the Cherokee Garden Library during the time much of my research was conducted, and to Staci Catron Sullivan, Director of Collections.

Individuals who generously gave of their time and talents include the late Dr. Joseph Ewan of Tulane University, Fred Meyer of the National Arboretum, Clermont Lee and Mary Helen Ray of Savannah, Georgia, Robert Gamble of the Alabama Historical Commission, Sally Reeves of the Notarial Archives in New Orleans, Mary Miller of the Historic Natchez Foundation, Brad Lyon and JoAnn Fuccello of Elisabeth Woodburn Books, and George Stritikus of the Alabama Extension Service. Other contributions include those of Eunice Robertson, Dale Jaeger, Flora Ann Bynum, Judith Ho, Glenn Halton, William Welch, Gregg Grant, Susan Hitchcock, Lucy Lawliss, Bill Scaife, Kent Brinkley, Elizabeth Boggess, Amelia Salmon, Jan Hardy, Gordon Chappell, Ken Thomas, and Florence Griffin.

Special appreciation also goes to the staff of the following research facilities, organizations, agencies, and institutions who provided invaluable assistance: the Charleston Library Society, the South Carolina Historical Society, the Library of Congress, the Historic Charleston Foundation, the Arnold Arboretum, the Atlanta History Center, the Atlanta Public Library, and the Tuscaloosa County Preservation Society. Others include the Hunt Institute for Botanical Documentation, the Historic Natchez Foundation, the Historic New Orleans Collection, the Southeastern Architectural Archive—Tulane University Library, and the State Historic Preservation Offices of South Carolina, Georgia, Alabama, Mississippi, and Louisiana.

No account would be complete without recognizing several special individuals who assisted with the production of text, editing, and illustrations. Among these were Susan

Evans, Mary Ann Eaddy, Jennifer Evans, Diane Friend, Robby Bryant, and Chad Baker. Each made important contributions that were essential to the completion of this work.

Finally, there are others too numerous to name who played a supporting role in the research and production of *Gardens and Historic Plants of the Antebellum South*. Each is to be thanked for their assistance, encouragement, and support.

# GARDENS AND HISTORIC PLANTS
## OF THE ANTEBELLUM SOUTH

# [1]

# HISTORICAL OVERVIEW

**THE ANTEBELLUM SOUTH,** often referred to as the Old South, encompassed a period from 1820 to 1860, when "cotton was king" and the plantation system produced great wealth for southern planters. During these years, the American South was characterized as much by its people and culture as by the physical boundaries and geography that comprised the region. Many of the mores, social values, and traditions established in the southern colonies during the colonial period prevailed throughout the antebellum era, not only in the coastal and Piedmont regions but also in the newly developed agricultural lands that became the southern frontier. Given a conducive climate, long growing season, fertile soil, and traditional ties of its people to the land, it was inevitable that an abiding interest and love of horticulture and gardening would develop throughout the region.

As a means of establishing a general understanding of the various cultural, social, and economic issues that characterized the antebellum South, a brief historical perspective is provided. While in no way complete, this overview is intended as an encapsulation of some of the major factors and events that helped shape and define the region. The primary focus of the following discussion is directed at the lower and middle South (South Carolina, Georgia, Alabama, Mississippi, and Louisiana); however, much of the material presented is also applicable to the upper South as well. Even though variations existed in these regions with respect to climate, growing conditions, agricultural practices, development patterns, and cultural traditions, many of these characteristics were similar or in some instances the same.

## AGRICULTURE

Prior to 1800, an agricultural economy based on the production of rice, indigo, tobacco, and, to a lesser extent, cotton dominated the American South. Although rice remained a profitable cash crop through the eighteenth century, the growth of tobacco greatly diminished, and the cultivation of indigo was largely abandoned as a result of increased Asian competition and the loss of the British market following the Revolution. Cotton continued as a minor cash crop until 1793, when Eli Whitney, a Massachusetts native who had moved South to accept a tutoring position, developed the cotton gin. This simple but remarkable machine provided an efficient method for separating seed from the cotton fiber.

Prior to the invention of the cotton gin, less than 140,000 pounds of cotton were exported from American ports. Yet only two years later, this figure had increased to 1,600,000 pounds, with the majority of production occurring in the coastal regions of the Carolinas and Georgia. The cotton rush was on, and "a cotton kingdom" was in the making. Cotton became the most important agricultural crop of the South, fueled by the ever-increasing demand of foreign markets, where inventors had perfected machines that could spin and weave cotton fiber into cloth with amazing speed. Cotton proved ideally suited to the American South, with its long growing season, intense summer heat, moderate amount of moisture, and fertile soil.

No. 1. GOSSYPIUM VITIFOLIUM, *LAMK*.

Original MS. Sketch made by Ehret in 1766 : preserved in the Library, Botanical Department, British Museum.

Cotton (*Gossypium vitifolium*) by George Ehret. Approximately two months following the time cotton seeds are planted, white hibiscus-like flowers develop. As the blossoms mature, they turn pink, then over time develop into oval-shaped pods (known as bolls) from which seeds and fibers are produced.

The cultivation of cotton in the antebellum South favored production on a large, rather than a small scale due to several factors: the availability of slave labor, a steady European demand for cotton fiber, and an abundant supply of undeveloped land.

Not only did cotton production reinvigorate older regions of the coastal South, it also created opportunities for a new generation of planters who were willing to move westward into the undeveloped regions of the southern frontier. Steadily, over time, cotton production shifted from the Piedmont region of South Carolina and middle Georgia to the fertile fields and rich river valleys to the west, which were thrown open by the removal of Indian tribes (Creeks, Choctaws, and Chickasaws). This area extended to the Mississippi River and into the undeveloped territory made available by the Louisiana Purchase. Many of those who moved west into the southern frontier were descendants of Virginia and Carolina lowcountry families who had maintained strong English ties and customs throughout the colonial period. A passionate interest in and love of gardening and ornamental plants were traditions many planters carried with them as they moved into the newly developing regions of western Georgia, Alabama, Mississippi, and Louisiana.

Coincidentally, the production of another great staple crop emerged in the lower South almost simultaneously with the beginning of the widespread planting of cotton. For generations, French and Spanish settlers in Louisiana had sought a dependable cash crop that would thrive in the moist, coastal lands of the Gulf region and the lower Mississippi Valley. While Louisiana's early settlers had speculated on the success of growing sugar cane for years, it was not until 1790 that concerted efforts were undertaken to determine if it could be effectively grown on a sizeable scale. These attempts proved successful and sugar cane production greatly increased following the Louisiana Purchase in 1803. Wealthy southern planters flocked to the newly acquired territory with a determined desire to succeed. The growing of sugar cane was attempted in parts of coastal South Carolina, Georgia, northern Florida, and Texas, but it was in Louisiana where ultimately more than 90 percent of the nation's sugar cane would be grown. By 1850 there were over 1500 sugar plantations in Louisiana that had a thousand slaves or more. This was at a time when the state produced nearly a fourth of the world's sugar supply. Like cotton, sugar cane production reached epic proportions, producing immense wealth that spawned the development of large plantations along the lower Mississippi and beyond.

While the cultivation of cotton and sugar cane greatly overshadowed rice production, rice remained a lucrative cash crop in the coastal regions of South Carolina and Georgia until the Civil War. By 1861, more than three-fourths of the entire output of rice produced in the United States was grown in South Carolina, North Carolina, and Georgia. Of these, South Carolina proved the leader, not only in quantity of rice produced but in quality as well. Following the return of rice as a staple crop in South Carolina, its production was greatly increased through selective breeding, sound research, and improved agricultural practices. Over time Carolina planters replaced white rice with a newer, larger grained variety known as "golden seed."

The increased production of rice in the coastal areas surrounding Charleston, South Carolina, and Savannah, Georgia, during the antebellum period had a marked impact on the prosperity of the region. The revenues generated from its successful production allowed many planters to build fine town houses or refurbish older plantations of an earlier era. Planters (particularly those in the coastal regions of South Carolina) fashioned their homes and gardens in a manner that reflected an intelligent regard for culture, refinement, and taste. Rice remained the great money crop for lowcountry planters throughout the antebellum period, although revenues were often supplemented by the planting of cotton.

*Gardens and
Historic Plants of the
Antebellum South*

The antebellum South was predominantly a region composed of a large number of independent farmers, but the economic and social structure was dominated by a small and elite class known as planters—a group that exercised power and influence far in excess of their numbers. Planter status was based on the ownership of at least twenty slaves and 500 to 1000 acres of land (at least 200 of which had to be in cultivation). Within this privileged

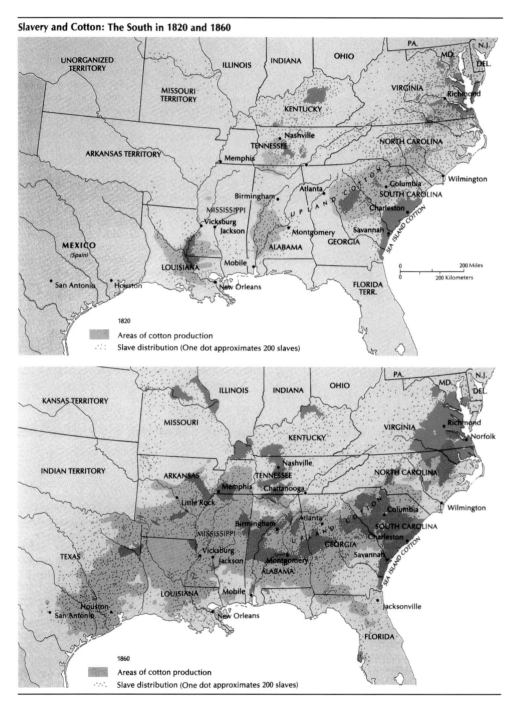

**Slavery and Cotton: The South in 1820 and 1860**

1820

     Areas of cotton production

     Slave distribution (One dot approximates 200 slaves)

1860

     Areas of cotton production

     Slave distribution (One dot approximates 200 slaves)

The Rise of King Cotton. The most important economic factors in the development of the antebellum South (1820–1860) were the dramatic growth in the production of cotton and the expansion of the plantation system into the undeveloped lands of the southern frontier. *From American History: A Survey* by R. N. Current, T. H. Williams, F. Freidel, and A. Brinkley, © 1987, Alfred A. Knopf. Printed with permission of The McGraw-Hill Companies.

*Ile Copal* by Marie Adrien Persac.

class there existed even a smaller echelon of so-called "large planters," which consisted of those owning 100 slaves or more. Census reports in 1860 indicate that while 43,000 met the planter classification, less than 2300 large planters were identified at that time.

Plantations developed by large planters exhibited many similarities in spatial organization and physical layout to the older colonial estates found along the eastern seaboard from Tidewater, Virginia, to the lowcountry of South Carolina. Many of the physical characteristics of these early estates were intrinsically tied to seventeenth and eighteenth-century English customs and traditions, traditions that included a large manor house and formal garden. This English manorial model, which was emulated by landed gentry during the colonial period, remained the ideal throughout the South during the antebellum era. Not only did this idealized image of an imposing house and garden extend into the Piedmont region of South Carolina and middle Georgia but was also carried into the southern frontier, as a new generation of planters ventured westward in search of the opportunity to gain immense wealth through the production of cotton and sugar cane.

In many respects a large plantation during the antebellum period functioned as a small village or self-contained enclave, consisting of a main dwelling (referred to not as a manor house but the "big house"), an ornamental garden, a grove of trees, a work yard, outbuildings, slave quarters, and fenced views of cultivated fields. (Within this spatial arrangement, house servants were customarily located close to the main house in order to facilitate the handling of a variety of household duties—cooking, washing, and food preparation—while quarters for field slaves were generally relegated behind or to the side of the work yard). Although this described layout was the ideal, in most instances it was never fully achieved—particularly in respect to a fine ornamental garden and a well-preserved grove of indigenous trees.

Emily Burke, a New England school teacher, provides the following account of the layout of a typical, large cotton plantation in *Reminiscences of Georgia in the 1840's:*

In the first place there is a paling [fence] enclosing all the buildings belonging to the family and all the house servants. In the center of this enclosure stood the principal house, then there was the kitchen, the store-house, corn-house, stable, hen-coop, the hound's kennel, the shed for the corn mill. All these were separate little buildings within the same enclosure. . . . Then, to increase the beauty of the scene, the whole establishment was completely shaded by ornamental trees, which grew at convenient distances among the buildings and towering far above them all. The quarters of the field servants formed another little cluster of dwellings at considerable distance from the master's residence, yet not beyond the sight of his watchful eye.

Another account by Frederick Law Olmsted in *The Cotton Kingdom* (1861) described the layout of a large Louisiana sugar plantation along the Mississippi River:

Fronting upon the river . . . was the mansion of the proprietor: an old Creole house, the lower story of brick and the second of wood, with a broad gallery, shaded by the extended roof, running all around it. . . . The gallery was supported by round brick columns, and arches. Between the house and the street was a yard, planted formally with orange trees and other evergreens. . . . In the rear of the house was another large yard, in which, irregularly placed, were houses for the family servants, a kitchen, stable, carriage-house, smoke-house, etc. Behind this rear yard there was a vegetable garden, of an acre or more, in the charge of a Negro gardener. . . . From the corner of the yard a road ran to the sugar works and Negro settlement, which were five or six hundred yards from the house.

As the cultivation of cotton and sugar cane varied in respect to processing and labor demands, variations often occurred in the physical layout of antebellum plantations in different regions of the South. Additional elements that also influenced the layout of plantations included climate, geography, cultural ties, architectural style, as well as regional differences in gardening and landscape traditions.

## ARCHITECTURE

Influenced by a desire for a fine house, wealthy southerners generally turned to the Greek revival style of architecture because of its purity and clarity of design and its association with democratic traditions and ideals. While the Greek revival style was not limited to the antebellum South, it was uniquely suited to the region at a time when the affluent class was eager to build fine homes that reflected both their wealth and political ideology. Several factors associated with the Greek revival style made it particularly popular in the South including an emphasis placed on the classics in a southern gentleman's education; support and endorsement of Greek independence and ideals; and the belief that the Greek temple was a metaphor of Grecian democracy. The monumental scale of the Greek revival style also allowed wealthy planters and others of financial means who lived in towns and cities throughout the American South to exhibit their success and to achieve social prestige.

Talbot Hamlin, author of *Greek Revival Architecture in America*, observed: "Never before or since, I believe, has there been a period when the general level of excellence was so high in American architecture, when the ideal was so constant, and its varying expression so harmonious, when the towns and villages, large and small, had in them so much unostentatious beauty and loveliness as during the forty years from 1820 to the

Civil War." It is interesting that the largest concentration of antebellum houses designed in the Greek revival style did not occur in the coastal regions of the South but in the newly developed lands of South Carolina, Georgia, Alabama, Mississippi, and Louisiana. This development pattern resulted because planters left the older regions of the South in search of new land for the production of cotton and sugar cane. Thus, pedimental temple-style houses of the Greek order are seldom found in Virginia or the coastal regions of the Carolinas and Georgia.

Because the professional study of architecture developed in America after 1865, individuals requiring a professional architect prior to this time had to turn to a European-trained practitioner or obtain the services of a craftsman-builder. As many southern planters were afforded leisure time to study building principles laid down in architectural pattern books, they often served as their own architects, working closely with craftsmen or with slaves trained as carpenters. As a result, many antebellum homes reflect variations in style because craftsmen and builders alike took liberties with the architectural details associated with the classical orders.

Houses designed in the Greek revival style with colonnaded porches, central hallways, high ceilings, and large windows were ideally suited to the hot, humid conditions of the southern climate—a condition visitors frequently spoke of when visiting the region. The following account appeared in *The Slave States of America* by James Silk Buckingham, an English traveler who toured America from 1837 to 1840: "We remained in Columbia

Melrose—Natchez, Mississippi. Built circa 1845, Melrose is a fine example of the Greek revival style.

[South Carolina] a week, during the whole of which the heat was intense. . . . During the hottest part of the day, the thermometer was from 98° to 99° in the shade, but the nights were even more oppressive." Not only did the Greek revival houses, with their verandahs, colonnades, and piazzas, help mitigate the heat of southern summers, but their designs also provided an architectural expression that supported and enhanced an elegant way of life that was inherent to southern society. As one authority observed, "The wide piazzas beneath the Greek porticoes were a distinct improvement on earlier Georgian houses, for they were admirably adopted for pleasant conversation and southern hospitality." In warm weather, porches and piazzas served as outdoor rooms, and during the hot summer months, doors and floor-to-ceiling windows were left open for ventilation, creating a strong relationship between the house and the surrounding garden or grounds. This interrelationship is noted in *Children of Pride* as described by Mary Jones of Montevideo, a Georgia sea-island rice and cotton plantation: "The doors and windows stand open now, and the bright sunshine peeps in, and the cool breezes, filled with perfume from the tea-scented olive and the sweet roses and flowers of the garden, came freely through the entry and halls." The Greek revival style also complemented the symmetrical gardens

Kolb-Pou-Newton Place (1851)—Madison, Georgia. While antebellum gardeners continued to rely on traditional European and native plants, by midcentury many newly introduced exotics were arriving from China and Japan.

and ordered landscapes, which prevailed throughout the antebellum period. Today, Greek revival homes remain an enduring symbol of the Old South much as the great manor houses of England and the Palladian villas of Italy continue to reflect the ideals and spirit of another age.

## GARDENS

During the colonial period, gardens of the southern colonies were of two distinct types—kitchen and pleasure gardens. Kitchen gardens were employed to produce a variety of fruits, vegetables, and herbs to satisfy dietary and medicinal needs, while pleasure gardens were created for the enjoyment of growing a variety of ornamentals. Commonly grown vegetables in kitchen gardens were cabbage, lettuce, carrots, squash, potatoes, and beans, while fruits included apples, pears, peaches, cherries, plums, quince, and figs. Traditional herbs for medicine and flavoring were basil, chives, fennel, rosemary, sage, tarragon, and thyme. The use of the word "garden" in eighteenth and early-nineteenth-century literature (books, journals, letters, diaries, etc.) generally referred to kitchen/vegetable gardens as opposed to pleasure or flower gardens.

Pleasure gardens of the colonial period, as a rule, consisted of parterres subdivided by paths of gravel or crushed oyster shells that divided the garden into equal parts. Their balanced, straightforward plans were simple versions of early seventeenth and eighteenth-century European designs. These patterned gardens were traditionally bordered in dwarf box, planted with flowers, bulbs and herbs, and enclosed by a picket fence or, in the case of coastal towns and cities, brick or tabby walls. Plants and flowers grown in colonial pleasure gardens were obtained either from Europe or collected from surrounding forests and fields. Traditional Old World favorites were marigold, hollyhock, larkspur, iris, calendula, daylily, pinks, pansy, and peony, along with daffodils, tulips, narcissus, jonquils, and hyacinths. Native plants selected for their fragrance, fruit, or flowers included the Carolina jessamine, fringe tree, American holly, sweet shrub, yaupon, trumpet vine, and the Cherokee rose.

In contrast to small parterre gardens of towns and cities, successful tobacco and rice planters of the colonial era often built fine homes and larger gardens along rivers or navigable streams, as evidenced by examples along the banks of the Potomac and James Rivers in the Tidewater region of Virginia and the Ashley and Cooper Rivers in the low-country of South Carolina. A distinctive feature that characterized many of these plantations was their accessibility from both water and land. When water was the primary access, an ornamental garden generally was located on the side of the house facing the river or navigable stream, while the land-side route often consisted of an axial drive lined with trees. Unlike the gardens in towns and cities, plantation gardens of the colonial period were larger and often included a variety of traditional European garden features such as formal avenues, bowling greens, terraces, and elaborate box-bordered parterres.

Plantation gardens, as a rule, were enclosed by fences to exclude livestock and restrict the encroachment of deer, which were prevalent throughout the region. Even though European styles influenced colonial town, city, and plantation gardens, they reflected a uniquely American character, resulting from the need to adapt to climate, terrain, vegetation, and local conditions.

With the successful development of cotton, sugar cane, and rice during the antebellum period, many southern planters accumulated vast wealth that allowed for the building of fine homes at an unprecedented scale. During the antebellum period, with few exceptions, southerners remained wedded to formality and the principles of geometric garden design that had prevailed throughout the colonial era. Not only did geometric elements fit within the context of a symmetrical house and garden plan, but formalized landscape features (avenues, parterres, and a structured plantation layout) reflected a control over nature and served as a means of conveying wealth, taste, and social prestige.

An Antebellum Garden. With few exceptions southerners remained wedded to formality and the principals of geometric design during the antebellum period.

With the increase of affluence during the antebellum period, interest in horticulture, gardens, and ornamental plants continued to expand. In response to these interests, trade for plants, bulbs, and seeds from European sources rapidly increased and a growing number of American nurseries began to emerge. While nurseries initially concentrated on providing fruit trees, by mid-century many were offering a wide selection of ornamentals from China and Japan. Mild winters and a long growing season (characteristic features of the lower and middle South) provided an ideal environment for many of the newly introduced Asian plants—camellias, tea olive, banana shrub, crape myrtle, wisteria, etc.—that were making their way into the American nursery trade.

## THE CIVIL WAR AND ITS CONSEQUENCES

By 1850 a growing number of regional differences had emerged between the North and South, the most important being over slavery and state rights. The North supported a free-labor economy, while the South held tenaciously to the use of slaves as a primary labor supply. Many southerners believed that the best course of action was to secede from the Union. Northerners on the other hand feared that if the South was allowed to leave the Union, the U.S. Constitution would be irreparably damaged and the democratic system of government would ultimately fail. In 1861, following continued differences and

Huntsville, Alabama. As Seen from General Logan's Headquarters. Union forces under General John Logan occupied Huntsville, Alabama, from December 1863 to April 1864. As depicted in the illustration, General Logan's headquarters was surrounded by a landscape containing fenced lots, large shade trees, clipped hedges, and a garden in a geometric design.

conflicts between the North and the South, South Carolina, Georgia, Alabama, Florida, Louisiana, Mississippi, and Texas seceded from the Union, setting in motion a series of events that resulted in the Civil War. Following four years of bloody conflict between the Union and Confederate armies, the North was resolved to initiate a military strategy that would bring the war to an end. To achieve this objective, Union troops initiated a twofold military campaign under General Grant and Meade in Virginia, and General Sherman in Tennessee and Georgia. Based on this strategy, Union forces set out to achieve the following objectives: secure Richmond and destroy General Lee's army; capture Wilmington and Charleston; complete the blockage of southern ports; and launch an aggressive campaign through Georgia and the Carolinas to deprive the Confederate army of needed supplies. General Grant moved aggressively to secure Richmond, while Sherman's army marched through the South creating a path of destruction and devastation.

After the fall of Atlanta and the capture of Savannah, Sherman moved northward into South Carolina, destroying virtually everything in his path. While the towns and villages of South Carolina were being sacked and burned, the rural districts of the state through which Federal troops passed were subjected to a similar fate, as described in the following account: "Upon arriving at *Woodlands*, a plantation owned by William Gilmore Simms (noted South Carolina poet, novelist, and author) Union soldiers purportedly burned the house, pilfered books and furnishings, and made away with the evergreens and rose bushes of the property's artistically arranged walks, flower-beds, and drives!" After reaching Columbia, the city was set on fire. Union soldiers openly looted houses as rapidly as they could enter them, just ahead of the fire. From the evening of February 17, 1865, until the following morning, the flaming city presented an appalling sight. One observer upon viewing the scene wrote, "All the business portion, the main streets, the old capital, two churches, and several public and private buildings were one pile of rubbish and bricks. Nothing remained but the tall specter-looking chimneys. The noble looking trees that shaded the streets, the flower gardens that graced them, were blasted and withered by fire." The route of the Union army from Columbia to the North Carolina line was marked with similar destruction. So effective was General Sherman's tactic of total war, carried out in concert with the combined military efforts of other Union forces throughout the South, that General Lee surrendered the once great Confederate army to Grant at Appomattox, Virginia, on April 9, 1865.

At the end of the Civil War, over 620,000 Union and Confederate troops and an estimated 50,000 southern civilians had died either in combat or from starvation or disease. In addition to the loss of human lives, the South was transformed from one of the richest regions of the country into an area of almost total ruin. Cities, towns, and villages throughout the South were damaged and destroyed, but more significantly the Civil War dashed the hopes and ideals of the southern states. A northern reporter upon visiting Charleston, South Carolina, shortly after the war described it as "a city of ruins, of devastation, of vacant houses, of widowed women, of rotting wharves, of deserted warehouses, of weed-filled gardens, of miles of grass-grown streets and acres of pitiful and voiceful barrenness." Many southerners found themselves in a state of poverty with little in the way of financial resources to rebuild their homes and gardens.

# [2]

# TRAVEL ACCOUNTS OF
# ANTEBELLUM GARDENS
# AND LANDSCAPES

BY THE MIDDLE of the nineteenth century numersous descriptive travel accounts, written by visitors who were fascinated with the region, documented life in the antebellum South. While most visitors followed well-defined coastal and river routes that included visits to Charleston, Savannah, Mobile, New Orleans, and Natchez, others with an intrepid taste for adventure often traveled inland by rail or stage to smaller towns and cities (Columbia, Augusta, Macon, and Montgomery). Not only did travel to these locations prove difficult, but personal accommodations were generally simple and austere. Visitors were assisted in planning their routes through the use of travel guides, such as one published in 1847 entitled *The Illustrated Hand-Book, a New Guide for Travelers Through the United States of America.* Travel guides provided descriptions of cities, towns, villages, watering places, and colleges, along with information on rail, stage, and steamboat routes, and fares.

Most travel accounts of the period were written by foreigners or northern journalists who had a keen eye for detail and sensitivity to the natural environment. Some of the more notable visitors included Fredrika Bremer (1801–1865), an influential Swedish novelist, social worker, humanitarian, and traveler; Joseph Holt Ingraham (1809–1860), a native of Portland, Maine, who moved South to teach at Jefferson College in Washington, Mississippi; Basil Hall (1788–1844), a retired British military officer who spent his retirement traveling in literary or scientific pursuits; Harriet Martineau (1802–1876), an English writer who toured the South in 1834, then visited other parts of the country before returning to England in 1836; James Silk Buckingham (1786–1855), a world traveler who wrote eight volumes describing his travels in the United States; and Frederick Law Olmsted (1822–1903), who became the father of American landscape architecture.

These individuals, along with others who visited the South during the antebellum period, frequently spoke of a verdant landscape of incredible beauty, resplendent with native flora that was unparalleled in other parts of the country—live oaks, magnolias, holly, beech, sycamore, red cedar, cypress, palms, and palmettos. Of particular interest are descriptions of urban and plantation gardens, extensive groves of indigenous trees, and Old World plants, along with newly introduced exotics from China and Japan, and a tradition of gardening and horticultural endeavors that reflected the spirit of the age. The following brief profiles and accompanying travel accounts offer descriptions and observations of selected cities, towns, and plantations of the antebellum South, providing insight into the nature of gardens, ornamental plants, and landscape scenes.

## SOUTH CAROLINA

South Carolina remained predominantly rural throughout the antebellum period. With the exception of Charleston, the state included only four cities in 1860 with a population of 1500 or more—Columbia, Georgetown, Camden, and Greenville. During this period, South Carolina could best be characterized not by its small towns and cities, but rather by a series of pleasant villages that consisted of a central courthouse, several churches, a school, and a cluster of modest homes. While Columbia prospered as the state capital and contained a respectable number of public buildings and imposing homes, it was Charleston that served as the center of commerce and culture during the antebellum era. Visitors were eager to visit this old port city, with its stately homes, handsome churches, public edifices, and walled gardens. Rice and long-staple cotton remained viable cash crops in the Carolina lowcountry throughout the first half of the nineteenth century, but it was the lucrative production of upland cotton in the Piedmont region, beginning in the 1820s, that brought the greatest prosperity to the state during the antebellum years.

### *Charleston*

**Travels Through North America, 1828**
    His Highness Bernard, Duke of Saxe-Weimar-Eisenach

ꝏ On entering the city, we seemed to be transported into a garden. Orange trees laden with ripe oranges, peach trees covered with blossoms, and flowering shrubs of a description which I had been accustomed to see only in hot houses, gave me impressions similar to those which I suppose you experience on visiting some of the cities

View of Charleston: Drawing by M. Duraad-Brager.

on the Mediterranean. . . . In the course of the morning we saw several other plantations in the neighborhood; on some of which were very handsome residences with grounds greatly resembling an English Park. The houses of the suburbs were, for the most part, surrounded by gardens, in which orange trees, with most splendid ripe fruit, monthly roses in full bloom, and a variety of other flourishing plants displayed themselves. . . . Upon the walls and columns ran creeping vines; we took notice of a great number of passion flowers.

### *Travels in North America,* vol. 3, 1829
Basil Hall

☞ Charleston is a very pretty-looking city, standing on a dead level, with the sea in front, and two noble rivers, the Ashley and Cooper, enclosing it on a wide peninsular called the Neck. This space is covered with the villas of the wealthy planters, many of which were almost hid in the rich foliage, which even at this early season [February 25] was in great beauty. In the streets, a row of trees is planted on each side, along the outer edge of the foot pavement, a fashion common to most of the southern towns of America. This tree is generally called the Pride of India, the botanical name being, I believe, Melia Azedarach. . . . What gives Charleston its peculiar character, however, is the verandah, or piazza, which embraces most of the houses on their southern side, and frequently, also, on those which face the east and west. These are not clumsily put on, but constructed in a light oriental style, extending from the ground to the very top, so that the rooms on each story enjoy the advantage of a shady, open walk. Except in the busy, commercial parts of the town, where building ground is too precious to be employed, the houses are surrounded by a garden, crowded with shrubs and flowers of all kinds, shaded by double and treble rows of orange trees; each establishment being generally encircled by hedges of a deep green, covered over with the most brilliant show imaginable of large white roses, fully as broad as my hand. The houses which stand in the midst of these luxurious pleasure grounds, are built of every form and size, generally painted white.

## *Illinois Magazine,* 1831
### Anonymous

↬ To a person that arrives in the city of Charleston on a moonlight evening of March or April, it seems that he has never seen or imagined so delicious a place. He will walk delighted through spacious streets, lined with the Pride of India; he will see the multiflora rose, with its clusters of a hundred flowers, clasping pillars and balconies; and he will breathe an air, perfumed with the blossoms of the orange and jessamine. He will see the dark green laurel shoot up its pyramidal form, covered with large glossy leaves, and studded with huge flowers of a delicate white; and he cannot fail to admire the slender palmetto, shaped like an enormous umbrella, with a straight shaft of sixty feet, and a cluster of hanging leaves at the top. The stranger will see in Charleston not only colonnades, piazzas, and domes, with other parts of good architecture, but he will find many trees and gardens, without which the best edifices lose half their proper effect.

## *Homes of the New World,* vol. 1, 1853
### Fredrika Bremer

Charleston, South Carolina, March 28, 1850

↬ Things have gone splendidly with me. I arrived this morning, after a voyage of three days and nights, expecting to have found here full summer, and somewhat annoyed,

A Garden in Charleston.

instead of that, to find the weather cold and gray, and to be obliged to go about in winter clothing. But it can not last long. The trees—for all the streets are planted with trees—are already clothed in tender green; roses, lilies, and orange-blossoms beckon from terraces and gardens, and the sun begins to break through the clouds. Probably, in the morning, it will be real summer again. . . .

I have been out wandering about the town for two good hours, pleased with my solitude, and by the great number of new objects which meet my eye everywhere; by the appearance of the town, with its numerous gardens (for it is like a great assemblage of country houses, each one with its veranda or piazza ornamented with foliage and flowers); by the many kinds of trees, all strange to me, and which are now in flower or in leaf (I only saw one without leaves, but with its stem and tops covered with pink blossoms); by the dark-green orange groves in the gardens, and which whisper and diffuse their fragrance on the breeze.

## Homes of the New World, vol. 1, 1853

Fredrika Bremer

Charleston, April 12, 1850

ॐ During these delicious days I have made some excursions into the country, round the city, with Mrs. H. and some kind acquaintances. In all directions, after we had plowed through an extent of deep sand—but they are now beginning everywhere to form wooden roads, which are very excellent to drive upon—we arrived at a forest. And the forest here is a sort of paradisaical wilderness, abounding with many kinds of trees and plants, which I have never before heard of or seen. Nothing is studied or trimmed, but everything grows in wild, luxuriant disorder: myrtles and fir trees, magnolias and cypresses, elms and oaks, and a great many foreign trees, the names of which I do not know. The most magnificent and the most abundant of all trees here is the live oak, an evergreen, an immense tree, from the branches of which depending masses of moss, often three or four yards in length (the *Tillandsia Umvides*), hung down in heavy draperies. These pendent gray masses upon the heavy branches produce the most unimaginably picturesque effect; and when these trees have been planted with any regularity, they form the most magnificent natural Gothic churches, with arcades, and lofty, vaulted aisles. Beneath these long-branched patriarchs of the forest flourish a number of lesser trees, shrubs, plants, and climbing vegetation, especially the wild vine, which fill the wood with perfume, and make a beautiful show in the hedges, and up aloft in the trees, whence they fling down their wild blossoming branches. Thus with the wild yellow jasmine, which was here and there yet in flower; thus with the white Cherokee rose, which also grows wild, and in the greatest abundance; thus with many other showy, creeping plants, which on all sides twine around the boles of the trees. . . . The magnolia is one of the most glorious of their trees, a tall, green-leaved laurel, the white blossoms of which are said to be the most beautiful flowers of the South; but it does, however, not begin to flower till the end of May.

The city itself is now in full bloom, for the city is like a great assemblage of villas standing in their gardens, which are now brilliant with roses of every kind. The fragrance of orange blossoms fills the air.

## The Soil of the South, 1853

Charles A. Peabody, Horticultural Editor

ॐ Gleanings of Horticultural Travel

In Charleston, we visited the Commercial Garden of Mr. Andrew Gray; he has a great variety of Camellias in the open ground, but from the moisture of the locality, many have died; this convinces us that they will flourish well in higher, drier regions. We saw in Mr. Gray's garden, a new yellow seedling rose of his own producing, which is the finest yellow rose we have ever seen, being a brighter yellow than the Cloth of Gold. We regret that Mr. Gray has no plants to spare this season. He will not be able to fill any orders until next season; as yet he has no name for this beauty [later to be named, Isabella Gray]. There are many beautiful private gardens in Charleston, which looked on Christmas day, as if they had put on their best holiday bloom, so dense was the bloom of sweet roses and magnificent Camellias.

### *From Cape Cod to Dixie and the Tropics,* 1864
J. Milton Mackie

〜 My first impressions of Charleston were extremely agreeable. . . . The whole town looks picturesquely dingy, and the greater number of buildings have assumed something of the appearance of European antiquity. The heavy brick walls and the high gateways are such as one sees in London and Paris. Many front doors and piazzas had

*Camellia japonica.* The noted French botanist André Michaux (1746–1802) introduced the camellia into Charleston circa 1787. By the middle of the nineteenth century, camellias had become a common feature in Charleston gardens.

been wrought after the graceful models brought from England in the old colonial period. The verandas, story above story, and generally looking toward the south, or the sea, form another pleasant feature in the prevailing style of building. Nor less attractive are the gardens and courtyards invariably attached to the best houses, where, in winter, the hedges are green with pittosporum and the dwarf orange; and where blow the first fragrant violets and daffodils of spring. Here, in February I beheld with delight the open rose, and camellias so numerous as to redden the ground they fell upon; also, the wild orange bursting with white buds, and the peach tree in full blossom, as well as the humble strawberry at its foot. . . .

These charming gardens, in connection with the piazzas resting on ornamental pillars, make the whole town graceful. One sits, in the morning, in these open chambers, inhaling the refreshing air from the sea, its perfume mingled with that of the flowers below; and, at midday, closing the Venetian shutters to exclude the sun, he rests in grateful shade. Here, too, throughout the longer portion of the year, may he spread, at evening, the tea table; while the heavens still glow with the purple and amber of the sunset. And here lingers the family until the bells from the tower of St. Michael's, sweetly ringing their silver chimes through the calm, starry air, announce, at last, the hour of repose. [Although the account was published in 1864, travel occurred prior to 1860.]

## Columbia

### The Western World; or, Travels in the United States in 1846–1847, 1850
Alexander Mackay

ᔕ Southern Travel and Travelers

Columbia, the seat of government in South Carolina, is situated on the banks of a river called the Congaree, a stream of petty dimensions in America, but one which would cut a very respectable figure in the geography of a European kingdom. . . . One would think that in selecting a site for their capital, fertility in the circumjacent region would be a *sine qua non* with any people. But not so with the Carolinians, who, in order to have it in as central a position as possible, have placed it in the midst of one of the most barren districts in the state. . . .

Notwithstanding all its disadvantages in point of position, Columbia is, on the whole, rather an interesting little town. There is about it an air of neatness and elegance, which betokens it to be the residence of a superior class of people—many of the planters whose estates are in the neighborhood making it a place of their abode; as well as the governor. . . . The streets, as in the majority of the southern towns of more recent origin, are long, straight and broad, and are lined, for the most part, with trees, prominent, amongst which are to be found the gay and flaunting "Pride of India."

### The Works of Daniel Webster, 1851
Daniel Webster

ᔕ The situation and the town are very beautiful. The College [South Carolina College] was established 40 or 50 years ago and is still flourishing; here is the seat of government, and here sit the principal courts. Great care was taken early to plant ornamental trees in the squares and along the streets, so that the town is now one of the handsomest and nicest looking of our little inland cities.

*Sumter Banner*

Reprinted *Columbia Banner*, Tuesday, May 24, 1853

〜 Columbia

A trip to the capital of the State last week has convinced us of the truth of the assertion, which we have often heard of late, viz: that Columbia was rapidly increasing in population, and business; everything about the town bears upon its face the mark of *progress*. . . . Columbia is at this season, certainly the garden spot of the South; the beautiful evergreens, which adorn and shade almost every street have put on the new and bright livery of spring, and the air is rich with the perfume of a thousand flowers; a dwelling without a garden, in this place, is hardly to be met with, and this passion for the beauties of nature must certainly be viewed as an evidence of the cultivated and refined taste of its inhabitants. Why Columbia has not been resorted to more during the summer months, we cannot imagine; it certainly presents all the advantages for such a retreat; health, air, scenery and polished society, what more can be desired.

## *The Horticulturist,* 1857

Jay Smith, Editor

Columbia, S.C.

〜 MR. EDITOR: I like this place surpassingly well. Columbia is certainly one of the most beautiful rural towns in the United States. The *Camellia, Pittosporum, Gardenias, Magnolias*, all the new *Pines, Firs, Spruces, Thuyas*, &c., are here perfectly hardy, and very common in nearly every garden in the place, and nearly every dwelling has attached to it from one to four acres of ground under the protectorate of accomplished gardeners. There is a *Magnolia grandiflora* here sixty feet high, with a top whose diameter exceeds seventy feet—a perfect colossus of arboricultural beauty. I saw a *Cryptomeria Japonica*, twenty feet in stature, and *Auracaria Imbrieata*, twenty-five feet high, a *Cedrus Deodarii*, thirty-two feet from the ground to its extreme apex. Roses are in great profusion, flouting their beautiful heads from miles of hedge, exulting in balconies and parapets, enshrining cottages, and making nature generally exceedingly gorgeous; in fact, it is just the place to locate a paradisaical garden. As soon as I can steal a little time from my present labors, I will send you a description of some of the beauties which make me love—or, as the poet sung:

"A wood coeval with himself he sees,

And loves his own *contemporary* trees."

I tried to purchase the *Horticulturist* here, but it wasn't to be had.

Yours, cordially,

C. Reagles

## *The Farmer and Planter,* 1861

R. M. Stokes, Editor

〜 Visits To Columbia Gardens . . . No. 1

Throughout the South, the city of Columbia has gained a high reputation in point of Horticulture. The interests in the products of the garden, manifested by the citizens generally, is well exhibited in the surroundings of their residences, remarkable to trees of unusual grandeur and beauty, so essential to the charm of landscape. The seat of Col. Preston is one of the most interesting in this neighborhood. The house is a large and respectable mansion of stone, surrounded by pleasure grounds of fine evergreens and deciduous trees. The most conspicuous ornament of the grounds, however is a magnificent specimen of the *Cedrus deadora* of large size, over thirty feet high, whose wide stretched branches give an air of dignity to the whole place. . . .

Among the deciduous trees, our attention was arrested by a fine specimen of that curious tree, the Japanese Ginkgo (*Salisburia adiantifolia*) twenty feet high; the *Paulownia imperialis*, forty feet high, and many others of great excellence. Many of the large old trees, are now venerable specimens, over eighty feet high, whose huge trunks and wide spreading branches are, in many cases, densely wreathed and draped with masses of English Ivy, forming the most picturesque sylvan objects so rarely met with. . . .

The grounds—a specimen of the ancient school—are laid out strictly in the geometrical style. All the symmetry, uniformity of the old school, introduced in Europe several centuries ago, are displayed here, in formal walks and small figures, mixed plantations, trellises, grottoes, artificial water, etc. The effect of this garden is striking, and its liberal proprietor, Col. Preston, by opening it freely to the public, no doubt, greatly increased the popular taste of the city.

W. R. Bergholz
Landscape Gardener and Rural Architect

# Georgia

By 1820 Georgia's population had grown to almost a quarter of a million people. Settlement continued along navigable rivers but also extended into the rich alluvial lands of the central interior and later into the southwest region of the state which was made available by the removal of the Creek Indians. The state's fertile agricultural lands, coupled with an improved system of roads, attracted newcomers from the South and North. While Savannah remained the primary center of trade and commerce during the antebellum period, numerous small and medium-sized cities and towns soon developed. Among these were Augusta, Athens, Madison, Milledgeville, Macon, Columbus, and Atlanta. Rice was a viable cash crop in coastal Georgia, but the phenomenal growth of the cotton industry dominated the state's economy. As cotton became king, a small elite planter class emerged, and by 1860, Georgia had the distinction of having more cotton plantations over 100 acres than any other state in the Union.

## *Savannah*

### Travels in the Old South, vol. 1, 1973

Eugene L. Schwab and Jacqueline Bull, Editors

Savannah, 1817

ॐ Savannah now exhibits an interesting and picturesque appearance to the northern visitor. Its streets are planted on both sides with a handsome tree, called the Pride of India; it is now in bloom, and emits a pleasing, odoriferous smell, and its foliage being very exuberant affords a convenient and agreeable shade in sultry weather— *Bay Street* is the principal street for business; it is parallel with the river, and being very wide, admits of a Mall in its center, which is now completely shaded from the rays of the sun by the approximation of the boughs of two rows of those umbrageous trees, which enclose a space convenient either as a promenade for walking, or an exchange for commercial transactions. Squares to the amount of 14 or 16 are judiciously interspersed through the town, relieving the monotony resulting from streets crossing each other at right angles, as those of this city do. Circular enclosures surround the centers of those squares, which together with the side walks, are planted with a number of similar ornamental trees.

A View of Savannah.

### *Travels in North America,* vol. 3, 1829
Basil Hall

↪ The showy town of Savannah, which stands at the height of about fifty feet above the river of the same name, on the very edge of the right or southern bank, is rendered particularly striking, when seen from the river, by several public buildings, either mingling pleasantly with the groves of trees planted in the streets, or standing boldly up against the sky above them.

    We were much surprised at Savannah, at the absence of verandas or piazzas, those useful and ornamental appendages, so general at Charleston and most other places in the south. In all the streets and squares of Savannah, most of which are very tastefully laid out, numerous rows of Pride-of-India trees have been planted, which serve to shade the walks, and give a tropical air to the scene. The grand mistake, however, as it appears to me, in all the towns of the southern part of the United States, is making the streets so wide, that little or no shade is afforded by the houses. They manage these things better in Italy and Spain; and the modern inhabitants of Georgia and Louisiana would have done well to imitate the founders of New Orleans, where the European plan has been followed, I think with great advantage.

### *The Gardeners Magazine,* 1832
John Claudius Loudon, Editor

Leicester, England, May 7, 1832

↪ *At Savannah,* I found the garden of Thomas Young, Esq., to surpass all others in the south. It is rich in the most choice and most expensive plants that can be obtained.

This most worthy gentleman spares no expense in obtaining every plant which will succeed in that climate; and, in a few years, his garden will surpass even his own most sanguine expectations. The genera Amaryllis, Pancrarium, and Crinum succeed admirably in the open air here; and Mr. Young has commissioned me to bring him from England as many of those delightful plants as I think proper. Mr. Young's garden is as numerously frequented as that of our great national Horticultural Society at Chiswick. As it respects gardening, he is a host within himself; his example is doing wonders. . . .

The Pride-of-India (*Melia azedarach*). The Pride-of-India, or chinaberry, was a popular street tree in towns and cities in the lower and middle South during the antebellum period.

Mr. Oemler of Savannah is a great amateur in gardening, and a most excellent botanist; the late Mr. Elliot of Charleston, the editor of the *Botany of South Carolina and Georgia*, frequently mentions the kind assistance of this gentleman; and also of two other gentlemen, Lewis le Conte, Esq., and his brother, Major le Conte, of the United States' army: than whom there are not two more scientific gentlemen in the United States of America. The assistance I received from these gentlemen, in making my collection of plants, I cannot give you the most distant idea of. They are most excellent botanists, and naturalists in every branch of science; and I hope to prevail on Major le Conte to become a contributor to your *Magazine of Natural History*. . . .

*The Garden of Lewis le Conte, Esq.*, near Riceborough, in Liberty County, Georgia, forty miles south of Savannah, is decidedly the richest in bulbs I have ever seen; and their luxuriance would astonish those who have only seen them in the confined state in which we are obliged to grow them in this country. M. Le Conte has discovered many new plants; and through his kindness I have been enabled to enrich our collections with some splendid treasures.

Alexander Gordon

### The South Atlantic States in 1833, as Seen by a New Englander, 1833

Henry Barnard

Its streets [Savannah] are planted so thick with the Pride of China that the small dark houses are hardly seen. The city is very regularly laid out, and open areas are planted with the above fragrant tree, and are quite frequent. The city could never be seen to better advantage than while I was there. The weather was not very warm . . . the gardens are filled with flowers, especially with a variety of roses . . . the Pride of China is in full bloom, which fills the air with the most delightful odor, especially at morning and evening when it is damp. . . . The splendid Magnolia, which flourishes in the low meadow lands, was occasionally putting forth its large white flowers.

## *The Rambler in North America,* 1835
Charles Joseph Latrobe

త Savannah is one of the most striking cities in the Union, regularly built on a high, sandy bluff, with a very regular ground-plan, and picturesque houses standing at intervals with rich gardens between. Its whole plan and arrangement fit it for the climate. The broad rectangular streets are lined with luxuriant Melia and Locust-trees, and there are frequent open squares with grass-plots.

## *Impressions of America,* 1836
Tyrone Power

త With this little city of Savannah I was exceedingly pleased. The weather was remarkably mild, the sun shone brightly; and I took much pleasure in wandering along the quiet sandy streets, flanked by double rows of the Pride-of-India tree.

Except the range of buildings immediately facing the river, the dwellings are nearly all detached; each surrounded by its own offices, many by a garden filled with orange and other evergreens: they are mostly built on the true Southern plan, of two stories, with a broad gallery running entirely round; being of wood and painted white, with bright green *jalousies,* they give to the streets a gay and lively look, which is exceedingly cheerful and attractive.

## *The Slave States of America,* 1842
James Silk Buckingham

త Savannah, the principal city and sea-port of Georgia, is agreeably and advantageously situated. The city is laid out with the greatest regularity, the streets running in parallel lines with the river from east to west, and these crossed by others at right angles running north and south. Philadelphia itself is not more perfect in its symmetry than Savannah; and the latter has this advantage over the former, that there are no less than eighteen large squares, with grass-plats and trees, in the very heart of the city, disposed at equal distances from each other in the greatest order; while every principal street is lined on each side with rows of trees, and some of the broader streets have also an avenue of trees running down their center. These trees are called by some, the Pride of India, and by others, the Pride of China; they give out a beautiful lilac flower in the spring. There are others also, as the live oak, and the wild cherry [*Prunus caroliniana*], both evergreens, and, when in full foliage, their aspect and their shade must be delightful. Even now, in February, when this is written, the prospect up and down every street in the city, intersected as it is by squares and rows of trees, is peculiarly pleasing, and gives the whole the most rural appearance imaginable.

Along the bank of the river, and on the edge of the bluff on which the city stands, is a long and broad street, having its front to the water, and built only on one side. The part nearest the water is planted with rows of trees, having seats placed between; and this street, which is called "The Bay," is the principal resort for business. The counting-houses, warehouses, and best shops, are along this Bay; the Exchange and Post Office, as well as the city offices, are here; and underneath the bluff, or cliff, are the warehouses and wharfs, alongside which the vessels load with cotton, while the tops of their masts are a little higher only than the level of the street, the height of the cliff from the water varying from forty to seventy feet.

Monterey Square (1855)—Savannah, Georgia. From a lithograph by J. Hill.

Every part of the town is level; and the general breadth of the streets varies from 80 to 150 feet. This ensures a thorough ventilation, from whatever quarter the wind may blow; and, with the fine shade of the trees around, makes it delightful to ride in; but the whole surface is sand, often as loose and deep as in the Deserts of Arabia, and, after dry weather for any length of time, it is as heavy to walk on as the loosest and on the sea-shore.

### *A Northern Army Officer in Antebellum Savannah: The 1849 Memoirs of Second Lieutenant John C. Tidball,* 2000
Eugene C. Tidball

April 20, 1849

෨ When I reached Savannah nature was in the springtime of loveliness. The beautiful crape myrtle bloomed in the yards of the wealthy while the lilac shed its fragrance around the abodes of the lowly. Roses, blooming and fresh, bordered the walks about the lawn, and from the wisteria twining itself over verandas hung clusters of flowers in reckless profusion. All nature was smiling with the freshness of spring and I thought to myself that I had landed in a haven of bliss.

### *Homes of the New World,* vol. 1 , 1853
Fredrika Bremer

Savannah, May 14, 1850

෨ Savannah is the most charming of cities, and reminds me of "the maiden in the green-wood." It is, even more than Charleston, an assemblage of villas which have come together for company. In each quarter is a green market-place, surrounded with magnificent, lofty trees; and in the center of each verdant market-place leaps up a living fountain, a spring of fresh water, gushing forth, shining in the sun, and keeping the green-sward moist and cool. Savannah might be called the city of the gushing springs; there cannot be, in the whole world, a more beautiful city than Savannah! . . .

There are many beautiful places in the neighborhood of Savannah, on the high banks of the river, and the number of beautiful trees and flowers is untold. It delighted me to hear Swedish family names in many of the appellations of these, and thus to recognize tokens of Linnaeus; as, for instance, I here found *Kudbeckia Lagerströmia,* a very pretty shrub with pale-red flowers, resembling *Tellandsia,* and many others. The kind ladies here—and I have become acquainted with some extraordinary women among them—drove me about in their carriages to see the places and forest parks in the neighborhood. Bonaventure is a natural park, and is one of the remarkable features of the place and the South. The splendid live-oaks, growing in groups and avenues, with their long hanging moss, form on all sides the most beautiful Gothic arcades, and when the evening sun casts his glowing beams through these deep, gloomy vistas, the most lovely effects are produced. The young artists of America ought to come here and study them.

A portion of this beautiful park is being converted into a burial-ground, and white marble grave-stones raise themselves below the hanging mosses of the live-oaks. This moss vegetation is now in blossom; the blossom is a small green button-like flower of the pentandria class, with a delicate scent. Other magnificent flowers of the South, the *Magnolia grandiflora,* the Cape jasmin, and many others, are now beginning to be generally in bloom, but the scent of these is strong, and too powerful for my taste.

## *Masonic Mirror and American Keystone,* 1853

Curtis B. Pyle

ᘐ Letters from the South, by Our Corresponding Editor

Savannah, Monday, March 28, 1853

Savannah is a city of trees and gardens. It reminds me of what William Penn wished that his beloved Philadelphia might be—"a green garden town." In the city here a large number of small squares are laid out, and these are planted with trees. In the outer portion of the town a large plot of ground, has been surrounded with iron railing, and set apart as a public park [Forsyth Park].

## *The Soil of the South,* 1853

Charles A. Peabody, Horticultural Editor

ᘐ Gleanings of Horticultural Travel

We were delighted with the floral beauties of Savannah and Charleston. The private gardens, though mostly small, are very beautiful. Here for the first time, we saw the *Camellia japonica* in all its glory, in the open air and ground. We visited the garden of Mrs. Marshall of Savannah, and saw a sight worth the pilgrimage over broken rail-roads and swimming stage roads—some twenty massive Camellias, from six to fourteen feet in height, covered with one dense mass of bloom. The plants looked uncommonly vigorous and healthy, as they stood in the open yard, of course the roots had plenty of room, and yet, we noted on one single bush more than two hundred blooms opened at one time. The cut flowers from that single plant, in one season in the New York market, would bring at least three hundred dollars. Mrs. Marshall's Camellias had been planted out in the open grounds twelve years. There were also many varieties of roses, in their fullest.

We experienced much pleasure in this visit and received much courtesy from this most excellent lady. She loaded us down with flowers, cutting here and there a Camellia, and then a Rose, until we could carry no more. May her spirit, like her flowers, ever repose in peace and beauty!

### *Journey in the Seaboard Slave States,* 1856
Frederick Law Olmsted

Savannah, which is but half a day's sail from Charleston, has . . . a curiously rural and modest aspect, for a place of its population and commerce. A very large proportion of the buildings stand detached from each other, and are surrounded by gardens, or courts, shaded by trees, or occupied by shrubbery. There are a great number of small public squares, and some of the streets are double, with rows of trees in the center.

Charleston and Savannah are so easily accessible from the North, and are, in consequence, so much visited, and so much written about, that there is no occasion for me to particularly describe them, or their vicinity. Both towns are chiefly interesting from that in them which is indescribable, and which strangers cannot be expected to fully appreciate.

### *From Cape Cod to Dixie and the Tropics,* 1864. (Travel occurred prior to 1860)
J. Milton Mackie

Savannah is a pretty town, half city, half village, and well deserves its graceful name. Beautiful shade trees have been planted in the streets, most of which are wide and straight, having originally been laid out, as it would appear, by line and compass. There are not crooked ones enough to give even a little variety to the monotonous right angles. Still, it is pleasant, in this early season of the year, when the leaves are new, and the heat of the approaching sun begins to assert its great power, to take one's promenade in checkered shade. For this exercise, the street of streets is Bull Street. Here reside many of the opulent families, and here walks all the fashion. . . .

At intervals, along the Corso, there are pretty green squares, likewise decorated with shade trees . . . continue your promenade to the end of Bull Street, and there you shall see the city park. It is an enclosure of a few acres, shaded by tall, resinous pines, which cast upon the green turf beneath them a pleasing shade. The place is laid out with much simplicity in paths, half sand, half shell, but you have permission, likewise to walk, or sit upon the grass and the wooden benches, and to admire the neat stone fountain, which, situated in the center of the grove, sends a few playful though feeble streams out of the horns of sundry Tritons and sea gods. It is a pretty work of art. . . . It brings pleasantly to the mind of the traveler the many beautiful fountains and gardens of the old countries.

Bull Street—Savannah, Georgia. Shaded by handsome street trees, Bull Street served as a prominent pedestrian promenade.

***The South Atlantic States in 1833, as Seen by A New Englander,*** 1918
Henry Barnard

⚘ Augusta is a very beautiful place—the great street of the city is the widest I have ever seen. . . . The streets of Augusta are planted with the China tree, which has a very bright green leaf. . . . Near the Arsenal which is three miles out of Augusta are the residences of the wealthy citizens. The houses are very small, about as large as the Wordsworth cottage, and are embowered in shrubbery and a small thick-leaved oak. I noticed several kinds of roses in thick blossom as well as various other flowers.

## *Macon*

***Masonic Mirror and American Keystone,*** **April 6–May 25, 1853**
Curtis B. Pyle

⚘ Letters from the South, by Our Corresponding Editor

Macon is a thriving town, and presents some points of attraction. . . . Outside the town are many very beautiful private residences, surrounded with gardens, now in the very luxuriance of their vernal bloom. I have nowhere seen a greater profusion of flowers than here. The cluster of residences a short distance from the town, known as Vinesville (now a part of the residential district of the city), is a collection of gardens, rich in floral wealth. While you are tormented with little April snaps of fair weather, just enough to make you think of spring, and then ending in a frost, here we are surrounded by roses and honey suckles, and a hundred of the sweet-scented blossoms.

# ALABAMA

In 1819 Alabama became the twenty-second state to join the Union. The port of Mobile was the state's largest city during the antebellum period and achieved its highest levels of prosperity between 1850 to 1860. Other cities and towns that developed on a more modest scale included Montgomery, Huntsville, Selma, Tuscaloosa, and Birmingham. The first real flush of cotton prosperity that took place in Alabama occurred in the agricultural region known as the Black Belt—an area of fertile land located between the northern and southern regions of the coastal plain. Cotton production also took place along the rich lands that lay along the Tombigbee, Alabama, Tennessee, and Chattahoochee Rivers. Many of the planters who moved westward into Alabama in search of wealth and prosperity came from the Carolinas and Virginia, bringing with them sizeable fortunes and English traditions that influenced their desire for a fine house and landscaped grounds.

## *Mobile*

***The Soil of the South,*** **1853**
Charles A. Peabody, Horticultural Editor

⚘ Gleanings of Horticultural Travel

Arrived at Mobile, and how shall we describe it?—*A city of Palaces filled with Princes*—a city of Gardens filled with Flowers. . . . In no city of the South has

View from the River (circa 1830)—Mobile, Alabama.

horticulture taken so strong a hold upon its people. The merchant, lawyer and Divine, take an interest in the development of horticulture; and in no part of the world do we believe exists a finer soil and climate for fruits, vegetables and flowers than Mobile and its environs. Here, we saw orange trees that last season produced eight thousand oranges, each, the same ground producing the apple, peach, plum, fig, grape, strawberry, and every vegetable known to culture, with all the gayest, wildest forms of flora in her most magnificent perfection. Verily, this is an Eden land, and the beauties of its soil and climate are shadowed forth in the hearts of its citizens.

We parted from many warm hearts in Mobile with regret, but duty called, and its mandates must be obeyed. We hope again to visit the fair city in May, and see her in her robes of beauty.

### *The Sunny South; or, The Southerner at Home,* 1860

Joseph Holt Ingraham, Editor

᠀ Letter LXVI

Mobile, Alabama, 1855

My Dear Mr. _____:

This lovely Southern metropolis has been our sojourn for a week past, and has presented so many attractions both to me and my husband, that, were we not desirous of being in New York early in June, we should yield to the solicitation of many kind friends and our own wishes, and enjoy its refined hospitality for some days longer.

The Mobileans are genuine Southerners by birth and feeling; that is, this city is not made up, like New Orleans of strangers, but mainly of those who are "to the manor born." It reminds me more of Charleston, South Carolina, in this respect; and gives, like that elegant city, a true representation of Southern manners. . . .

The environs of Mobile are charming. Some of the roads for a league west are lined with country houses adorned with parterres; and few houses are without the greatest variety of shade trees. Orange trees abound; but the live oak everywhere rears its majestic Alp of foliage, casting beneath shade broad enough to shelter from the sun a herd of cattle. This tree is always "a picture" in the scenery—a study for the artist. It combines the grandeur of the English oak with the grace of the American elm. There are superb groups of them in and about this city. They shade the lawns and give dignity to the mansions that lift their roofs above them.

The drives to Spring Hill and the Bay Road are the favorite avenues of the Mobileans. The former leads to a fine elevation, two leagues from the city, and commanding a view of it and of the beautiful bay. It is covered with the suburban retreats of the Mobile merchants, whose families generally retire here for the summer, if a northern tour does not tempt them. The Bay Road is a delightful drive for four miles, with the open bay on one side and villas and woodlands on the other.

I may write one more letter from this charming city, and then we proceed northward.

Kate

## *The Cotton Kingdom,* vol. 1, 1861

Frederick Law Olmsted

Gathering Magnolia Blossoms in the South. Courtesy of the Charleston Library Society, Charleston, South Carolina.

ꙅ Mobile, in its central, business part, is very compactly built. . . . Out of the busier quarter, there is a good deal of the appearance of a thriving New England village —almost all the dwelling-houses having plots of ground enclosed around them, planted with trees and shrubs. The finest trees are the magnolia and live oak; and the most valuable shrub is the Cherokee rose, which is much used for hedges and screens. It is evergreen, and its leaves are glossy and beautiful at all seasons, and in March it blooms profusely. There is an abundance, also, of the Cape Jessamine. It is as beautiful as a camellia; and, when in blossom, scents the whole air with a most delicate and delicious fragrance. At a market-garden, near the town which I visited, I found most of the best Northern and Belgian pears fruiting well, and apparently healthy, and well suited in climate, on quince-stocks. Figs are abundant, and bananas and oranges are said to be grown with some care, and slight winter protection.

*From Cape Cod to Dixie and the Tropics,* **1864. (Travel occurred prior to 1860)**

J. Milton Mackie

The most striking feature of the landscape seen on the road to Spring Hill [a residential suburb of Mobile], is its lofty and wide-spreading live oaks. They make a pleasant contrast with the pines, which stand thickly clustered together, and have tall, straight, tapering stems and crowns tufted with needles. In passing through the groves composed of these latter trees, so full of sap in this warm climate, one scents at a considerable distance the pleasantly aromatic perfume. . . . Accordingly, in passing along the road to Spring Hill, I came in sight of some pretty little villa, peeping out of its shrubbery, with rows of orange and lime trees, of mock orange and pittosporum, of crape myrtle and jessamines from Mexico. . . . Spring Hill is, of course, a hill—a slight natural elevation on these sandy shores and level plains of woods. From its summit, looking over an intervening distance of green tops of trees, one sees the city of Mobile; and, beyond, Lake Pontchartrain. Getting out of the carriage, he [the driver] strolls for a few minutes in the pleasant shade, and breathes the hilltop air, pure from all odors unless it be that of flowers. Returning through the little cluster of villages called Somerville, he again descends from his carriage; for who could pass these magnificent live oaks, these lofty pines, with bark of purple and foliage so deeply green, and these poplars growing as vigorously here as in their native Lombardy, without lingering to admire the luxuriant display of vegetation? He wishes also to inspect more closely the roses of the Cloth of Gold, and the white Lamarques. The Malmaison, too, is so delicately tinted, and its petals are so gracefully folded, that the lover of flowers is never tired of looking at it. How effulgently the Giant of Battles glows, spotting the surrounding green with crimson! Are here the Lady Banks climbs the China tree, adding its yellow to their blue. How sweetly sleeps the sunlight of the noon of these beds of flowers! Reposing on rose leaves; lying hid in the cups of the lilies; basking on the crimson carpet of the verbenas; poised on the out-spread calyxes of the pinks; and cradled in the large blossoms of the magnolias, which on the tops of the trees are gently swinging in the wind.

I could have spent the whole morning in these lanes and gardens; but, the morning being already gone, I returned to town.

## MISSISSIPPI

Mississippi was admitted to the Union as the twentieth state in 1817. By 1832, the remaining Indian tribes that had once inhabited the region had relinquished their rights to the territory, making possible the influx of settlers from the East who were searching for new land for the production of cotton. The most productive agricultural region extended from the southwest along a central band north to the Tennessee line. Another important section that was ideally suited for cotton production was the Tombigbee region, which included the towns of Columbus, Aberdeen, and Macon. The port of Natchez, with its strategic location along the mighty Mississippi became an important center of trade and commerce. By 1860, Natchez was inhabited by more millionaires than any other city of its size in the nation. This concentration of wealth sparked a building boom that included not only fine town houses but suburban villas sited in spacious landscaped parks.

### Three Years in North America, 1830

James Stuart

∽ Natchez ... is very beautifully situated on high grounds on the east side of the river, at the distance of about three-quarters of a mile from the shore, and is the largest town of the State of Mississippi, containing a population of 5000 or 6000 people. . . . One of the passengers, with whom I had got well acquainted, agreed to walk with me to the town, which is well laid out, containing many handsome houses, and which commands delightful views. Indeed, this is one of the most beautiful towns in the United States, but occasionally very unhealthy. The Pride of India tree, shading the streets, was in blossom, and the odour charming. The top of this tree is full of blossoms, having a greater resemblance to the lilac than to any other of the flowering shrubs.

Dunleith—Natchez, Mississippi. Dunleith represents one of numerous so-called "suburban villas" that were built in the environs outside Natchez during the antebellum period.

### Southern Sportsman, 1843

Thomas Bangs Thorpe

∽ Our Visit To Natchez

We were always encouraged to believe that Natchez and its vicinity possessed great natural and artificial beauties, but we had very little conception of the country; or the improvements it possessed until we made personal observation. The bold bluff on which reposes in so much quiet the most beautiful city of the South, is one of the most striking peculiarities that meets the eye of the traveler on the Mississippi. It rises up with singular and startling effect from among the low lands with which it is surrounded, and is exaggerated by the contrast. . . .

Everywhere the stranger is met with elegant and tasteful display. The mansions of the rich, hid with foliage, festooned and trimmed, and variegated, full of graveled walks and choice flowers, finds a fit companion in every little cottage, however poor, that has, too, its flowers and modest trees, and little vines; showing that the prevailing taste is elegant, and appreciates those ornaments that are Nature's most beautiful, and yet within the reach of the poor and the rich alike.

The country around Natchez is broken, and the soil, like all lands of the kind in the South, very rich, and covered with the finest forest trees. We have traveled through some of these beautiful specimens of Nature's handy-work, before the axe had made a single waste, and we were struck with the great beauty of the groves of trees which met our eye everywhere, and we could not help expecting the palace of some wealthy landholder would suddenly peep out among the trees of the distant landscape. Around Natchez, though one of the oldest settled countries in the Union, these beautiful natural groves have been spared, and every road leading from the city is lined with elegant mansions, the abodes of luxury and taste, hid partially from view by the rich magnolia and oak, the frowning gum and delicate beech. In the immediate vicinity of these mansions are all the delicate shrubbery and flowers that grow with such profusion in the South—a perfect fairy land; and yet, for want of time, what we saw was said to be the least remarkable of all the improvements in the vicinity of Natchez.

### *The Horticulturist,* 1858

Jay Smith, Editor

A Trip To Cuba and the Southern States

Natchez reached, our first visit was paid to the great plantation of Dr. Mercer, Laurel Hill. The road, of some ten miles, passes many fine plantations and excellent houses. . . . Here began to be visible the miles upon miles of hedges of the Cherokee Rose, which, we must say, is one of the most beautiful objects of the kind ever presented to the eye. It was in full bloom—the leaves of dazzling brilliancy, and the coming buds most vigorous and graceful. These hedges occupy the great breadth of ten feet, and fall about in regular festoons of exquisite beauty, which no description can bring vividly to the reader. What a pity this rose is not hardy north of the Carolinas!

But if the hedges were so magnificent, what was the Northern lover of trees to say to the evergreen magnolias, *M. grandiflora,* which soon became as common as our oaks in the forests? *Thousands* line the road in every coppice with their glorious dark foliage and of dimensions like our tulip-trees. This experience of hedges and magnolias alone compensated for all our fatigues. Sometimes the Cherokee Rose festooned the magnolia, a sight we hope never to forget. On entering Dr. Mercer's park and woods of four thousand five hundred acres, these trees became giants; intermixed with oaks, the contrast was lovely beyond our powers of description. Dr. M.'s house is . . . built to suit a Southern climate, and might be likened somewhat to a first class East India bungalow, enriched with every elegance. Built round a hollow square, and of one story, it presents an appearance of comfort such as one would select to repose in for a few centuries, if the lease of life were to be so extended. Its verandas and projecting shades exhibit on every side the finest old trees of evergreen magnolias, casting their dark green shadows on the lawns; these, and the fine oaks, record their planting by nature's hand long anterior to the occupation of the white man; they would be the pride of the oldest family in Christendom. Their enormous stems were covered with running vines, while the limbs of one magnolia we paced, extended in a circle of three hundred feet! As we drove through the park, an occasional *whirr* marked the rising of a wild turkey; so completely is the scene one of nature's own glorious formation, that we wished *all* our readers could enjoy it with us. The Bignonia capriolata here grows wild, and festoons itself from the highest limbs.

In the garden (ably controlled by the ladies of the mansion), the Camellia lives in the open air, and attains a height of fifteen feet. Pomegranates require no housing, but issue a succession of scarlet flowers and excellent fruit. But what shall we say of the roses? A white Lady Banks Rose we took the pains to measure; the stem, at three inches from the ground, is twenty-one inches in circumference, and it covers a circuit of ninety feet, running, and hanging *full* of bloom from every tree within its reach, to the height of thirty or more feet! Hedges of Pyrus japonica, Magnolia purpurea (eighteen feet high), Wax-trees (*Ligustrum lucidum*), Crape Myrtles (*Lagerstroemia*),

A Southern Garden. The above illustration from *Appleton's Journal* appears to fit the description of gardens located outside Natchez, Mississippi, as observed and documented by Frederick Law Olmsted in *The Cotton Kingdom* (1861): "The country is entirely occupied by houses and grounds of a villa character; the grounds usually paltry with miniature terraces, and trees and shrubs planted and trimmed with no regard to architectural or landscape considerations."

twenty-five feet in height, Coral plants, Pittisporums, and similar greenhouse pets with us, run riot in this delicious climate. The finest red roses mounted the pine-trees to the upper branches, forty feet from the ground. Moss roses, the Olea fragrans, white Tea roses (whose bloom measured eleven inches in circumference), peaches, pears, and so forth, were as numerous and superb as heart could wish. Grapes do not succeed very well.

Dr. Mercer possesses eight thousand acres here, less than one-half being a cotton plantation, occupying four hundred and seventy hands. When we say that we dined on asparagus and strawberries at this early date (April 3), we must leave the reader to imagine the rest.

### The Sunny South; or, The Southerner at Home, 1860

Joseph Holt Ingraham, Editor

 Letter XXXI

Suburbs of Natchez

Dear Mr. _____:

We have at length reached Natchez, and I write once more from a plantation, but one situated in Mississippi instead of Tennessee, and in the bosom of the most opulent and cultivated portion of the South. I have already spoken of the town of Natchez, which possesses all the charming features of a tropical city. Its streets lined with the Pride of China tree, now in full flower, its verandah-ornamented residences, with their wide, airy halls and piazzas; the sweet gardens that fill all the atmosphere, even in the business streets, with the perfume of flowers. . . . Then there are the handsome suburban villas embedded amid flower gardens, their white columns glancing here and there, from openings in the foliage of the umbrageous trees that shade them.

Many of the more wealthy cotton planters, whose estates lie on the river where it is unhealthy to reside, live in the vicinity of Natchez, in country houses, on which they lavish taste and expense without limit. There is, therefore, a beautiful wilderness of architectural and horticultural elegance around the city. The pleasant drives carry you winding among these tasteful homes now rolling over a graveled lawn-road, now traversing hedges enclosing gardens that contain nearly all the tropical plants; now catching sight of a summerhouse, now of statuary, and on all sides beauty.

It is in these homes, which extend a league or more around the town, that are to be found the families that have given to the society of Natchez so much celebrity. Here are to be found persons who have traveled abroad, and cultivated their tastes by European discipline. Their parlors are adorned with pictures from pencils of the first masters. Their halls are not deficient in fine statuary. Their private libraries are often large and well chosen. The furniture, equipages, and style of living are all in keeping.

The Southern ladies are all natural gardeners. The taste with which they lay out and arrange their parterres would delight and surprise a Northern eye. The garden of this house where we are now visiting, though by no means regarded as the finest in this vicinity, I will describe, and it will give you some idea of others here. But first let me describe our drive hither from town.

After we had driven half an hour amid the most luxuriant hedgerows, which extended miles further, we came to a white gateway, set in the hedge. It was the entrance to the estate. Passing through it, we rode a quarter of a mile beneath the majestic branches of a fine old forest, and then emerged into an open road, which was bounded on both sides by cotton fields. . . .

The villa, or "great house," was visible half a mile off, fairly embowered in an island of the deepest verdure, for an island it seemed, surrounded by the ploughed, brown fields of the plantation. As we advanced, we could catch sight of a column between the trees, then of a wing, and get a glimpse of the portico. At length, after two or three times losing sight of it as we would round the undulations of the fields, we emerged full in front of its handsome arched gateway. The enclosure was many acres, entirely shut in by a hedge that was spangled with snow white flowers. A slave opened the gate for our carriage. We drove through, and found ourselves within a horticultural paradise. The softest lawns, the loveliest groups of trees of the richest leaf, the prettiest walks, the brightest little lakes, with swans upon their bosoms, the most romantic vistas, met our enraptured gaze. Through this lovely place we drove over a smooth avenue, at one time almost in complete darkness from the overarching limbs interlaced above; at another rolling in sunlight upon the open sward.

At length we drew near the mansion, which was an Italian villa of the purest style, elevated so as to be ascended by a broad flight of steps. There were immense vases, three feet tall, standing in front, just where the eye of taste would have them, containing West Indian plants, with gorgeous leaves, and flowering splendidly, the names of which I do not know. The color of the edifice was a shade under the lemon tint, which relieved finely the foliage about it. In the center were broad folding doors, which were thrown open, and presented a prospect, through a noble central hall with a polished oak floor, of the garden in the rear of the house. Standing in the door of this hall, we could command the main avenue of the garden, which descended in a succession of terraces to a small lake glittering at the extremity. This lake lay in deep seclusion beneath a grove of overhanging oaks and sycamores, of magnolia trees, elms, and orange trees. The south piazza commanded the whole garden, which was a labyrinth of beauty and floral magnificence. Upon descending into the garden, one passed through an avenue of tropical plants, many of which I had never seen, nor could have believed they ever existed, their loveliness and grandeur were so novel and extraordinary. In some of the flowers it seemed as if "the Angel of flowers" had tried to see how beautiful a thing it could make. Such exquisite forms and colors! Ah me! How beautiful, thought I, as I gazed on them, must things in Heaven be, if things, their shadows on earth, are so lovely! . . .

Yours,

Katharine Conyngham [*sic*]

## LOUISIANA

The United States purchased Louisiana from France in 1803, and nine years later became the eighteenth state to enter the union. New Orleans served as the first capital until it was moved to Baton Rouge in 1850. The Mississippi River was the primary inland waterway of the region, and by 1846 nearly 1200 steamboats traveled up and down this mighty river, transporting goods and passengers on a regular basis. By 1830, New Orleans had become one of the fastest growing cities in America, shortly thereafter, becoming the second busiest port in the nation. Both cotton and sugar cane production fueled the state's economy during the antebellum period. Thousands of new settlers arrived in Louisiana each year, many gaining tremendous wealth, which lead to the construction of fine homes and ornamental gardens. Many large plantations including the Hermitage, Oak Alley, St. Louis, Mulberry Grove, Evergreen, Ashland, Whitney, and Houmas House were located along the Mississippi River between New Orleans and Baton Rouge, on the historic route known as the River Road. Additional large plantations that were developed during the antebellum period were located in Feliciana Parish and the fertile lands of the Red and Cane River valleys.

## *New Orleans*

### *Retrospect of Western Travel,* 1838
Harriet Martineau

꙳ We were taken to the Battle-ground [the Battle of New Orleans, 1814] the native soil of General Jackson's political growth. Seeing the Battle-ground was all very well; but my delight was in the drive to it, with the Mississippi on the right hand, and on the left gardens of roses which bewildered the imagination. I really believed at the time that I saw more roses that morning than during the whole course of my life before. Gardens are so rare in America, from want of leisure and deficiency of labor, that, when they do occur, they are a precious luxury to the traveler, especially when they

New Orleans from the Lower Cotton Press (1852) by J. Hill and B. Smith.

are in their spring beauty. In the neighborhood of Mobile, my relative, who has a true English love of gardening, had introduced the practice; and I there saw villas and cottages surrounded with a luxuriant growth of Cherokee roses, honeysuckles, and myrtles, while groves of orange-trees appeared in the background; but not even these equaled what I saw, this warm 4th of May, on our way to the Battle-ground. One villa, built by an Englishman, was obstinately inappropriate to the scene and climate; red brick, without a gallery, or even eaves or porch; the mere sight of it was scorching. All the rest were an entertainment to the eye as they stood, white and cool, amid their flowering magnolias, and their blossoming alleys, hedges, and thickets of roses. In returning, we alighted at one of these delicious retreats, and wandered about, losing each other among the thorns, the ceringas, and the wilderness of shrubs. We met in a grotto, under the summer-house, cool with a greenish light, and veiled at its entrance with a tracery of creepers. There we lingered, amid singing or silent dreaming. There seemed to be too little that was real about the place for ordinary voices to be heard speaking about ordinary things.

### The Magazine of Horticulture, 1846
C. M. Hovey, Editor

꙾ I send you the following brief account of a few plants I saw on my arrival, the fifth of November, in bloom, in the garden of Charles L. Bell, Esq., . . . in the vicinity of New Orleans. . . . I think it may possibly prove interesting to a number of your northern readers.

I found the weather, at my arrival, very warm and perfectly delightful—a beautiful Italian sky, and almost no wind. Mr. Bell's garden presented to me very much the appearance of a vast conservatory, studded with West Indian plants, growing in the greatest profusion. Great numbers of tree-like oleanders, eugenias, jasmines, pomegranates, and myrtles, with their dark, somber foliage, gave a stateliness and grandeur to the scenery, while their blossoms spread a delicious fragrance around, and their branches afford shelter to the mocking-bird. The contrast of these dark evergreens with beds of bright and dazzling flowers beneath, proved to my northern eyes pleasing and unique in the extreme.

The following I noticed in flower: *Tecoma capensis*, some large specimens, covered with their gorgeous flowers and growing most luxuriantly; Mr. Bell informed me, they had proved hardy the last two winters. *Datura arborea*, covered with its fragrant flowers, is quite hardy here; *Hibiscus rosa sinensis*, all the varieties made a splendid show, and stood out the last two winters. I cannot help remarking here, that it is a great pity, this splendid flowering, half hardy Chinese shrub, so easily propagated and procured by every florist, is not more extensively cultivated in the gardens of the north. From my own experience I can assert, that, treated perfectly hardy, planted out in Spring, in an open border, and taken up and sheltered in the fall, in a cold pit or cellar, it will flower abundantly during the Summer. *Jasminum revolutum, sambac fl. pl., grandiflorum and multiflorum*, covered with its large, fragrant white blossoms, is a particularly fine object here during November and December. . . . *Lantana odorata purpurea*, large specimens, covered with flowers, made a pretty, showy appearance; *Plumbago capensis, Zeylanica rosea*, very luxuriantly covered with blossoms. A beautiful shaped and large *Metrosideros (Kallistemon) lanceolata* in full bloom; it proved so hardy, that by early and unprecedented hard frost in December, even the flowers were not injured. *Poinciana pulcherrima*, raised in fall from seed flowers the first Summer here; *Jatropha multifida* (tender). *Erythrina crista-galli* forms a large tree here, as in its native country, and flowers three or four times a season; *Pittosporum tobira* is perfectly hardy and splendid evergreen here; *Cerbera Thevetia* covered with seed pods. *Nerium coronarium*, with its dark foliage, and white fragrant blossoms, is a beautiful plant here. Double and single pomegranates.

Mr. Bell has a large and splendid specimen of *Melaleuca alba*, which has proved for several winters a perfectly hardy evergreen with him. *Thunbergia alata*, covered with bloom. *Vinca rosea* and *alba*, very large seeding freely. *Gomphrena globosa* grows to a great size, seeds itself, and the new seedlings flowering the same summer. A handsome variety of Chinese chrysanthemums, made a most lively display. This is the country for the chrysanthemums to show their beauty to perfect advantage. Roses of all kinds, Noisette, tea, bourbon, etc. grow and flower here in great perfection. Mr. Bell showed me a very showy, yellow flowering shrub, which he raised from seeds received from Mexico. It has attained a height of eight feet and branches well off, forming handsome sized shrubs. Mr. Bell calls it *Bignonia fraxnifolia;* it formed plenty of seed pods, but the seeds did not ripen. Mr. Bell has potted several large plants and sheltered them in a room this season, with a view of forwarding their blossoming and ripening the seed. If Mr. Bell succeeds, he will be enabled to disseminate this valuable plant to the extent it deserves. The flowers are of the size and shape of *Gloxinia formosa*, but of a bright yellow color. I have not doubt it will prove in the North a half-hardy shrub, similar to *Hibiscus sinensis*. I never saw this plant before, but it may perhaps be known to you. The *Mespilus japonica* grown here in some situations to a magnificent tree, producing bushels of fine fruit.

J. W. Paulsen

C. M. Hovey, Editor

Baton Rouge, Louisiana, May 8, 1849

ꝕ DEAR SIR,—A long period has elapsed since I raised my pen to address you. Since then, I have traversed many a dreary waste, and many fertile regions, having twice, during the interim, extended my researches to the Rocky Mountains, California, Oregon, and New Mexico, on botanical pursuits; but, now having a leisure hour, I shall occupy the time in making a few Remarks on Gardening and Gardening Productions in the state of Louisiana.

ORANGER FRANC

*Arancio Silvatico dolce.*

Tab. 5.

*The Orange* by Antoine Risso. Oranges along with lemons and limes were frequently grown in the gardens and sheltered courtyards of New Orleans.

Gardening, in this section of the Union, differs widely, in many respects, from the system practiced in the North and middle States; this semi-tropical climate affording numerous advantages unattainable in a more northern clime. During the month of February, I visited a vast number of gardens in New Orleans—its vicinity, and for 130 miles up the Mississippi. Even at that unfavorable season, from the mildness of the winter, I found a tolerable display of Flora's beauties, the gardens, as it were, conjuring up a spring-like appearance in the gloomy season of winter. The various plants, &c. in bloom were, to me, equally astonishing as gratifying. Many varieties of the rose were displaying their gaudy flowers, and exhaling their fragrance in profusion. Many exotics, planted in the open ground, were then blooming freely, and most of them had been so during the previous season from the months of April and May. My attention was particularly arrested by a magnificent Crìnum amábile. I had never seen this rich gem, under the most fostering care, present such a splendid appearance. Most of the following were blooming vigorously:—Heliotrope, Plumbàgo, Petunia, Russéll*ia*, *Cé*strum, Achània, Justic*ia*, Verbèna, Manétt*ia*, Brugmáns*ia*, Hibiscus (Chinese sp.,) Strelitz*ia*, &c. &c. In many gardens the camellia was flowering to admiration, and, in favorable situations, several Chinese azaleas were truly magnificent. Many other species might be mentioned, did time and space permit; but the above will convey some idea of a Louisiana *winter's* vegetation.

You are well aware the ornamental department of gardening is my more particular province, and here I find a rich and varied field. 'Tis most astonishing to witness with what luxuriance every variety of the rose grows, and, in many instances, without the least attention or care. Here the Noisettes and Tea roses develop their magnificent flowers in full perfection. The carnation, pink, and picotee succeed well; Gardenias and Lagerstroemias are perfect pictures in their season. The dahlia thrives to admiration. Oleanders, Night and Day scented jesamines, (Cestrums,) Alloysia, citriodòra, Erythrinas, Plumbagos, and Clerodendrons are all planted in the open ground. In severe winters, they may be killed down, but they again shoot vigorously in the spring, and grow and flower most luxuriantly. Pittosporum, Olea fragrans, and the Chinese magnolias, attain a size which is most astonishing; but neither tulip nor hyacinth succeed well, although I am inclined to attribute the failure more to the soil, (which could be obviated,) than to the climate, as I have seen the latter in great perfection one degree south of Savannah, State of Georgia. . . .

There are some very extensive gardens in this state; that of Mr. Valcouraam, in the Parish of St. James, about 60 to 70 miles above New Orleans, would bear a comparison with any garden in the United States. If we take into consideration its extent, the vast and varied collection of plants, trees, and shrubs, its hothouses and ornamental buildings, I am inclined to think it is unsurpassed, if equaled, by any in the Union. It was intended, as I have understood, to make this a transcript of an English pleasure ground, but I must confess, in that respect, the designer has been by no means successful. This leads me to remark, in general, the French style in the ornamental department of gardening is that most frequently adopted, particularly among the Creole portion of the population, and there are some very unique and judiciously arranged gardens laid out and kept according to that system, which, however much it may be repudiated by some, possesses a fascination under peculiar circumstances. For instance, within a few minutes walk from where I now write, I could find magnificent groves of magnolias (now in full bloom,) with an abundance of choice trees and shrubs. All that would be required to form the scene into a perfect *fac simile* of an English shrubbery would be to introduce walks, and judiciously thin out and regulate the mass. To those, therefore, who have such scenes daily under their view, a perfect contrast—something displaying the art and ingenuity of man—has a far greater tendency to arrest the attention, and call into requisition the approbation of the community; but I would by no means be understood as advocating the adoption of straight lines and clipped shrubs in a general way. The parks, groves, and squares, formed by Le Notre, the father of that system, can never, in my estimation, bear a comparison with the scenic beauties formed by the principles advocated and practiced by Kent, Price, Knight, and Repton.

Alexander Gordon

## *The Horticulturist*, 1851
Andrew Jackson Downing, Editor

✒ Random Notes on Southern Horticulture

New Orleans, March 20, 1851

I was taking a stroll the other morning among the old fashioned gardens of New Orleans, which are just beginning to be inviting, after the gloomy and cheerless winter, when it occurred to me that a few random notes on the subject of what does or does not, grow in this region, might be acceptable to your columns. I plucked a Chromatella rose, such in size and color as would make your heart glow to look on, and sauntered home to fulfill my intention. . . .

There are many families in New Orleans, highly respectable, who make a handsome support from the products of their gardens, principally flowers, which here are always in demand, particularly when the city is filled with strangers, as is usual for about two-thirds of the year. But their flowers are usually of the most ordinary kind, and that require but little labor or care in the cultivation, such as roses, acacias, violets, and camellias. . . . There are many quaint, smug little gardens and delicious retreats, scattered here and there, through the city and suburbs.

Sylvanus

### De Bow's Review, 1853

James D. B. De Bow, Editor

᠅ Editorial Miscellany

We lately had the pleasure of visiting the garden and grounds of Mr. Lawrence, in the lower part of the city of New Orleans. This gentlemen gives great attention to the culture of the best and rarest varieties of fruits, flowers, vines, vegetables,

A New Orleans Courtyard. Service courts in the older section of New Orleans evolved into today's so-called courtyards. Plants used in courtyards traditionally were selected for their fragrance, color, and ability to thrive in cool, shaded spaces.

&c., and is prepared to execute orders for the same. Among the fruits, we noted cherries, plums, currants, gages, raspberries, gooseberries, nectarines, apricots, peaches, oranges, lemons, quinces, figs, pears, bananas, apples, pineapple, mangoes, guavas, &c. His greenhouse is supplied with rare exotics, and upwards of 10,000 rose-trees are set out in the garden. We saw beautiful strawberries in January. Among grape vines, we noted the Black Hamburg, the Chasselas de Fontainbleau, the Muscat, Spanish and Sweet Wate &c.

### Letters from the United States, Cuba, and Canada, 1856

Amelia M. Murray

᠅ All of the houses here, except some in the old town [Vieux Carré] and center streets, have gardens—not very extensive . . . but the soil and climate are such that everything grows luxuriantly. Magnolias, jessamines, roses, oranges, lemons, loquats, and a hundred other things beautiful and good; and then the mocking birds and butterflies, and the pretty little chameleons!

## The Horticulturist, 1858

Jay Smith, Editor

❧ A Trip to Cuba and the Southern States

New Orleans reached, we took an early stroll through its level streets, and were again interested to see the trees in full leaf and bloom before the advent of April. The sour-orange trees were loaded with golden fruit as in Cuba; the roses were magnificent, climbing to the tops of the houses; the Locust and the Pride of India, favorite street trees, the latter especially, were in full beauty. At the shops a few strawberries without much flavor had made their appearance, and we were delighted to see at this early date at the fruit stores a ripe yellow fruit of the medlar family, here called the Mespilus Plum [*Eriobotrya japonica*], which blossoms in December, and is now sought for here with greater avidity than any fruit planted at the north. It is oblong, with small seeds said to contain much prussic acid, and possesses an agreeable acidity.

The Place d' Armes—New Orleans, Louisiana.

## The Sunny South; or, The Southerner at Home, 1860

Joseph Holt Ingraham, Editor

❧ As we approached the city [New Orleans] through a level landscape, level as a lake, we flew past now a garden on this side, now a Spanish-looking little villa on that, the gardens richly foliaged with lemons and banana trees, and far over-stretching verandahs shut in by curtains to keep out the sun from the piazzas. Such gardens and villas one after another in great numbers we passed for a mile or so, when the houses grew numerous, the gardens narrower and narrower, and shops and small tenements were crowding together, where once had stood the orange, lemon, and banana tree. Side-walks of brick, as we darted forward, now took the place of green way-side paths by walks and fences, and stone pavements were substituted for natural dirt roads.

## From Cape Cod to Dixie and the Tropics, 1864. (Travel occurred prior to 1860)

J. Milton Mackie

❧ But to escape this clatter, you can take a drive to the southern part of the city, which is made beautiful by flowers. It is the garden of the town [the Garden District]. Here every house is built in an enclosure well filled with ornamental shrubs and trees, which, during the spring season, are fresh with green leaves and fair with blossoms. From the live oak hung with moss, to the blue violet which scents the air, all the forms of vegetation are full of sap and vigor. The flowering trees are of many colors—white, blue, yellow, purple, crimson. The roses grow on tall stems, or climb to the roofs of the houses. The walls and trellises are covered with the blushes of the most lovely flowers; or they are straw-colored; or they peep out of the green leaves in spotted white, and in the midst of them stands the solemn, graceful cypress, making strong contrast with oleanders and pitosporums. How gracefully the locust hangs out its tassels in the air; the orange trees glow with the yellow of our sweet maples in autumn; the Chinese viburnums are only less fair in their dress of green and white; while the mocking birds in cages mock the wild birds which sing to their young in the tall laurel trees.

## River Plantations along the Mississippi
## New Orleans to Baton Rouge

**The South-West, vol. 1, 1835**

Joseph Holt Ingraham

During the afternoon, we passed successively many sugar plantations, in the highest state of cultivation. Owing to the elevation of the levee, and the low situation of the lands, we could see from the deck only the upper story of the planter's residences upon the shore; but from the main top, we had an uninterrupted view of every plantation which we passed. As they very much resemble each other in their general features, a description of one of them will be with a little variation applicable to all. Fortunately for me, a slight accident to our machinery, which delayed us fifteen or twenty minutes, in front of one of the finest plantations below New Orleans, enabled me to put into practice a short system of *espionage* upon the premises, from the main top, with my spy-glass, that introduced me into the very *sanctum* of the enchanting ornamental gardens, which the palace-like edifice was half-embowered.

The house was quadrangular, with a high steep Dutch roof, immensely large, and two stories in height; the basement or lower story being constructed of brick, with a massive colonnade of the same materials on all sides of the building. This basement was raised to a level with the summit of the levee, and formed the ground-work or basis of the edifice, which was built of wood, painted white, with venetian blinds, and latticed verandas, supported by slender and graceful pillars, running around every side of the dwelling. . . . At each extremity of the piazza was a broad and spacious flight of steps, descending into the garden which enclosed the dwelling on every side.

Situated about two hundred yards back from the river, the approach to it was by a lofty massive gateway which entered upon a wide graveled walk, bordered by dark foliaged orange trees, loaded with their golden fruit. Pomegranate, fig, and lemon trees, shrubs, plants and exotics of every clime and variety, were dispersed in profusion over this charming *parterre*. Double palisades of lemon and orange trees surrounding the spot, forming one of the loveliest and most elegant rural retirements, that imagination could create or romantic ambition desire. . . . By the time I had completed my observations . . . the engineer had arranged the machinery, and we were again in motion, passing rapidly by rich gardens, spacious avenues, tasteful villas, and extensive fields of cane, bending to the light breeze with the wavy motion of the sea.

Once more I am floating upon the "Father of rivers," New Orleans, with its crowd of "mingled nations," is seen indistinctly in the distance. We are now doubling a noble bend in the river, which will soon hide the city from our sight; but scenes of rural enchantment are opening before us as we advance, which will amply and delightfully repay us for its absence. . . . The banks are lined and ornamented with elegant mansions, displaying, in their richly adorned grounds, the wealth and taste of their possessors, while the river, now moving onward like a golden flood, reflecting

Oak Alley Plantation. Located along the Mississippi River in Vacherie, Louisiana, Oak Valley Plantation is well known for its imposing avenue of live oak trees.

the mellow rays of the setting sun, is full of life. . . . A glimpse through the trees now and then, as we move rapidly past the numerous villas detects the piazzas, filled with the young, beautiful, and aged of the family, enjoying the rich beauty of the evening, and the objects upon which my own eyes rest with admiration. . . .

These plantations have been, for a long period, under cultivation for the production of sugar crops. As the early possessor of large tracts, they portioned off parallelograms to each; which, to combine the advantages of exportation and wood, extended from the river to the flooded forest in the rear. . . . Other plantations retain their original dimensions, crowned, on the borders of the river, with noble mansions, embowered in the ever-green foliage of the dark-leaved orange and lemon trees.

### *The South-West,* vol. 1, 1835

Joseph Holt Ingraham

ᘓ A gentleman to whom I brought a letter of introduction called yesterday—a strange thing for men so honoured to do—and invited me to ride with him to his plantation, a few miles from the city [New Orleans]. . . . An hour's drive, after clearing the suburbs, past a succession of isolated villas, encircled by slender columns and airy galleries, and surrounded by richly foliaged gardens, whose fences were bursting with the luxuriance which they could scarcely confine, brought us in front of a charming residence situated at the head of a broad graveled avenue, bordered by lemon and orange trees, forming in the heat of summer by arching naturally overhead, a cool and shady promenade. . . .

Around the semi-circular flight of steps, ascending to the piazza of the dwelling —the columns of which were festooned with the golden jasmine and luxuriant

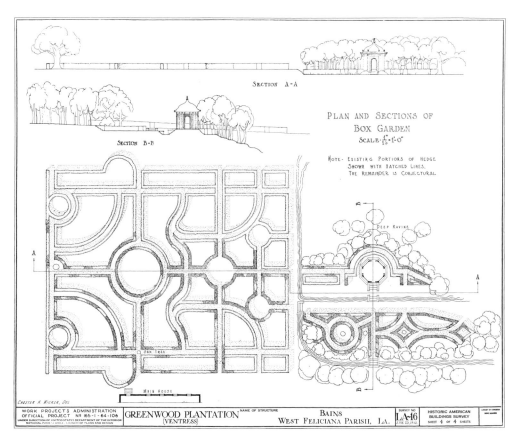

Greenwood Plantation Garden Plan—West Feliciana Parish, Louisiana. The garden includes a formal parterre, a lower terrace garden connected by a series of steps, and a fanciful summer house or folly. This garden is one of only several documented as part of the early efforts of the Historic American Building Survey (HABS).

multiflora—stood, in large green vases, a variety of flowers, among which I observed the tiny flowerets of the diamond myrtle, sparkling like crystals of snow, scattered upon rich green leaves—the dark foliaged Arabian jasmine silvered with its opulently-leaved flowers redolent of the sweetest perfume—and the rose-geranium, breathing gales of fragrance upon the air. . . .

Passing from this scene through the airy hall of the dwelling, which opened from piazza to piazza through the house, to the front gallery, whose light columns were wreathed with the delicately leaved Cape-jasmine, rambling woodbine, and honey-suckle, a lovelier and more agreeable scene met my eye. I stood almost embowered in the foliage of exotics and native plants, which stood upon the gallery in handsome vases of marble and China-ware. The main avenue opened a vista to the river through a paradise of althea, orange, lemon, and olive trees, and groves and lawns extended on both sides of this lovely spot,

"Where Flora's brightest broidery shone,"

terminating at the villas of adjoining plantations. . . . As I was under the necessity of returning to the city, I took leave of the young family of my polite host.

### *Adventures in the Wilds of the United States,* vol. 2, 1856
Charles Lanman

That portion of the Mississippi valley lying between New Orleans and Baton Rouge is altogether the *sweetest* section of country in the United States, since it is here that the sugar-cane attains its greatest perfection and the largest quantity of sugar is made. Both sides of the Great river are lined with extensive plantations. . . . All the residences that you see are pleasant and picturesque, and many of them have a stately bearing; the gardens which surround them, bloom almost perpetually with hedges of rose and hawthorn and with groves of the lemon and orange. . . . About all the sugar plantations there is a rural charm which never fails to interest the stranger; and though the levees which line the banks of the Mississippi for more than a hundred miles are indispensable as well as curious, the amount of ditching which has to be performed on some of the plantations is astonishing. Many of the estates are enormous, and I have heard of one which contained a thousand acres of land and had netted for its proprietor, in one year, the respectable sum of one hundred and fifty thousand dollars. . . . All through the winter the Cherokee rose sports itself luxuriantly on every plantation, and upon green lawns children play with their toys and throw the ball— in continuous fields you see the cattle grazing, and droves of horses kicking up their heels.

### *From Cape Cod to Dixie and the Tropics,* 1864. (Travel occurred prior to 1860)
J. Milton Mackie

This plantation is one of the largest on the Mississippi. It lies lower, indeed, than the river, as do the others all the way to New Orleans; the water being kept in its channel by an embankment ten or more feet in height. The whole estate, extending three or four miles back from the river, is well-nigh as level as a house floor. . . . During our visit, there occurred a succession of beautiful days, beautiful as pearls upon the string. The sunrise, so praised by the poets, we here found to be no fable; and all that had been said by this fibbing class of writers respecting the beauty of the early dewdrops, nestled in rose petals pendent from honeysuckles, cradled in the hollows of leaves, and flashing like gems from every spear of grass and blade of clover, we discovered to be simple verity. . . . What calmness of joy to walk in these paths where the myrtle blooms, and the sweet-scented violet! The wild olive, also, is fragrant and so is the banana shrub, bearing corollas chocolate-colored. Here, on the lawns, is a perfect harmony of flowers of every hue; and here, besides, grow great numbers of strange, semi-tropical plants, and trees which love the sun. At the same time, the ear is captivated with a chorus of mocking birds, and other sweet-throated songsters; for the birds all fly to these gardens, taking delight, apparently, in this beauty of foliage and flower, and made also more cheerful themselves from the addition they bring to the happiness of man. Such mornings are like nosegays, which never fade, and live forever in the memory.

# [3]

# FORMS AND FEATURES
# OF ANTEBELLUM GARDENS
# AND LANDSCAPES

ANTEBELLUM GARDENS AND grounds, like earlier colonial examples, were characterized by a variety of physical forms and features (avenues, groves, parterres, lawns, hedges, fences, etc.), which were based on standards and traditions found in Italian, French, and English gardens of the seventeenth and eighteenth centuries. When employed in gardens and landscapes during the antebellum period, many of these elements were modified and altered in response to a variety of local and regional conditions including climate, terrain, economics, fashion, taste, and cultural traditions. For example, parterres in antebellum gardens were smaller in size and simpler in design than their European counterparts; avenues of live oaks and cedars, typical of southern plantations, were neither as long nor as grand as those of the great estates of Europe, and unlike the carefully planted ornamental groves in the English landscape, those of the antebellum South generally consisted of existing stands of indigenous trees—poplars, oaks, magnolias, hickories, beeches, cedars, catalpas, maples, and pines.

Other common features of gardens and landscapes were an assortment of fences and hedges. Fences were used to enclose ornamental gardens, screen work yards, protect crops and orchards, confine livestock, and delineate property boundaries. Fences were generally decorative or utilitarian in nature depending on their use, location, or need. Like fences, hedges were also employed for a variety of purposes. Commonly used hedge plants selected for decorative uses included common box (*Buxus sempervirens*), cherry laurel (*Prunus caroliniana*), privet (*Ligustrum vulgare*), and yaupon holly (*Ilex vomitoria*). Popular hedge plants employed to meet utilitarian needs included the Cherokee rose (*Rosa laevigata*) and the Osage orange (*Maclura pomifera*). Each was used either to create impenetrable barriers to protect agricultural lands or to serve as livestock enclosures.

Another landscape feature of the antebellum period, employed on a limited scale, was the use of lawns. While in no way comparable to the expansive lawns of England or the manicured turf of contemporary times, these early so-called "lawns" of the southern landscape generally consisted of native or pasture grasses or in some instances rough stands of turf comprised of mixtures of clover, herd, bluegrass, Italian rye, and other imported grasses. Because of intense summer heat and extended periods of drought, lawns in the South were generally confined to areas beneath groves of trees and to areas adjacent to the house and garden.

## GARDEN DESIGN

The age-old practice of creating gardens in decorative geometric patterns using box and low-growing herbs as edging material is a gardening tradition that dates back to ancient times. Initially conceived by the Greeks and Romans, this ancient practice spread to northern Europe during the Middle Ages. By the seventeenth century, the French had refined and perfected the design of geometric gardens, which came to be known as parterres. The term parterre has a dual derivation, the Latin verb partire, "to divide," and the French word parterre meaning "on the ground." As a general rule, parterres were laid out in intricate patterns on flat or level ground and were best viewed and enjoyed from an elevated position, such as a raised terrace, a portico, or upper-story window.

Two of the earliest books on parterres were French publications: *Le Jardinier Solitaire* (1704) by Francois Gentil and *Le Jardinier Fleuriste et Historiographe* (1704) by Louis Liger. Both were translated into English in 1706 and combined into a single volume entitled *The Retired Gard'ner.* Three years later, A. J. Dezallier d'Argenville, a French engraver and writer on art, published *La Théorie et la Pratique du Jardinage.* This comprehensive work included a chapter on the design of parterres, accompanied by illustrations on a variety of prototypical designs. John James translated Dezallier's treatise into English in 1712 under the title *The Theory and Practice of Gardening.* According to this authoritative source, parterres were divided into four distinct types: parterres of embroidery, parterres of compartment, parterres after the English manner, and cutwork parterres—the oldest form of parterres. Cutwork parterres are based on a variety of geometric patterns, incorporating box-bordered planting beds separated by sand or gravel paths.

The French style of garden design (featuring the extensive use of parterres) remained popular in Europe through the early part of the eighteenth century, at which time the English naturalistic style of gardening began to emerge. Even with the introduction of this new style of gardening, many English landowners continued to adhere to the traditions of formal design, for unlike architecture and the decorative arts, gardens

The Batersby-Hartridge Garden—Savannah, Georgia. The Batersby-Hartridge Garden is one of the oldest cutwork parterres in Savannah. Characterized by geometric patterns, box-bordered planting beds, and sand or gravel paths, cutwork parterres proved popular in the antebellum South.

often required fifty years or more to evolve into an entirely new style. Parterre gardens proved popular in colonial America, particularly in the southern colonies where strong ties with England prevailed. Of the four types of parterres, cutwork parterres were most often employed in southern gardens. Their geometric patterns, reliance on box to define their design, and the use of sand or gravel paths proved the most practical for the southern climate. Southern gardeners, no doubt, felt comfortable with the rigid formality of cutwork parterres and their implied expression of control over nature. As the southern landscape abounded in natural and irregular forms, the use of straight lines and geometric shapes in the design of formal landscapes and gardens established a mark of distinction, implying a sense of wealth and a refinement of taste.

Parterres remained a central feature in southern landscapes during the antebellum period when spatial organization extended beyond the house to the garden, outbuildings, work yard, and surrounding fields. A typical house and garden plan of the antebellum period reflected a highly structured arrangement that created an overall sense of organization and formality. Parterres also were well suited to the conservative nature of southern planters and their resistance to change. In an address delivered at the Central Agricultural Society of Georgia in 1851, the Right Reverend Stephen Elliott Jr., Episcopal bishop of Georgia, educator, and agricultural advocate spoke of the independent nature of southern planters: "Living separate and apart, each upon his own estate, the planter is an independent power; he is lord of all he surveys, and he frames his own conduct upon the basis of this individual sovereignty. . . . It is very difficult to move such a being out of the routine of old practices and traditional modes of action . . . and to engage him in any new-fangled scheme for the improvement of his homestead or his grounds."

The question is frequently raised as to who was responsible for the design and layout of gardens in the South during the antebellum period. While some were designed by cultured and educated southern gentry who relied on English and French garden books or personal knowledge of garden design gained through European travel, others were designed by itinerant garden designers who came from England, France, Scotland, Ireland, and other European countries to practice their trade. Many of these individuals had an intuitive sense of design. Others were trained under the tutelage of recognized garden designers. Upon arriving in America, these itinerant designers quickly adapted their skills to local conditions and demands. The designs of many antebellum gardens can be credited to the talents of these dedicated practitioners, who traveled about the South offering their services to discerning property owners in cities, towns, and rural areas. Evidence of itinerant designers advertising their services appears in newspapers, periodicals, and agricultural journals of the period. The following notices reflect the diversity of professional services available to gentlemen and ladies of the South shortly before and during the antebellum period:

> **J. Bryant.** The subscriber, well acquainted with the European method of gardening, being a native of England, and likewise well acquainted with it in this state [South Carolina] . . . proposes superintending ladies and gentlemen's gardens in or near the city whether intended for pleasure or profit—he also plans and lays out gardens in the European taste on moderate terms.
>
> *The Charleston City Gazette*, June 6, 1795

*The Compleat English Gardner: or, A Sure Guide to Young Planters and Gardners*, Eleventh Edition, 1710. *The Compleat English Gardner* by Leonard Meager provided practical information on the management of fruit, kitchen, and pleasure gardens, as well as prototypical plans for the layout of formal gardens.

**Mr. J. C. G.\*\*\*** gardener and florist planter, and cutter of trees, and vines, puts in order new gardens and repairs old ones. Having learned his profession under the most celebrated master gardeners of Europe, and who having constantly exercised his art in this country since several years past, he has perfect knowledge of the cultivation of vegetables both indigenous and exotic. He will make arrangements with persons who may wish to employ him by the month.

Reference, to Mde. Matossy, and Mr. Willoz, Orleans street, and to Mr. St. George, corner of Levee and Ursuline streets.

*The Bee,* New Orleans, Louisiana, February, 1828

**Landscape Gardening. Robert Nelson, Augusta, Georgia.** The subscriber will devote a portion of his time, the coming winter to *landscape gardening, laying out grounds, planting ornamental trees, shrubbery,* etc. When the distance is not too great, he will superintend all operations in person; and will furnish plans to remote applicants who will describe their grounds and state clearly their desires.

*The Southern Cultivator,* Augusta, Georgia, December, 1857

**Landscape Gardening. Wm. H. Hamilton** is now ready to visit any part of the South to *layout, and improve ornamental grounds and gardens,* having completed the improvement of the Capital Grounds at Raleigh, N.C. plans, drawings and estimates given on application. Also, plans and instructions given to persons to execute their own work. All letters addressed to WM. H. HAMILTON, FLORIST, Raleigh, N.C., will be promptly attended to.

*The Southern Cultivator,* May, 1858

**W. R. Bergholz. Landscape Gardener and Rural Architect, Columbia, S.C.** Will devote particular attention to the improvement and laying out of Country and City Residences, Public parks, Cemeteries, and all kinds of Ornamental and Flower Gardens and Garden Architecture, the construction of Green-Houses, Conservatories, Graperies, etc. His plans and designs are drawn up so as to be practically applicable to the purposes for which they are intended; the position of every tree and shrub carefully indicated, with accompanying references and remarks, explanatory of the particular features to be developed, and a list of the kind and quantity of plants required for their completion.

*The Farmer and Planter,* Pendleton, South Carolina, August, 1861

Numerous references in diaries, letters, and travel accounts of the antebellum period reveal that many southerners often engaged the services of itinerant gardeners to design their gardens and grounds. One such account is contained in the family papers of Alfred and Millicent Battle of Tuscaloosa, Alabama. In 1835, Alfred Battle, the son of a prominent North Carolina planter, and his wife, Millicent, built an imposing town house on Market Street (now Greensboro Avenue) in Tuscaloosa, Alabama. The Battle's new home with its monumental portico and handsome facade proved to be one of the finest residential structures in the city at the time. Shortly after its completion, Millicent Battle commissioned an English landscape gardener to design an elaborate parterre garden as a compliment to their newly constructed home. In 1844, the Battle's son, William Augustus, in a letter to his cousin, Virginia Clay (who was married in the Battle's house the previous year), wrote that his mother had recently "had her yard laid off most beautifully by a Trans-Atlantic gardener who boasts in his skills and taste, and in truth, he is proficient in his trade. He says he has lavished profusely his skill and talent on Lord Ashburton's garden, which is quite a recommendation." (Tuscaloosa County Preservation Commission.) The garden was laid out using an intricate pattern of walks and interlocking, diamond-shaped beds, enclosed by a decorative fence. From all accounts, the Battle's ornamental garden was one of the most notable in the state.

Another account documenting the use of an itinerant landscape gardener is contained in a letter to Louisa Collins Harrison of Faunsdale Plantation (outside Uniontown, Alabama) from her sister Henrietta Collins Page of Eatonton, North Carolina. In her letter Henrietta notes that her neighbors, Dr. and Mrs. Thomas Warren, had secured the services of a landscape gardener to layout the grounds of their stylish new home: "Their house is a very fine large one; but many persons think it looks gloomy and heavy. It strikes me, however, as imposing. [Dr. Warren] . . . has imported an English or Irish gardener this spring to lay off his grounds and I have no doubt they will have a pretty place. Every improvement he makes adds to the beauty of our view." (Faunsdale Plantation Family Papers.) Given that the Warren's new home was situated on a spacious site, and that its design was based on a plan contained in an architectural pattern book by William H. Ranlette entitled *The Architect*, with a subtitle containing the phrase *Connected with Landscape Gardening*, it can be safely assumed that the resulting design of the Warren's garden and grounds were executed in a fashionable and stylish manner.

In 1841, Andrew Jackson Downing (1815–1852), the noted American horticulturist, author, and landscape gardener of Newburgh, New York, published *A Treatise on the Theory and Practice of Landscape Gardening*. This work provided design principles specifically adapted to the layout of gardens and grounds of North America. Downing's principles were strongly rooted in English landscape theory of naturalistic design, which relied on the use of lawns and the informal planting of trees and shrubs. While Downing strongly opposed the use of geometric forms, southerners continued to adhere to the landscape traditions of formal design. The southern gardeners' reluctance to follow Downing's advice was based on the belief that recommendations contained in his *Treatise* were inappropriate for the southern climate, with its mild winters, long hot summers, and periods of extended

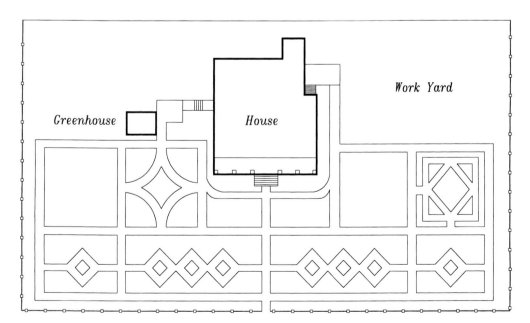

The Battle-Friedman Garden Plan—Tuscaloosa, Alabama. The garden was laid out using an intricate pattern of walks and interlocking, diamond-shaped beds.

drought. This position is reflected in a letter by an unidentified correspondent to the editor of the *Southern Cultivator* in 1856:

> I have an idea of writing something (if capable of doing it) on laying out, planting and ornamenting Southern gardens. Downing, as well as many European authors, have written volumes about it; but our Southern climate is very different from theirs. . . . An entirely different style ought to be introduced with us, and I have not yet seen anything on the subject, *Landscape Gardening in the South.* Do you know anything about it? Then please let me know. . . . I have this winter been laying out a garden, and met with some difficulties following the "Downing style" and it struck me at once that we, of the South, ought to find out some other method, but, as yet I do not know what to do.

Evidence also suggests that many gardeners in the North, like their southern counterparts, rejected Downing's principles of landscape gardening and continued to adhere to the principles of geometric design. A letter to the editor of the *Horticulturist* written in 1852 by George Jacques of Worcester, Massachusetts, confirms this assertion: "I venture to offer for publication . . . a few hints, having a somewhat local bearing upon the subject of landscape gardening. . . . Although modern writers recognize two grand divisions of styles of this art, the *geometrical* [or ancient] *style,* and the *natural* [or modern] *style.* . . . The taste of New England people generally for the beautiful and picturesque in rural scenery is either vitiated, or totally uncultivated. . . . Hence, the great mass of the people prefer symmetry, stiff formality, straight lines, and the geometric forms of the ancient or artificial style of laying out grounds. Nearly all our first class places in Yankeedom are so arranged."

It is interesting that while Downing strongly espoused the principles of the natural or modern style of gardening in his *Treatise* on landscape gardening, he reluctantly condoned the use of the geometric or "ancient style" in specialized situations, for instance "in very small gardens, in which variety and irregularity are out of the question . . . or where a taste for imitating an old and quaint style of residence exists." Southerners who read Downing's book likely interpreted his advice in each of these instances to validate the use of parterres in urban settings where space restrictions left little room but for a small geometric garden, or in association with houses of the Greek Revival or classical styles. Justified or not, parterres remained a central feature of southern gardens throughout the antebellum period.

## GARDEN PLANS

A variety of factors played an important role in determining the design of antebellum gardens. These included cultural differences, gardening traditions, skill and expertise of the designer, resources for upkeep and maintenance, the availability of garden books and horticultural literature, and the influence of travel. While differences existed in urban and rural areas, surprising similarities occurred between city and town gardens and those of rural plantations. Regardless of space or location, formality and strict adherence to rules of geometry generally characterized ornamental gardens of the antebellum South, creating patterns that reflected symmetry, balance, proportion, and scale. Although designs of earlier eighteenth-century, colonial gardens served as prototypes for nineteenth-century garden plans, distinct variations in garden patterns developed during the antebellum period. Triangles, rectangles, squares, and circles were combined into a variety of new designs. By 1850, the designs of many parterres not only reflected variations in geometric patterns but also often included the use of curves and fluid lines. It was also during this time that parterre beds were often planted with a wide variety of ornamentals (many from China and Japan) to create a diverse palette of plants including shrubs, roses, flowers, and bulbs. The following is a description of a parterre garden in Savannah, Georgia, in 1855:

### *The Magazine of Horticulture,* 1855

H. Andrew Gray

᠅ Ornamental Gardening in the South

On the south side of the house it [a parterre] is divided into numerous small figures, while on the north side the figures are larger, and better adapted to the kind of plants grown in them; the former has fifty figures or beds, while the latter has only thirty. They have an aggregate of about nine yards of walks, from four to six feet wide. Oyster shells broken fine are substituted for gravel, and make a very fine walk. Formerly these walks were all laid down with box edgings, but are now superseded with the Euonymus japonica; while it is not so neat as the box, it looks very well, having so fine a green, and it can be kept in due proportion as an edging for five or six years, after which relaying will be desirable. The beds are planted chiefly with roses and a few of the finer varieties of shrubs, interspersed with such herbaceous and bulbous plants as we find stand the climate, viz: —Liliums, Amaryllis, Pancratiums, Hyacinth, Gladiolus, Narcissus, Phlox, Chrysanthemum, Asclepias, Carnation Pinks, Wall Flowers, Stocks, Sweet William, Alyssum, Verbenas, Violets, &c., and a good number of annuals.

Once a desired pattern for a parterre had been achieved, it was essential that some form of edging be used to define the beds, walks, and paths that comprised the design. Of all materials employed for edging during the antebellum period, dwarf box (*Buxus sempervirens suffruticosa*) was the most commonly used. Its slow growth, evergreen foliage, and ability to remain sheared to a height of eight to ten inches made it ideal for use in parterre gardens. Additional features that encouraged and enhanced the use of box was its ease of propagation, tolerance of heat and drought, its ability to thrive in a variety of growing conditions, and its resistance to insects and diseases. Box also was sometimes planted to create design motifs within individual beds. While hardy in the upper and middle South, the inability of box to thrive in areas of high humidity limited its use in many areas of the

San Francisco—St. John's Parish, Louisiana. Located outside New Orleans on the east bank of the Mississippi River, San Francisco (circa 1850) was originally enhanced by a formal garden in a geometric pattern. It is believed that common privet (*Ligustrum vulgare*) was used in the layout of the garden.

lower South. In these locations, yaupon holly (*Ilex vomitoria*) was often used as a substitute. The records of Dr. Alexander Garden (1728–1791) of Charleston, South Carolina, noted that yaupon holly "makes a very good and most beautiful hedge that can be kept as short and as neat as box." Many of the early parterre gardens of New Orleans and plantations along the Mississippi River employed common privet (*Ligustrum vulgare*) as an alternative to box. It is seldom used today, but common privet has long been recognized as good edging material because of its compact habit of growth, evergreen foliage, resistance to drought, and small leaves that are not disfigured by clipping. Toward the end of the antebellum period, Japanese euonymus (*Euonymus japonica*) was used as edging material in the middle South, but it never proved as popular as box.

The Low House Garden—Savannah, Georgia. Similar to other old gardens in the city, the Low House Garden was bordered with decorative edging tiles. While originally imported from England, edging tiles were eventually produced in the region.

Brick, in association with box, was frequently used during the antebellum period to define walks and paths of parterre gardens. Brick used for this purpose was either obtained from commercial operations in towns and cities or was manufactured on plantations by slaves. In coastal towns and cities, bricks were often brought over from Europe in the ballast of ships and sailing vessels. The ease with which bricks could be purchased or made, their modest cost, and freedom from maintenance made them ideal as permanent edging material for parterre beds. Bricks used for edging usually were placed in the soil in a vertical position with at least half or one-third of the surface extending above ground. This practice allowed individual beds to be raised two to three inches above the elevation of a walk or path, facilitating good drainage and creating clean, crisp lines to define and accentuate a design. In some cases, brick was placed in the soil at a forty-five degree angle to add visual interest and refinement of detail. While bricks were usually of a standard size (2.5 to 3 inches high, 4 to 4.5 inches wide, and 8 to 9 inches long) differences frequently occurred in shape, color, and texture, depending on the skills of the manufacturer or craftsman, type and color of clay, and the purpose for which they were made.

References are sometimes found in garden literature documenting the use of decorative brick and tile as edging material. In a letter to the editor of the *Gardeners Magazine* (1839), a subscriber who identified himself simply as M. A. W. of Athens, Georgia, referred to the use of brick and tiles specifically designed for garden edging: "Brick or tiles molded expressly for the purpose [edging], are next resorted to, and if sunk so that the earth in the beds shall not be more than from one to two inches above the level of the paths . . ." While specially molded brick and tiles are occasionally found in antebellum gardens, it is difficult to establish their age or place of origin. In some cases, garden tiles appear as square or rectangular paving or roof tiles, while others are similar in design to English garden edging tiles that were popular during the Victorian era. Garden tiles used for edging are frequently found in old gardens of Savannah, Georgia. As Savannah avoided destruction during the Civil War, one can speculate that old garden tiles found in the city came into use after 1865, at a time when gardeners in other areas of the South lacked the financial resources to keep up with changing garden styles and fashions of the day.

Wood also was used to edge garden beds. Wood was readily available, inexpensive to use, and easy to install, but its tendency to warp and rot made it costly and difficult to maintain. Native stone from surrounding fields was also frequently employed as edging material. Stone used for edging was usually selected for its consistency of color, appropriate size, and visual appeal. Stone, like brick, was used to define and articulate a design and to allow the soil within individual beds to be raised several inches above ground level, in order to improve drainage. Materials traditionally used for walks during the antebellum period included sand, compacted soil, crushed oyster shells (in coastal areas), or brick laid in patterns of running bond or herringbone.

## AVENUES

Tree-lined avenues are as old as antiquity, dating to Persian and Roman times. While avenues declined in importance during the Middle Ages, they reappeared during the Renaissance, at which time they were planted with evergreen or deciduous trees at regular intervals in single or double rows. Avenues served as ceremonial entrances to a manor house or estate to arouse expectations of the visitor and to convey a sense of ownership, power, strength, and control. In England during the seventeenth and eighteenth centuries, noblemen and gentry often planted grand avenues of lime (*Tilia europaea*), elm (*Ulmus campestris*), and horse chestnut (*Aesculus hippocastanum*) trees. Each was selected for their imposing size, strong trunks, and uniform habit of growth.

Upon arriving in North America, early settlers of the southern colonies remained tied to English landscape traditions, including the planting of grand avenues of trees. During the eighteenth and early nineteenth centuries, many fine avenues of live oak trees were planted in the lowcountry of South Carolina, where they were nurtured by warm winters, mild summers, and a long growing season. A traveler on his way to Charleston in 1827 described one of these imposing avenues: "The county seats of South Carolina are monuments of feudal pride,

A Live Oak Avenue at Chelsea Plantation—Beaufort, South Carolina. Among North American trees, none is more majestic than the live oak (*Quercus virginiana*).

and lordly sway. They are not unlike, in this respect, the vast baronial possessions of the earlier period of English history. . . . The dwelling house is usually located at the head of a high and dense avenue of oaks; which afford an extremely picturesque view in long perspective, perhaps a mile or more from the road."

An Avenue of Live Oaks leading to Boone Hall Plantation—Mount Pleasant, South Carolina. Originally owned by Major John Boone, the Horlbeck family, who produced sea-island cotton, purchased the property in 1817.

The live oak (*Quercus virginiana*), indigenous to the lower coastal plain from Virginia to Florida and westward to the Rio Grande, proved to have no equal as an avenue tree. The beauty of this magnificent tree is found in its dark, evergreen foliage, vast size, beautiful symmetry and gnarled, pendulous branches. Many live oak avenues were planted on rice plantations located outside Charleston, South Carolina, along the Ashley and Cooper Rivers, as noted by Herbert Ravenel Sass in a selection from Alice Smith's book *A Carolina Rice Plantation of the Fifties:*

> The house stood as a rule among trees, some of them the original forests growth, others planted around the house-site in the Colony's early days. . . . Besides these trees around the house and in the plantation yard, there was often, though not invariably, the avenue, lined with live oaks, usually of great size, through which carriages of visitors approached the house from the main road. . . . The avenue generally formed by single rows of oaks on each side, occasionally by double rows, was likely to be the most impressive feature of the place, and it was hard to say which was more beautiful—the view of the river and rice fields . . . or the view from the landward piazza whence one looked straight down the long wide isle of the avenue—a shadowy, colonnaded, high-ceilinged vista, festooned and tapered with Spanish moss.

The cathedral-like arches formed by avenues of live oak trees often evoked a sense of awe and admiration. As described in Frederick Law Olmsted's account in *A Journey in the Seaboard Slave States* of an avenue approaching a lowcountry plantation: "On either side, at fifty feet distance, were rows of old live oak trees, their branches and twigs

slightly hung with a delicate fringe of gray moss, and their dark, shining, green foliage, meeting and intermingling naturally but densely overhead. The sunlight streamed through and played aslant the lustrous leaves, and fluttering, pendulous moss; the arch was low and broad; the trunks high and gnarled, and there was a heavy groaning of strong, rough, knotty branches. I stopped my horse and held my breath; for I have hardly in all my life seen anything so impressively grand and beautiful."

Like Olmsted, J. Milton Mackie (a northern traveler from Great Barrington, Massachusetts) also observed several magnificent live oak avenues outside Charleston, as referenced in *From Cape Cod to Dixie and the Tropics*, a recounting of his trip through the South on the eve of the Civil War:

Before leaving Charleston, I did not fail to take a look at its environs. On a bright, sunny afternoon, the soft southwest wind gently blowing, I was driven out by a friend to his farm, situated a few miles out of town. The rather quiet landscape was made attractive by numerous live oaks, with sturdy, broadly spreading branches, by tall, dark-leafed magnolias, and by the graceful wild oranges [*Prunus caroliniana*], all being evergreens. . . . But the most pleasing feature of the scenery which came within my observation, on this excursion, was an avenue, or, rather, a couple of avenues, of live oaks of unusual size and beauty. The trees being fully grown, the crooked branches stretched themselves high in the air, numerous as the masts in a crowded seaport, and strong enough to supply the joints and knees of the proudest ships of war. They stretched high overhead, and apparently half-way to heaven, until gradually lost in the tapering twigs, and evergreen leaves, and gracefully pendent mosses. The stems had the strength of the columns of some great temple in Thebes or Palmyra. And yet, I was told that these monarchs of the plain had scarcely attained their threescore years and ten. When the old men of Charleston were in their cradles, these oaks were tiny acorns, such as I trod under foot as I walked thoughtfully in the vast, checkered shade of these green avenues. . . .

Another account of a live oak avenue, this time outside Savannah, Georgia, can be found in *Life and Liberty in America* (1859) by Charles Mackey. The author describes an avenue of live oaks at Bonaventure Cemetery, established in 1850 on the site that was originally the home of Josiah Tattnall:

> This gentleman [Mr. Tattnall], though he came to a forest land where trees were considered a nuisance, admired the park-like beauty around the great country mansions of the nobility and gentry in his native England, and, while everyone else in the colony was cutting down trees, made himself busy in planting them. Having built himself a house on the estate of Bonaventure, he planted an avenue or carriage drive leading up to its porch, and the tree he chose for the purpose was the evergreen oak, next to the cypress and magnolia the noblest tree in the Southern States of America In due time, long after the good man's death, the trees attained a commanding height, and from their boughs hung the long, feathery festoons of the *tillandsia*, or Spanish moss, that lends such melancholy beauty to all the southern landscape.

Live oak avenues were in no way limited to the coastal regions of South Carolina and Georgia but occurred throughout the lower South. Some of the finest oak avenues were on plantations located along the Mississippi River from New Orleans to Baton Rouge. One of the most impressive of these was Oak Alley Plantation, situated sixty miles upriver from New Orleans. This spectacular avenue of live oaks is believed to have been planted a century before a large plantation house was constructed on the site in 1839. The avenue at Oak Alley is composed of twenty-eight magnificent oaks that extend a quarter of a mile from the house to the river's edge. J. W. Dorr, a nineteenth-century journalist, provided a brief description of Oak Alley in the *New Orleans Crescent* shortly before the Civil War: "I noticed particularly the plantations of Valcour Aime and . . . Henry J. Roman [Oak Alley], which is one of the handsomest, most costly and tasteful on the coast. . . . The avenue of ancient live oaks on his plantation is . . . magnificent . . . and the grounds are a paradise of rare and beautiful plants, trees and shrubs." Additional live oak avenues found along the Mississippi include those at Rosedown, Afton Villa, and The Oaks Plantation, all in or near St. Francisville, Louisiana.

Outside the coastal regions of the lower South, planters had to rely on other trees as a substitute for the live oak. One of the most popular of these was the eastern red cedar (*Juniperus virginiana*). The great respect and admiration southerners had for this noble evergreen tree is reflected in the names frequently given to antebellum plantations— Cedar Grove, The Cedars, Cedar Lane, Cedar Hill, etc. Several factors influenced the use of the eastern red cedar as an avenue tree: its longevity, hardness, evergreen nature, and availability from the fields and forests of the

The Eastern Red Cedar (*Juniperus virginiana*)

middle and upper South. Another factor that led to the popularity of the eastern red cedar as an avenue tree was its similarity in shape and size to the Italian cypress (*Cupressus sempervirens*). This plant was used extensively as an avenue tree in southern Europe and was frequently seen and admired by southern travelers who made the grand tour. As the Italian cypress was neither available from American nurseries nor adaptable to the southern climate, planters turned to the eastern red cedar as a substitute. While many avenues of eastern red cedars have survived from antebellum times, one of the finest is found at the Hermitage, former home of President Andrew Jackson, located outside Nashville, Tennessee. This stately avenue extends from the main entrance of the property to the monumental facade of the house. It serves as an outstanding example of the formal effect achieved from use of the eastern red cedar as an avenue tree. The following reference to the use of cedar avenues along the Mississippi River is provided in *Lafayette in America in 1824 and 1825* by A. Levasseur: "For some miles after leaving New Orleans, the eye rests agreeably on scenes of fine sugar and cotton plantations which border the stream. . . . There are avenues of oaks, cedars, and numerous pecan trees."

The southern magnolia (*Magnolia grandiflora*), while frequently employed in contemporary times to line streets and boulevards, experienced limited success as an avenue tree prior to 1860. While many romantic novelists have written of magnolia avenues as a common feature in the antebellum South, there is little evidence to support this view. There is evidence, however, indicating that magnolias were occasionally used as an avenue tree, especially in the lowcountry of South Carolina, as noted in an advertisement in the *South Carolina and American Gazette*, dated January 1, 1778: "For Sale . . . Magnolia or Laurels fit for Avenues . . . any height from three feet to twenty."

One of the few surviving magnolia avenues of the antebellum period is found at Redcliffe Plantation, along the Savannah River in Aiken County, South Carolina. Completed in 1859, Redcliffe Plantation was the home of South Carolina governor James Henry Hammond (1807–1864), a successful cotton planter who coined the phrase "Cotton is King" in a speech to the U.S. Senate in 1858. Tradition has it that the Belgian horticulturist and nurseryman, P. J. Berckmans, proprietor of Fruitland Nurseries in nearby Augusta, Georgia, planted the avenue of magnolias leading to the plantation house. It is noteworthy that the avenue at Redcliff Plantation does not lead to the front of the house but instead to the side. This surviving magnolia avenue attests to the longevity and enduring nature of this stately tree.

Although infrequently used as an avenue tree during the antebellum period, the southern magnolia was planted during the period in groves and grounds as a "specimen tree." It was greatly revered for its handsome evergreen foliage, fragrant flowers, and majestic size as described in the following account in *The Sunny South; or, The Southerner at Home* (1860):

> The appearance of the country from the plantation [outside Natchez] where I am now sojourning for a few days, is very beautiful, diversified as it is to the eye with woodlands, broad cotton fields, and county seats in the center of surrounding estates. The magnolia here is the pride and glory of all trees. . . . When the sun at a certain angle glances upon the polished surface of its large leaves, every tree seems as if encased in emerald armor. Then the grand, huge flowers, that glitter here and there amid the masses of foliage like large silver stars, fill all the air around with their fragrance. Some of these trees rise to the height of ninety feet tall, proud cones of beauty that seem to be conscious of their elegance.

MAGNOLIA *altissima Lauro cerasi folio flore ingenti candido*

The Southern Magnolia (*Magnolia grandiflora*) by George Ehret. Colonial Williamsburg Foundation.

Orange trees, while less imposing than live oaks, cedars, or magnolias, were frequently employed to form avenues in rural and urban settings of the lower South. In addition to the use of orange trees to develop avenues, they were also frequently planted to create ornamental groves. A visitor to Charleston, South Carolina, in the early 1800s observed that "the houses of the suburbs were, for the most part, surrounded by gardens, in which orange trees, with most splendid ripe fruit, monthly roses in full bloom, and a variety of

Faye-Webster Plantation—St. Mary's Parish, Louisiana.

other flourishing plants displayed themselves." References to the use of orange trees for similar purposes in other coastal cities can be found in travel accounts of the antebellum period. Of the numerous types of oranges, the sweet orange (*Citrus sinensis*) was the most commonly grown. Low-branched with a rounded crown and dense evergreen foliage, the sweet orange produces an abundant supply of white, highly-fragrant flowers in March and April. Flowers are followed in late fall and winter by round to oval-shaped, edible fruit.

While stately avenues were a common feature in older regions of the antebellum South, there were many areas where avenues were an infrequent sight. This is evidenced in Joseph Holt Ingraham's account written in *The South-West* (1835):

> A long avenue of trees, ornamenting and sheltering the approach to a dwelling, is a rare sight in this state [Mississippi], though very frequently seen in Louisiana, yet, in no region of the south can fine avenues of beautiful trees be made with such facility. . . . No state surpasses this in the beauty, variety, and rapid growth of its ornamental shade trees; the laurel, sycamore, locust, oak, elm, and white bay with the "pride of China,"—the universal shade tree in the southwest—arrive here at the most perfect maturity and beauty. Every plantation residence is approached by a drive, often nearly a mile in length; yet so little attention is paid to this species of ornament and comfort, in a climate where shade is a synonym for luxury, that scarcely one of them is shaded, except where . . . nature has flung the broad arms of majestic trees across the path.

The infrequent use of avenues in some regions of the South, particularly in the southern frontier, no doubt resulted from a changing attitude regarding the use of avenues as an important landscape feature or because newly planted avenues had limited time to develop and mature before being destroyed or damaged during the Civil War. In either case, there is little evidence that avenues were a prominent landscape feature in western Georgia or the interior regions of Alabama, Mississippi, and Louisiana.

The Reynolds House—Camden, South Carolina. This handsome, three-story structure was constructed circa 1820. As evidenced in the photograph, the house was surrounded by an extensive grove of majestic trees.

## GROVES

Groves represent one of the oldest forms of garden art, dating back to Greek and Roman times. The use of groves continued throughout the Middle Ages and by the eighteenth century had become an essential element in English landscapes. According to Philip Miller, author of the *Gardener's Dictionary* (1731), groves were "the central feature of a garden, being a great ornament to all the rest of its parts." Groves were occasionally composed of a single species, but in most cases they included both native and imported trees in an informal or naturalistic arrangement. Upon arriving in North America, European explorers found impressive groves of indigenous trees in the coastal region of South Carolina and Georgia. In 1592, Loudonniere, a French naturalist, provides the following observation of the Carolina coast: "We found the place as pleasant as possible, for it was covered with mighty oaks and an infinite store of cedars and with Lentiskes [myrtles] growing underneath them, smelling so sweetly, that the very fragrant odor made the land seem exceedingly pleasant. On every side were to be seen palm trees and other sorts of trees bearing blossoms of very rare shape and very good smell." Another account by an English voyager tells of "odoriferous and fragrant woods flourishing in perpetual and constant Verdure, vis, the lofty pine, the sweet smelling Cedar and Cypress trees, the Wild Walnut or Hickory Tree."

Many early planters in the southern colonies preserved native trees for shade and for their natural beauty. E. T. H. Shaffer in *Carolina Gardens* notes that during the colonial period, "The first settlers of Carolina, loyal to the traditions and clinging to the memories of England, a land whose stately county seats were proud and mindful of ancient groves and avenues, were quick to preserve imposing specimens of the New World forest for their groves and woodland parks." Of all existing trees, it was the live oak, *Quercus virginiana* (known at the time as *Quercus virens*), that was held in the greatest esteem. Its imposing size, dark foliage, and moss-draped branches created a presence unequaled by other species. The use of native trees, following the English manner, was a common landscape practice among southern planters throughout the antebellum period, as confirmed in the following account by Adam Hodgson, an English traveler who visited Natchez, Mississippi, in 1820: "Indeed there is something in the vicinity of Natchez which perpetually reminds me of home. The thick clover, the scattered knolls with their wood-crowned summits, differing only from those most familiar to me in the magnificence of the foliage with which they are shaded, and the neat husbandry of the intervening plantations, give the whole country the appearance of an English park." Hodgson further noted that many residents in the neighborhood of Natchez lived much in the manner and style of English gentry, possessing polished manners and fine homes surrounded by ornamental groves. "Their houses are spacious and handsome," he wrote, "and their grounds are laid out like a forest park."

In 1843, Thomas Bangs Thorpe in "Our Visit to Natchez" provides another account of the natural groves in and around Natchez: "The country around Natchez is . . . covered with the finest forest trees. We have traveled through some of these beautiful specimens of Nature's handy-work, before the ax had made a single waste, and we were struck with the great beauty of the groves of trees which met us everywhere. . . . Around Natchez . . . these beautiful natural groves have been spared, and every road leading from the city is lined with elegant mansions, the abodes of luxury and taste, hid partially from view by the rich magnolia and oak, the gum and delicate beech."

In his *Treatise on the Theory and Practice of Landscape Gardening* (1841), Andrew Jackson Downing, America's first landscape gardener, encouraged the preservation of groves of native trees. Downing strongly promoted the preservation of American forest as a means of achieving the "natural style of landscape design," and observed that "in many parts of the Union, where new residences are being formed, or where old ones are to be improved, the grounds will often be found, partially, or to a considerable extent, clothed with belts or masses of wood, either previously planted, or preserved from the woodman's ax [*sic*]. How easily we may turn these to advantages in the natural style of landscape gardening; and by judicious trimming when too thick, or additions when too much scattered, elicit often the happiest effects, in a magical manner." Downing also encouraged the planting of newly introduced Asian trees into existing groves to create visual interest and diversity.

The Stevens Thomas Place—Athens, Georgia.

Groves appear to have remained an important landscape feature throughout the antebellum period, for as late as 1855, G. M. Kern in *Practical Landscape Gardening* offered American gardeners guidelines for establishing ornamental groves:

A beautiful grove of trees has many attractions, and adds much to the appearance of a place. . . . A grove shows to most advantage when placed along a gentle slope or hill-side, where the eye can at once take in its extent and beauties, and where likewise the noble trees of which it may consist be brought prominently into view. Where there already exists, on the grounds to be improved, a grove, or collection of trees planted there by Nature, the gardener should not fail to take advantage of them. They should not be disturbed, unless very much interfering with the levels of the ground or the lines of walls. If the outlines can be improved, this may be done by a careful use of the ax [*sic*], but it is often more advisable to plant additional trees on the margins or projections, to give greater apparent depth to the woods, than to make the incision deeper by cutting down trees. In planting a grove, the improver should be careful to avoid any regular recurrence of particular trees, nor should they be set at regular distances apart, but scattered irregularly over the surface, here wider apart—there closer—here two or three together—yonder an open space, admitting the sun to the grass, and making a bright spot to contrast the surrounding shade. None but straight-growing, widespreading trees should be used in planting a grove, that we may have an arch of foliage formed overhead which will effectively protect from the rays of the sun.

Contributors to agricultural journals published shortly before the Civil War provided additional advice for both preserving groves and forming "plantations" (informal planting of trees). As an example, W. R. Bergholz, a landscape gardener in Columbia, South Carolina, offered the following recommendations in *The Farmer and Planter* in 1860:

The American Beech (*Fagus grandiflora*). Andrew Jackson Downing referred to the beech in his *Treatise on the Theory and Practice of Landscape Gardening* as a notable ornamental tree.

> The house should be sheltered by shade trees. The air keeps the trees in motion, yielding a cooling and refreshing breeze, which, during the heat of the summer months, is not only animating, but pleasing; and, in winter, these also serve to break off the keenness of the blasting winds. . . .
>
> In forming plantations near the house, either to hide the offices [outbuildings], or to form ornamental groups, there should always be dispersed among them a great portion of our best evergreen trees and shrubs, to preserve a lively and interesting appearance, as well in winter as in summer; but in planting, great care must be taken not to plant too thick; a free circulation of air and breadth of light must be admitted, to display the form and effect of the surrounding plantations. The trees and shrubs should be grouped in the natural style, and be allowed to develop their beauties. . . .

Trees when grouped, should present regular forms, nor be crowded into masses, or carelessly scattered without any references to effect, their height or habit; however they be planted, they should partake of what is considered rural beauty, and natural simplicity. Single specimens of trees, if placed consistently with beauty, and left alone, will ornament our pleasure grounds very much—stretching its leader upwards to the sky, and its branches outward to the winds, and downward, touching the earth with a graceful sweep. We love to see a tree with all its natural beauties, full of health and majesty, shaped by Nature to delight the eye and gratify the beholder. . . .

Trees were often planted to commemorate the birth of a child, a marriage, or other special events. The most frequently selected ceremonial trees included oaks, cedars, elms, beech, and magnolias—trees that not only were long lived but also developed over time into handsome specimens. While trees planted for practical and aesthetic reasons varied throughout the South (depending on location and climate), a pallet of favorite trees developed during the antebellum period. Some of the more important of these included the following:

Native Trees—live oak (*Quercus virginiana*); catalpa (*Catalpa bignonioides*); eastern red cedar (*Juniperus virginiana*); southern magnolia (*Magnolia grandiflora*); water oak (*Quercus nigia*); willow oak (*Quercus phellos*); American holly (*Ilex opaca*); winged elm (*Ulmus alata*); black locust (*Robinia pseudoacacia*); tulip tree (*Liriodendron tulipifera*); beech (*Fagus grandifolia*), and pines (numerous species).

Imported Trees—maiden hair tree (*Ginkgo bioloba*); mimosa (*Albizia julibrissin*); tree of heaven (*Ailanthus altissima*); crape myrtle (*Lagerstroemia indica*); Osage orange (*Maclura pomifera*); royal paulownia (*Paulownia tomentosa*); Chinese parasol tree (*Firmiana simplex*), and the sweet orange (*Citrus sinensis*).

## FENCES

Throughout the antebellum period, wooden fences were employed to define, enclose, and protect kitchen and ornamental gardens, work yards, and cultivated fields. An established hierarchy of fences within distinct landscape zones was an American tradition that had its origin in colonial times. As a general rule, decorative fences were located in close proximity to the main house or dwelling, and simpler and more practical fences were relegated to work yards and outlying areas. The ornamental zone, located in front of or to the side of the house or dwelling, was generally enclosed by a fence to protect and define a formal garden or simple plantings of flowers, trees, and shrubs. Fences within this zone were generally decorative in character, ranging from simple to elaborate designs. The utilitarian zone, which defined the work yard, relied on the use of crude board fences to protect the kitchen garden and to enclose or screen an assortment of outbuildings including a detached kitchen, barn, stables, sheds, well, privy, etc. Fences in the utilitarian zone were practical in nature and generally exhibited a respectable honesty of purpose and design. Outlying areas, referred to as the pastoral zone, contained groves, orchards, pastures, farmland, and cultivated fields, which were typically enclosed either by worm fences or by fences referred to as post-and-rail. Worm fences normally protected crops and farmland against stray animals, while post-and-rail fences were traditionally employed as livestock and cattle enclosures.

View of Christiansburg by Edward Beyer. This 1855 illustration of a Virginia landscape reflects the use of a variety of decorative and utilitarian fences that were employed during the antebellum period.

## Decorative Fences

Decorative fences enclosed ornamental and kitchen gardens and provided protection against roaming livestock, farm animals, and household pets. The earliest decorative fences constructed in the South were made of simple pales, which were secured vertically to horizontal rails and supported by posts that were firmly anchored in the ground. Pales functioned as visual and physical barriers and provided protection to gardens and work yards, dwelling houses, and associated outbuildings. Pales ranged in height from three to five feet, were generally two to six inches wide, and contained upper ends that were flat or fashioned into triangular, truncated, or single slope designs. Individual placement of pales was either flush against each other or spaced several inches apart. In most instances, fences made of pales were whitewashed or painted to provide protection against the weather and to improve their visual appeal.

Catalpa Plantation—Coweta County, Georgia.

Unlike pales, which were simple and basic in design, picket fences were composed of thinner and more delicately fashioned vertical members, having rounded or pointed tops. Throughout the eighteenth century there was a clear distinction between pales and pickets, but by the beginning of the antebellum era, the term "picket" was used to describe all board fences containing vertical components regardless of the size, spacing, or design. Picket fence designs in the South were initially based on drawings found in English garden and architectural books. Later, American pattern books were used, most notable was Asher Benjamin's *The Architect or Practical House Carpenter* (1830). In addition to the standard designs offered in these early works, American craftsmen and builders created many imaginative designs. While picket fences were utilized primarily in domestic settings, they were also used to enclose and embellish public buildings and grounds including town halls, courthouses, schools, institutions, churchyards, as well as college and university campuses.

The design of picket fences varied considerably throughout the first half of the nineteenth century, but typically their height, spacing, size of pickets, posts, and bases were generally the same. Gates incorporated into fences were, as a rule, located on the main axis of a walk or path to provide ease of access and create a symmetrical design. While picket fences were traditionally built three to four-feet high, in situations where privacy and security were required, pickets were generally taller, sturdier, and more formidable in size. For instance, in Charleston, South Carolina, where city lots were small and privacy was desired, fences were often built five to six-feet tall. In an effort to disguise their size and enhance their visual appeal, Charleston fences were traditionally painted a dark receding green. Charleston artist, Charles Fraser (1782–1860), in *A Charleston Sketchbook, 1796–1806*, provides numerous examples of early nineteenth-century fences that graced the gardens and grounds in and around the city.

Decorative and utilitarian fences remained prominent in the southern landscape through the antebellum period. However, Andrew Jackson Downing, in his *Treatise on the Theory and Practice of Landscape Gardening* (1841), called into question their appropriateness. Downing found fences objectionable and ill-advised, noting that, "Fences are often among the most unsightly and offensive objects . . . scarcely advisable even in country farms, but for which there can be no apology in elegant residences." While Downing's advice found a more receptive audience in the North, in the South, where one's livelihood was generally tied to an agricultural base, fences remained an essential element in daily life through the end of the nineteenth century.

## Utilitarian Fences

Utilitarian fences were employed to delineate property boundaries, enclose and screen work yards, and protect kitchen gardens, pastures, agricultural crops, and farmland. As early as 1722, Mark Catesby, the noted English naturalist and author of *The Natural History of Carolina, Florida and the Bahama Islands*, wrote of seeing the extensive use of rail fences in South Carolina: "The fields are bounded by wooden fences, which are usually made of pine, split into rails of about twelve or fourteen feet long; the frequent removing of these fences to fresh land, and the necessity of speed erecting them, are partly the reasons that hedges are not hitherto made use of, besides

The worm fence, also known as the Virginia rail or zigzag fence, was employed throughout the southern states to protect crops and contain livestock.

the facility of making wooden fences in a country abounding in wood." The fences described by Catesby were common worm or zigzag fences, which were in continuous

The Wallace House—Onslow County, North Carolina. This postbellum image reflects the continuous use of a variety of wooden fences in the American South throughout the nineteenth century.

use in the South from the late 1600s through the nineteenth century. This fence type (sometimes referred to as the Virginia rail fence) was generally constructed of split rails of cedar, oak, locust, or pine—each selected because they were resistant to decay and could remain in continuous use for extended periods of time. Building a worm fence required an abundant supply of wood, but if properly constructed, this versatile fence could last fifty years or more. A worm fence could be constructed from as few as five, or as many as ten or more rails, each stacked one on top of the other in a zigzag fashion. Its strength was based on the appropriate length of rails, the angle at which the horizontal sections were connected, and the use of vertical props at intersecting points to provide strength and stability. For a strong, effective fence that could be easily installed and quickly removed, the worm fence proved extremely serviceable. In 1861, one authority estimated that the worm fence represented over ninety percent of all fences employed in the southern states.

Another commonly used utilitarian fence that was popular during the antebellum period was the post-and-rail. This fence was constructed by inserting horizontal rails into vertical posts. Two, three, and sometimes as many as four horizontal rails were used to create a strong and secure fence that could either contain or exclude cows, horses, sheep, goats, and even pigs. The post-and-rail fence was also used to enclose town lots, the grounds of public and private buildings, orchards, pastures, and cultivated fields. Wood that was durable and long lasting, such as cedar and locust, was selected for vertical posts, while pine and poplar were favored for rails. Rails were usually mortised, not nailed, into posts to insure greater strength and stability. Evidence suggests that post-and-rail fences were seldom painted but were allowed to weather naturally, as a means of reducing upkeep and maintenance.

By 1860, most southern states had enacted fence laws, which regulated the height, construction, materials, spacing, and maintenance of utilitarian fences. A sampling of early fence laws in the South reveals that in 1827 South Carolina enacted a law that required planters to construct and maintain a five-foot fence either of rails, boards, or post and rails around cultivated land. In Georgia, all fences had to be five or six-feet tall, depending on the type and method of construction. In North Carolina, property owners were subject to indictment for failure to maintain their fences, and removal of an existing fence was forbidden if an adjoining property owner was preparing his property for the planting of crops or for livestock production. Mississippi defined a lawful fence as one that was "strong and sound, five feet high, well staked . . . sufficiently locked, and close enough to prevent animals from creeping in." While fence laws varied from state to state, they often shared many similarities regarding design, material selection, and construction requirements. With decreasing sources of timber, experimentation with wire fencing began, and by 1860, wire fencing was being advertised in southern agricultural journals both for farm and residential use. Although wire fences proved less costly and easier to maintain than those made of wood, adherence to the use of traditional wooden fences continued in the southern states until the end of the nineteenth century.

## HEDGES

Hedges played an important role in the antebellum South both for ornamental uses, as well as for a variety of practical purposes. In all cases, the selection of appropriate hedge plants was an important decision and was based on a number of considerations including ease and ability to clip or shear, height and spread, existence of thorns or spines, availability of plants, cost, and maintenance requirements. In the lower and middle South, a number of native and imported plants proved ideal for ornamental hedges. The following descriptions of plants commonly used as ornamental hedges appeared in John A. Warder's *Hedges and Evergreens* (1858), one of the most definitive works published on the subject during the antebellum period:

> Cassine—*Ilex Cassine* is a low, evergreen tree, of Carolina and Florida, and some other southern states. The leaves are small, like the Arbutus; but the berries are large in proportion, red and persistent during winter. . . . Other species of *Ilex* are found in the southern states, some of which have merit; but they are not so well known. [Of equal importance was the native yaupon holly, *Ilex vomitoria*, which occurs from Virginia to Florida and Texas and was among the native hollies the most frequently used for ornamental hedges.]

> *Junipers virginiana*, or Red Cedar, is one of our most valuable evergreen trees. . . . It grows from forty to fifty feet high; the branches spring horizontally and low down the tree. . . . As an ornamental tree or large shrub it is of great value for grouping, and especially for shelter. This plant is highly esteemed in Europe, but quite too much neglected in our own country; perhaps, because it is so common: its growth is rapid, and it is very hardy.

> Certain deciduous shrubs, which hold their leaves late in the season, may be found to answer a very good purpose for those who cannot procure the expensive evergreens. . . . Of these, the commonest and most easily propagated is the Privet (*Ligustrum*

View from a Garden Overlooking Augusta, Georgia. Hedges were employed during the antebellum period to define and enclose a variety of ornamental spaces.

*vulgare*), which will grow readily from cuttings. . . . It bears pretty, white, fragrant flowers in summer, and affords a nice shelter. The chief objection to this plant is, that it has been found subject to blight.

For southern gardens there are many beautiful shrubs, that are well adapted to the purpose we are now considering [hedging]. . . . Among these are our beautiful Wild Orange (*Cerasus caroliniana*), that is much planted about southern residences, for hedges; because of its beautiful dark and shining leaves, and early white blossoms; it grows rapidly, and bears the knife well: I have seen perfect hedges of this material in Louisiana and Alabama. [This plant is known today as cherry laurel, *Prunus caroliniana*.]

Several other plants are well adopted to hedging; one of the very best and most beautiful is the Holly (*Ilex opaca*), which will form a beautiful evergreen hedge, and a pretty good barrier against cattle. It is of exquisite green, and, ornamental in the depth of winter with its scarlet berries, it is very attractive. This plant is of very slow growth, and does not succeed in many of our limestone soils; hence it cannot be applied in such locations.

The Box, *Buxus sempervirens*, is a well-known evergreen shrub of great beauty. There are several varieties, belonging to the greater or tree sort, and the less or dwarf. The principal plants representing these classes are: *B. sempervirens, var. Arborescens* and *suffruticosa*. The larger kind seldom exceeds twelve or twenty-five feet in height. . . . The small, coriaceous, bright-green and shining leaves, are very persistent, and make a beautiful evergreen. As the Box-tree bears clipping well, the smaller is adopted to garden-edging, and the larger to hedges. . . .

The *Pittosporum tobira* is a half-hardy evergreen, with entire leaves, somewhat lanceolate. In its native country, it sometimes attains a height of twelve feet. The flowers are creamy-white, in clusters appearing in March to August. In the Southern states, it may be treated as a hardy plant; in the North, it needs the protection of a glass-house.

The Laurustinus, *Viburnum tinus*, is an evergreen with dark foliage and fragrant white corymbosa flowers. It is a native of the south of Europe, hardy in Great Britain, but a green-house plant in the northern and middle states. It flowers from November until April. This plant is used for forming low hedges in flower-gardens, where hardy.

The use of several of the referenced plants for ornamental hedges was described by Miss Almira Coffin of Buxton, Maine, in a letter to her friend, Mattie Osgood. Miss Coffin provided an account of her visit, in the spring of 1851, to Midway Plantation, located some twelve miles outside Georgetown, South Carolina, on the Waccamaw River. After discussing events surrounding her arrival, she proceeded to elaborate on the fascinating features of Midway's gardens and grounds:

> We walked from the wharf several hundred yards through the rice field . . . then we came to the high land and entered through a big gate on either side of which was a tree called the "Pride of India" [*Melia azaderack*] covered with purple flowers and a Cherokee Rose climbing to the top, and a multiflora the other, both having hundreds and perhaps thousands of roses on them. Wild orange *hedges* [cherry laurel, *Prunus caroliniana*], as high as my neck and some six feet broad we walked between to the house, which is a two-story square one, white with green blinds, a piazza on the north and south side. . . . There is a large circle in front of each piazza surrounded by *hedges*, filled with roses, flowering vines and evergreens. . . . I forgot one other feature upon this landscape, which was a labyrinth of *hedges*. You enter it, near the house, and the path will lead you about in a zigzag direction, in the center is a circle with a summer house covered with flowering vines etc., then you go on and on, round and round, first coming to a *hedge* of wild oranges then again to Arbor-vital then to Casina [*Cassine holly* or *Ilex cassine*], and between them are plots in a variety of shapes, filled with flowers. Some of the *hedges* are so high and broad that you can just peep over them and so thick a chicken couldn't get through, and trimmed beautifully, looking like one mass of deep green leaves. . . .

Another account, this time of a garden in Savannah, Georgia, describing the extensive use of hedge plants, appeared in the *Magazine of Horticulture*, 1855.

## "Ornamental Gardening in the South" by Andrew Gray

འ The area at the front door, which is about thirty yards wide and of an oval form, has in the centre an elliptical figure, running athwart the door, and twelve by six yards in size, planted round with red cedars at about three feet apart, which are cut into a hedge about five feet high, arched between the plants. The arches are about three feet high, and from the top of them to the summit of the hedge, it forms a semicircle. Formerly this was a magnificent affair, but the cedars now begin to decay, and they, unlike many other evergreens, will not admit of severe cutting in. At each end of this ellipsis and about eight yards from it, is a cassine [*Ilex cassine*] hedge, forming a kind of crescent, which divides the area from the shrubbery. I have heretofore spoke of this plant; its adaptation for ornamental hedges cannot be surpassed. This hedge fully proves the assertion it stands about four feet high and three wide, cut square and perfectly close from top to bottom. . . .

We are now in the flower gardens [parterres], and shall speak of them jointly, as they differ only in the plan of laying out. A hedge of the Cérasus caroliniénsis [*Prunus caroliniana*] encloses the whole space; this plant answers pretty well as a hedge, but is liable to get thin at the bottom, owing to the old branches decaying. A border of shrubbery surrounds the whole, widening at the corners and at two sides of the house into considerable space, divided from the flower beds by a hedge of cassine. This, in my opinion, tends to give the whole a stiff and confined appearance; but when the shrubs are in flower they somewhat compensate for that evil. Both gardens are laid down geometrically.

Hedges also were used for a variety of practical purposes, such as screening of service yards, delineating property lines, and as livestock enclosures. Hedges were also used as a substitute for traditional wooden fences, thus conserving timber, and reducing maintenance and replacement costs. To achieve the desired results, plants for hedges were selected based on their adaptability to location, soil, climate, and other physical characteristics. Plants recommended for use as functional hedges included pyracantha, Cherokee rose, red cedar, hawthorn, and Osage orange. Of these, the Cherokee rose and Osage orange were most commonly used in the southern states. The Cherokee rose (*Rosa laevigata*) was utilized in the South as far west as the Mississippi River. The outstanding beauty of its shining evergreen leaves and numerous large, white blossoms in spring made the Cherokee rose a handsome object in the southern landscape. One writer in the *Southern Farmer and Planter* described the Cherokee rose in the following manner:

The Cherokee Rose (*Rosa laevigata*). In addition to its use as an ornamental, the Cherokee rose was frequently employed in the antebellum South as a hedge plant to protect crops and cultivated fields.

> A great many shrubs and trees have been used for the formation of hedges, but none is better adapted to this purpose than the Cherokee or Carolina Rose. This plant is of a hardy nature, rapid growth, ease of cultivation, and makes a durable, compact, and perfectly impenetrable hedge, and, so far has been ascertained, is not subject to any disease, nor the attacks of any deprecations. This rose is propagated from roots, seeds, layers, or cuttings. . . . In about three years from the insertion of cuttings, if the soil has been well prepared, and well worked, a hedge will be formed, which, by its impenetrability, will repel the attacks of any animal, and by its beauty soften, in a degree, the desolate and gloomy appearance of our winters.

Frederick Law Olmsted in *A Journey in the Back Country* (1860) provides the following account of Cherokee Rose hedges in the vicinity of St. Francisville, Louisiana:

> For some miles about St. Francisville the landscape has an open, suburban character, with residences indicative of rapidly accumulating wealth, and advancement in luxury among the proprietors. For twenty miles to the north of the town, there is on both sides a succession of large sugar and cotton plantations. Much land still remains uncultivated, however. The roadside fences are generally hedges of roses—Cherokee and sweet brier. These are planted first by the side of a common rail fence, which, while they are young, supports them in a manner of a trellis; as they grow older they fall each way, and mat together, finally forming a confused, sprawling, slovenly thicket, often ten feet in breadth and four to six feet high. Trumpet creepers, grapevines, gree-briers, and in very rich soil, cane, grow up through the mat of roses, and add to its strength. It is not as pretty as a trimmer hedge, yet very agreeable. . . .

An equally useful hedge plant was the Osage orange (*Maclura pomifera*), which is native to the central section of the United States but capable of thriving as far north as New England. The Osage orange was collected and introduced to the eastern states by members of the Lewis and Clark Expedition. A deciduous tree with thorny branches, rich green foliage, and large orangelike fruit, the Osage orange made both a handsome and useful hedge. Its superior merits as an ideal hedge plant included its ease of propagation, quick growth, formidable spines, freedom from the attack of insects and diseases, longevity, and its ability to bear pruning well and to form an impenetrable barrier.

While the Osage orange was promoted as one of the finest of all hedge plants, it was more widely employed in the central and western states than in the South. This was largely because the southern economy was based on large-scale cotton farming, not livestock production, which required fencing and physical enclosure and was more common in other regions of the country. Another reason for the extensive use of hedges in the prairie states instead of fences was the limited availability of timber and forest trees. The Osage orange was sometimes used as a hedge plant in the southern states, a fact supported from accounts in farm and agricultural journals, but it was the Cherokee rose that was generally preferred, as indicated in a letter to the editor of the *Southern Cultivator* in 1855:

The Osage orange (*Maclura pomifera*) was used both as a hedge plant and an ornamental. When allowed to grow in a natural state, the Osage orange develops into a fifty- to sixty-foot tree, producing large, orangelike fruit.

I am astonished that one of your taste in rural matters would prefer the Osage Orange to all other plants for a hedge. On my part I much prefer the Cherokee Rose to the Osage Orange. I have seen hedges 12 feet high of the latter in Texas, growing in the wild unpruned state, and they present an uncouth, jagged, naked appearance, not at all "a thing of beauty," though a very effective barrier to any kind of depredators. But so is the Cherokee Rose formidable to stock, while with its evergreen leaves and flowers of snow, it is gloriously beautiful. Unfortunately it has never received the care, as it needs little, which is bestowed on other hedges. . . .

Truly yours,

Jenkins                                                        Montgomery, Alabama, July 1855

## LAWNS

The meaning of the word "lawn" has evolved over time. Beginning in the sixteenth century, the term was used to describe an open area in woods and forests. By the seventeenth century, the reference had changed to indicate a section of earth covered with grass. A century later, a lawn referred to an area within a garden or pleasure ground of neatly mown grass. Finally, in the nineteenth century a lawn was used to describe an area of turf, or greensward, in the vicinity of a house. The earliest use of lawns as a landscape element occurred in France during the mid-seventeenth century when André Le Nôtre (1613–1700), the famous French garden designer, incorporated carpets of grass known as *tapis vert* [carpet of green] in the designs of elaborate parterres. In the eighteenth century, lawns became an integral component of the English landscape movement, which was characterized by grassy lawns, sweeping meadows, sinuous lakes, and sheep and cows grazing in parklike settings.

The use of lawns as a landscape element was slow to arrive in North America. Prior to the Civil War, few Americans had lawns, and those that did were generally well educated, considerably wealthy, and had traveled extensively both in America and abroad. Lawns not only had to be cut once or twice a month, using a lawn-scythe, but also required a mild climate and adequate rainfall. Some of the earliest attempts at establishing lawns in America occurred in the northeast, particularly in the Hudson River Valley. Here the climate was more conducive to creating lush, green lawns, and appropriate seed mixtures were readily available from northern seedsmen in Boston, New York, and Philadelphia. Comparable efforts in the South were far less successful as few lawn grasses could tolerate the heat and drought of southern summers.

Throughout the antebellum period, lawns remained an uncommon feature in the southern states. Bishop Stephen Elliott confirmed this in an address made to the Southern Agricultural Society in Macon, Georgia, in 1851. Bishop Elliott commented that "Two-thirds of the year, in our climate there is a conflict with heat. Everything, therefore which *art* can do ought to be done to mitigate its fervor and make life comfortable, and yet, strange to say, very little is done toward that end." Elliott recommended that houses be built with deep piazzas and verandahs, that existing trees around dwellings be protected, and that grounds be planted in grass. In regard to the latter, he emphatically asked, "But where are our lawns? Where are the green spots that are to relieve the eyes and cheer the exhausted nature. There are literally none. A green sward is almost as rare in Georgia as a pavement of jasper." To establish a successful lawn in the South, Bishop Elliott offered the following advice:

Montgomery Place. Located along the Hudson River near Tarrytown, New York, Montgomery Place was one of several notable homes described by Andrew Jackson Downing in his *Treatise on the Theory and Practice of Landscape Gardening* as having a picturesque landscape that contained stately trees, spacious lawns, and sinuous walks and drives.

If the desire is to have a perfect lawn, pains and labor have to be bestowed upon it. Deep spading, a free use of lime where it does not exist in the soil, clean weeding, nice harrowing, a mixture of blue grass, white clover and English lawn seed rolled in plaster before planting, constant top dressing of plaster or charcoal, all these will be necessary, not once but often, to enable it to stand the heat of our sun, and the interminable droughts of our summers. . . . In land prepared and dressed as above recommended, a very fair lawn can be obtained. The white clover protects the other grasses for two or three years and then dies out leaving them to form the smooth body of the sward. To the labor above detailed must be added frequent scything and rolling with a heavy stone roller. All weeds and intrusive grasses must be carefully handpicked until you shall have destroyed all that was left in the original preparation of the soil. The seed ought to be placed in such a lawn by October, so as to give it a firm root and a steady growth before the trying heat of summer.

In addition to this method of establishing a lawn, Bishop Elliott also recommended use of native grasses, of which there are more than 100 varieties in the southern states. He advised that the site first be cleared of excess trees and underbrush to allow light to filter in. Then, using the wisdom taught by the American Indians, the fallen leaves should be burned. Elliott explained that "out of this will spring a variety of native grasses that will give in a few years the impression of a very pretty sward provided you will use the scythe upon it freely. This will not be, of course, such a lawn as an artificial one . . . but it will afford a most delightful relief to the eye, and covered with fine cattle, will give an idea, at least, of the English lawn." The occurrence of native grasses throughout the South in cleared forests and beneath groves of native trees did, in effect, create the impression of lawns as referenced in William Bartram's *Travels Through North and South*

*Carolina, Georgia, East and West Florida* (1791), as well as in travel accounts by visitors to the South during the antebellum period:

### *Travels Through North and South Carolina, Georgia, East and West Florida* (1773–1776)

William Bartram

ॐ We rode a long time, through magnificent high forests, extensive green fields, meadows and lawns . . . [the] next day proceeding on eight or ten miles, generally through spacious forests and flowery lawns. . . . We arrived after riding over a level plain, consisting of ancient Indian plantations, a beautiful landscape diversified with groves and lawns. . . .

### *The Sunny South; or, The Southerner at Home,* 1860

Joseph Holt Ingraham, Editor

ॐ Letter XXIV

The road now divides a green and verdant landscape, more woodland than field, but made up of both . . . you gaze with admiration into the sun-dappled forests, whose broad patches of light and shade look like scenes in Claude Lorraine's pictures, and remind you of them. You wonder at the green sward beneath the trees being so green and soft, as if it had been the work of trained English gardeners; when the extent of these lawn-like forests convinces you that they are as nature's gardening left them.

ॐ Letter LVIII

On my way up from New Orleans to Louisville, I determined to stop and see my fair friend, in her own home; and having obtained the direction, I embarked at New Orleans on board the steamer "Dr. Beattie," for Thibodiaux. We steamed up the Mississippi to Donaldsonville, eighty miles, and thence diverged into a narrow stream called Bayou La Fourche. Along this winding water we sailed thirty miles more, through a lovely land of groves, sugar fields, meadows, villas, and villages. . . . Silence and beauty reign there. One fine feature of this land is, that the forests have natural lawns, like the leveled sward of an English park. . . .

Prior to the publication of Andrew Jackson Downing's *Treatise on the Theory and Practice of Landscape Gardening* (1841) most Americans acquired their knowledge of lawns either from English garden books, European travel, or through the services of an itinerant landscape gardener. Even after the publication of Downing's monumental work, little information on lawns or lawn care was offered specifically to gardeners in the southern states. Thus, in an effort to obtain advice and information on growing lawns in the South, many southern gardeners directed inquiries to the editors of agricultural journals:

English Parks. During the eighteenth century, naturalistic or landscaped parks surrounded many English country estates.

∿ Grasses for Lawns

    Messrs. Editors—I notice in the columns of your invaluable paper much written on grasses for pasturage, but see nothing on grasses for *lawns.* I desire to know, either from you or some of your correspondents, what kind of grass or assortment of grasses will best beautify lawns, and thrive in this part of Georgia; the quantity of seed per acre; the time and manner of sowing, etc. with the whole *modus operandi.* . . .

                                    Oglethorpe County, Georgia, 1853

∿ Reply—It is very difficult to raise a good lawn in this arid and scorching climate, and those who are not prepared to foster and nourish their favorite grass plots with care and patience, need not undertake it. Several fundamental principles are absolutely necessary to success, viz: 1st, Deep plowing, (i.e. 12 to 18 inches) and thorough pulverization of the soil. 2nd, an abundant supply of the best compost or manure, turned under and intimately mixed with the earth. 3rd, a very liberal application of mixed seed, embracing the different clovers, Blue Grass, the English Eaver, Texas Mesquite, Herds Grass, and etc. (Some people prefer Bermuda Grass alone, and we have seen it used with success.) 4th, close and frequent cutting and mowing of the grass after it is well "set"—generous top dressings of the best manure every Spring and Fall afterwards; and showerings, during dry weather, with a weak infusion of Guano, or nitrate of soda. All this, properly carried out, will give . . . a verdant and velvety lawn, gladdening to the eye and yielding to the footstep. . . .

                                              Editors

Another request several years later to the editors of the same publication indicated that southern gardeners still had little in the way of instructions for establishing successful lawns in the South:

## *The Southern Cultivator,* 1857

∿ Lawn Grass for the South

    Editors, Southern Cultivator. You will confer upon me a personal favor, and no doubt upon others of your readers, if you will give me, in your paper, the information you have in relation to the best Lawn grass for the South, the mode of preparing the land, sowing seed, etc.

    I have several acres of old field, high and dry, with clay subsoil, in front of my house which I wish to set in grass of some sort suited to our climate. The only instance I know of complete success in our District in making a beautiful plot has been with the little white Clover. Most other grasses, you are aware, die out under our hot summer sun. It is, however, not very suitable for a lawn—it grows too high.

    If you think the subject would be of interest to your readers, I would be pleased to see an article in your journal which would give us your best information.

                                    Very respectfully, A. C. G.

                         Newberry, South Carolina, August 1857

∿ Remarks—The Lawn grasses of cool and humid England are little adapted to the hot and dry climate of the southern states. Southern grown Blue Grass seed is, perhaps, the best single seed. . . . Will not some of our readers, long familiar with both annual and perennial grasses of the South give the public a few suggestions of this interesting subject?

Editors

Various mixtures of lawn grasses were tried in the South with limited success. Most would thrive during the fall, winter, and spring, but almost all were intolerant of the heat and drought of the summer. From all accounts, references to lawns or greenswards in the lower and middle South prior to the Civil War were to stands of native grasses or pasturelike lawns seeded with clover, orchard grass, redtop, timothy, herd, and common rye. Over time, experimentation with various pasture grasses in the South led to the discovery that Bermuda grass (*Cynodon dactylon*) was also useful for lawns. While it is believed that Bermuda grass first arrived in North America in the ballasts of European sailing ships, it was not officially introduced until around 1751. In the South it proved ideal for pastures because of its ability to grow in almost any soil and its tolerance of heat and drought. Its greatest disadvantage was its aggressive nature, which made it difficult to control, especially in row or cultivated crops.

Bermuda lawns were not extensively planted in the southern states until after the lawnmower was patented in 1868. However, there is evidence that Bermuda grass was occasionally used for lawns in the antebellum South. Mr. Andrew Gray, in an article published in *The Magazine of Horticulture* in 1855, provides one such account in his description of a garden at a country residence outside the city of Savannah, Georgia: "No proper lawn grass has yet been found to stand in this soil and climate. . . . There are, however, several sorts of coarse native grasses which grow here, and except in a very severe season keep green throughout; but the one most adaptable in this section is the Bermuda grass; it never rises above the surface over eight or ten inches. It has long creeping roots and sends up stems at every joint, and by planting the roots in the ground, it is not many years before it becomes completely matted; and, in Spring and early Summer, if kept mown,

Lawns. The "lawns" of the antebellum South were generally comprised of a mixture of annual/perennial pasture grasses or native species.

looks as well as many of the grass lawns I have seen in the North." In the upper south, Kentucky bluegrass (*Poa protensis*) proved to be an excellent lawn grass, but in areas south of Tennessee, it was intolerant of the summer heat and long periods of drought.

As a substitute for a lawn, there developed in the South the so-called "swept yard." The term swept yard refers to an area of compacted soil or loose sand that was routinely "swept" with a brush broom for the purpose of creating a clean, neatly maintained space, completely free of grass or vegetation. Brush brooms were made of branches of native trees or shrubs, such as inkberry (*Ilex glabra*), wax myrtle (*Myrica cerifera*), and dogwood (*Cornus florida*). These yards were, as a rule, enclosed by a picket or paleing fence to limit access and define and articulate the space. While swept yards are frequently associated with the antebellum period, the term appears to have a late-nineteenth or early-twentieth-century origin.

In addition to insuring a neat and well-maintained surface, swept yards also were employed to discourage the encroachment of vermin (small animals, rodents, and insects) and to provide protection against the potential spread of fire from surrounding fields and forests. Some historians contend that swept yards were of African origin, introduced into the South by slaves during the antebellum period. Others speculate that swept yards simply evolved over time, initially as a practical means of maintaining a clean and orderly work yard, and then expanding to other areas adjoining the dwelling. As a rule, when a swept yard was employed in an area other than a work yard, it was usually associated with a house of modest means and seldom with the houses of planters or the professional class. This conceivably was based on the prevailing belief that an ornamental garden and the planting of trees and shrubs were a display of status and social prestige. As swept yards were completely devoid of all vegetation, they did little to convey a sense of wealth or refinement of taste.

## *Formulas for Mixtures of Grasses for Southern Lawns*

Commercial formulas for grass seed mixtures viable for southern lawns were not widely available until the latter half of the nineteenth century. One of the earliest references describing mixtures of grass seed that were ideally suited for lawns in the South was published in 1890 in Bulletin Number 73, issued by the North Carolina Agricultural Experiment Station in Raleigh, North Carolina. As copies of this bulletin are quite rare and difficult to locate, portions of this document are reprinted here:

> All of these mixtures contain only low-growing grasses, and will not need mowing, nor should they be mown more frequently than every six weeks. Where cost is not an object it is advised to sow upon two acres the quantity of seed, sufficient according to the formula for three acres. This will give a very thick and close sward, so much admired in lawns.

| Name of Grass | Portion of Ground Occupied | Quantity of Seed Per Acre |
|---|---|---|
| #21—For Lawns—Rich Soil, Considerably Shaded: | | |
| Kentucky Blue | 50 percent | 12–1/2 pounds |
| Crested Dog's-Tail | 20 percent | 7 pounds |
| Fiorin | 20 percent | 2–1/2 pounds |
| Perennial Sweet-Vernal | <u>10 percent</u> | <u>4 pounds</u> |
| | 100 percent | 26 pounds |

| Name of Grass | Portion of Ground Occupied | Quantity of Seed Per Acre |
|---|---|---|
| **#22—For Lawns—Poorer Soil Than Above:** | | |
| Creeping Red Fescue | 30 percent | 12 pounds |
| English Blue | 30 percent | 7–1/2 pounds |
| Fine-Leaved Fescue | 30 percent | 15 pounds |
| Perennial Sweet-Vernal | 10 percent | 4 pounds |
| | 100 percent | 38–1/2 pounds |
| **#23—For Lawns and Parks—Rich Soil, Not Much Shade:** | | |
| Perennial Rye | 30 percent | 24 pounds |
| Crested Dog's Tail | 20 percent | 7 pounds |
| Kentucky Blue | 40 percent | 11 pounds |
| Perennial Sweet-Vernal | 10 percent | 4 pounds |
| | 100 percent | 46 pounds |
| **#24—For Lawns and Parks—Poorer Soil Than Above:** | | |
| Perennial Rye | 10 percent | 8 pounds |
| English Blue | 50 percent | 12 pounds |
| Creeping Red Fescue | 30 percent | 12 pounds |
| Perennial Sweet-Vernal | 10 percent | 4 pounds |
| | 100 percent | 36 pounds |

These formulas are for one acre only and to be taken as many times as there are acres.

# [4]

# ANTEBELLUM GARDENS

**PREVIOUS RESEARCH ON** the landscape history of the antebellum South generally focused on plantation gardens. This is unfortunate, for many of the finest gardens of the antebellum period were developed in towns, cities, and their surrounding areas. It was in these locations that resources for the creation of high-style gardens were in greatest supply, including garden designers, artisans, craftsmen, seed and plant merchants, and nurseries. In an effort to provide a comprehensive overview of the development of gardens of the antebellum period, the following material examines gardens and gardening practices in both urban and rural settings.

Affluent citizens developed many of the fine houses and ornamental gardens found in southern cities during the antebellum period. Among those that created beautiful gardens were prosperous merchants, bankers, lawyers, and cotton brokers as well as wealthy planters from surrounding areas. Planters often resided in cities on a full-time or seasonal basis either for cultural and social benefits or to escape the threat of malaria and yellow fever that was often prevalent in rural areas. Members of the professional class and wealthy planters developed urban properties that typically included a fine house, a formal garden, work yard, servants' quarters, detached kitchen, and a variety of out buildings, creating an urban complex that approached the dimensions of a miniature plantation.

While city gardens of the antebellum South were generally formal, variations in design often occurred as a result of differences in cultural traditions, architectural styles, and a city's physical plan. For instance, Charleston's strong English ties, vernacular architecture, and physical layout were responsible for the development of gardens that were distinctly different from those in New Orleans, where French and Spanish culture, classical architecture, interior courts, and a compact city plan had a strong influence on garden design. Variations also occurred in the use of paving and edging material, fences, gates, and garden furnishings.

Although differences existed in urban gardens of the antebellum South, consistency generally prevailed in the use of geometric shapes to create formal designs. As a rule, city gardens contained a wider selection of ornamental plants than did those in small towns or on plantations. This occurred because city gardeners had greater access to plants, seeds, and bulbs than did those living in rural areas. In fact, many northern nurseries hired local agents in southern cities to secure orders that were then shipped at the appropriate season. City residents also had a greater opportunity to exchange and share ornamental plants with other gardeners than those in isolated areas. The exchange of cuttings of ornamental plants among urban gardeners is documented in the following correspondence between Joel Poinsett and J. B. Campbell of Charleston, South Carolina, in 1833:

> I wish you would make a collection of cuttings and send them up [to Joel Poinsett's plantation, located outside Georgetown, South Carolina] by the John Stoney, the Schooner in our employ, which must be leaving town now. Lewis and Robertson will inform you all about where abouts and probable times of sailing. Cuttings of all manner of Roses, Pittisporum [*sic*], Myrtles, Etc. Etc. Seeds of the wild orange, a peck at least. At Belvedere the Doctr. [Dr. Joseph Johnson] can give you a great variety of cuttings for all which we shall be thankful. Think nothing too common, we have literally nothing here. Even a Multiflora will be acceptable. Lots of daily roses, cuttings will do and we will strive to make them grow. Seeds of Arbor vitae etc. etc. Cuttings of Cape Jessamine, the Japanese honey suckle, and above all a few roots of Ivy to be had at the Grove at Mr. Wagner's who can give you other things and at Noisettes in profusion. Send lots of cuttings of the Tamarisk it grows at Judge Richard's cottage.
>
> The Poinsett-Campbell Correspondence
> *The South Carolina Historical and Genealogical Magazine*

The best examples of city gardens of the antebellum South are found in Charleston, South Carolina, Savannah, Georgia, and New Orleans, Louisiana.

Following the destructive effects of the Revolutionary War, Charleston regained its position as a major seaport city, and with the increased planting of rice and the production of sea-island cotton (*Gossypium barbadese*), prosperity soon returned to the region. Following the Revolutionary War, houses built in Charleston began to depart from the established style and included piazzas or open galleries that extended along the south or west side of the house. There were usually as many tiers of piazzas as there were stories to a building. Piazzas served several functions. During cold weather, they provided an ideal spot to enjoy the typical sunny days of a Carolina lowcountry winter, and in intense summer sun, they prevented the house from becoming unbearably hot. In the late afternoon and evening, piazzas caught the cool, refreshing ocean breezes and became delightful outdoor living spaces. Piazzas also served as outdoor rooms from which Charleston's small-patterned gardens could be viewed year-round. Many of these small gardens were simple versions of English or French parterres, fashionable in Europe in the seventeenth and eighteenth centuries. These garden plans were based on various designs and combinations of geometric shapes including circles, squares, rectangles, triangles, and diamonds. Parterres were usually bordered with dwarf box or oversized English brick and planted with flowers, bulbs, and ornamental shrubs. Paths were generally made of sand shell, gravel, or crushed oyster shells. In *Charleston, the Place and the People*, Harriott Horry Rutledge Ravenel provides a description of Charleston's vernacular architectural style and accompanying gardens from around 1790:

> The houses many of them wood and airy, and the fashion of piazzas were becoming general. People were adopting the peculiar style of house stretched long to catch the breeze with gable end to the street and long piazzas. It was not as handsome, but cooler and better suited to the climate than the square colonial mansion. This manner of house presupposes a garden, for the door upon the street is in truth only a sort of gate, and the true front door opens from the piazza, and gives upon the garden opposite. . . . In the town, behind their high walls grew oleanders and pomegranates, figs and grapes, and orange trees both sweet and bitter, and bulbs brought

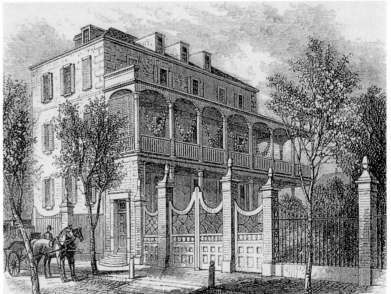

A Charleston Single House—Charleston, South Carolina.

> from Holland, jonquils and hyacinths. The air was fragrant with the sweet olive, myrtle and gardenia. There were old-fashioned roses! The cinnamon, the York and Lancaster, the little white musk, and the sweet or Damascus. The glossy-leaved Cherokee clothed the walls with its great white disks, and was crowned by jasmine and honeysuckle.

Construction of Charleston's so-called "single houses" evolved in response to several factors: the city's semitropical climate, narrow urban lots, and the need to provide ample space for a variety of outbuildings and a small side garden. The single house was typically built with its gabled end facing the street and its rooms strung out in a single line, which allowed for cross ventilation. The first floor was usually raised several feet above the ground to provide protection against flooding during hurricanes and tropical storms and as a health measure, as it was considered unhealthy at the time for a house to be built on damp ground. An outer door that opened directly onto a piazza provided access from the street into the house, with the piazza traditionally overlooking a small side garden. The real front door was located in the center of the piazza facing the garden. Charleston's antebellum gardens were simplified versions of earlier European designs. They were comprised of a combination of geometric shapes and symmetrical forms, with individual beds being interrelated to create a unified design. A distinctive feature of nearly all gardens in Charleston during this period was their containment behind brick or stucco walls, which were employed both for security and as a means of providing a sense of privacy, a needed feature because of the closeness of individual houses that resulted from the city's dense urban plan.

The Jenkins Mikell House—Charleston, South Carolina. Built in 1853 by I. Jenkins Mikell, a wealthy cotton planter, this structure represents one of Charleston's great town houses.

In addition to Charleston's single houses, there developed during the first half of the nineteenth century many fine classically styled town houses. Many of these structures were built by the wealthy planters who retreated from their rural plantations to the society and culture of the city. Descriptions of several of Charleston's large town house gardens are provided in Alice Lockwood's *Gardens of Colony and State* (1931–1934). One of the most renowned gardens in Charleston during the antebellum period was that of Thomas Bennett, who employed the services of two English gardeners: "The grounds were most extensive, including a vegetable garden in the rear, numerous fruit trees and a group of large Live Oaks. The garden was laid out in the Flemish style, square beds and broad, straight walks. Many foreign plants were brought from Europe; they were constantly being added to by things strange and beautiful. There were extensive greenhouses in which delicate plants and pineapples were raised."

Another important garden of the period was that of William A. Hayne. Located on the corner of Ashley Avenue and Cannon Street, the garden was described as very formal with box-bordered flower beds in shapes of diamonds. The following description provides additional details:

Very formal were the box-bordered flower beds—diamonds, circles, squares, etc. At one end of the garden were three pieces of topiary. . . . At the other end and at each side were large lattice trellises covered with white and yellow climbing roses. Large *Camellia japonica* trees, white, red and variegated, single and double varieties, were planted in favorable spots. There was the delicate pink, Lady Hume, and a very small tree of pure white flowers, the petals of which were fringed, as though clipped with scissors. . . . A row of magnolias with their handsome white and purple blossoms stood at the rear of the garden, and every available space was filled with roses, day lilies, clove pinks, and other small sweet-scented plants. Many of the box beds were filled with a delightful variety of spring bulbs. The garden was separated from the street by an open wooden fence, and the paths were of pounded white oyster shells.

Another city garden, known as the Lucas Garden, was located at the western end of Calhoun Street. This elaborate garden contained long alleys hedged with laureltinus (*Viburnum tinus*), which ran through the main garden to the rear of the property. The centerpiece of the Lucas garden featured a large oval bed that contained a magnificent camellia, which each spring produced a profusion of single-flowered, crimson blossoms. One account of the garden tells of as many as eighty camellias planted throughout the garden, the choicest being housed in a structure known as the "Japonica House"; a structure simi-

lar to a greenhouse that was twenty or thirty feet long and about twenty feet wide. The garden consisted of a series of brick-edged beds planted with roses and flowering shrubs including such old-time favorites as flowering quince, crape myrtle, forsythia, along with Maréchael Neil and cloth of gold roses.

The Nathaniel Russell House on Meeting Street also contained an elegant nineteenth-century garden. It was here that Nathaniel Russell, a prominent shipping merchant from Rhode Island, maintained a large garden in a geometric arrangement with patterned beds planted with flowers, ornamental shrubs, and large orange and grapefruit trees. In 1819, William Faux, an English traveler and author of *Memorable Days in America*, told of a visit with the venerable Mr. Russell, which occurred only a year before his death. Russell was found "living in a splendid mansion surrounded by a wilderness of flowers, and bowers of myrtles, oranges and lemons, smothered with fruits and flowers." Russell's youngest daughter continued to live in the house until the mid-1850s. In 1857, it became the house of R. F. W. Allston, a prominent planter and the governor of South Carolina.

Many of Charleston's urban elite also owned country seats north of the city, on the upper peninsula along the Ashley and Cooper

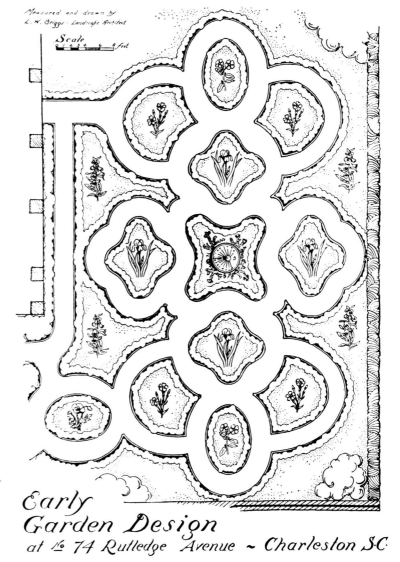

*Early Garden Design at №74 Rutledge Avenue ~ Charleston S.C.*

A Parterre Garden—Charleston, South Carolina.

Rivers, and on neighboring sea islands along the coast. These retreats were visited on a regular or seasonal basis, offering their owners the opportunity for a variety of horticultural and gardening pursuits. Many country seats had simple, two-storied plantation houses characterized by high, hipped roofs, simple piazzas, and ornamental gardens surrounded by stately trees, native groves, and cultivated fields. Watercolor drawings of many of Charleston's country seats are contained in Charles Fraser's (1782–1860) *A Charleston Sketchbook*. Fraser, a distinguished Charleston artist, also captured in his sketchbook views of churches, town houses, and landscape scenes in and around the city.

While English garden traditions are well documented in Charleston's gardening past, the French also made important contributions to the area's garden heritage. The many French Huguenots who immigrated to Charleston following the Edict of Nantes in 1685 and later French refugees who arrived in the city following a slave uprising in the French colony of Santo Domingo strongly influenced the social customs, fashions, architecture, and garden design in Charleston and the surrounding area. The French who settled in Charleston were particularly well known for their fine, small gardens, before and during the antebellum period. Prominent French names associated with Charleston's horticultural and gardening past include Michaux, Noisette, Poinsett, Legare, Manigault, and Porcher, to mention but a few.

## Savannah, Georgia

Founded by James Edward Oglethorpe in 1733, Savannah's physical development was greatly influenced by its innovative plan, which was based on a formalized arrangement of wards and squares. Each ward contained forty tithing lots for private residences, four trustee lots reserved for public buildings, and a central open space or square. It was envisioned that each square would become a center of commercial, social, and religious activity. As early as 1822, the Savannah city council appointed a tree committee that was instructed to formulate a list of trees to be planted in Savannah's squares. Trees selected by the committee included the chinaberry (*Melia azedarach*), live oak (*Quercus virginiana*), laurel oak (*Quercus laurifolia*), willow oak (*Quercus phellos*), wild orange (*Prunus caroliniana*), sycamore (*Platanus occidentalis*), American elm (*Ulmus americana*), and southern magnolia (*Magnolia grandiflora*). In 1853, Curtis B. Pyle, a corresponding editor for the *Masonic Mirror and American Keystone*, offered the following account of Savannah and its overall plan: "Savannah is a city of trees and gardens. It reminds me of what William Penn wished that his beloved Philadelphia might be—'a green garden town.' In the city plan a large number of small squares are laid out, and these are planted with trees." By 1860, Savannah had developed twenty-four squares and a large public park named for John Forsyth, the former governor and secretary of state under presidents Andrew Jackson and Martin Van Buren. Forsyth Park not only served as a public park but also as a military parade ground.

Savannah, unlike Charleston and other southern cities, avoided destruction during the Civil War by surrendering to federal troops. Following occupation of the city in December of 1864, General W. T. Sherman dispatched a telegram to Washington in which he offered to President Lincoln as a Christmas gift "the City of Savannah, with one hundred and fifty guns and plenty of ammunition, also, about twenty-five thousand bales of cotton." While detrimental to the Confederate cause, this historic event was responsible for preserving the city's historic homes, public buildings, parks, squares, and gardens. General Sherman appeared to have been duly impressed with Savannah's beauty and charm

Fountain in Forsyth Park.

Fountain in Forsyth Park—Savannah, Georgia. This ornate, cast-iron fountain was added to Forsyth Park in 1858.

for in his *Memoirs* he wrote, "The city of Savannah was an old place, and usually accounted a handsome one. Its houses were of bricks or frame, with large yards, ornamented with shrubbery and flowers; its streets perfectly regular, crossing each other at right angles; and at many of the intersections were small enclosures in the nature of parks. These streets and parks were lined with the handsomest shade trees of which I have knowledge, viz., the willow-leaf live-oak, evergreens of exquisite beauty; and these certainly entitled Savannah to its reputation as a handsome town."

Similar to Charleston, Savannah developed numerous long, narrow residential lots. An important difference between the two cities is that Savannah's city plan included the placement of central alleys (referred to locally as lanes) that extended behind the city's residential blocks. These public easements permitted the building of traditional row houses that could be positioned so that their front facades were close to the street, leaving adequate space for a small front garden and room at the rear of the property for outbuildings and servants' quarters. In some instances, variations of the Charleston single house, with its accompanying piazza and small parterre garden, were developed in Savannah. The following account by Laura Palmer Bell in the *Georgia Historical Quarterly* (1944) describes several of Savannah's early parterre gardens:

The garden I knew best has been called a crown garden, probably because some of the beds are shaped like a crown [see Knapp Garden below]. It is a fairly elaborate parterre, with beds finished with scalloped tile, and bordered with violets that were more lavish with leaves than with blossoms. The paths were of hard beaten black sand, and the beds farthest from the huge live oaks (there used to be two of them) were filled with bush roses. . . . Rhincospernum or Confederate Jessamine covered the arched gateway between the garden and the brick paved backyard, with its fig trees and Pride of India. Blue morning glories were on the fence, and in the garden from early winter on, there were paper white narcissus, pink and blue hyacinths, Easter lilies, rain lilies, snow drops and other bulbs blooming in their season. In the very center, covering even the violet border of the round bed, was a watermelon pink azalea, so large that passers-by used to stop to admire it when it was in bloom. . . . There were other azaleas and several camellias, hibiscus and hydrangeas, dahlias, chrysanthemums, phlox and verbenas, sweet alyssum, spice geraniums, Jacob's ladder under the veranda, a dwarf lemon tree that used to produce with an exhaustive effort one giant lemon, and a dwarf orange tree, with small hard tasteless fruit after fragrant blossoms. There were pepper bushes too, the lady finger, the African, the variegated and the inevitable bird's eye, in the narrow bed at the foot of the veranda steps that roofed a diminutive greenhouse. . . . Many of these plants, or their descendants . . . are in the garden today, a garden almost exactly as it used to be.

In contrast to the previously described layout, many large town houses were built on trustee lots—sites that were originally set aside for public buildings. These structures were handsomely designed and positioned so as to provide space for a front garden and ample room at the rear for a service yard. The Owens-Thomas House, which was designed by William Jay, a young British architect who came to Savannah to practice his trade in 1817, is one example of this type of structure and layout. Considered one of the

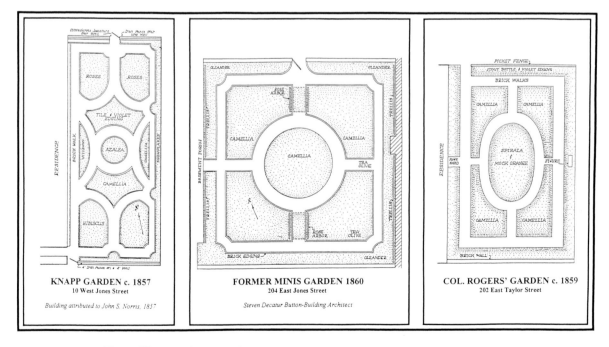

**KNAPP GARDEN c. 1857**
10 West Jones Street

*Building attributed to John S. Norris, 1857*

**FORMER MINIS GARDEN 1860**
204 East Jones Street

*Steven Decatur Button-Building Architect*

**COL. ROGERS' GARDEN c. 1859**
202 East Taylor Street

Plans of Parterre Gardens—Savannah, Georgia. The illustration shows plans for several parterre gardens developed in Savannah during the antebellum era.

finest examples of Regency architecture in America, this elegant town house was built for Richard Richardson, a successful cotton merchant and banker. According to early accounts, a small garden was located between the front facade and a balustrade wall that enclosed the intervening space. The garden was reported to have contained ornamental plantings of camellias, oleanders, and crape myrtles. The Richardsons also developed a larger garden on a lot they owned across the street. According to an account contained in *Gardens of Colony and State*, this garden was "laid out by M. M. Kollock, Esq., on a lot

sixty by ninety feet, and was enclosed on all sides by a high brick wall, topped with broken glass bottles to discourage marauders. . . . The pattern of the garden was a rather unusual one . . . with oval beds which were all edged with dwarf box." The garden contained extensive plantings of *Camellia japonica*, including such varieties as *Donklaeri*, *Ochraleuca*, and *Mutabilis* among others. Additional plants grown in the garden included "banana shrub, sweet olive, purple and white wisteria, English jasmine, ivy, a great many roses, syringa, Guernsey lilies, scillas, iris, narcissus, Roman hyacinths, snowdrops, ixias, anemones, asters, pansies and larkspur." The Richardsons lost their elegant town house during the financial depression of 1820, and for ten years the structure served as a lodging house. During that time it housed many notable visitors including the Marquis de Lafayette, the Revolutionary War hero, who delivered an address from the decorative cast-iron balcony located on the south side of the house. In 1830, George Welchman Owens, congressman, lawyer, and one-time

The Richardson-Owens-Thomas House—Savannah, Georgia.

mayor of Savannah, purchased the house for $10,000. The property remained in the Owens family until 1951, when Margaret Thomas, Owens's granddaughter, bequeathed the house and grounds to the Telfair Academy of Arts and Sciences. Today, the Richardson-Owens-Thomas House is a national historic landmark and serves as a house and garden museum. The site includes the original carriage house and a recreated period garden behind the house in an area that originally served as the service yard.

Another important town garden in Savannah still extant today is the parterre garden of the Batersby-Hartridge House on the south side of Lafayette Square. The house, designed in the Charleston style, was built by William Battersby, an English cotton broker who came to Savannah about 1852. The garden extends the full length of the property and is enclosed by a high brick wall. The design of the garden includes a series of circles and ovals forming a variety of interconnected beds bordered with scalloped edging tiles. The original garden contained plantings of camellias including *Donklaeri*, *Camellia reticulata*, Lady Hume's Blush, Ella Drayton, Legeman and Abby Wilder, alba plena. Additional ornamentals once grown in the garden included a tea plant (*Thea sinensis*),

The Green-Meldrin House—Savannah, Georgia. The Green-Meldrin House is enhanced by a formal parterre that retains its original design. The garden is bordered by a cast-iron fence of mid-nineteenth century origin.

flowering quince (*Chaenomeles lagenaria*), tea olive (*Osmanthus fragrans*), Devoniensis and General Jaqueminot roses, and lilac bignonia (*Clytostoma callistegioides*), a purplish, ever-green flowering vine which at one time covered the walls surrounding the garden.

Other old gardens in Savannah include those of the Green-Meldrin House, which serves as the parish house of St. John's Episcopal Church, and the Andrew Low House, now the home of the Georgia Society of the Colonial Dames. Andrew Low, an English cotton merchant, originally developed the Low House and garden in the 1840s. The house faces Lafayette Square and was Juliette Gordon Low's home at the time she founded the American Girl Scouts. The front garden retains its original "hourglass" design. The entrance walk is paved with flagstone from England and the parterre beds are edged with garden tiles. John S. Norris of New York designed the Green-Meldrin House, which was used by General Sherman as his headquarters during the occupation of Union forces in 1864. The garden reflects its original 1850s design. The parterre is comprised of a series of interlocking beds, bordered by decorative edging tiles. Walks between individual beds consist of loose sand and crushed oyster shells. Decorative, cast-iron fences, which were often found in southern coastal cities during the antebellum period, enclose the gardens of both the Andrew Low and the Green-Meldrin Houses.

## New Orleans, Louisiana

New Orleans is located approximately 100 miles upstream from the mouth of the Mississippi River. Founded in 1718 by Jean Baptiste le Moyne of France and named in honor of the Duc d'Orleans, New Orleans became an American city when the United States acquired the Louisiana Territory from France in 1803. At the time of the transaction, New Orleans had a population of around 8000—comprised of a cultural mix of Indian, French, African, Acadian, Spanish, and American inhabitants. During the antebellum period, New Orleans experienced unprecedented growth due to the regional production of cotton and sugar cane, the coming of the steamboat, and the city's position as a strategic port involved in both national and international trade. During the Civil War, Union troops captured the city in 1862 under the command of Admiral David Farragut and remained under federal control through the remainder of the war. Today, New Orleans represents one of the country's most interesting cities. It is well known for its unique location along the east bank of the Mississippi River, its cultural heritage and traditions, historic architecture, secluded courtyards, beautiful gardens, and rich urban fabric.

Nineteenth-century New Orleans gardens are well documented in drawings held at the New Orleans Notarial Archives. A product of French civil law, these legal documents extend from 1802 to 1918 and include surveys, plans, elevations, and perspective drawings of numerous New Orleans properties prepared by surveyors, engineers, architects, and artists. The larger drawings (usually two feet by four feet in size) in the collection were generally executed in watercolor and were either displayed in the auction room where the property was sold or accompanied acts of sale or building contracts in the notary's records. These drawings provide a graphic record of courtyard designs, garden layouts, and landscape details for properties throughout the city. Research confirms that the Notarial Archives are faithful recordings of what actually existed at the time. Drawings in the Notarial Archives reveal that the majority of gardens in antebellum New Orleans were formal in design, as simple geometry and symmetry were a logical extension of lot layouts and space constraints. Garden planting beds in New Orleans were typically rectangular, circular, or triangular in shape with walks composed of brick or flagstones.

When the Vieux Carré (the oldest section of the city) was laid out, surveyors configured building lots that were long and narrow. L-shaped houses with interior courtyards (originally referred to as courts and later as courtyards) were constructed in the area's restricted spaces. Plants frequently grown in the Vieux Carré's protected urban spaces included citrus, roses, jasmine, gardenias, sweet olive, myrtle, ginger lilies, and tuberoses. In describing a trip to New Orleans in 1830, a northern visitor commented on the "gales of fragrance" that were experienced throughout the Vieux Carré. New Orleans's subtropical climate, long growing season, and protected urban spaces fostered the use of many exotic and fragrant plants, which were purchased from local and foreign sources or

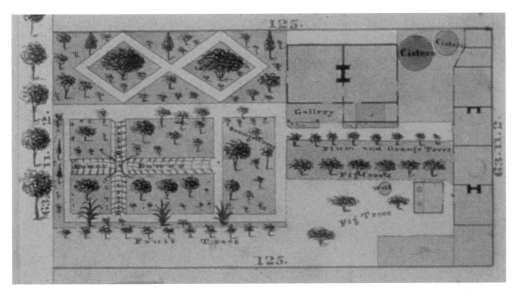

House and Garden Plan—New Orleans, Louisiana. This plan for a structure located on Josephine Street in the lower Garden District between Chestnut and Camp Streets reflects an extensive garden designed in a formal manner. New Orleans Notarial Archives, Plan Book 64, Folio 27.

obtained from friends from near and afar. In addition to growing ornamentals in geometric beds, many were raised in containers fashioned in iron, terra cotta, or clay. Courtyards not only served as pleasant retreats from the noise and activities of the city, but also functioned as the center of various service and social activities including food preparation, washing and drying, gardening, and family events. In addition, they also accommodated a variety of ancillary structures including garçonnières (quarters for adolescent boys), servants' quarters, stables, storage buildings, cisterns, and privies.

During the antebellum period, two or more lots in the Vieux Carré were often assembled for the purpose of constructing large town houses. These imposing structures were traditionally built to the edge of the sidewalk to maximize space for an interior court and a variety of outbuildings. The court was traditionally connected to the street by a narrow corridor or carriage-way, which provided access to the interior of the property and facilitated the removal of trash, delivery of food, access to stables, wood piles, and storage bins. Joseph Holt Ingraham in *The South-West* described a typical building in the Vieux Carré:

> The majority of structures in the old, or French section of New Orleans, are after the Spanish and French orders. This style of building is not only permanent and handsome, but peculiarly adapted, with its cool, paved courts, lofty ceilings, and spacious windows, to this sultry climate. . . . Dwellings of this construction, have, running through their center, a broad, high-arched passage, with high folding doors, or gates, leading from the street to a paved court in the rear, which is usually surrounded by the sleeping-rooms and offices, communicating with each other by galleries running down the whole square. In the center of the court usually stands a cistern, and placed around it, in large vases, are flowers and plants of every description. In their love for flowers the Creoles [individuals of Latin extraction born in the colonies] are truly and especially French. The glimpses one has now and then, in passing through the

Hermann-Grima House Site Plan and Courtyard—New Orleans, Louisiana. Built by William Brand for Samuel Hermann in 1831, the property was purchased in 1844 by Judge Felix Grima and remained in the Grima family until 1921.

streets, and by the ever-open doors of the Creoles' residences, are of brilliant flowers and luxuriantly blooming exotics.

An excellent example of an antebellum town house and interior court is the residence of Samuel Hermann, built in the Vieux Carré in the 1830s. Like other urban dwellings of the antebellum period, the court of the Hermann-Grima House (as it is presently known) served as a pleasant sanctuary from the congestion of the city and functioned as a service yard. The court contained several raised, rectangular planting beds described as "parterres." The long narrow shape of these beds permitted easy maintenance and fit nicely within the available space. While planting beds in many Vieux Carré courts are referred to as "parterres," one authority notes, "their origins appear to be more akin to utility and order than ornament, and are more straight-forward attempts to provide adequate space to cultivate ornamental plants and yet provide for simple maintenance, good space utilization, and ease of circulation."

With the expansion of the city, new residential developments occurred outside the Vieux Carré and into the Garden District. In the first half of the nineteenth century, prosperous merchants, bankers, and cotton brokers built large houses and villas in this early suburban neighborhood. Houses in the Garden District were constructed in a variety of eclectic styles and were adorned with formal gardens generally in the French style. Many of these ornamental gardens included decorative fences, tasteful garden furnishings, and a wide assortment of ornamental plants. Large lots in this and other suburban areas allowed for the construction of freestanding residential structures in spacious landscaped settings. Gardens were usually located in front or along the side of the dwelling and included formal parterres in geometric designs. Parterres in the Garden District were generally characterized by patterns that exhibited a high degree of geometric complexity. Little evidence exists that indicates any attempt at developing gardens during this period in the naturalistic style. Work yards located at the rear of Garden District properties were similar to those of the Vieux Carré with the exception that additional space was allocated for the stabling of horses and storage of carriages.

Thomas K. Wharton, an English-born architect who served as superintendent of construction for the New Orleans Custom House, provided descriptive accounts of New Orleans and the Garden District in his journal, which he kept from 1853 until shortly before his death in 1862. The following is one of several of Wharton's accounts in which he described various aspects of suburban development in and around the city:

> In the afternoon I took a wider circuit thru Lafayette than yesterday, and in broad daylight, enabling me to judge more correctly of the suburban improvements of the summer. Indeed I find several handsome new private residences, especially on Nagades Street [now St. Charles Avenue] and between it and Magazine, and the gardens in this neighborhood are still very beautiful, the leaves cling lovingly to the deciduous trees, and some, as the Weeping Willows &c., are in full foliage, while numerous Live Oaks, and abundance of glossy evergreen shrubs, give richness and mass to the general verdure, and the Rose trees are covered with splendid blooms from the purist white, to the rich damask scarlet. Indeed but for the keen racy air, there is nothing here to remind one of Winter, blossoms, green leaves and sunshine everywhere. (*Queen of the South, New Orleans, 1853–1862*)

A keen observer of his surroundings, Wharton also provided descriptive accounts of new houses, evolving landscapes, and lush gardens. Among the ornamental plants he observed

The Bosworth House—New Orleans, Louisiana. Located at 1126 Washington Street in the Garden District, the Bosworth House was designed by English-born architect Thomas K. Wharton for A. W. Bosworth, a native of Maine.

were China trees, live oaks, oranges, mulberries, pecan trees, bananas, yellow jasmine, century plant, yucca, oleander, gardenias, hibiscus, amaryllis, salvias, chrysanthemums, larkspurs, sweet peas, nasturtiums, bachelor buttons, gladiolus, verbenas, heliotropes, geraniums, mignonette, violets, and a wide variety of roses.

As evidenced in travel accounts and historical records, one of the most interesting aspects of New Orleans during the antebellum period was the great diversity of ornamental plants grown in the city's gardens. While ornamental plants were initially obtained from European sources, over time, they were available from local merchants and nurseries. The following newspaper advertisements reflect the variety of ornamental plants offered to gardeners in New Orleans:

> **The French Florist Gardeners,** have the honor of informing the public of their arrival in this city from Paris, with a beautiful collection of exotic plants, fruit trees of all kinds, shrubs, 150 varieties of the rose, hyacinths, daffodils, jonquils, tuberoses, amaryllis (very scarce), imperial crowns, and a complete assortment of flower and kitchen vegetable seeds . . . may be seen at their store, in Mr. Andry's house, Toulouse Street.
>
> *Louisiana Courier*
> February 14, 1825

> **Fruit Trees, Dwarf Oranges, Camellias, Roses.** The subscriber in addition to his already splendid collection of flowering shrubs, plants, etc. has just received from Tennessee in a short passage, a collection of fruit trees, Camellia Japonica, Dwarf Oranges, Roses . . . also a number of hardy flowering plants such as Snow Balls, Syringas, Lilacs, Chinese and French, Viburnums, Strawberry Tree, Sweet scented Vitex, Blue Jasmine or Chinese Bos, Thorn, Evergreen Privet, Honey Suckles, Double Dahlias with the new and most improved varieties of the Fig Tree, consisting of 10 varieties of those most cultivated in Italy and South of France.
>
> *The Courier*
> January 4, 1832

**H. Hafner, 139 St. Charles.** Evergreens, Magnolias, Mespilus, Japonicas, Cedars, Cypresses, Pyramidilis, Arbor vitaes, Pittosporum, Vibernums, Sweet Olives, Laureltinus, English Laurel; A fine collection of roses and greenhouse plants; Camellia Japonicas, Strawberry Plants; and flower pots.

*Daily Picayune*x
December 15, 1857

John M. Nelson established the first commercial nursery in New Orleans, Magnolia Nurseries, in 1859. Located at two separate sites, one on the outskirts of the city and the other downtown at the corner of Camp Street and Lafayette Square, Magnolia Nurseries offered a wide variety of "fruit, shade, and ornamental trees, evergreens, roses, and miscellaneous plants." The 1860 *City Directory* lists John Nelson as a horticulturist with a business in Jefferson City, a suburb of New Orleans.

Travel accounts also provide additional insights and clues into garden designs and the use of ornamental plants in New Orleans prior to 1860. One of the most informative was written by Alexander Gordon (a British plant collector) and published in the *Magazine of Horticulture* in 1845:

During the month of February, I visited a vast number of gardens in New Orleans. Even at that unfavorable season, from the mildness of the winter, I found a tolerable display of Flora's beauties, the gardens, as it were, conjuring up a spring-like appearance in the gloomy season of winter. The various plants in bloom were, to me, equally astonishing as gratifying. Many varieties of the rose were displaying their gaudy flowers, and exhaling their fragrance in profusion. Many exotics, planted in the open ground, were then blooming freely, and most of them had been so during the previous season from the months of April and May. . . . Most of the following were blooming vigorously: —*Heliotrope, Plumbago, Petunia, Russellia, Cestrum, Achania, Justicia, Verbena, Manettia, Brugmansia, Hibiscus* (*Chinese sp.*) and *Strelitzia.* In many gardens the camellia was flowering to admiration, and, in favorable situations, several Chinese azaleas were truly magnificent. Many other species might be mentioned, did time and space permit, but the above will convey some idea of a Louisiana winter's vegetation. . . . You are well aware the ornamental department of gardening is my more particular province, and here I find a rich and varied field.

Tis most astonishing to witness with what luxuriance every variety of the rose grows, and, in many instances, without the least attention or care. Here the Noisettes and Tea roses develope [*sic*] their magnificent flowers in full perfection. The carnation, pink, and picotee succeed well; Gardenias and Lagerstroemias are perfect pictures in their season. The dahlia thrives to admiration. Oleanders, Night and Day scented jesamines, Cestrums, *Alloysia citriodora,* Erythrinas, Plumbagos, and Clerodendrons are all planted in the open ground. In severe winters, they may be killed down, but they again shoot vigorously in the spring, and grow and flower most luxuriantly. *Pittosporum, Olea fragrans,* and the Chinese magnolias, attain a size which is most astonishing; but neither tulip nor hyacinth succeed well. . . . The summers appear to be too long, the heat too intense, or the aridity of the atmosphere during the summer months is too much for these beautiful genera, and either kills them entirely, or they become so exhausted that they scarcely recover during the winter, and the succeeding season puts a *finale* to their existence.

New Orleans gardeners often turned to the use of a variety of structures including greenhouses, plant pits, hot houses, and cold frames to provide protection for tender ornamentals during the winter months. In the 1840s, one New Orleans gardener, George T. Dunbar, a Baltimore native, maintained a large collection of camellias that he overwintered, along with other tender species, in a greenhouse at his home on Common Street (now downtown New Orleans). Another gardener in the city, Louis de Feriet, built a fine home and elaborate garden with a two-story greenhouse covered with slate and glass. This structure had a southern exposure in order to capture the heat of the winter sun. It also was situated in close proximity to the stables, allowing ready access to rotting manure to provide additional heat to warm the greenhouse during periods when the weather was extremely cold. De Feriet enlarged his greenhouse on two separate occasions, first in 1837 and then a year later, to accommodate a large collection of oranges, lemons, guava, and tender ornamentals.

A Garden in the Lower Garden District—New Orleans, Louisiana. New Orleans Notarial Archives, Plan Book 97, Folio 18.

Dunbar and De Feriet, along with other nineteenth-century Louisiana gardeners, relied almost exclusively on French and English garden books for advice on gardening. However, in 1838, Louisiana gardeners were provided a garden book that attempted to adapt and translate European gardening information and techniques to the unique growing conditions of the region. Prepared by Jacques-Felix Lelièvre, a French-trained horticulturist who arrived in New Orleans in 1834, this small but informative work entitled, *Nouveau Jardinier de la Louisiane* or *The New Louisiana Gardener* was a hallmark in southern garden literature, providing gardening information that addressed the special growing conditions of the Gulf Coast region with its mild winters and hot, humid summers. Lelièvre's work covered a wide range of subjects including planting schedules, cultivation and maintenance procedures, grafting and pruning techniques, along with a comprehensive list of recommended fruit trees, vegetables, and flowers.

## TOWN GARDENS

With the rapid expansion of the southern frontier many towns developed in the lower and middle South. These were river ports, seats of government, market towns, educational centers, or rural hamlets where various trade and manufacturing activities were conducted. While some were modest in size, others were no more than simple villages with several fine homes built by affluent merchants or wealthy planters from the surrounding region. Planters and their families often elected to reside in towns or villages rather than live on a rural plantation. In town they could enjoy the benefits of social interaction, cultural and educational opportunities, and hopefully escape the threat of malaria and yellow fever that plagued rural areas. Town gardens, like those in cities, were often designed by itinerant gardeners who traveled about the South offering their services to southern gentry. Others were laid out by discerning property owners who had an eye for

Boxwood—Madison, Georgia. In 1851, Wildes Kolb of Madison, Georgia, built a unique townhouse that contained not one, but two box-bordered parterres, each of which exhibited different designs.

design, or who based designs from those found in English pattern books or from observations made when traveling abroad. Unlike city gardens, those in towns, particularly those developed in the interior regions of the southern frontier, generally contained a smaller variety of ornamental plants. This occurred for a number of reasons including fewer sources from which ornamental plants could be obtained; limited access to major ports and transportation routes; and a smaller number of local gardeners from which cuttings, slips, roots, seeds, and newly introduced ornamental plants could be exchanged or shared. The following historical accounts provide evidence of ornamental gardens in towns and villages in the antebellum South:

> Immediately adjacent to our town [Madison, Georgia] is a most beautiful and tastefully laid out Garden, planted with a great variety of shrubbery and flowers, many of which are very rare and curious.
>
> *Southern Miscellany,* 1842

> With the town of Huntsville, Ala., I am quite delighted, and do not wonder at its reputation. . . . Some of the private hot-houses and gardens in the place would delight the most fastidious of horticulturists.
>
> *Adventures in the Wilds of the United States,* 1856
> Charles Lanman

> Columbus [Mississippi] is one of the largest and most beautiful interior towns in the South, and has long been celebrated for the wealth of its inhabitants. . . . The private residences are beautiful, and are adorned with the choicest gardens.
>
> *DeBows Review,* 1859

> Passed through Madison [Georgia]. Found it the prettiest village I've seen in the state. One garden and yard I never saw excelled, even in Connecticut.
>
> *Diary of Rufus Mead, Jr. of the Federal Army,* 1864

Examples of town gardens of the antebellum period are best represented in Columbia, South Carolina, Athens and LaGrange, Georgia, Tuscaloosa, Alabama, and Natchez, Mississippi.

## Columbia, South Carolina

The capital of South Carolina was moved from Charleston to Columbia in 1787. Located geographically in the center of the state, Columbia was laid out along the banks of the Congaree River on a site known as Taylor Hill, which according to early accounts was "covered with a magnificent growth of immense oaks, hickories, and pines." Columbia remained relatively small until 1830 when it became the center of state government and the location of the South Carolina College (now the University of South Carolina). In *The Western World; or Travels in the United States*, Alexander Mackay, an English traveler, provided a description of the town in 1846: "Columbia is, on the whole rather an interesting little town. There is about it an air of neatness and elegance, which betokens it to be the residence of a superior class of people—many of the planters whose estates are in the neighborhood making it the place of their abode. . . . The streets, as in the majority of the southern towns of more recent origin, are long, straight, and broad, and are lined, for the most part, with trees, prominent amongst which are to be found the gay and flaunting 'Pride of India' [*Melia azedarach*]." On February 17, 1865, General Sherman and his Union army arrived on the outskirts of Columbia. General Sherman met with the town's mayor advising him to "Go home and rest assured your town will be safe in my hands, as if under your control." But on the following morning, Columbia lay in total ruin, destroyed by fire, with only a few public buildings, churches, and residential structures surviving.

### Hampton-Preston House and Gardens

In 1818, Ansley Hall, a successful merchant and cotton factor of English origin, built a fine town house for himself and his new bride on the outskirts of Columbia. Only five years after its completion, Mr. Hall sold the house to General Wade Hampton, a hero of the Revolutionary War and who upon his death in 1835 was purported to have been one of the wealthiest men in America. General Hampton indulged his wife's interests in gardening. He engaged the services of an English landscape gardener, who designed a fine garden for their new home. Documented accounts describe the gardens as being laid out in a symmetrical manner with formal walks and beds, trellises, grottos, and an artificial water feature. Once completed, Mrs. Hampton eagerly set out collecting a great variety of native and exotic plants to embellish the gardens. Mrs. Hampton's love of gardening was instilled in her oldest daughter, Caroline. Upon returning to Columbia in 1848 with her husband, John Preston, to live at the Hampton residence, Caroline assisted her mother with improvements and management of the gardens. It was during this time that the Hampton-Preston House became the center of social activity in Columbia, with such notable guests as Senator Daniel Webster, Henry Clay, John C. Calhoun, General Winfield Scott, and presidents Millard Fillmore and Franklin Pierce.

Through Mrs. Hampton's and her daughter's continued efforts the gardens of the Hampton-Preston House obtained local and regional acclaim. What had begun as a modest endeavor, developed into extensive gardens with winding paths, formal beds, alleys of box, and arched trellises covered with a variety of flowering vines. The gardens were adorned with fine statuary and a fountain designed by the noted American sculptor, Hiram

Powers (1805–1873). A large greenhouse, located at the rear of the property, was filled with an extensive collection of exotic and tender plants collected from around the world.

The following accounts provide descriptions of the Hampton-Preston gardens as they appeared in 1853, and eight years later in 1861, on the eve of the Civil War:

### *The Waterford N.Y. Sentinel,* **May 10, 1853**

I arrived at the Capital of the Palmetto State on Saturday last. . . . The gardens [of Columbia] as a whole, surpass anything I have ever seen for cultivation and beauty. The garden of Mr. Hampton, of Revolutionary memory, contains four acres. The grounds are laid out with elegant taste. The whole front fence is covered with the Cherokee rose, now in full bloom, presenting the appearance of a hedge. The wild orange [*Prunus caroliniana*] also, is trimmed and trained into almost every shape. It makes a thick complete hedge from 2 to 15 feet, as you prefer it, and is as regular in its appearance as the boxwood borders. The cedar [*Juniperus virginiana*] is also sheared and trained in the same manner. A description of the many flowers and plants would be endless. The greenhouse for beauty and variety rivals that of the government one at Washington. In it the orange and lemon are covered with the ripe golden fruit, and at the same time with a white delicate blossom. Also the banana, the plantain and the bread fruit are all vying for distinction.

The Hampton-Preston Garden Plan—Columbia, South Carolina.

Columbia, S.C., April 15, 1853

### *The Farmer and Planter,* **1861**

The house is a large and respectable mansion of stone, surrounded by pleasure grounds of fine evergreens and deciduous trees, our attention was arrested by a fine specimen of that curious tree, the Japanese Ginkgo (*Salisburia adiantifolia*) twenty feet high; the Paulownia imperialis, forty feet high, and many others of great excellence. Many of the old trees are venerable specimens, over eighty feet high, whose huge trunks and widespread branches are, in many cases, densely wreathed and draped with masses of English ivy, forming the most picturesque sylvan objects so rarely met with. After passing through many fine walks and a neatly arranged flower garden we came to an extensive range of glass, and through the kindness of Mr. Schol, the present intelligent gardener, were admitted to see the exotic treasures of the charming green-houses. Here our attention was first attracted by a collection of Pelargoniums in full bloom, some fine Fuchsias, and well-grown specimens of Acacia pendula, Inga, Pulcherrima, Musa cavendishii and Paradisiaca, Nepenthes destillatoria, Ficus elastica, Maranta zebrina, with its beautiful variegated leaves, Caladium bicolor, the interesting Dionaea muscipula, and some fine species of Lycopodium, etc. . . . The collection of Camellias and Azaleas, composed of many old and fine varieties, is represented in quite large plants. The effect of this garden is striking, and its liberal proprietor, Colonel Preston, by opening it freely to the public, no doubt, greatly increased the popular tastes of the city.

W. R. Bergholz
Landscape Gardener and Rural Architect

The Hampton-Preston property served as a college for women from 1890 to 1930. While the house survives, the gardens were destroyed in 1946.

During the Union occupation of Columbia in 1865, tradition has it that General Sherman offered the Hampton-Preston House as a sanctuary for an order of Urselin nuns whose convent had been destroyed by fire during the pillage of the town. General Sherman's gesture of good faith (the Mother Superior purportedly had taught Sherman's daughter) provided protection to the Hampton-Preston House and gardens from the wholesale destruction that beset the town. After occupying the house for only four months, the nuns returned the estate to its rightful owners. Because of depleted economic resources following the Civil War, the Hampton-Preston House passed out of the family's hands on January 14, 1872. Following several changes of ownership, the Presbyterian Institute for Young Ladies purchased the property around 1890. The gardens remained intact until they were destroyed in 1946. Today, the Historic Columbia Foundation, a private, non-profit organization founded in 1961, manages the Hampton-Preston House as a house museum.

### Caldwell House and Gardens

The Caldwell House is located at the corner of Richland and Gadsden Streets in Columbia's historic Arsenal Hill District. The house and gardens occupy a site originally owned by the Taylor family at the time the town was founded in 1787. Built about 1830 by John Caldwell, a prosperous cotton broker and president of the South Carolina Railroad, the Caldwell House represents one of the finest examples of Greek revival architecture surviving in Columbia. The symmetrical layout of the house distinguishes it from similar styled houses of the period. It features a central hall, four large rooms on two floors, and double porches supported by round, fluted columns. When originally constructed, the house offered unobstructed views to the south and west, making its location one of the finest in the town. Some believe that the Caldwell House avoided destruction by General Sherman's Army in 1865 because of its isolated location, while others speculate that Union troops spared the property because of Mr. Caldwell's coolness to the idea of succession prior to the Civil War.

Today, the Caldwell House and grounds contain a series of gardens that have evolved over time. The earliest of these is an elaborate parterre laid out shortly after 1830. Located along the west side of the house and extending to the middle of the block, the parterre is composed of four rectangles of varying sizes divided by intersecting walks. Each of the quadrants of the parterre are connected by an informal arrangement of sanded paths bordered with English box (*Buxus sempervirens suffruticosa*). Individual beds are planted with evergreens including camellias, tea plants, anise, cherry laurel, etc., creating a harmonious carpet of green throughout the year. Many of the old trees, which are strategically located throughout the garden, provide shade and seasonal color. Included among these are a towering ginkgo (*Ginkgo biloba*), evergreen magnolias (*Magnolia grandiflora*), and an enormous incense cedar (*Calocedrus decurrens*). Additional plants that enhance the garden include crape myrtle, mountain laurel, banana shrub, azaleas, sweet shrub, althea, spirea, nandina, and chaste tree. There is speculation that a trained landscape gardener laid out the Caldwell garden, but no documentation exists to substantiate this claim.

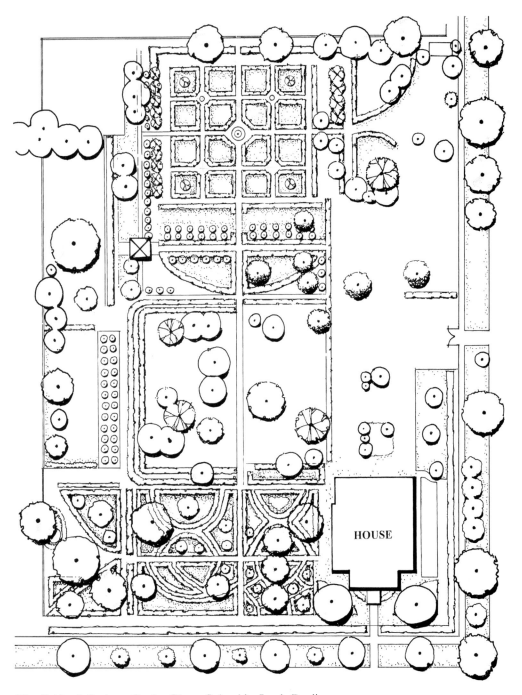

HOUSE

The Caldwell-Boylston Garden Plan—Columbia, South Carolina.

A View of the Caldwell Garden. The view reflects a portion of the original box-bordered parterre, with a rich tapestry of evergreens and ornamental trees.

Following Mr. Caldwell's death, the property was sold to Daniel Chamberlain, who became governor of South Carolina in 1874. Upon his retirement from public office in 1877, the house and garden passed through several owners until Samuel and Sarah Boylston purchased it in 1909. The Boylstons expanded the grounds. They acquired additional acreage and expanded the gardens, which served as an ideal setting for their lavish parties given for Columbia society. Sarah Boylston's devotion to the property continued until her death in 1962, at the age of ninety-two. Presently, the state of South Carolina owns the site, and it is open to the public as a historic house and garden museum. The original box-bordered garden remains much as it did in Mr. Caldwell's time, reflecting the love and care provided by its owners throughout the years.

## Athens, Georgia

Athens was incorporated in 1801 as the site of the University of Georgia, then known as Franklin College. The college was located on the west bank of the Oconee River on property containing stately trees, several springs, and extended views in every direction. Athens remained a small town until 1820, when it began to develop into a thriving center of industry, commerce, and trade. By 1831, the town could boast a botanical garden (a five-acre site at the intersection of Dearing and Finley Streets) that was designed by John Bishop, a landscape gardener. The garden was placed under the administration of Matthus Ward, Professor of Natural History at Franklin College. A visitor in 1849 described the garden as containing a "handsome collection of flowers, flowering plants, and shrubs, scattered over . . . several acres in which is preserved a large portion of the original forest-trees, consisting of oaks, hickory, chestnut, maple, and locust."

By midcentury, many prominent individuals were drawn to Athens, and the town became well known for its many fine homes and beautiful gardens. Wealthy residents, as well as cotton planters from the surrounding region, built large federal or Greek revival houses on large lots along the principal streets of the town. James Silk Buckingham, an English traveler, provided the following description of Athens following a visit to the town in June, 1839: "The appearance of the town is very pretty, especially at this, the summer season. . . . The mansions are almost all detached buildings constructed of wood, with porticos, pediments, and piazzas, surrounded with spacious and well-planted gardens; and all the houses are painted white, with green venetian blinds, they afford a striking relief to the deep-green foliage in which they are embosomed. There is but one regular street of business, in which the houses are continuous; and this is as yet built on one side only, the rest of the dwellings are scattered like separate villas, and the surface being greatly undulated, and the wood or forest-trees approaching close to their borders, the whole appearance of the village is picturesque and romantic." Athens escaped the destructive effects of the Civil War and continued to prosper throughout the nineteenth century, retaining many fine homes, old gardens, and its historic character.

### The Thomas Grant House and Garden

The Thomas Grant House is located on Prince Avenue, one of Athens's most fashionable residential streets. Built in 1857 as a fashionable town house by John Thomas Grant, a successful railroad contractor and plantation owner in nearby Walton County, the house is considered by many architectural historians as one of the finest examples of Greek revival architecture in America. Its plan consists of a brick ground floor, two frame stories, and a spacious porch with Corinthian columns that extend across the front of the house and along both sides. A list of building expenses recorded during the construction of the house confirms that the Thomas Grant House was one of the most expensive residential structures built in Athens during the antebellum period. The original layout of the property included a large parterre garden at the front, fenced side yards, and a work area at the rear with servants' quarters,

The Thomas Grant House—Athens, Georgia.

a detached kitchen, well, and privy. The back portion of the property served as a miniature farm with an orchard, vegetable garden, pasture, and several outbuildings.

The parterre garden, which still reflects its original design, encompasses an area of approximately 2000 square feet and, according to tradition, was designed by an itinerant landscape gardener. The house and garden present a unified and harmonious plan, complementary both in scale and design. The pattern of the garden is based on a series of circles and symmetrical forms interlaced by an intricate network of walks and paths. Individual beds were bordered with box and originally planted with bulbs, peonies, iris, daylilies, violets, pinks, roses, crape myrtle, and cherry laurel. Over time, these plantings were supplemented with a variety of ornamental shrubs including spirea, sweet shrub, yucca, tea olive, flowering quince, lilacs, althea, mock orange, snowball, and tea plants. The garden originally contained a number of large trees, which added balance and scale to the overall plan. Prominent among these were southern magnolias, American elm, oaks, red cedars, and white mulberries. A decorative picket fence separated the garden from the street and a clipped evergreen hedge enclosed it along the sides.

The Thomas Grant House and Garden Plan.

The Thomas Grant House was sold to Benjamin Hill in June 1869 and over the following years passed through a number of owners until the Georgia Board of Regents purchased it in 1949 to serve as the home of the president of the University of Georgia. Through the university's efforts, the property has been carefully preserved and remains as an outstanding example of architecture and garden design of the antebellum era.

## LaGrange, Georgia

Established along the western frontier of the Piedmont plateau, LaGrange was chartered in 1828 as the seat of Troup County on lands purchased from the Creek Indians in 1825. LaGrange was named in honor of the Marquis de Lafayette (beloved hero of the American Revolution) who after traveling through the area in 1825 remarked that the town and surrounding area reminded him of France and his ancestral home, the Chateaux de LaGrange. The town prospered because of its mild climate, fertile soils, and abundant water supply. During the antebellum era, LaGrange became a center of commerce and government as well as the site of several educational facilities including the Troup County Academy for Boys, Brownwood University, the Southern Female College, and LaGrange Female Academy. LaGrange also became the location where many wealthy cotton planters built fine town homes. Because of its strategic location and extensive system of rail lines, the town served as an important hospital zone for wounded Confederate soldiers and a haven for southern refugees during the Civil War. Near the end of the war, Union troops occupied LaGrange. Its homes were spared from damage, but the business district, depot, and several industrial sites were burned and destroyed.

## Ferrell Gardens

In 1828, Mr. Blount Ferrell and his wife Sarah, built a modest home on an eighty-acre site located on the outskirts of LaGrange. Twelve years later, Mrs. Ferrell initiated the development of a formal garden along the south facing slope of the property, which had previously been used for the cultivation of cotton. While tradition has it that Mrs. Ferrell laid out the earliest phase of the garden, it is believed that at some point the services of an itinerant landscape gardener was secured to prepare a comprehensive plan for an elaborate parterre garden. One authority described Ferrell Gardens as "a splendid example of Italianate Renaissance work at a time of the Baroque period, when informalism was creeping in." The plan included a series of terraces, intricate box-bordered beds, an elaborate system of walks and paths, and an ornamental grove.

As Mrs. Ferrell carried out the garden plan, she incorporated various religious symbols and motifs into its design as a confirmation and testimony of her belief that a garden should be a reflection of faith and religious piety. Dispersed throughout the garden are various personal themes executed in box. For her motto, Mrs. Ferrell selected "God is Love" and for her husband, a circuit court judge and Mason, she chose the Masonic emblem with the inscription "Fiat Justitia" (let justice be done). In the southwest corner of the garden, which Mrs. Ferrell first developed and referred to as "the sanctuary," are a number of ecclesiastical icons. Among these are a lyre, an organ, a bishop's chair, a collection plate, and a cluster of grapes, all having a religious or biblical connotation. Each was executed in box and regularly clipped to maintain their individual shape and design.

Sarah Coleman Ferrell

While Mrs. Ferrell grew a great variety of plants, dwarf box (*Buxus sempervirens suffruticosa*) dominated the garden. Dwarf box was planted as individual specimens and also employed to edge planting beds, garden walks, and paths. Its evergreen nature, slow growth, and ability to be clipped into various shapes and forms made dwarf box ideal edging material to articulate and define the garden's intricate patterns and geometric designs. Additional plants employed in the garden included cherry laurel (*Prunus caroliniana*), magnolias (*Magnolia grandiflora*), cedars (*Juniperus virginiana*), crape myrtle (*Lagerstroemia indica*), tea plants (*Camellia sinensis*), and a ginkgo tree (*Ginkgo biloba*). An interesting feature of the garden was the use of local quarried stone to create walls, steps, and terraces.

The Ferrell house and gardens were spared when federal troops marched through LaGrange during the final days of the Civil War. Some believe the property survived because Mrs. Ferrell urgently pleaded with Union soldiers to save her beloved gardens, while others contend it was out of respect for the religious symbols and Masonic emblems that were prominently displayed throughout the gardens. Mrs. Ferrell's care and devotion to the gardens continued long after the war, as evidenced in the following account of a visit to the property that appeared in *The Reporter* (a local newspaper) on May 28, 1888:

> Approaching the garden through the majestic grove of oaks, the scented breeze and the happy songs of feathered minstrels foretoken a sylvan retreat; and yet, when we entered the gate, we were speechless with astonishment at the bewildering paradise opening before us. . . . We immediately repaired to the mansion and met Mrs. Ferrell—the priestess of this temple of beauty. Her benevolent features beamed with pardonable pride and pleasure as she exhibited and explained to us this charming creation of her hands. Sometimes, when I have long gazed at a beautiful flower and wondered as to the hidden fountains of life whence it grows, I think of such souls as hers. . . . They must draw their substance from some sacred source hidden from the worldly eye. The gardens were begun about the year 1842. Mrs. Ferrell and her mother, who then lived at the old Ferrell homestead, . . . vied with each other in this lovely pursuit. It was her great desire to beautify the grounds. Small was the beginning, yet with indefatigable industry she added plant after plant, and built terrace after terrace, until now, at the end of forty-five years, she has a monument to her perseverance, the fairest in the land.

> T. J.

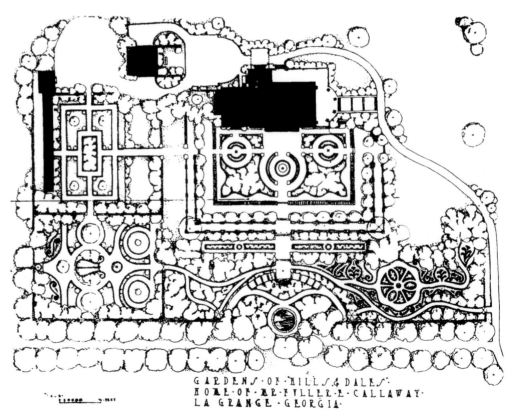

Plan of Ferrell Gardens—LaGrange, Georgia.

Hills and Dales—LaGrange, Georgia. Following the sale of the Ferrell property to Mr. and Mrs. Fuller E. Callaway Sr. in 1912, Atlanta architect Neel Reid was commissioned to design a new house to replace the original Ferrell home. This new structure was designed to both respect and compliment the existing garden. During the Callaway's ownership, the property became known as Hills and Dales.

In 1912, following Mrs. Ferrell's death, Fuller E. Callaway, Sr., purchased the property, and, since that time, it has been carefully maintained under the stewardship of the Callaway family. Mrs. Ferrell's beloved gardens survive as one of the South's finest horticultural treasures. The property (known today as Ferrell Gardens at Hills and Dales) is open to the public as a house and garden museum.

## Tuscaloosa, Alabama

Established in 1819, Tuscaloosa, Alabama, remained a small conservative town until it became the site of the state capital in 1825. Tuscaloosa's strategic location as a center of trade, as well as its selection as the location for the state university in 1831, propelled the town into a period of growth and prosperity. During the antebellum period, Tuscaloosa became well known throughout the region for its fine homes and gardens, tree-lined streets, and beautiful college campus. Upon visiting the town in 1845, Juliet Coleman of Connecticut wrote that the campus buildings exceed "any I have seen for a college—or even any others except for the public buildings of Washington." The state capital was relocated to Montgomery in 1847 and subsequently Tuscaloosa slowly declined, resulting in part from its isolation due to poor roads, limited steamboat access, and few rail lines.

Throughout the Civil War, Tuscaloosa remained unscarred until the final days of the conflict. On the morning of 1 April, 1865, Confederate General William H. Jackson assured the residents of Tuscaloosa that "the threat of the vandal hoards shall not pollute the streets of their fair city." Contrary to Jackson's claim, Union forces under General John T. Croxton entered the town, destroying university buildings, industrial facilities, and

View of the Battle-Friedman House and Garden—Tuscaloosa, Alabama.

strategic military sites. Fortunately, many of Tuscaloosa's fine homes and gardens miraculously survived.

## The Battle-Friedman House and Garden

Alfred Battle was born in 1803 to Matthew and Anne Battle of Asheville, North Carolina. Alfred attended the University of North Carolina, and at the age of twenty-two, relocated to Warren County, Georgia, where he met his future wife, Millicent Bradley Bealle. Following their marriage in 1823, the couple moved westward to Alabama, settling in Tuscaloosa where Alfred became a prosperous cotton planter. In 1835, Battle built a handsome town house that was expanded in the 1840s to include an imposing portico with six massive columns. At the time the portico was added, the front facade of the house was plastered, scored, and painted to resemble a Greek temple, a common practice during the antebellum period.

In 1844, Millicent Battle secured the services of Peter M'Arthur, an English landscape gardener, to design an ornamental garden that would complement the house. M'Arthur had at one time been employed by Lord Ashburton (1774–1848) a well-known English figure who owned the Grange, one of England's finest country estates. M'Arthur designed a garden for Mrs. Battle following a pattern similar to one suggested in 1812 by J. C. Loudon, the noted English garden writer and designer, for "parterres on sites of limited size." The design included a complex arrangement of walks and formal planting beds in a diamond motif. A unique feature of the garden was a greenhouselike structure that served as a large cold frame or miniature greenhouse where annual and perennial seeds could be started for early spring planting and as a miniature greenhouse for the overwintering of tender plants.

Following Millicent Battle's death in 1872 and Alfred's eventual financial demise, the house was sold in 1875 to Bernard Friedman, a self-educated Hungarian immigrant who, after moving to Tuscaloosa, operated a prosperous dry goods business and textile mill. Several accounts attest to Mrs. Friedman's love and care of the garden and of her tenacious efforts to preserve its original design. Family history holds that Mrs. Friedman's brother, poet Robert Loveman, who wrote the poem "Rain Song" with its familiar verse "It isn't raining rain to me, its raining violets," was inspired by beds of purple violets that were a prominent feature in the Friedman garden. The property remained in the ownership of the Friedman family until it was deeded to the city of Tuscaloosa in 1968. Since 1987, the Tuscaloosa County Preservation Society has cared for the house and gardens and managed it as a house and garden museum.

## Natchez, Mississippi

Often described as the "center of antebellum culture in the South," Natchez was one of the wealthiest and most sophisticated towns of its size during the antebellum period. Prior to the Civil War, many wealthy merchants, as well as planters from outside the town, built grand homes and purchased the finest in material goods—furnishings from New York, silver and china from London, and fashionable clothing from Paris. Travel accounts and letters dating to the 1820s attest to the growing sophistication of life in Natchez, particularly in respect to gardens and landscaped grounds. Visitors spoke of Natchez's ornamental groves, avenues, parterres, lawns, flower beds, hot houses, and a variety of exotic plants. Natchez boasted many elegant homes close to the center of the town and fostered the development of numerous large, so-called "suburban villas" in outlying areas. Distinctive among these were Melrose, Auburn, Monmouth, Dunleith, Elmscourt, Linden, Gloucester, and Longwood. Each reflected a sense of beauty, charm, and elegance unparalleled in the South during the antebellum period. As noted in Edward King's *The Great South* (1873), "There were before the war, a great number of planters' residences in the suburbs—beautiful houses, with colonnades and verandas, and rich drawing and dining-rooms, furnished in heavy antique style, and gardens modeled after the finest in Europe."

Travelers to the region frequently described the gardens and grounds of Natchez's suburban villas, providing clues as to their nature and design. One account is provided in *The Sunny South* (1860) edited by Joseph Holt Ingraham: "Many of the more wealthy cotton planters, whose estates lie on the river where it is unhealthy to reside, live in the vicinity of Natchez, in country houses, on which they lavish taste and expenses without limit. There is, therefore, a beautiful wilderness of architectural and horticultural elegance around the town. The pleasant drives carry you winding among these tasteful homes now rolling over a graveled lawn road, now traversing hedges enclosing gardens that contain tropical plants, now catching sight of a summer-house, now of statuary, and on all sides beauty. It is in these homes, which extend a league or more around the town, that are to be found the families that have given to the society of Natchez so much celebrity. Here are to be found persons who have traveled abroad, and cultivated their tastes by European discipline."

In *A Second Voyage to the United States of North America* (1849), Sir Charles Lyell describes a visit to Natchez and the beauty of the gardens: "Many of the country houses in the neighborhood are elegant, and some of the gardens belonging to them are laid out in the English, others in the French style. In the latter are seen terraces, with statues and evergreens, straight walks with borders of flowers, terminated with a view of the wild forest, the charm of both being heightened by contrast." This contrast between formal and natural landscapes is a consistent theme frequently referenced in the South throughout the antebellum period.

Rosalie—Natchez, Mississippi. Completed in 1823.

One of the most important gardens in Natchez was that of Mr. Andrew Brown, located several miles outside the town along the banks of the Mississippi River. While the house was less distinctive than were others in the area, the garden from all accounts was one of the finest and most beautiful in the town. Brown's garden was described in the *Horticulturist* (1858) in an article entitled "A Trip to Cuba and the Southern States":

A View of Brown's Garden—Natchez, Mississippi.

Natchez is pre-eminently the "Persia of roses." In no part of the Union have we ever seen them attain such perfection and beauty. It so happened that we were in this Paradise at exactly the "happy moment," the 4th of April, when there was a *gush* of bloom that was as delightful as surprising. The best exhibition was at the garden of Mr. Andrew Brown, on the river, a short distance above the town, sheltered by a high bank. Here reside Mr. and Mrs. Brown, in the handsomest garden, without exception, we have seen for many years. Both are enthusiasts, directing and enjoying to the fullest extent their beautiful domain, and by their liberality and goodness in dispensing novelties brought at great expense from long distances, have created a gardening spirit in this region. The entrance view of their long garden vista tells the story at once; an eye accustomed to looking after effects is delighted, and knows what to expect.

After this *coup*, the details are highly satisfactory; the borders of each bed, where we should depend upon box edgings, are formed of dwarf pompom roses, little miniatures of a few inches in height, and all of them in the fullest bloom. Nothing of the kind can be more beautiful; it blooms all winter except January, and is an evergreen.

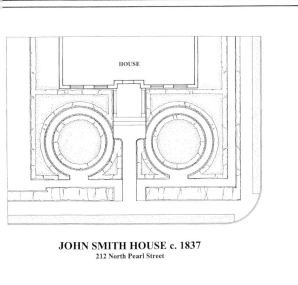

**JOHN SMITH HOUSE c. 1837**
212 North Pearl Street

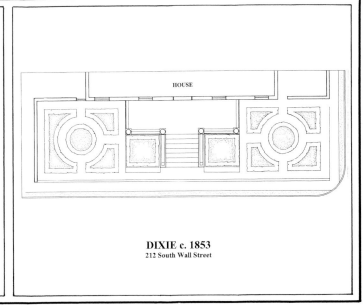

**DIXIE c. 1853**
212 South Wall Street

Garden Plans of Natchez Town Gardens—Natchez, Mississippi. Plans for the John Smith House and Dixie are represented in the illustration above. Each reflects geometric patterns and symmetrical designs.

> Mr. Brown's Chromatella, Luxemburg, La Reine, Belle Isidore, Solfaterre, Cloth of Gold of a really gold color, it was difficult to designate, and we had to ask their names, so very superior in size and color are they to the same kinds at home. The Sanguinea climbs to the height of eighteen feet over evergreens that add to its beauty. Moss roses are quite superior to those of Paris. The Gloire de France was never exceeded anywhere. Reine de la Gultare measured thirteen inches in circumference. Myrtle is used for borders and hedges, and over these clamber in wild luxuriance the Red Hermosa and the Lamarck. Ivy seems as if it would encircle every mound and tree, knowing no limits.
>
> Then the fruits: peaches, pears, plums, fig-trees as large as our apple-trees, all conspire to carry the garden lover out of his former experiences. Grapes damp off, and though Mr. Brown has planted long acres of them, he has not a satisfactory return. The Pittisporum is cut like box bushes, and was full of bees and bloom. The evergreen magnolia has been made much of in this garden, and Mr. and Mrs. Brown deserve great praise for showing what a garden may become with intelligence and love of the subject. Mr. B. is a correspondent of several learned societies, and has done good service to science by exploring the geology of the Mississippi Valley.

S. B. Buckley of Shreveport, Louisiana, provided another description of Brown's garden in an article entitled "Notes on the Garden of A. Brown, Esq., Natchez, Miss.," also appearing in the *Horticulturist* in 1858:

> About the first of last June, on the route north up the Mississippi River, I stopped at Natchez to visit Mr. Andrew Brown, who had said that if I would call on him he would show me a fine garden. I did not expect to see anything extra, but was happily disappointed. It is situated under the hill, on the banks of the river; while the high bluff back of the garden is covered with native trees and shrubs. The part devoted to ornamental trees, shrubs, and flowers contains about seven acres, at the farther end of which up the river is the residence of Mr. B. Near the entrance of the

large gate on each side of the carriage-way are two large green mounds, covered with Bermuda grass, which here makes a fine lawn. Each of these mounds is ascended by a spiral walk to the top, which is flat, with a live oak in the center, beneath which is an iron settee, where one can sit and look at the river; and close beneath are crooked walks extending far among Magnolias, Camellias, and thousands of Roses, scattered amid a profusion of rare tropical plants and flowers. Evergreen arbors, and screens, and other mounds add to the scene, which certainly combines more beauty and has a greater variety than any other garden in the Southern States. It far exceeds the Hampton garden, at Columbia, S.C., or any in the vicinity of Charleston, S.C. Many beautiful evergreens thrive in the climate of Natchez which cannot endure the winters of the Northern States. Mr. B. has a great abundance of the Magnolia grandiflora, the most beautiful of native evergreen trees. Some of his Magnolias begin to flower in early spring, and continue to bloom occasionally during the summer until early autumn. I lingered about this charming spot for several days.

Town gardens in Natchez were similar to those found in other urban settings throughout the South. Like other parterre gardens of the period, they were formal in nature and bordered with dwarf box (*Buxus sempervirens suffruticosa*) or privet (*Ligustrum vulgare*). Paths between parterre beds were usually of fine gravel, crushed oyster shells, or brick laid in a herringbone pattern on beds of gravel or sand. An 1864 map of the Defenses of Natchez, prepared by the Union army, provides visual documentation of numerous parterre gardens that existed in and around Natchez at the time of the Civil War.

## PLANTATION GARDENS

By 1860 there were approximately 2300 "large plantations" (those with sizable land holdings and a hundred slaves or more) in the southern states, with the greatest concentration occurring in three distinct areas. The first was located in the lower coastal region from South Carolina to northern Florida, extending no further inland than about 100 miles. A second concentration was situated along an arc (50 to 100 miles wide) through

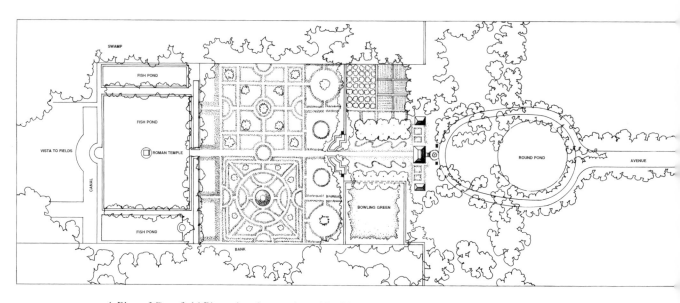

A Plan of Crowfield Plantation. Located outside Charleston, South Carolina, this colonial estate was developed in 1730 by Williams Middleton. Crowfield was reminiscent of an English country estate, having a fine house and garden.

the central portions of South Carolina, Georgia, and the south-central region of Alabama to eastern Mississippi. The third concentration stretched along the fertile lands of the lower Mississippi Valley from Natchez, south to New Orleans.

The layout of a large plantation during the antebellum period was usually based on the English manorial model of a large house and garden. This model was emulated in the southern colonies during the colonial period (exemplified by Westover, Carters Grove, and Berkley Plantations in Virginia and Middleton, Crowfield, and Medway Plantations in South Carolina) and served as inspiration for a new generation of planters who moved westward into the southern frontier.

While the colonial manorial model of a fine house and ornamental garden remained the ideal throughout the antebellum period, in most instances it was seldom achieved. Many wealthy planters were successful in building a large plantation house embellished with plantings of ornamental trees and shrubs, but few developed high-style gardens. This may have occurred for a number of reasons: the lower priority of a fine ornamental garden in comparison to a large house as a means of conveying wealth and status in rural settings; the lack of professional garden designers in remote regions of the South; the reluctance to commit the necessary resources of money, time, and labor to establish and maintain an elaborate garden; the practice of many planters to own a large house in a nearby town or city where they resided much of the year, leaving the management of the plantation in the hands of an overseer; and finally, the practice of many wealthy planters to travel to northern resorts or Virginia's therapeutic springs during the summer months, leaving little time for the care and upkeep of a high-style garden.

In an article entitled "Random Notes on Southern Horticulture," printed in the *Horticulturist* in 1851, Sylvanus of New Orleans described large plantations along the Mississippi and offered the following observations of ornamental gardens:

> Though nature has done much to adorn the scene, art has done little or nothing. . . . You would be astonished at the few varieties of trees and shrubs, and flowers, you would meet with, and surprised at the meagerness of what seemed so powerfully attractive in the approach. Notwithstanding all the praises bestowed upon the sunny south, in this part of it, at least, Landscape Gardening is half a century behind the age. I say this with many years' [*sic*] acquaintance with the gardens of both town and country. Even with the wealthiest planters, those who count their slaves by hundreds and their acres by thousands, and have the incomes of the nobles of England, a garden seems a superfluity, except, a kitchen-garden.

In Joseph Holt Ingraham's *The South-West* (1835), he observed the absence of ornamental gardens and grounds surrounding many of the mansions in and around Natchez, Mississippi:

> There are many private residences, in the vicinity of Natchez . . . whose elegant interiors, contrasting with the neglected grounds about them, suggest the idea of a handsome city residence, accidentally dropped upon a bleak hill, or into the midst of a partially cleared forest, and there remaining, with its noble roof grasped by the arm of an oak, and its windows and columns festooned by the drooping moss, heavily waving in the wind. Thus are situated many of the planters' dwellings, separated from the adjacent forest by a rude, white-washed picket, enclosing around the house an unornamented green, or grazing lot, for the saddle and carriage horses, which can regale their eyes at pleasure, by walking up to the parlour windows and gazing in

upon handsome carpets, elegant furniture, costly mantel ornaments, and side-boards loaded with massive plates; and, no doubt, ruminate philosophically upon the reflection of their figures at full-length in long, richly-framed mirrors. Very few of the planters' villas, even within a few miles of Natchez, are adorned with surrounding ornamental shrubbery walks, or any other artificial auxiliaries to the natural scenery, except a few shade trees and a narrow, graveled avenue from the gate to the house.

Ingraham offers the following explanation as to why a taste for horticulture was often little cultivated in the South:

> In the southern United States, nature enamels with a richness of colouring and a diversity of materials which she has but sparingly employed in decorating the hills and valleys of other lands. The grandeur of the forests in the South, and the luxuriance of the shrubs and plants, have no parallel. But southerners tread the avenues, breathe the air, and recline under the trees and in the arbours of their paradise, thankfully accepting and enjoying their luxurious boon, but seldom insinuating, through the cultivation of flowers, that nature has left her work imperfect. There are it is true, individual exceptions. . . . But as a general rule, southerners, with the exception of the cultivation of a few plants in a front yard, pay little regard to horticulture.

The exploitative agricultural practices commonly employed by planters who owned several large plantations was another factor that played an important role in discouraging the development of ornamental gardens, particularly in the interior agricultural regions of Alabama, Mississippi, and Louisiana. These practices quickly depleted the soil, requiring frequent relocation from one area to another in search of more fertile land, leaving little time to establish roots and the incentive to develop an ornamental garden. Additionally, many wealthy planters moved to towns or cities during the summer months to avoid the dangers of malaria, leaving their properties in the hands of overseers who had minimal interest in maintaining an ornamental garden. The Reverend Abel Abbott (1770–1828) notes in his journals, *The Abel Abbott Journals—A Yankee Preacher in Charleston Society, 1818–1827*, the dilemma many southern planters encountered in justifying the time and resources necessary to develop an ornamental garden when six months of the year were spent away from the plantation: "It has been the plan of the present proprietor [Izard Plantation] to cultivate the more profitable fields [rice and cotton] with his laborers and expend less money and sweat on the ornamentals of a garden, which 'wastes its sweetness on a desert air' from which he is obliged to flee for his life by the first of June, while it is in all its splendor and beauty."

Casulon Plantation, High Shoals, Georgia.

While many plantation owners never developed high-style gardens, research reveals that numerous planters did achieve the manorial model and successfully built a fine house and developed an ornamental garden. The manorial model was most often employed in the Piedmont region of South Carolina, middle Georgia, central Alabama, eastern Louisiana, and the Mississippi River corridor from New Orleans to Natchez. It was in these locations that planters of many old-line families from Virginia and the Carolinas settled, bringing with them traditional values that included a strong desire for a fine house and an ornamental garden. Additionally, resources for the design and planting of a high-style garden were more readily available in these areas than in the interior regions of the southern frontier.

To convey the typical site plans and spatial organizations of several large plantations (including a fine house and an ornamental garden), descriptions of several properties are provided. Although layouts vary from one region of the South to another, due to variations in climate, geography, local conditions, cultural differences, agricultural practices, and gardening traditions, similarities generally prevailed in the overall arrangement of buildings, gardens, and open space.

## Eden Hall–McCormick County, South Carolina

Located in the Piedmont region of western South Carolina, Eden Hall is a large plantation home that was built in 1854 by John Wardlaw Hearst. Born in 1813 in Abbeville, South Carolina, the son of Colonel John Hearst and Sarah Wardlaw, John Wardlaw Hearst attended Miami University in Oxford, Ohio, where he obtained a medical degree. After completing his education, John returned home to practice medicine and, in 1835, married Anne Chiles. The couple resided at Dr. Hearst's parents' home, known as Sylvania, until 1847, at which time they moved nearby to a beautiful wooded site located at the intersection of the Charleston Road and the old Indian trail in what is now McCormick County. Here Dr. Hearst and his wife resided in a small cabin until Eden Hall was completed.

Designed by architect Henry Jones of Atlanta, Georgia, Eden Hall is a two-story, four-columned Greek revival structure. Similar in scale and size to other large plantation houses of the antebellum period, Eden Hall is characterized by a large veranda, central hall, spacious rooms with large windows and high ceilings, and beautiful hardwood floors. As was the custom of the day, a detached kitchen and various outbuildings were located to the rear of the house. According to family records, once the house was finished, Dr. Hearst and his wife secured the services of an itinerant landscape gardener to design a formal garden:

> The garden which was designed by an English landscape gardener was symmetrical in design with circular pathways edged with brick. There were

Eden Hall—McCormick County, South Carolina.

plantings of English boxwood, lilacs, crape myrtle, spice wood, purple magnolias, tea plants, and sweet olive. Both house and garden were enclosed by a white picket fence. There were two gateways into the garden, the front entrance and the east side. The gate columns for both entrances were four-sided and were made with brick and covered with plaster, as were the posts that supported the fence panels. The brick walk from the east gate was bordered with cherry laurel.

The layout of the garden was a symmetrical pattern that featured a circular motif with curvilinear paths and a central walk leading from the main gate to the entrance of the house. A mixture of both formal and informal elements reflected a design theme that became more prevalent toward the end of the antebellum period. White, picket-fence panels, positioned between vertical, plaster-covered brick columns, enclosed the garden. A large grove of native trees (oaks, hickories, poplars, and pines) was located outside the fenced, ornamental garden and gave the impression of an English park.

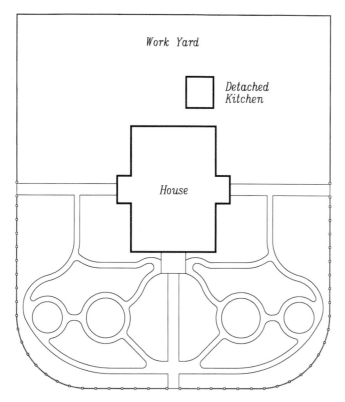

Work Yard

Detached
Kitchen

House

Eden Hall House and Garden Plan. The design of the garden is based on a symmetrical pattern featuring a circular motif with curvilinear paths and a central walk.

During Dr. Hearst's nineteen-year tenure at Eden Hall, he distinguished himself in agriculture, politics, and military service. In the field of agriculture, he was recognized for his progressive farming methods and his efforts to develop new seed varieties that would produce greater yields. In politics, Dr. Hearst represented Abbeville County in the South Carolina legislature before and after the Civil War. In 1861, he became a surgeon in the Confederate army. He was also a first cousin to Senator George Hearst, a wealthy mining engineer and the father of William Randolph Hearst, a newspaper magnate who built the palatial California estate, San Simeon. Dr. Hearst died in 1873, leaving Eden Hall and all of his assets to his wife Anne.

Following Anne Hearst's death in 1891, Eden Hall remained in the hands of family descendants until 1995. At that time, Mr. and Mrs. Emmett Davis Jr. of Greenwood, South Carolina, purchased the property, and under their attentive care Eden Hall has been carefully maintained. Through the devoted stewardship of all who have called Eden Hall home, both the house and garden remain today much as they did when completed in 1854.

## Valley View—Bartow County, Georgia

Located outside of Cartersville, Georgia, in historic Bartow County, Valley View was built in the late 1840s by John Caldwell Sproull, who relocated his family from South Carolina to the fertile lands along the Etowah River. Situated on an elevated site overlooking the broad valley below, Valley View was developed as a large cotton plantation. The imposing Greek revival house built on the property contained massive columns and a spacious piazza, which extended along the front facade and around both sides. A decorative picket fence enclosed a parterre garden that was designed with a central walk that extended from an entrance gate to the front of the house. A clipped-box and cherry laurel hedge bordered the walk. According to family records, the Sproulls brought the boxwood used to plant the garden at Valley View from their home in Abbeville, South Carolina.

In her memoirs, Rebecca (Sproull) Fouche, the Sproull's daughter, recalls some of the important ornamentals included in the gardens at Valley View: "Mother loved evergreens, roses, violets, cape jasmine, tulips, mignonettes, hyacinths, etc., and there was room for all of her favorites because the hedge

Valley View—Bartow County, Georgia.

Valley View House and Garden Plan. The house is entered from a central brick walk, flanked on both sides by parterre gardens of different designs.

was always kept one yard square and the boxwood one foot wide. I have never seen such lovely straw-colored double hollyhocks anywhere, and the violets seemed indigenous to the soil." Additional ornamental plants known to have been grown in the garden included Persian lilac (*Syringia persica*), crape myrtle (*Lagerstroemia indica*), mock orange (*Philadelphus coronarius*), flowering quince (*Chaenomeles speciosa*), forsythia (*Forsythia virdissima*), evergreen euonymus (*Euonymus japonica*), along with a variety of old roses and flowering bulbs.

The surrounding grounds of Valley View were naturalistic in character, including groves of indigenous trees, broad pastures, and cultivated fields. From the front of the house was a spectacular view of the long rolling terrain of the river valley below. Obviously, this imposing view influenced the Sproulls in naming their plantation Valley View. Like the Sproulls, other southern planters who moved into the Etowah River Valley found the area a desirable place to settle because of fertile soils, a good water supply, and its proximity to several small towns.

During General Sherman's march on Atlanta in the final stages of the Civil War, the Sproulls fled to Alabama, leaving their property in the care of a German immigrant, Mr. Vitenger. In their absence, General Schofield of the Union army occupied the house, keeping his horses stabled in the parlor to protect them from Confederate snipers. Upon returning to Valley View at the end of the war, the Sproulls discovered that their house and garden had miraculously survived. Over the years, Valley View has remained in the Sproull family under whose stewardship the house, garden, work yard, and outbuildings have been preserved and maintained.

## Rosedown—St. Francisville, Louisiana

In 1828, Daniel Turnbull and Martha Hilliard Barrow were married in West Feliciana Parish, Louisiana, in an elaborate wedding ceremony that united two of the South's most prominent families. Following their marriage, the couple set out on a grand tour of Europe. During their travels, Daniel and Martha were impressed with the elaborate gardens they visited in England, Italy, and France. Upon returning to Louisiana, they dreamed of having a garden that would combine the formal elements of Italian and French landscapes with the romantic features of English gardens. In the 1840s, the Turnbulls secured the services of a landscape gardener to design a garden for their plantation home, known as Rosedown. Following its completion, Martha devoted her energies to Rosedown's garden for the next sixty years.

Similar to other ornamental gardens of the antebellum period, the garden at Rosedown featured a central avenue of live oaks and formal parterres. The Turnbulls prosperity (derived from the lucrative production of cotton) allowed them to expand the gardens to include an elaborate system of meandering paths, informal plantings of trees and shrubs, and a variety of decorative features. Not only was Martha interested in creating a garden that reflected good taste but also one that contained a fine collection of ornamental plants. To achieve this goal, she imported many trees and shrubs from European sources and regularly ordered camellias, azaleas, roses, and other exotics from northern nurseries including William Prince and Son in Long Island, New York, and Robert Buist of Philadelphia, Pennsylvania.

As the gardens at Rosedown expanded, they evolved into a wonderful blend of formal and natural elements. In time, the gardens at Rosedown overshadowed the plantation house, an anomaly that seldom occurred during the antebellum period. Martha

View of Rosedown Garden—St. Francisville, Louisiana.

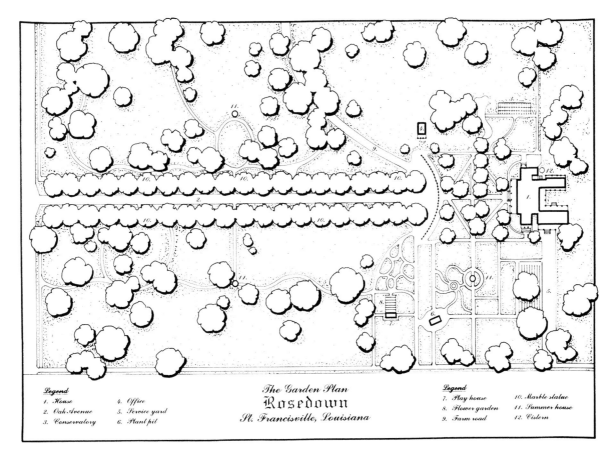

Legend
1. House
2. Oak Avenue
3. Conservatory
4. Office
5. Service yard
6. Plant pit

The Garden Plan
Rosedown
St. Francisville, Louisiana

Legend
7. Play house
8. Flower garden
9. Farm road
10. Marble statue
11. Summer house
12. Cistern

Rosedown House and Garden Plan. Approached by a central avenue of live oaks, the garden designs at Rosedown incorporate both formal and informal elements.

Turnbull's garden diary is a fascinating aspect of Rosedown's garden history. In addition to providing a comprehensive account of her day-to-day gardening activities, the diary also provides a rare and insightful look at gardening during the antebellum period. The diary represents a testament of Martha Turnbull's love for her gardens at Rosedown.

Following the death of her husband Daniel in 1861 and the ensuing hardships imposed by the Civil War, Martha faced economic hard times. Although she underwent continued adversity, Martha Turnbull maintained and managed Rosedown until her death on September 14, 1896, at the age of 87. Martha willed her property and assets, including Rosedown, to her only surviving child, Sarah Turnbull Bowman. Sarah and her husband John, maintained Rosedown until 1914, at which time the property was conveyed to their four unmarried daughters, Carrie, Isabel, Sarah, and Nina. Rosedown remained in their hands until 1955. In 1956, Catherine Underwood of Houston, Texas, purchased the estate and eagerly set about to restore the house and gardens to their former glory. The state of Louisiana currently owns Rosedown and maintains the property as a historic house and garden museum.

### Evergreen Plantation—Edgar, Louisiana

Evergreen represents one of Louisiana's finest antebellum plantations. The main house at Evergreen plantation is characterized by broad galleries, towering columns, and an imposing facade in the Greek revival style. Located along River Road on the west bank of the Mississippi River in St. John the Baptist Parish, Evergreen was developed when the principal cash crop in the region was sugar cane. The original house, built around 1800, was extensively remodeled in 1832 by Pierre Cledamont Becnel, several years after he purchased the property from his grandmother, Magdelaine Haydel Becnel. The remodeling, as recorded in historic records, included the construction of a new hipped roof and belvedere, removal of several existing rooms, addition of a new Greek revival facade, and the addition of double, free-standing stairs. At the time of the changes, Evergreen consisted of the main house as well as a complex of thirty-nine outbuildings including garçonnières (quarters for adolescent boys), a detached kitchen, office, carriage house, stables, pigeonnaires, a privy, and twenty-two slave cabins ceremoniously placed along an alley of live oak trees.

As originally designed, the grounds at Evergreen were based on a symmetrical arrangement of roads, drives, and paths that were spatially organized to meet a variety of aesthetic and utilitarian needs. The original complex included a formal parterre, vegetable garden, orchards, service yard, slaves' quarters, and cultivated fields. These individual elements were articulated by a series of well-defined avenues, hedges, and fences. The central feature of the property was a large formal parterre located in front of the house and extending east to the perimeter of River Road. The parterre consisted of

Evergreen Plantation—Edgar, Louisiana. Located north of New Orleans on the east bank of the Mississippi River, Evergreen represents one of Louisiana's great sugar cane plantations.

geometric beds symmetrically placed along both sides of a central axis. Clipped evergreen borders of box or privet were employed to define and maintain the design.

Another prominent feature that characterized the landscape of Evergreen was a series of linear plantings of live oaks (*Quercus virginiana*), magnolias (*Magnolia grandiflora*), and red cedars (*Juniperus virginiana*). Collectively, these trees formed two long avenues that extended from the river's edge to the rear of the property. While each of these individual species were used during the antebellum period to form imposing avenues, the combination of the three is unique to the property; the name Evergreen was derived from this combination. J. Frazer Smith in *Plantation Homes and Mansions of the Old South* (1933) described the gardens and grounds at Evergreen plantation as follows:

> There are three rows of trees forming two alleys that flank each side and form an enormous formal park between the river and the house. The outer row is giant live-oaks, the next row is magnolias slightly smaller in scale, while the third or inner row is of dwarf cedars still smaller. Similar taller garden shrubs border the alleys and taper down to the small formal blossoms of the flower beds which form a blanket of colors while silvery-shelled paths divide it in patterns. The whole, seen from the river, forms an arena of myriad colors at the end of which proudly reposes the simple white-pillowed great house.

Evergreen was originally laid out to create the impression of a small, self-contained village. While the property retains much of its original integrity, the house and grounds reflect only a glimpse of what was originally one of the South's finest plantations. Today, Evergreen is operated as a historic house museum.

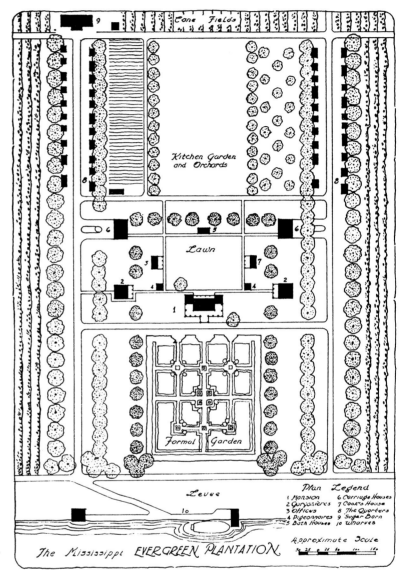

Evergreen House and Garden Plan. Evergreen, like other large plantations of the antebellum period, was designed to function as a small, self-contained village.

# [5]

# SUMMARY OF ANTEBELLUM GARDENS AND LANDSCAPE TRADITIONS

**THE ANTEBELLUM ERA** represents a period in U.S. history (1820–1860) when a variety of economic, social, cultural, and environmental factors were responsible for the development of a prescribed set of landscape topologies that were unique to the American South. Prominent among these were a standardized site plan, a distinctive garden style, and a structured arrangement of outdoor spaces. While regional differences played an important role in fashioning variations in these established patterns, general design consistency prevailed throughout the antebellum period. Another characteristic that was unique to antebellum gardens was their special collection of ornamental plants, which included a blend of American natives, Old World favorites, and newly introduced exotics from China and Japan.

As a general rule the physical layout for a fine antebellum house with an ornamental garden (whether located in an urban or rural setting) was based on a site plan in which the house served as the central feature. The garden was located either in front or to the side of the dwelling. This standardized arrangement relegated functional activities and associated outbuildings to the rear of the house, creating an overall layout of symmetry and order. Integral to this layout was the use of a variety of fences or hedges to assist in defining and articulating outdoor space. While variations occurred in this prototypical arrangement, the basic organization of individual elements generally remained the same.

## Garden Style

Ornamental gardens of the antebellum period were traditionally formal in design, consisting of a parterre enclosed by a decorative fence or formal hedge, which defined the space and provided protection against the intrusion of livestock and domestic animals. Parterres were composed of a combination of geometric shapes, including squares, triangles, rectangles, and circles, arranged to create a variety of patterns. The designs of parterre gardens at the beginning of the antebellum period were based almost exclusively on standard geometric shapes, but by 1850, many designs began to reflect the use of ovals, curves, and flowing lines. Whether this change was the influence of the informal style of landscape gardening or simply an effort to create variations in traditional designs, parterres of the late antebellum period took on a recognizable character that can be described as a regional or vernacular style.

*Myrtle Land* by Father Joseph M. Paret. Located approximately thirty-three miles from New Orleans, in St. Charles Parish, Louisiana, Myrtle Land reflects a typical layout of a large plantation.

## *The Organization of Outdoor Space*

The organization of outdoor spaces in cities and towns was normally based on a simple plan that included a house, garden, and work yard. In rural areas, the layout of plantation grounds generally was more elaborate, including several distinct and separate spatial zones: an ornamental zone including a house and garden; a functional zone comprised of a work yard and vegetable garden, outbuildings, and slaves' quarters; a transitional zone of native trees or groves of indigenous and exotic trees (with an undergrowth of pasture grasses); and finally, an agricultural zone consisting of cultivated crops and open fields. Integral to this layout was the use of a hierarchy of fences that were employed to define and articulate each of the separate areas. While regional variations often occurred in the size, layout, or location of individual elements, consistency in arrangement and overall layout generally remained the same in each of the separate zones.

## *Ornamental Plants*

Early antebellum gardens generally relied on a limited number of ornamental plants, mainly comprised of a combination of American natives (e.g., sweet shrub, cherry laurel, American holly, southern magnolia, fringe tree, yaupon) and a variety of Old World favorites that were introduced during colonial times (e.g., boxwood, althea, chaste tree, mock orange, oleander, laurustinus). By 1840, an extensive array of newly introduced Asian plants were beginning to make their way into the American nursery trade. While these newly introduced exotics (e.g., camellia, azalea, tea olive, banana shrub) were grown in the northern states as greenhouse plant, it was discovered that most would thrive outdoors in the lower and middle South. This expanding array of imported plants, with bright and colorful blossoms, fragrant flowers, and evergreen foliage, along with native and European selections, created a pallet of ornamental plants grown in antebellum gardens that had a distinct regional character.

## *High-Style Ornamental Gardens*

Although the production of cotton and sugar cane during the antebellum period generated immense wealth, not every southern planter or prosperous professional owned a fine ornamental garden. In fact, ownership of a high-style garden—one that was outstanding with respect to design, planting, and details—was the exception, and certainly not the rule. While southerners of the antebellum era had a great interest in horticulture, gardening, and ornamental plants, recent research reveals there were far fewer high-style ornamental gardens than historians have led us to believe, and that the largest concentration of high-style gardens during the antebellum period occurred most often in cities and towns rather than on large plantations. This was particularly true for plantations located in the isolated agricultural regions of Alabama, Mississippi, and Louisiana, because of the following reasons:

> ↗ Plantations located in remote areas of the southern frontier were the last to be developed prior to the Civil War, leaving little time to establish an ornamental garden before the devastation of the war changed the South's economic stability and well-being.
> ↗ A large number of plantations located in interior regions of the developing frontier were owned by planters who resided in towns and cities, placing an overseer in charge of day-to-day operations and activities. Thus, planters who served as

Rosemary—Newnan, Georgia. Ownership of a fine garden during the antebellum era was not necessarily based on one's wealth or social class, as many notable gardens of the period were developed by individuals of modest means—especially those with a passionate interest in gardening and ornamental plants.

"absentee owners" of rural plantations had little interest or desire to build a fine house or develop an ornamental garden on property that was only visited for brief periods throughout the year.

↶ At the time the interior lands of the southern frontier were actively being developed, many planters were employing exploitative agricultural practices that quickly depleted the land. These practices required frequent relocation, generally leaving little time to establish roots and to build a large house and establish an ornamental garden.

↶ Remote regions of the southern frontier had few cities and towns from which ornamental plants or the services of a garden designer could be easily obtained.

Although high style ornamental gardens were fewer in the antebellum South than originally believed, there were numerous examples that reflected excellence in design, physical layout, and unique planting schemes. While variations often occurred in respect to size, individual design, physical character, and detail of ornamental gardens, they typically followed an established arrangement in respect to their location in regards to the house, outbuildings, and open space.

# [6]

# GARDEN BOOKS,
# AGRICULTURAL JOURNALS,
# AND NURSERY CATALOGUES

## GARDEN BOOKS

PRIOR TO THE nineteenth century, southern gardeners had limited instructional material that provided advice and recommendations on ornamental gardening. With the exception of agricultural and commercial almanacs and two early garden guides, *The Gardeners Kalendar* (1779) by Martha Logan and *The Gardeners Kalendar for South Carolina* (1787) by Robert Squibb (both Logan and Squibb resided in Charleston, South Carolina), southerners had to rely almost exclusively on English and French garden books for advice on planting schedules, procedures, practices, and design. The material contained in European garden books was of limited use. Much of the information they contained was inappropriate for the unique growing conditions of the southern states. Several of the more important English garden books used by southern gardeners prior to the nineteenth century included Philip Miller's *The Gardener's Dictionary*, Mawe and Abercrombie's *Every Man His Own Gardener*, Thomas Whately's *Observations on Modern Gardening*, and A. J. Dezallier d'Argenville's *The Theory and Practice of Gardening* (translated from French into English by John James in 1712).

It was not until the beginning of the nineteenth century that American garden books first appeared on the scene. The earliest of these, *The American Gardener* (1804) by John Gardiner and David Hepburn and *The American Gardener's Calendar* (1806) by Bernard M'Mahon, were soon followed by additional works that addressed a variety of topics ranging from the cultivation of fruits, vegetables, vines, flowers, and ornamental plants to the construction of greenhouses, cold frames, and hot houses of various sizes and designs. All but a few of these early works were compiled and written by American nurserymen. This is understandable, considering that nurserymen possessed the greatest knowledge of plants and seeds that were adaptable to local conditions, as well as their desire to provide American gardeners with the necessary information needed to stimulate the growth and expansion of the American nursery trade.

As most early American garden books were written by northern nurserymen from Philadelphia, New York, and Boston, instructional material relating to the specific needs of the southern gardener remained almost nonexistent prior to 1840. One of the earliest attempts to rectify this deficiency was undertaken by Francis S. Holmes in the preparation of *The Southern Farmer and Market Gardener*, published in Charleston, South Carolina, in 1842. The author's primary objective was to collect material from both European and northern sources and, using his own personal experience and observations, adapt it to the growing conditions of the lower South. While Holmes's efforts were directed primarily at the cultivation of fruits and vegetables in the lowcountry of South Carolina, *The Southern Farmer and Market Gardener* represented the first comprehensive effort by a southern author to provide specialized instruction for the unique growing conditions of the South —a region characterized by mild winters, a long growing season, high humidity, and extended periods of heat and drought.

Phineas Thornton, a nurseryman in Camden, South Carolina, with over forty years of practical gardening experience, provided southerners with another book directed at gardening in the South, *The Southern Gardener and Receipt Book* (1840). Even though its main focus was directed at fruit and vegetable gardening, this publication included additional topics such as cooking, beverages, dairy, medical, veterinary, and other miscellaneous subjects. After Thornton's death, Mary L. Edgeworth of Fort Valley, Georgia, printed a revised edition, which was published by the Philadelphia firm of J. B. Lippincott in 1860. Mrs. Edgeworth noted that the title, *The Southern Gardener* was somewhat deceiving as its usefulness was in no way limited to the South, but was "equally applicable to all sections of the Country with some little variation in time, dependent on latitude and climate."

It was not until 1856 with the publication of William Nathaniel White's *Gardening for the South* that southerners were provided with a comprehensive garden book that included advice for cultivating vegetables, fruit trees, and a selected list of ornamentals "adapted to the states of the Union, south of Pennsylvania"—an area that encompassed the upper, middle, and lower South. A native of New York, White relocated to Athens, Georgia, in 1847. In Athens, he combined his literary skills as the editor of various agricultural journals with his personal knowledge of gardening to produce a practical publication that was adapted to the climate, habits, and requirements of the South. In the introduction to the book, White stated, "If this treatise, with all its imperfections, shall in any degree increase the love of Gardening among us; if it shall cause orchards to flourish, shade-trees to embower, and flowers to spring up around any southern home, the author's purpose is accomplished."

The only garden book published in the South prior to the Civil War that dealt exclusively with flowers and ornamentals was Mary Catherine Rion's *Ladies' Southern Florist*. Published in Columbia, South Carolina, in 1860, this small but informative document was intended to provide "every lady of education in the South" a garden book that was practical and easily understood. Born in Sparta, Georgia, in 1829 to northern parents, Mary Catherine's knowledge of plants and botany was gained from William Preston, president of South Carolina College (now the University of South Carolina), under whose care she was entrusted following her mother's return to the North and her father's death in 1847. Mary Catherine married James Henry Rion in 1851 and settled in Winnsboro, South Carolina, forty miles north of Columbia. *Ladies' Southern Florist* was the first garden book written specifically on flowers and ornamentals for southern gardens and was the first book of its kind in the South written by a woman. Like other authors of the time, Mrs. Rion combined her own personal gardening experience with that contained in prominent American garden books of the period including Robert Buist's *American Flower Garden Directory* (1839) and Joseph Breck's *The Flower Garden* (1851).

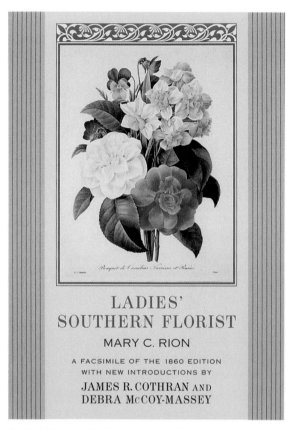

LADIES'
SOUTHERN FLORIST
MARY C. RION

A FACSIMILE OF THE 1860 EDITION
WITH NEW INTRODUCTIONS BY
JAMES R. COTHRAN AND
DEBRA McCOY-MASSEY

*Ladies' Southern Florist* by Mary C. Rion. Published in 1860, *Ladies' Southern Florist* was the first book in the South written specifically about flowers and ornamentals for southern gardens, and the first book of its kind in the South written by a woman.

Andrew Jackson Downing's *A Treatise on the Theory and Practice of Landscape Gardening*, published in 1841, was the only American garden book written before the Civil War that was devoted solely to landscape gardening. In this comprehensive work, Downing, a northern nurseryman and landscape gardener located in Newburg, New York, set out to adapt the concepts and principles of the English naturalistic style of garden design to the American landscape. In compiling and formulating his *Treatise*, Downing relied heavily on the writings of John Claudius Loudon (1783–1843), an English author described by Downing as "the most distinguished gardening authority of the age." While Downing endeavored to provide recommendations on landscape gardening that were applicable to all areas of the country, his ideas and principles of design were met with greater acceptance in the North than in the South. The resistance of southern gardeners to Downing's ideas was largely based on the South's continued adherence to the traditional principles of geometric design and their belief that Downing's recommendations failed to meet their needs and interests. Comments by the editor of *Farmer and Planter* regarding Downing's *Treatise* reflected these concerns:

America has been too busy in opening the forests during the two centuries which
have been marked by her rapid progress, to pay much attention to beautifying the

landscape, by the application of rules of art, or studies tending to improve natural advantages around the homesteads, even of the most wealthy of our citizens. . . . Such was the state of things when Downing published his *Landscape Gardening*—a book which, in the norm, was well adopted to the needs of the Middle and Northern States of the Union. . . . Unfortunately for the South and South-West, it was not adopted to our wants. Indeed, the landscape author who could awaken our people to a general improvement of our broad-tilled acres, we think, has not yet appeared.

*The Farmer and Planter*
Pendleton, S.C., 1859

In addition to his *Treatise on the Theory and Practice of Landscape Gardening*, Downing also wrote *Cottage Residences* (1842) and *The Architecture of Country Houses* (1850). From 1846 until his death in 1852, Downing served as editor of *The Horticulturist*—a periodical containing current information including reports of numerous American horticultural societies and foreign journals/periodicals dealing with agriculture, horticulture, and gardening. The *Horticulturist* remained in publication until 1875 when it was combined with the *Gardener's Monthly*.

With only a limited number of garden books devoted specifically to gardening in the South, southern gardeners generally relied on books published in the North and adapted the material to meet the unique requirements of the southern climate. This demanded constant experimentation. Over time, southern gardeners learned that a wide variety of exotics grown in the North as greenhouse plants proved perfectly hardy when planted outdoors in the South, providing southerners with a wide range of ornamentals to enhance and embellish their gardens and grounds through spring, summer, and fall. Some of the more important garden books published during the Antebellum period included the following, listed in chronological order:

Andrew Jackson Downing. While Downing's *Treatise on the Theory and Practice of Landscape Gardening* (1841) provided recommendations that were accepted in the North, his ideas on gardening were generally rejected in the South.

| Date of Publication | Author and Title |
| --- | --- |
| 1804 | John Gardiner and David Hepburn. *The American Gardener Containing Ample Directions for Working a Kitchen Garden Every Month in the Year; and Copious Instructions for the Cultivation of Flower Gardens, Vineyards, Nurseries, Hop-yards, Green Houses and Hot Houses.* City of Washington. |
| 1806 | Bernard M'Mahon. *The American Gardener's Calender Adapted to the Climate and Seasons of the U.S.* Philadelphia. Eleven editions (second edition, 1818), with the last printed in 1857; remaining basically unchanged until the last edition, which had a memoir of the author, revisions, and illustrations by J. J. Smith, Philadelphia. |

1807    Thomas Main. *Directions for the Transplantation and Management of Young Thorn or Other Hedge Plants.* City of Washington.

1817    William Coxe. *A View of the Cultivation of Fruit Trees and the Management of Orchards and Cider.* Philadelphia.

1820    William Prince. *A Treatise on Fruit and Ornamental Trees and Plants Cultivated at the Linnaean Botanic Garden.* Flushing, Long Island, New York.

1828    Roland Green. *A Treatise on the Cultivation of Ornamental Flowers.* Boston and New York.

1830    William Robert Prince, aided by William Prince. *A Treatise on the Vine Embracing Its History from the Earliest Ages to the Present Day, with Descriptions of above 200 Foreign and 80 American Varieties; Together With a Complete Dissertation on the Establishment, Culture and Management of Vineyards.* Frontis. New York.

1831    ———. *The Pomological Manual; or, A Treatise on Fruits; Containing Descriptions of a Great Number of the Most Valuable Varieties for the Orchard and Garden.* 2 parts, 2nd edition. New York, 1832.

1832    Hibbert and Buist. *The American Flower Garden Directory, Containing Practical Directions for the Culture of Plants in the Hot-house, Garden-house, Flower Garden and Rooms or Parlous, for Every Month of the Year. With a Description of the Plants Most Desirable in Each. Instructions for Erecting a Hot-house, Green-house and Laying out a Flower Garden. With Lists of Annuals, Biennials, and Ornamental Shrubs, Contents, a General Index.* Frontis. Philadelphia. A second printing of this with frontis issued in 1834.

1833    William Kenrick. *The New American Orchardist or an Account of the Most Valuable Varieties of Fruit, Adapted to Cultivation in the Climate of the U.S. Uses, Mode of Management, Remedies; also a Brief Description of the Most Ornamental Forest Trees, Shrubs, Flowers, etc.* Boston. Last edition published 1848.

1838    J. F. Lelievre. *Nouveau Jardinier de la Louisiane* (The New Louisiana Gardener). Nouvelle-Orleans.

1838    Robert Manning. *Book of Fruits.* First series, Salem, Massachusetts. Later revised editions; see 1844 and 1847.

1838    Edward Sayers. *The American Flower Garden Companion Adapted to the Northern States.* Second Edition, Boston. Boston 1839 edition adds *"and Middle States"* to title. Third edition published in Cincinnati, Ohio, 1846.

1839    Robert Buist. *American Flower Garden Directory,* second edition, with Buist as

*Nouveau Jardinier de la Louisiane* (The New Louisiana Gardener) by J. F. Lelievre. Published in 1838, *Nouveau Jardinier de la Louisiane* was an important contribution to southern garden literature, providing gardening information and advice that addressed the special gardening conditions of the Gulf Coast region.

only author (see 1832, Hibbert and Buist) continuing through printings to 1854. No frontis piece. Philadelphia.

1841 Andrew Jackson Downing. *A Treatise on the Theory and Practice of Landscape Gardening Adapted to North America with a View to the Improvement of Country Residence.* New York. Revised editions published 1853 to 1875.

1842 Francis S. Holmes. *The Southern Farmer and Market Gardener.* Charleston.

1844 Robert Buist. *The Rose Manual Containing Accurate Descriptions of all the Finest Varieties of Roses . . . Their Character and Mode of Culture, with Directions for Their Propagation and the Destruction of Insects.* Philadelphia. Revised editions 1847, 1851, 1854.

1845 Andrew Jackson Downing. *The Fruits and Fruit Trees of America, or the Culture, Propagation, and Management, in the Garden and Orchard, of Fruit Trees Generally; with Descriptions of the Finest Varieties of Fruit, Native and Foreign, Cultivated in the Country.* New York. Fourteen editions until 1853. Revised and corrected by Charles Downing, with large editions printed through 1900 (1847 to 1850, some issues have sixty-six to seventy color plates).

1845 Phineas Thornton. *The Southern Gardener and Receipt-Book.* Philadelphia.

1846 William Robert Prince. *Prince's Manual of Roses Comprising the Most Complete History of the Rose Including Every Class, and All the Most Admirable Varieties that have Appeared in Europe and America; Together with Ample Information on the Culture and Propagation.* New York.

1847 Robert Buist. *The Family Kitchen Garden . . . Descriptions of All the Different Species and Varieties of Culinary Vegetables, with Their Botanical, English, French and German Names.* New York. Printings through 1867.

1847 Parsons, Samuel B. *The Rose: It's History, Poetry, Culture, and Classification.* New York. Revised editions, with last entitled *Parsons on the Rose* being reprinted in 1910. First edition only had two color plates.

1851 Joseph Breck. *The Flower Garden; or Breck's Book of Flowers in Which Are Described . . . Hardy Herbaceous Perennials, Annuals, Shrubby Plants, and Evergreen Trees, Desirable for Every Ornamental Purpose, with Directions for Their Cultivation.* Boston.

1853 Thomas Meehan. *The American Handbook of Ornamental Trees.* Philadelphia.

1856 William Nathaniel White. *Gardening for the South; or the Kitchen and Fruit Garden; with Best Methods for Their Cultivations . . . Hints upon Landscape and Flower-gardening. Containing Modes of Culture and Descriptions of the Species and Varieties of the Culinary Vegetables, Fruit Trees and Fruits, and a Select List of Ornamental Trees and Plants Found by Trial Adapted to the States of the Union South of Pennsylvania, with Gardening Calendars for the Same.* New York. Revised editions last published in Richmond, Virginia, in 1901.

1858 John A. Warder. *Hedges and Evergreens. A Complete Manual for the Cultivation, Pruning and Management of All Plants Suitable for American hedging; Especially the Maclura or Osage Orange, Fully Illustrated with Engravings of Plants, Implements and Processes. To Which is Added a Treatise on Evergreens; Their Different Varieties; Their Propagation, Transplanting, and Culture in the United States.* New York.

1860 Mary C. Rion. *Ladies' Southern Florist.* Columbia, South Carolina.

The above-referenced material was adapted from a list of American horticultural texts prepared by Elisabeth Woodburn, as presented in *Agriculture Literature: Proud Heritage, Future Promise* (1975).

## AGRICULTURAL JOURNALS

In addition to garden books, numerous agricultural and farm journals were also published during the first half of the nineteenth century. These publications were primarily directed at providing recommendations on various farm and agricultural practices along

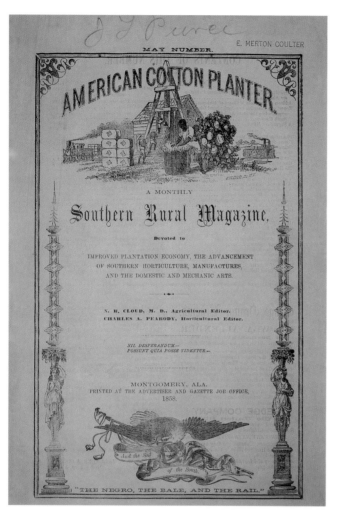

*American Cotton Planter.* Initially published in 1843, the *American Cotton Planter,* along with other southern agricultural and farm journals and magazines of the antebellum period, frequently contained information on horticulture and gardening that proved valuable to gardeners in the South.

with advice on a wide variety of social, moral, aesthetic, health, and economic issues. They often included instructional material on various aspects of horticulture and ornamental gardening. Baltimore, Maryland is credited as the city that produced the first agricultural journal, *The American Farmer* in 1819. Additional publications soon followed, and by 1860, as many as eighty agricultural and farm journals were being published in the South alone. A comprehensive list of nineteenth-century agricultural journals can be found in *A List of the Agricultural Periodicals of the United States and Canada, July 1810 to July 1910* by Stanley Conrad Stunty, published in 1914.

Of all the southern states, Georgia published more agricultural journals than any other state, producing over five such publications before the Civil War. Of these, *The Southern Cultivator,* founded in 1843, was the most successful. From 1845 to 1847, James Camak, an agricultural activist, served as editor of *The Southern Cultivator* bringing the publication respect and acclaim, not only in Georgia but throughout the southeast. Camak was succeeded by Daniel Lee, a northerner with excellent editorial and management skills, under whose editorship from 1847 to 1859 subscriptions to *The Southern Cultivator* doubled. In addition to providing readers with editorials and articles on a vast array of information on agricultural affairs, Lee instituted a "question and answer" column that soon became a regular feature in *The Southern Cultivator* and in other agricultural journals as well. Under Lee's direction, attention was also given to including material relating to various aspects of horticulture and gardening, specifically directed at the needs and interests of gardeners in the South.

The following list of southern agricultural journals, with the initial date of publication, proved particularly valuable to southern gardeners during the antebellum period:

Alabama

*American Cotton Planter*, Montgomery, 1853

*Alabama Planter*, Mobile, 1843

Georgia

*Southern Cultivator*, Augusta, 1843

*Soil of the South*, Columbus, 1851

*South Countryman*, Marietta, 1858

*Southern Field and Forest*, Augusta, 1859

Mississippi

*Mississippi Farmer and Mechanic*, Jackson, 1819

Maryland

*American Farmer*, Baltimore, 1819

Virginia

*The Southern Planter*, Richmond, 1841

*Southern Farmer*, Petersburgh, 1854

South Carolina

*Southern Agriculturist*, Charleston, 1822

*The Farmer and Planter*, Pendleton, 1850

North Carolina

*North Carolina Planter*, Raleigh, 1845

Tennessee

*Southern Homestead*, Nashville, 1856

*The Southern Agriculturist*, Memphis, 1828

Kentucky

*Kentucky Farmer*, Frankfort, 1840

## NURSERY CATALOGUES

Nineteenth-century American nursery and seed catalogues also serve as a valuable source of historic information on ornamental plants available to gardeners. Originally published as single, oversized sheets, (known as "broadsides") they later developed into multipage catalogues. Early nursery catalogues not only provide documentation as to what was being offered for sale at a particular place and time, but frequently included valuable information on the growing of plants and seeds, as well as practical advice on cultivation, planting schedules, and growing requirements. As early as 1807, the catalogue of the famous Bartram Nursery in Philadelphia contained instructional material regarding the "soil and situation" for each plant offered for sale along with an indication as to which of the offerings required winter protection. In 1823, the Prince Nursery of Long Island, New York (America's first commercial nursery), offered patrons a nursery catalogue that contained a short treatise on the management of both fruit and ornamental trees. In the preface of the catalogue, the proprietors explained, "in supporting orders for trees, shrubs, etc. from the most remote parts of the Union" it was deemed necessary to provide adequate directions to subscribers as to planting and management procedures.

In addition to Bartram and Prince, other nurseries offering useful instructional material included Landreth, M'Mahon, and Buist of Philadelphia; Thorburn and Parsons of New York; and Breck of Boston. Each of these nurseries advertised in southern periodicals or had agents that represented their interests in the major cities of the South.

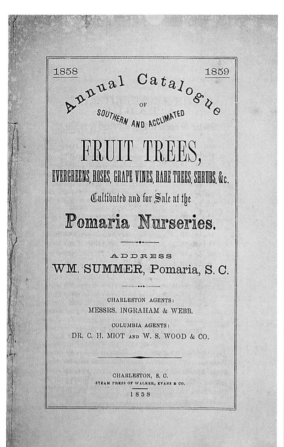
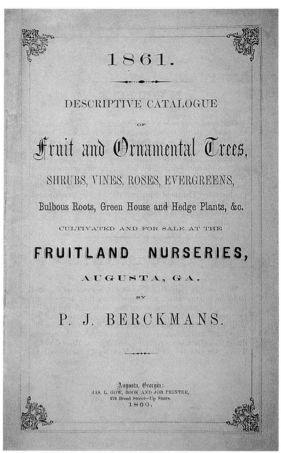

Pomaria Nurseries of Pomaria, South Carolina, and Fruitland Nurseries of Augusta, Georgia, provided southern gardeners with a wide variety of fruit trees, shrubs, vines, roses, and evergreens during the antebellum period.

Regarding southern nurseries, Pomaria of South Carolina, Fruitland of Georgia, and Southern Nurseries of Mississippi were the most notable in providing subscribers with advice on planting and cultivation procedures. In addition to offering instructional material, nineteenth-century nursery catalogues also were instrumental in standardizing the use of botanical names according to the binomial system of nomenclature. The use of acceptable Latin names, including both genus and species, played an important role in the proper identification of plants offered in the nursery trade. Nineteenth-century nursery catalogues generally arranged plants according to the following categories: fruit trees, ornamentals, exotics, greenhouse plants, herbs, flower and vegetable seeds.

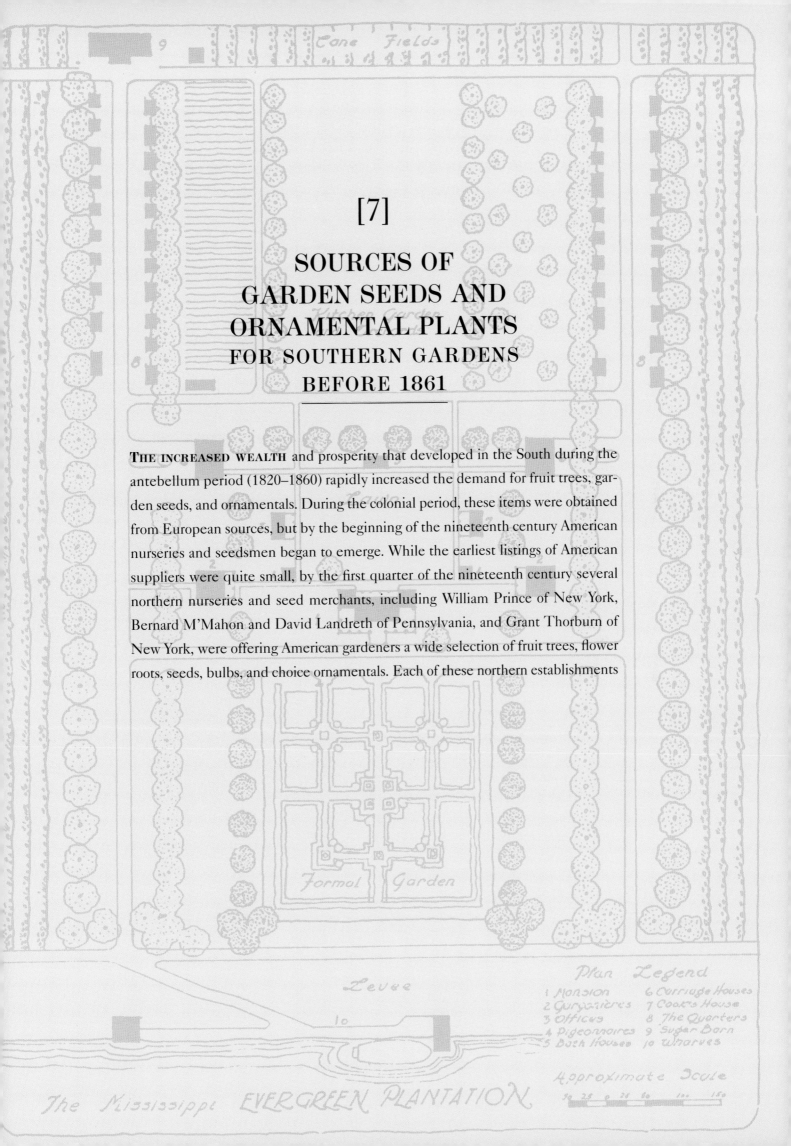

# [7]

# SOURCES OF
# GARDEN SEEDS AND
# ORNAMENTAL PLANTS
## FOR SOUTHERN GARDENS
## BEFORE 1861

**THE INCREASED WEALTH** and prosperity that developed in the South during the antebellum period (1820–1860) rapidly increased the demand for fruit trees, garden seeds, and ornamentals. During the colonial period, these items were obtained from European sources, but by the beginning of the nineteenth century American nurseries and seedsmen began to emerge. While the earliest listings of American suppliers were quite small, by the first quarter of the nineteenth century several northern nurseries and seed merchants, including William Prince of New York, Bernard M'Mahon and David Landreth of Pennsylvania, and Grant Thorburn of New York, were offering American gardeners a wide selection of fruit trees, flower roots, seeds, bulbs, and choice ornamentals. Each of these northern establishments eagerly promoted sales in the southern market either by opening branch offices in southern cities, hiring local agents to represent their interests, or advertising in regional newspapers, magazines, or agricultural journals. Northern nurseries and seedsmen dominated the horticultural field until midcentury, when southern nurseries began to appear. These regional nurseries promoted the position that locally grown stock was more adaptable to the southern climate than that grown in the North. Southern nurserymen also appealed to the sentiment of gardeners in the South to support southern establishments during a time of growing political differences with the North. The following discussion provides an historical overview of the various sources of indigenous and imported seeds and ornamental plants available to southern gardeners prior to the Civil War.

✧

Throughout the eighteenth century Charleston, South Carolina, served as the center of horticulture and gardening in the lower South. Charleston's development as a major seaport city tied it to the vast trade routes between England and other European ports, providing ready access to a wide variety of flower and vegetable seeds, bulbs, and ornamental plants. The first recorded reference of imported garden seeds being sold in Charleston was in 1732 when Samuel Evelyn advertised for sale in the *South Carolina Gazette*, Charleston's first newspaper, "divers [diverse] sorts of the best garden seed." In the same year, "garden seeds just in from London" could be purchased from Mr. Charles Pinckney of Charleston at his newly established mercantile business on the bay. The earliest offering of fruit trees in Charleston occurred in 1745 when Richard Lake offered for sale "lemon trees with lemons on them in boxes, lime trees and orange trees." Shortly thereafter, enterprising merchants and entrepreneurs were offering Charleston's garden enthusiasts flower roots, bulbs, and roses. Charleston had the distinction of having one of the first nurseries in the South, established in 1765 by John Watson, a trained English gardener who came to America to tend the garden of Henry Laurens, one of Charleston's leading citizens. Watson offered Charleston gardeners "a great variety of seeds and plants of flowering trees, shrubs, evergreens . . . and the natural growth of South Carolina, along with a great variety of garden tools."

Many new and exotic trees and shrubs were introduced into Charleston when André Michaux (1746–1802), the noted French botanist, established a plant nursery outside the city in 1786. It was from this nursery that Michaux exported to France many important native American plants that had economic potential. He also introduced into Charleston a wide variety of ornamentals from the Jardin des Plantes in Paris. Initially distributed to prominent plantation owners along the Ashley River, many of these plants soon found their way into the gardens of Charleston and ultimately into the American nursery trade. Michaux is credited with introducing into Charleston the camellia (*Camellia japonica*), the tea olive (*Osmanthus fragrans*), the crape myrtle (*Lagerstroemia indica*), the mimosa or silk tree (*Albizia julibrissin*), the ginkgo (*Ginkgo biloba*), the varnish tree (*Firminana simplex*), and according to some accounts, the Chinese azalea (*Azalea indica*).

Additional contributions to Charleston's horticultural heritage were made by Philippi Noisette, brother of Louis Noisette, a prominent French horticulturist, nurseryman, and writer. Philippi Noisette came to Charleston by way of Santo Domingo around 1783. Upon arriving in Charleston, Noisette accepted a position as director of the Charleston Botanic Society and Garden. He subsequently purchased a large tract of land outside the city where he established a nursery. Noisette soon became a respected nurseryman in Charleston, offering many new and exotic plants to Charleston gardeners. While on a tour of some of the principal nurseries in the United States in 1831, Alexander Gordon, a British botanist and plant collector, made a visit to Noisette's nursery, which he described in the *Gardener's Magazine:*

The last five years have wonderfully changed the features of gardening in Charleston; and the number of botanists to whom I was introduced was convincing proof that this delightful science is duly appreciated in that beautiful city, while the surrounding country furnishes them with ample resources for their exertions. There are two seedsmen in Charleston, Mr. James Wilson, and a relation of the Messrs. Landreth of Philadelphia. The only nurseryman is M. Noisette, brother to the celebrated nurserymen of that name at Paris. But for me to describe the beautiful specimens his garden contains would occupy a whole magazine. Camellias 16 to 20 ft high, and 20 ft in circumference; a most splendid Cycas revoluta at least 20 ft in circumference, in the open ground, and with all our plants of the same nature and habits in equal proportion. I cannot pass over some beautiful specimens of the Noisette rose. I venture to assert that few, if any, ever saw such beautiful specimens of that excellent variety of that delightful genus as are in this garden; but I must drop the subject; I am not competent to do it justice. This garden must be seen to be duly appreciated. Mr. Noisette has a most thorough knowledge of the plants in the southern states; and there are many varieties, strangers to our gardens, which it would be highly gratifying to possess, and which few but himself can furnish.

*Camellia japonica,* "Reine des Fleurs," was introduced to Middleton Place Gardens outside Charleston, South Carolina, before the end of the eighteenth century by the noted French botanist André Michaux.

Equal in importance to the early horticultural activities in Charleston were the many contributions made by the Trustees' Garden in Savannah, Georgia. Established by General James Oglethorpe in 1733, the Trustees' Garden consisted of a ten-acre plot devoted to growing a wide variety of potential economically important fruit trees, vines, plants, and vegetables. A descriptive account of the Trustees' Garden in 1735 is provided by Frances Moore, an English traveler, in *A Voyage to Georgia:*

There is near the town, to the East, a Garden belonging to the Trustees', consisting of ten acres, the situation is delightful, one half of it is upon the top of a hill, the foot of which the Savannah River washes, and from it you see the Woody Islands in the

The Tea Plant (*Camellia sinensis*). While seeds of the tea plant were brought from the East Indies and cultivated in the Trustees' Garden in Savannah (circa 1735), they failed to survive.

Sea. . . . The garden is laid out with cross-walks planted with orange trees. In the squares between the walks, were vast quantities of mulberry trees, this being a nursery for all the province, and every planter that desires it has young trees given him gratis from the nursery. These white mulberry trees were planted in order to raise silk. . . . Besides the Mulberry-trees; there are in some of the Quarters in the coldest part of the Garden, all kinds of fruit-trees usual in England such as apples, pears, etc. In another Quarter are olives, figs, vines, pomegranates and such fruits as are natural to the warmest parts of Europe. At the bottom of the hill, well sheltered from the north-wind, and in the warmest part of the garden, there was a collection of West-Indian plants and trees, some coffee, some coconuts, cotton, Palma christi, and several West-Indian physical plants.

The orange trees, according to Moore's account, were planted along the crosswalks that divided the garden into various squares. Thus, they not only served an experimental purpose, but when in bloom produced a delightful fragrance for those who might stroll the walks. Moore also reveals that the Trustees' Garden was supplied with tea seed (*Camellia sinensis*) from the East Indies, olive trees from Venice, caper plants from Marseilles, and grapevines from France. Within ten years of its founding, the Trustees' Garden was abandoned and the land regranted to the settlers. Though the Trustees' Garden had a short-lived success, this innovative endeavor yielded peach seeds, figs, and a wide variety of vegetables and herbs as well as upland cotton (*Gossypium hirsutum*), which had a profound influence on the economic future of the antebellum South.

The increased development of the southern Piedmont and the westward expansion into Georgia, Alabama, Mississippi, and Louisiana during the first quarter of the nineteenth century contributed greatly to the heightened demand for fruit trees, ornamentals, and garden seed. As few nurseries developed in the lower and middle South until the late 1840s, most gardeners in the region had limited sources to meet their horticultural and gardening needs. To fill this demand, many large, well-established northern seed merchants and nurseries actively solicited the patronage of southern gardeners. They regularly advertised in southern newspapers and agricultural journals, and many mailed catalogues to southern clients or employed local agents in cities throughout the South to serve as sales representatives. In his unpublished diary, James P. Waddel of Athens, Georgia, notes that on 12 April, 1845, he received catalogues from C. M. Hovey, a nurseryman and seed merchant from Cambridge, Massachusetts, and from the famous Prince Nursery in New York. Waddel, like many other gardeners in the South, appears to have fulfilled his gardening needs from the regular placement of orders with northern nurseries and seedsmen. Plants were shipped from the North along coastal routes, or by rail during the winter months when they were in a dormant state. However, many plants were lost due to adverse weather and the extended travel time required before reaching their intended destination.

Prominent among the northern nurseries that solicited southern customers was the Prince Nursery, the first commercial nursery established in North America. Founded by Robert Prince of Flushing, New York, around 1750, the Prince Nursery continued under the management of four generations of the Prince family, offering an extensive array of fruit trees and ornamentals to America and foreign clients until the middle of the nineteenth century. Prince's earliest catalogue (known at the time as a broadside) was published in 1771. As evidenced in the nursery's 1841 catalogue, the Prince Nursery led all other American nurseries in size and number of offerings. The catalogue included an extensive collection of fruit trees, 196 deciduous ornamentals, 111 evergreens, 72 vines, 680 varieties of roses, and over 800 perennials. In 1823, William Prince and Company ran the following advertisement in the *Times*, a Savannah paper:

> Proprietor of the Linnean Garden on Long Island, near New York, offers for sale his usual extensive collections of Fruits and Ornamental Trees and Plants, among which are twenty-six kinds of Orange, Lemon, Citron, and Shaddock Trees, and seventeen varieties of the Camellia Japonica or Japan Rose. Orders will be received by the subscriber and executed during the month of March, and shipped pursuant to orders. *August G. Omler, Druggist, Corner of Jefferson and St. Julian Streets, Savannah, Georgia.*

Undoubtedly advertisements like these were quite effective given the numerous records that document southerners' regular patronage of the Prince Nursery. The following notice-of-sale appeared in the *Huntsville Southern Advocate* on December 1, 1832:

> LAND FOR SALE—The PLANTATION [Belle Mont] on which I lately reside, lying in Franklin County [Alabama] 5 miles south of Tuscumbia, containing 1,680 acres, of which 1,175 are cleared; about 70 acres in clover and grass; 26 are planted in the choicest fruit trees of every kind from *Prince's Nursery on Long Island*—the balance in corn and cotton. On the premises is a Brick Dwelling House 76 feet front, with two wings 42 feet, and all necessary out houses. In point of fertility of soil, health, and local advantages, it is not surpassed by any tract of land in North Alabama.

Bois de Fléche—St. Martins Parish, Louisiana. In addition to obtaining fruit trees and vegetable seed from northern nurseries for orchards and kitchen gardens, southerners also purchased ornamentals, flower seeds, and bulbs from a growing list of offerings from northern establishments including Prince Nursery and Grant Thornburn of New York, and David Landreth and Robert Buist of Philadelphia.

For terms apply to W. A. Moseley on the premises, who is fully authorized to sell. —
November 1, 1832, A. W. Mitchell.

David Landreth, founder of America's first seed business in Philadelphia, Pennsylvania, also advertised his extensive seed collection in the southern media. Established in 1784 and continuing from father to son through four generations, Landreth Seed Company was highly respected both in America and Europe. Landreth's success was achieved by providing top-quality flower and vegetable seeds. Some of the firm's early patrons included such notable Americans as George Washington, Thomas Jefferson, and James Monroe. The firm opened a branch office in Charleston, South Carolina, in 1818, under the management of David Landreth, the eldest son of the founder. The business remained open until 1862, when the Civil War forced its closure. In addition to garden seed, David Landreth offered Charleston gardeners a vast assortment of flowers, bulbs, and ornamentals as evidenced in a notice in the 1841 issue of the *Charleston Courier:* "Flowers and Plants. The conservatory of Mr. D. M. Landreth, sign of the Garden Plough, 289 King Street, is worthy of the attention of notaries of Flora. His Camellia japonicas are very numerous, and covered with buds ready to burst into their wintry bloom. The Daphne odorota already diffuses a delicious fragrance; and his assortment generally of hyacinths, tulips and flower roots and plants are rich and various."

The rose proved to be a popular ornamental during the antebellum period. In 1841, the Prince Nursery of New York offered over 600 different varieties of roses in its catalogue.

Another prominent Philadelphia establishment that catered to southern gardeners was owned by Robert Buist (1805–1880). Trained at the Edinburgh Royal Botanic Garden, Buist immigrated to America to work as a gardener for Henry Pratt in Philadelphia. In 1830, Buist joined Thomas Hibbert in the management of a florist business. Upon Hibbert's death, Buist continued the business, combining a successful florist trade with the sale of seeds. Buist soon became one of America's most successful seedsman and over time expanded his business to include the sale of a wide selection of camellias, roses, and other ornamentals. It was Robert Buist who authored the *Rose Manual* in 1844, a popular publication that contained descriptions of twenty-two classes of roses along with cultural instructions for each. In addition to developing one of the country's most successful seed and nursery businesses, Buist is also credited with introducing the poinsettia (*Euphorbia pulcherrima*) to the florist trade, around 1830. Grant Thorburn (1783–1863), a prominent seedsman and florist in New York City, also actively sought the southern market. Initially established under the name of Grant Thorburn, Seedsman and Florist, the business later became, G. Thorburn and Son and finally, Thorburn and Co. The firm's catalogues offered an extensive listing of garden seeds along with advice and instructions on planting, fertilizing, and cultivation.

By the late 1840s, many prominent leaders in the South felt the time for the development of southern nurseries had arrived. It was felt that regional nurseries could better meet the horticulture and ornamental gardening demands and needs that had resulted from the increased wealth of southerners and the expanding gardening interests that was occurring throughout the southern states. The first major nursery to develop in the lower and middle South was Pomaria Nursery, located in Pomaria, South Carolina. Established in 1840 by William Summer (1815–1875), some forty miles north of Columbia, South Carolina, Pomaria Nursery proved to be one of the most important southern nurseries of the antebellum period, offering a wide variety of fruit trees and ornamentals to gardeners in South Carolina and surrounding states. A notice by the editor of the *American Cotton Planter* in 1859 indicated that "again we have the catalogue of Wm. Summer, Esq., of Pomaria, South Carolina. Mr. Summer offers to our Eastern friends a large, well selected and thoroughly tested variety of fruit trees at very reasonable prices. We can confidently recommend this nursery to our subscribers in eastern Georgia and the Carolinas, having grown . . . many excellent fruit trees and handsome flowering shrubs from there, all true and of the best quality." While most of Pomaria's business was conducted in South Carolina, the nursery's ledgers included listings of clients in Georgia, Alabama, Mississippi, and North Carolina, with agents in Charleston and Columbia, South Carolina, and in Fernandino, Florida. So extensive were Pomaria's offerings of fruit trees and ornamentals that shortly before 1861 the catalogue contained over 1000 varieties of apples, pears, peaches, plums, figs, apricots, and grapes, as well as an equal number of ornamentals, including 400 varieties of roses.

Another important southern nursery was developed by Thomas Affleck (1812–1868) in Washington, Mississippi, around 1842. Born in Scotland in 1812, Affleck immigrated to the United States in 1840 and became an associate editor of the *Western Farmer and Gardener*—one of the first agricultural journals to be published in the west. Affleck traveled widely in the South studying agricultural methods. He settled in Washington, Mississippi (located a short distance north of Natchez), and established Southern Nurseries, one of the first commercial nurseries in the region. In 1846, Affleck became editor of a series of almanacs published by B. M. Norman. Initially known as *Norman's Southern Agricultural Almanac*, the name was changed to *Affleck's Southern Rural Almanac and Plantation/Garden Calendar* in 1851. The publication offered practical advice to southern farmers and gardeners and served as a means for Affleck to advertise plants available from his nursery. Seldom did Affleck miss the opportunity to express his belief that in order for plants to be grown successfully in the South, they should be purchased from southern nurseries. In the mid-1850s Affleck moved to

Home of Thomas Affleck—Washington, Mississippi. In 1842, Thomas Affleck established Washington Nurseries, one of the first commercial nurseries to develop in the region.

Texas where he continued his work as a nurseryman, educator, and writer until his death in 1868.

While the Pomaria and Washington nurseries were able to partially meet the southern gardeners' demand for fruit trees and ornamentals, a call for additional nurseries in the southern states continued, as is evidenced in the following 1847 letter to Andrew Jackson Downing, Esq., editor of the *Horticulturist:*

> There are no intensive *nurseries* and commercial gardens in the South, or at least accessible from which we can procure such fruits, flowers, shrubbery, etc., as may be desired. This is unquestionably felt as a sore inconvenience. Many in the South are deterred from sending to the North for their things, because the cost of transportation, and other expenses connected therewith, especially when the orders are not large, would be very considerable. Besides, there is a danger of being imposed upon by nurserymen and gardeners, where orders are sent to them to be filled—and again, there is a great danger that the precious package of good things, being long as the way, may be received in a very unsound condition. I am well aware, our people are generally much averse to sending orders for fruits, flowers, etc., and would invariably patronize home gardens and nurseries if we had them here. . . . I will also remark that on account of our southern climate, vegetation grows so rapidly that the nurserymen would be remanded for his labor in, grafting, budding, etc., in half the time that it required in the north.
>
> George W. Fish
> Macon, Georgia, September 10, 1847

Mr. Fish's request soon came to fruition, for in 1847 Robert Nelson, a highly competent horticulturist from Denmark, established Troup Hill Nursery in Macon, Georgia. A notice in a Macon newspaper, the *Journal and Messenger,* dated November 1, 1848, noted that "a catalogue of fruit and ornamental trees, shrubs, vines and green-house plants, also bulbous and tuberous roots" had recently been received from Mr. Robert Nelson at his "Commercial Garden and Nursery." This neatly printed sixteen-page catalogue represented a sound testament to the industry and enterprise of this promising establishment. After being engaged in this enterprise for less than a year, Mr. Nelson developed a collection of fruit trees and ornamentals that rivaled many of his northern competitors. A later notice reveals that Nelson's nursery stock contained over ten thousand fruit trees of all descriptions, sixteen varieties of strawberries, four hundred varieties of roses, and an endless variety of evergreens and ornamental shrubs. His collection of greenhouse plants was purported to have contained over two thousand rare and valuable specimens. While Troup Hill Nursery remained a viable business for almost ten years, in 1856 Robert Nelson closed the nursery and relocated to Augusta, Georgia, where he assisted in the management of Fruitland Nurseries. In addition to his involvement in the nursery trade, Nelson wrote many definitive articles on horticultural and gardening subjects (many appeared in the *Southern Cultivator*) that addressed the special needs and interest of southern gardeners. In 1858, Nelson moved to Montgomery, Alabama, where he served as horticultural editor for the *American Cotton Planter and Soil of the South.*

The first nursery established in Alabama was Vineland Nursery, located twenty-nine miles north of Mobile at Langdon Station. Mr. C. C. Langdon, a native of Southington, Connecticut, came to Mobile in 1834. Shortly after arriving in the city he became engaged in politics and the brokerage business. As a trustee of the Agricultural and

Mechanical College in Auburn, Alabama, Langdon expressed a great interest in horticulture and scientific farming. In formulating his plans for Vineland Nursery (later known as Langdon Nursery), Langdon was guided by three primary objectives: a desire to satisfy his own personal taste, to substantiate his belief that the South could produce all the principle fruits and ornamentals presently grown in the middle and northern states, and finally, to establish a nursery that was of an appropriate size that could provide the South with a reliable product.

Another nursery that had a profound impact on the South was the well-known Fruitland Nurseries, located about three miles west of the city of Augusta, Georgia. In 1853, Dennis Redmond purchased 315 acres of land from Benjamin H. Warren and named the property Fruitlands. The following year, Redmond built Fruitland Manor, the first concrete dwelling to be constructed in the South. (Today, this structure serves as the clubhouse of the Augusta National Golf Course.) Redmond developed a nursery on the property, which he managed until 1857. He then sold the business to P. J. Berckmans and his father, Dr. Louis Berckmans, horticulturists from Belgium. The Berckmans began importing, selecting, and distributing a wide range of fruit trees and ornamentals throughout the South under the name of Fruitland Nurseries.

Louis A. Berckmans, Robert Craig Berckmans, P. J. Berckmans Jr. (standing, left to right), and P. J. Berckmans Sr. (seated in the chair). In 1858, P. J. Berckmans Sr. established Fruitland Nurseries in Augusta, Georgia.

The Berckmans' 1858 order ledger (located in the collection of the Cherokee Garden Library, Atlanta, Georgia) indicates that plants were sent to locations throughout the southeast. Each purchase had a written record that included an order number, the client's name, the client's address or pick up point, the date of the order, the scientific and common name of each plant, the price, and the date when the order was filled. The ledger also reveals the names of northern nurseries from which the Berckmans ordered many of their stock plants. The most important of these were William Prince of Long Island, New York, and Robert Buist and Thomas Meehan of Philadelphia, Pennsylvania. Over time, Fruitland Nurseries offered southern gardeners many new fruit trees and ornamental plants. Ultimately, the nursery would have its greatest impact in the South after 1865, but it established its reputation for unusual and high-quality plant material in its few short years of operation before the Civil War. Although additional nurseries developed in the southern states prior to 1861, few were as important or offered as great a variety of nursery stock as Fruitland. Interestingly, the Berckmans' 1861 catalogue listed over twenty varieties of camellias, an ornamental that by this time had gained great popularity throughout the lower and middle South.

Among the several smaller nurseries that developed in the lower and middle South during the antebellum period were Downery Hill Nursery (Atlanta, Georgia), Georgia Nursery (Augusta, Georgia), Glooming Nursery (Clarksville, Georgia), Magnolia Nurseries

(New Orleans, Louisiana), West Feliciana Nurseries (Bayou Sara, Louisiana), and Wilson's Nursery (Montgomery, Alabama). Several foreign nurseries, including Vilmarin, Andrieux and Co. in Paris and Andre Leroy in Anglers, France, also supplied plants to southern gardeners in New Orleans and the Gulf Coast region.

By the mid-1800s, many southern leaders and agricultural journals joined southern nurserymen in urging gardeners in the southern states to purchase plants from nurseries in the South instead of patronizing northern establishments. This position was based on the belief that had long been promoted by southern nurseries that plants grown in the South were better acclimated to the southern climate and because uninformed buyers who purchased plants from northern nurseries frequently found these nurseries to be unreliable in regards to plants' names or descriptions. The following passage taken from an 1857 letter written to the editor of the *Farmer and Planter* in Pendleton, South Carolina, addresses this issue:

> Our people should instead of going to the North for their fruit trees, patronize home nurseries where they will not be humbugged and disappointed by having trees palmed on them, that will be altogether worthless in our climate; heretofore we were compelled to resort to the North for fruit trees, and we have paid dearly for most of them. Not so now, we have in every Southern State, nurseries almost at our door.

Another letter written to the editors of the *Southern Cultivator* in 1859, encouraged the patronage of southern nurseries, while also exhibiting the undertones of a growing division between the North and South on the eve of the Civil War:

> Southern Nurserymen are now fully prepared to supply all desirable varieties of fruit and ornamental trees, vines, roses, etc.—grown with special reference to our climate; and the southerner who sends or gives his orders to Northern Nurseries or the peddlers (while he is, perhaps, politically advocating discussion and non-intercourse!) can hardly be a *consistent* man or a true *patriot.*
>
> *Home Place, Ga., June 1859.*

Growing political differences between the North and South in the years preceding the Civil War undoubtedly influenced many southern agricultural writers to attempt to undermine the integrity of northern nurseries. While it is difficult to determine what impact this had on the balance of trade between the two regions, southern nurseries continued to flourish and grow, and by 1861, gardeners in the lower and middle South were, as a general rule, able to fulfill their horticultural and gardening needs from southern sources.

# HISTORIC PLANTS OF
# THE ANTEBELLUM SOUTH
## AND DATES OF INTRODUCTION

THROUGHOUT HISTORY THE southern states, particularly those comprising the lower and middle South, have yielded a wealth of native trees, shrubs, and vines with outstanding ornamental value. From early times, European explorers were enthralled with the beauty and diversity of southern plants and eagerly collected specimens to send back to the Old World as newfound treasures that would embellish the gardens and landscapes of Europe. Conversely, American colonists were generally inclined to favor plants they had known and loved in Europe. In time, however, they recognized the value of using native American plants and often included selected specimens as ornamentals in their gardens. Indigenous plants also were used as substitutes for traditional Old World favorites that the colonists found difficult or impossible to obtain from European sources. A lively exchange of plants took place between America and England up until the American Revolution, at which time the practice was greatly curtailed, only to be renewed again at the turn of the century. With the arrival of many new Asian plants into England throughout the first half of the nineteenth century, American nurseries became eager to obtain these newly introduced exotics to help promote the American nursery trade. In the North, many of these new introductions were grown as greenhouse plants, while in the South most proved perfectly hardy as outdoor plants. Thus, gardens of the antebellum South became a blend of Old World favorites, American natives, and newly introduced Asian plants.

A variety of factors contributed to the richness and diversity of plants grown in gardens of the antebellum South, including a favorable climate, a long growing season, economic prosperity, and a desire for new and exotic plants. The great variety of plants grown in antebellum gardens is documented in numerous letters, diaries, and travel records of the period, as reflected in the following account in *The South-West* (1835) in which Joseph Holt Ingraham described a garden located outside of Natchez, Mississippi:

Oak Lawn—Thomasville, Georgia. Gardens of the antebellum South were comprised of a blend of Old World favorites, American natives, and newly introduced Asian plants.

> Among them—for I will mention a few—which represented every clime, were the crape myrtle, with its pure and delicately formed flower, the oak geranium, the classical ivy, and the fragrant snowdrop. The broad walks were, as usual in southern gardens, bordered by the varnished lauria mundi [*Prunus caroliniana*], occasionally relieved by the cape jessamine, slender althea, and dark green arbor vitae . . . amaryllis, the purple magnolia, the Arabian and night-blooming jessamines, the verbenum, a lemon-scented geranium, with the majestic aloe. . . . The sweet-scented shrub and oleander, with countless other shrubs and flowers, breathing forth the sweetest fragrance, gratified the senses and pleased the eye wherever it was turned. . . . The moss, and wild rose, the last a native, in which the creative power of horticulture annually unfolds new beauties, the dwarf cape jessamine, the Washita willow, with its pretty flower, the laurustinus, hibiscus, and citrinella, or fragrant lemon grass, the tea-tree, three feet high, with orange and lemon trees, bending under their golden fruit, and a guava tree . . . presented on every side the most delightful offerings to the senses.

Many of the newly introduced plants from China and Japan could be grown outdoors in the lower South with little or no winter protection. In other parts of the region, these exotics generally required shelter from freezing temperatures and during occasional periods of ice, sleet, and snow. To provide winter protection for tender and exotic plants and to assist in the germination of seeds for early planting, gardeners in the middle and upper

Center Hall—Darlington County, South Carolina. A hothouse (as shown in the lower right-hand corner) was a free-standing brick or stone structure with wooden-framed glass, which provided light and captured the heat from the sun.

South often used a variety of structures as substitutes for greenhouses including *cold frames*, *plant pits*, and *hothouses*. These structures were not comparable in cost or size to a traditional greenhouse, yet each provided similar benefits on a more modest scale. With the increasing number of imported exotics being grown in southern gardens during the first half of the nineteenth century, cold frames, plant pits, and hothouses became common features in the South during the antebellum period.

Cold frames were small garden structures used to provide protection for frost-sensitive plants (generally from November through March, depending on location and prevailing weather conditions) and to facilitate the germination of vegetable and flower seeds for spring planting. In its simplest form, a cold frame usually consisted of a shallow pit covered by a wooden sash (a frame that held glass panels). The sash was placed at a sufficient angle to capture the rays of the sun and to provide adequate water runoff during inclement weather. Cold frames had no source of artificial heat but were oriented in a southerly direction, thus allowing the sun to strike the sash and trap the heat inside. In instances where a cold frame was used primarily to grow seedlings or cuttings, the sash was usually no more than eighteen inches high at the rear and nine inches in front. This design permitted newly germinated seeds and young cuttings to remain close to the glass. The sash covering the cold frame was periodically removed during warm, winter weather to permit the circulation of fresh air, which helped prevent the spread of disease and allowed young seedlings to acclimate to outside conditions. During days when temperatures were extremely cold, fermenting manure was often added to the cold frame as a means of generating additional heat.

A plant pit, while similar to a cold frame, was generally larger and more elaborate in design. A plant pit generally consisted of an excavated area that extended three to four feet below the surface of the ground. The pit was lined with brick or stone so that the back wall was somewhat higher than the front. This arrangement permitted the placement of a sash over the pit at an angle that was appropriate for capturing the heat of the sun which would warm the interior space. A plant pit (sometimes referred to as a flower pit, fern pit, green pit, or simply a pit) required good drainage and generally was fitted with a series of shelves to accommodate potted plants or trays of cuttings or germinating seeds. When a plant pit was used primarily to germinate vegetable and flower seeds or to encourage continuous growth of tender ornamentals during the winter months, it was oriented to the south. In cases where its intended purpose was simply to protect and keep tender plants in a dormant condition during winter, it was oriented to the north, northeast, or northwest.

In areas of the South where winters were mild, a plant pit was often protected with wood frames covered with oiled homespun (a coarse cloth made of yarn) instead of glass. This material provided the same benefits as glass but was far less expensive and easier to maintain. In an address to the Southern Central Agricultural Society in Macon, Georgia, in 1851 (reprinted in *Georgia's Planting Prelate*, 1945), Stephen Elliott, Episcopal bishop of Georgia, extols the benefits of a plant pit covered with cloth:

> In our mild climate there is a very excellent substitute for a greenhouse, requiring no expenditure exceeding five or ten dollars. This substitute is a pit dug in the earth to the depth of five or six feet, or any size the party may desire, and furnished with benches rising over above the other like the staging of a theater. Around the upper edge of this pit, run a wooden frame-work of a foot in height in front and two feet in the rear, with its sides sloping from rear to front, cover the top with frames attached by hinges to the rear, and instead of glass, enclose these frames with the common ten cent homespun of our factories, well saturated and tacked lightly as they can be drawn over the sides and ends of the frame. Such a pit as this will answer all the practical purposes of a green-house, and will give you through the winter, a succession of exotic flowers.

Plants frequently referenced as being overwintered in plant pits included geraniums, salvias, petunias, ferns, azaleas, camellias, hydrangeas, gardenias, oranges, lemons, limes, along with a selection of newly introduced exotics from South America, Africa, and Asia. References conveying the joys of owning a plant pit appear in numerous diaries and letters of the antebellum period. Mary Louisa McMurran of Natchez, Mississippi, in a letter dated April 7, 1851, to her sister, Frances Connor, writes of her "green pit" which was "brilliant with the show of geraniums, cactus and etc." (Leumel P. Connor Papers). In another letter dated November 15, 1866, taken from the *Granit Farm Letters*, Sallie Bird of Hancock County, Georgia, conveys to her daughter, Sadie, a student at the Convent of the Visitation in Georgetown, D.C., of her desire to share with her "precious child" the floral treasures of her pit. "I wish, darling, I could send you a bouquet from the pit. The salvias are superb and white camellias, fuschias and heliotropes are in bloom too, and I so wish, I could send you a sweet cluster."

A hothouse refers to a freestanding garden structure constructed of brick or stone and heated by a wood or coal-burning furnace. The standard orientation of a hothouse was directly south, with any deviation being inclined to the east. A hothouse was usually built over an excavated area that extended three to four feet below the surface of the earth. Glass was placed in a wooden frame to provide light and to capture the heat of the sun. Robert Buist, a respected nurseryman and seedsman in Philadelphia, recommended in *The American Flower Garden Directory* (1839) that the angle of the glass be varied depending on the height of the structure and the size of the plants enclosed. Buist also noted that "where ornamentals are to be the principal object, the angle should be about thirty-three degrees from the level line; but a few degrees of inclination either way is of minor

*Azalea indica* from Flore Des Serres (1856). Azaleas were grown out-of-doors in coastal regions of the antebellum South, but they were generally treated as tender exotics in the upper and middle South.

importance." For easy access a small door was located at one end of the structure along with a series of steps leading into the space below.

While the use of artificial heat was necessary in hothouses in the North, in most areas of the South, heat generated by the sun proved adequate, except during the coldest of winters. Thus, the term hothouse in the southern states described a small, detached structure that relied solely on the heat of the sun to provide winter protection for exotics and ornamentals. A hothouse often was referred to inappropriately as a greenhouse, creating confusion in the use of the term. Hothouses in the South sometimes exhibited interesting and unique designs, depending on the imagination and skill of the builder. When a hothouse occupied a prominent location in a garden, it often served as a focal point or feature in the overall design.

The following account in the *Columbia Banner* on May 24, 1853, references Henry Lyons's use of hothouses in his garden in Columbia, South Carolina: "Meeting with an old friend from Sumter [South Carolina], I gladly accepted his invitation to pay a visit to the magnificent gardens, and orchards of H. Lyons, Esq., [famous for his fine collection of choice fruits and flowers] where we spent a profitable and delightful hour in visiting his luxuriant vineyards and graperies, fine vegetables, luscious fruits, and elegant hot-houses."

## PLANT PROFILES AND DATES OF INTRODUCTION

Unlike in England, where introduction dates of imported plants were accurately documented in such notable works as Philip Miller's *Gardeners' Dictionary*, William Aiton's *Hortus Kewensis*, Stephen Clark's *Horticus Anglicus*, and J. C. Loudon's *Arboretum et Fruticetum Britannicum*, no comparable effort was undertaken in North America. Because the majority of exotic plants imported into the United States before 1860 arrived by way of England, the date a plant was initially introduced into England offers an important clue as to when it was first available to American gardeners—keeping in mind that after a plant was first introduced into England, it generally took five years or more before it made its way into the American nursery trade. By midcentury, this time had been greatly reduced due to improvements in the maritime trade and the aggressive efforts of American nurserymen to offer new and exotic plants.

Another factor responsible for hampering research regarding the introduction dates of plants into America was the use of varied plant names. Prior to 1753, when Carolus Linnaeus, the noted Swedish botanist, developed the modern system of nomenclature, which gives a plant or animal a unique two-part Latin name (the first being the genus, and the second the species—for example, *Magnolia grandiflora*), no standardized system of plant identification had been established. Even after Linnaeus's binomial system of nomenclature was introduced, it took many years before it was widely adopted. This was particularly true in the American nursery trade where many practitioners continued to list plants only by their common names. Continued use of common names was employed by American nurseries for the benefit of the average gardener, who had little knowledge of scientific names. As common names varied from one location to another, their use in accurate plant identification can be extremely confusing. Among the earliest American nurseries to list plants by their common and scientific names were those owned by William Prince, Bernard M'Mahon, and David Landreth. Others soon followed, and by 1860 most American nurseries had adopted this system as a standard practice.

In an effort to develop a comprehensive list of ornamental plants available to southern gardeners during the antebellum period, along with approximate dates of introduction, the following methodology was employed:

- ↶ Review of historical plant lists, diaries, travel accounts, and literature of the antebellum period.
- ↶ Site visits to extant antebellum gardens.

↗ Examination of dates when plants of the antebellum period were first introduced into England.

↗ Review of over one hundred pre-1861 American nursery and seed catalogues, compiled from various archival collections, to determine approximate dates when selected plants of the antebellum period were first offered in the nursery trade. (See appendix C "Composite List of Pre-1861 American Nursery Catalogues" for a list of the nursery and seed catalogues consulted.)

Of the 164 trees, shrubs, vines, and ground covers surveyed, detailed profiles of seventy-nine of the plants most commonly used during the antebellum era were compiled. Each profile includes the current botanical name (genus and species), previous botanical name(s) (if relevant), and common name(s), as indicated in the following example:

Albizia julibrissin—(Botanical name)
(*Acacia julibrissin, Albizzia julibrissin*)—(Previous botanical names)
Mimosa, Silk Tree—(Common names)

Additional information includes a general and historical overview, date first offered in an American nursery or seed catalogue, and relevant references found in books, magazines, and journals of the period. While the date a plant was first listed in an American nursery or seed catalogue provides an indication as to when a commercial nursery initially made it available to gardeners, it cannot be assumed that it had not been grown in American gardens prior to that time. This is obviously true with respect to native or indigenous plants, which could have been collected from surrounding fields and forests. In the case of European and Asian species, some could have arrived earlier through the efforts of European botanists and naturalists, or obtained by American plant collectors who imported plants directly from foreign sources to embellish their gardens and grounds before they were available in the nursery trade. (For additional information on plant introduction dates see appendix B "Historic Resources for Documenting the Past.")

In addition to the seventy-nine detailed profiles provided in the following section, information on all 164 plants surveyed is presented in a table that lists the botanical and common name(s), place of origin, date first introduced into England, and the date the plant first appeared in an American nursery or seed catalogue.

## Ailanthus altissima

(*Ailanthus glandulosa*)
Tree of Heaven, Chinese Sumac, Tanners Sumac, Celestial Tree

Native to China, *Ailanthus altissima* is a fast-growing, deciduous tree characterized by large, compound leaves, small yellowish flowers, and green or reddish brown winged seeds. Growing to a height of 100 feet, *Ailanthus altissima*, or tree of heaven as it is generally known, produces plants of two types: those having only male flowers and those having both male and female flowers on the same plant. A disagreeable or offensive odor distinguishes plants producing only male flowers from those with male and female flowers on a single plant.

*Ailanthus altissima* was introduced into England in 1751 when Philip Miller of the Chelsea Physic Garden received seeds from Father d' Incarville, a French Jesuit stationed in Peking, China. The tree first arrived in America in 1784 when William Hamilton of Philadelphia received specimens from England for his estate gardens at The Woodlands, located on the Schuykill River. The tree of heaven was first offered by an American nursery when it was listed in Prince and Mill's 1823 *Catalogue of Fruit and Ornamental Trees.* The catalogue described the plant as having "quick growth and handsome foliage."

Originally revered as a prized ornamental in gardens and groves of the antebellum South, the popularity of this exotic tree began to wane during the second half of the nineteenth century, primarily because of its vigorous growth and the undesirable odor associated with the flowers of male trees. Today, the tree of heaven grows rampantly along roadsides and in cities throughout the eastern and central United States. While once regarded as a popular ornamental, *Ailanthus altissima* is now considered commonplace and labeled as a second-class tree.

### A Short Treatise on Horticulture, 1828
William Prince

৵ Chinese ailanthus

It was introduced from one of the London nurseries by the author, under the name of Tanner's Sumac, and the error remained uncorrected for a number of years. It is now becoming extensively planted for ornament, as it forms one of the most beautiful trees when at maturity, and withstands the severest cold. . . . As few trees are calculated to make as fine an appearance in

*Ailanthus altissima* (tree of heaven)

so short a space of time, it is particularly suitable for purposes where trees are required to promptly form an ornament.

### A Treatise on the Theory and Practice of Landscape Gardening, 1841
Andrew Jackson Downing

৵ THE AILANTHUS TREE *Ailanthus*

Ailanto is the name of this tree in the Moluccas, and is said to signify Tree of Heaven; an appellation probably bestowed on account of the rapidity of its growth, and the great height which it reaches in the East Indies, its native country. When quite young, it is not unlike a sumac in appearance; but the extreme rapidity of its growth, and the great size of its pinnated leaves, four or five feet long, soon distinguish it from that shrub. During the first half dozen years, it outstrips almost any other deciduous tree in vigor of growth. . . .

In New York and Philadelphia, the Ailanthus is more generally known by the name of the *Celestial Tree*, and is much planted in the streets and public squares. . . . The Ailanthus is well adopted to produce a good effect on the lawn, either singly or grouped; as its fine long foliage catches the light well, and contrasts strikingly with that of the round-leaved trees.

### The Horticulturist, 1852
Andrew Jackson Downing, Editor

৵ Down with the Ailanthus! is the cry we hear on all sides, town and country—now that this "Tree of Heaven" . . . has penetrated all parts of the union, and begins to show its true character. "Its blossoms smell so disagreeable that my family are made ill by it," says an old resident on one of the squares in New York, where it is the only shade. . . . In some cities southward, authorities, taking the matter more seriously, have voted the entire downfall of the species. . . . In the first place it smells horribly . . . in the second it suckers . . .

### *Prince's Select Descriptive Catalogue,* 1860–1861
William Prince

❧ The Ailanthus has lately fallen into disrepute on account of the odor of its blossoms: an evil easily remedied . . . by proper selection, as the odor proceeds only from one sex, latterly introduced, and therefore this objection does not apply at all to the tree originally introduced, which was of the other sex.

## Albizia julibrissin

(*Acacia julibrissin, Albizzia julibrissin*)
Mimosa, Silk Tree

Native to Iran, central China, Japan, and Korea, *Albizia julibrissin* or mimosa, as it is commonly known, is a deciduous, medium-sized tree with a spreading, picturesque form. The genus, *Albizia*, sometimes spelled *Albizzia*, was named in honor of Fillippo delgi Albizzia, a noted eighteenth-century Italian naturalist who introduced the mimosa into the Tuscany region of Italy around 1749. The species name, *julibrissin*, is derived from the Persian word *ghulibrechim* meaning silk rose, from which it derives one of its common English names, silk tree. Reaching a height of thirty to forty feet, the mimosa has dark green, doubly compound leaves, comprised of numerous small leaflets. The mimosa produces fragrant, pompomlike flowers that are borne from June through August. The plant's showy clusters of pink, silky flowers are followed by brown seed pods, four to six inches long, which remain on the tree well into winter.

*Albizia julibrissin* (mimosa)

In 1745, *Albizia julibrissin* was introduced into England, where it was grown as a prized ornamental. The mimosa arrived in North America around 1785 when André Michaux, the noted French botanist, brought seeds from France. Michaux had obtained seeds of this exotic tree from Persia, where he had traveled under the auspices of the French government from 1782 to 1785. Michaux provided mimosa seeds to William Bartram of Philadelphia, who in turn shared them with Thomas Jefferson. Michaux cultivated the mimosa at his botanic garden in Charleston, South Carolina, where it proved highly adaptable to the southern climate. *Albizia julibrissin* was first offered for sale by an American nursery when listed in Bartram's *1807 Catalogue of Trees, Shrubs and Herbaceous Plants*. The mimosa was popular in gardens of the antebellum South, where it was greatly admired for its fragrant, showy flowers, rapid growth, and tolerance of heat and drought.

ᴖ William Bartram to Thomas Jefferson, October 29, 1808

Dr. Say will hand your excellency a small packet containing a few seeds of a beautiful flowering tree together with a catalogue of our collection. The tree is the Mimosa julibrescens [Silk Tree], a native of Persia and Armenia; lately brought to us by the celebrated Michaux the Elder.

### A Short Treatise on Horticulture, 1828

William Prince

ᴖ This tree, a native of the Levant, is the only species which has yet been found hardy enough to endure our winters in this latitude. Even in Charleston, it has become so completely acclimated as to appear almost indigenous; but in the vicinity of New York and Philadelphia, they are not numerous. The foliage of the tree is of a most delicate and beautiful description, being numerous pinnated, and of a very pleasant green.

### The Soil of the South: A Monthly Journal, 1852

James A. Chambers and Charles A. Peabody, Editors

ᴖ But of all God's beautiful trees, there is nothing more exquisite than the Mimosa, now in bloom. How graceful it rears its feather-tufted blooms—how delicately it blends the rainbow—how sweetly it exhales its scented breath, and yet how humbly closes its myriad leaves at evening! If, as Downing [Andrew Jackson] says, it is worth a trip to England to look upon one of her velvet lawns, it is richly worth a trip to the South to look upon a full-grown Mimosa tree in bloom. They are easily propagated by their seed, and flourish like the China Tree amongst any kind of soil.

### The American Cotton Planter, 1855

N. B. Cloud, Editor

ᴖ [From the *Natchez Daily Courier*, October 28, 1854]

The *Acacia julibrissin*, or Flowering Acacia, though by no means rare, is yet too showy, with its myriads of pink and yellow flowers, to be omitted in pleasure grounds, or even small yards.

Thomas Affleck

## Aucuba japonica variegata

Japanese Aucuba, Gold Dust Plant, Variegated Laurel, Blotch Plant

*Aucuba japonica variegata* or gold dust plant, as it was originally known, is native to Japan. It is a striking evergreen shrub best known for its handsome variegated foliage. This exotic ornamental is a multi-stemmed, upright shrub which reaches a height of five to six feet and has long been prized for its dark green, leathery leaves and contrasting splotches of yellow gold. *Aucuba japonica variegata* is particularly valuable for its tolerance of dense shade and its ability to grow in locations where few other shrubs will survive. Being a dioecious plant (meaning the male and female flowers are borne on different plants), specimens of both male and female plants are required for this Asian native to produce its long, crimson red berries.

*Aucuba japonica variegata* was introduced into England in 1783 by John Groeffer, a former pupil of Philip Miller, author of *The Gardener's Dictionary.* The original introduction, a variegated female plant, was extensively grown both as a greenhouse and an outdoor plant for its striking, evergreen foliage. In 1861, Robert Fortune secured a solid green male plant from Japan, which was dispatched to England where it was used for cross-fertilization with the variegated form. Numerous varieties soon resulted, and the plant's popularity continued among English gardeners for use in city and suburban gardens, parks, squares, and as a favorite greenhouse plant. Gold dust plant was first offered by an American nursery when listed as an "exotic" in Bartram's *1807 Catalogue of Trees, Shrubs and Herbaceous Plants*. This striking ornamental proved popular in antebellum gardens, where it was grown either as a specimen in a shady, protected location or as a hothouse plant.

*Aucuba japonica variegata* (Japanese aucuba)

### The American Flower Garden Directory, 1839
Robert Buist

> ✣ *Aucuba japonica*. The flowers are small and almost insignificant, color purple; but the foliage is a desirable object, being yellow-spotted, or blotched. It is tolerably hardy, and withstands our winters. It prefers shade, and, if the situation were such when planted out, it would grow more freely. The hot rays of the sun are very prejudicial to its growth. It is an evergreen shrub and very desirable.

### The Horticulturist, 1855
P. Barry and J. Jay Smith, Editors

> ✣ *Aucuba japonica* (*variegata*). There are many individual specimens in gardens. It requires continual shade. The summer sun seems more harmful than the frost of winter. Its beautiful foliage affords a pleasing feature, and might be more frequently introduced in shady places.

### The Southern Cultivator, 1856
Daniel Lee and Dennis Redmond, Editors

> ✣ *Aucuba japonica* (*variegata*)
> Its only beauty consists in yellow blotches on the dark green, shining leaves. When planted on the north side of a building, where it is always cool and shady, this shrub will do well, but the sun kills it without fail. Any kind of soil. 4 to 6 feet high. Propagated by cuttings.

### Ladies' Southern Florist, 1860
Mary Rion

> ✣ *AUCUBA JAPONICA*, or Blotch Plant, is of slow and precarious growth, and only attains an inconsiderable height. It has yellow spotted or blotched leaves, hence its name. The flowers are small and insignificant. If planted at all, it requires a shady situation to grow more freely. The hot sun is fatal to the Aucuba japonica.

# Azalea indica

*(Rhododendron indicum)*

Indica Azalea, Indian Azalea, Chinese Honeysuckle, Chinese Azalea

*Azalea indica* was introduced into Europe at a time when the Orient was referred to as India or the Indies. Thus, the plant's Latin name, *indica*, a name given by Linnaeus in 1753, is misleading, as *Azalea indica* is a native of Japan, not India or the Indies. First introduced into Holland from Japan around 1680, *Azalea indica* was hailed as a newfound treasure, flourished for a brief period of time, and then faded from the European horticultural scene for over 120 years.

In 1808, *Azalea indica* reappeared in England, arriving from China on a sailing ship manned by a Captain Wallback of the famous East India Company. Originally grown as a greenhouse plant, *Azalea indica* was greatly appreciated for its brilliant red to scarlet flowers and fine evergreen foliage. With the advent of increased trade with the Orient in the first half of the nineteenth century, many new azalea species began to arrive in Europe, first from China and later from Japan. From these introductions, crosses were made, producing many single and double-flowering hybrids in colors ranging from white, pink, and rose to crimson and salmon. These new varieties came to be known collectively as Chinese Indica or Indian azaleas.

While the exact date of introduction of *Azalea indica* into North America is unknown, this showy ornamental was first offered by an American nursery when listed in Bartram's *1814 Catalogue of Trees, Shrubs and Herbaceous Plants*. Additional varieties were soon offered by other northern nurseries, and by 1847, William Prince included seventy varieties of "Chinese azaleas" in his *Descriptive Catalogue of Fruits, Ornamental Trees, Shrubbery, Vines, and Plants*.

By 1845, indica azaleas were being grown as outdoor plants in the coastal South, with the largest collection occurring at Magnolia Gardens in Charleston, South Carolina. Plantings of this prized ornamental soon followed in other southern cities including Savannah, Mobile, and New Orleans. During the antebellum period, indica azaleas generally were grown in the middle and upper South as greenhouse or cold-frame plants based on the belief that they were too tender to survive in these regions as outdoor garden plants. Fruitland Nurseries, located in Augusta, Georgia, was the first southern nursery to offer indica azaleas. Their *1857–1858 Catalog* included a listing for "*Azalea indica*—Chinese Honeysuckles of many different colors."

*Azalea indica* (indica azalea)

**A Short Treatise on Horticulture, 1828**

William Prince

☙ *Azalea indica*, an Indian shrub of great beauty and fragrance. It grows in sandy, turfy peat well drained, and requires a warm part of the Green-house.

## *The Southern Cultivator,* 1857

Daniel Lee and Dennis Redmond, Editors

☙ *Azalea indica* (Chinese Honeysuckle)—This beautiful shrub, so well known as a greenhouse plant, is perfectly hardy in this latitude. . . . It is a flower of unsurpassed beauty in its season, March and April; and those only who have seen it in its perfection can form an idea of its richness and grandeur. The Azaleas are near kin to the far-famed Rhodendron, almost as beautiful, and much easier of cultivation. The colors are very different, as crimson, purple, white, red, salmon, scarlet and variegated. . . . New varieties are raised from seed which should be saved as soon as ripe.

Robert Nelson, Fruitland Nurseries, Augusta, Georgia

## *The American Cotton Planter and the Soil of the South,* 1859

N. B. Cloud, Editor

☙ Chinese Honeysuckle (Azalea indica)

It is surprising, indeed, that this magnificent shrub—the beauty and glory of the Northern greenhouses in the early spring—is hardly ever to be met with here in the South. True, a few specimens in pots may now and then (though seldom) be seen, in a very poor condition. But why keep them in pots? Turn them out of doors, into the open ground, give them but one-tenth of the attention which you bestow on the plant, while in a pot, and you will have the most beautiful blooming shrub in your garden, during March and April, that your eyes ever beheld. . . . Two of the most brilliant varieties I have had, were the two old, well-known kinds, A. phoenicia, and A. hibbertia purpurea; but in fact all the Azalea indica will thrive in this latitude.

Robert Nelson, A. M.

Horticultural Editor

## Azalea nudiflorum

(*Rhododendron nudiflorum, Rhododendron periclymenoides*)
Wild Honeysuckle, Bush Azalea, Pinxter Bloom Azalea

Native to eastern North America, *Azalea nudiflorum* is a large to medium-sized, deciduous shrub with an upright, open form reaching a height of six to eight feet in its natural environment. This native azalea is best known for its long, trumpet-shaped flowers, which occur in late April and May on leafless stems, giving rise to the species name, *nudiflorum*. The plant's showy flowers are slightly fragrant and range in colors from white, pale pink to violet. Light green leaves develop in late spring, changing to a bright yellow in fall.

*Azalea nudiflorum* was first introduced into England in 1734 when John Bartram of Philadelphia sent seeds to Peter Collinson, a wealthy woolen merchant in London. Thomas Jefferson in *Notes on the State of Virginia* referred to this native shrub as the "upright honeysuckle, *Azalea nudiflora*," and it was described by Stephen Elliott in *A Sketch of the Botany of South Carolina and Georgia* (vol. 1, 1821) as "one of the most beautiful plants which adorn the forests of North America." It was first offered to American gardeners when listed in Bernard M'Mahon's 1804 *Catalogue of Garden, Herb, Flower, Tree, Shrub, and Grass Seeds,* thus making it available to American gardeners. *Azalea nudiflorum,* along with other native azaleas, including *Azalea calendulacea, Azalea visocsa,* and *Azalea carnescens*, were among the first native shrubs to be grown as ornamentals in southern gardens. Throughout the South, these indigenous plants were originally known as bush azaleas or wild honeysuckles, names that are still in use today.

### *Abrustrum Americanum: The American Grove,* 1785
Humphry Marshall

✌ AZALEA nudiflora. *Red Flowered Azalea*

This grows most common upon a moist, clayey, gravelly soil, rising two or three, to five or six feet in height. The leaves are produced in clusters at the extremity of the branches; they are oblong, inverse, egg-shaped, and a little hairy upon their edges and midribs underneath. The flowers are produced early in the spring before the leaves are expanded, in heads of clusters at the ends of the stalks and chief branches, of a red colour, and hairy, with very long red stamina. There is a great variety in the colour of the flowers, from red to almost white.

### *A Sketch of the Botany of South Carolina and Georgia,* vol. 1, 1821
Stephen Elliott

✌ *Azalea nudiflora*–A shrub 2–8 feet high, producing many stems from the root. . . . This is one of the most beautiful plants which adorn the forests of North America. Some of the varieties are considered by many persons as the most ornamental of our shrubs. . . . Grows in rich, dry soils and along the margins of swamps and creeks. Flowers March–May.

### *A Treatise on the Cultivation of Ornamental Flowers,* 1828
Roland Green

✌ AZALEA NUDIFLORA.—Several species—commonly called American Honeysuckle. This shrub blows profusely—very fragrant, and makes a fine appearance in a border.

### *Ladies' Southern Florist,* 1860
Mary Rion

*Azalea nudiflorium* (wild honeysuckle)

✌ AZALEAS

This genus of highly ornamental shrubs are, many of them, indigenous with us, being known as the Wild Honeysuckle. The colors vary from white to a deep red, which last is rare. The azalea is a flower of great elegance, and not difficult of culture in this its native clime, if some attention is paid to give it a good situation and suitable soil. Azaleas require moist, black, sandy loam, and a *shady* situation. If the wild azaleas are procured from the woods, they should be cut down to the ground, and they will send up numerous shoots and form healthy plants. No *animal manure* should ever be applied to an azalea. During the heat of the first summer after planting, they should be shaded by pine boughs placed upon the south side.

## Broussonetia papyrifera

Paper Mulberry

Native to China and Japan and widely grown in many of the South Sea Islands, *Broussonetia papyrifera* was named in honor of Pierre Broussonet, a French naturalist and botanist. While included in the mulberry family (*Moraceae*), *Broussonetia papyrifera* is not a true mulberry. The common name, paper mulberry, was derived from the Chinese who used the plant's inner bark for making paper. A small to medium-sized, deciduous tree with a wide-spreading canopy, the paper mulberry grows to a height of twenty to thirty feet with a trunk seldom more than a foot in diameter. Older trees are characterized by gnarled and twisted trunks with brown to grayish bark. The plant's leaves are ovate or irregularly lobed with male and female flowers occurring on separate plants. In late summer, female plants develop orange to red fruit.

Peter Collinson introduced paper mulberry into England in 1751 from China. The leaves of the paper mulberry were originally believed to have economic value in the silk industry but proved too rough and coarse in texture for the finicky taste of the silkworm. Arriving in North America before the end of the eighteenth century, this Asian native was first grown by William Hamilton at The Woodlands outside Philadelphia. An American nursery first offered paper mulberry for sale when it was listed in Bartram's *1807 Catalogue of Trees, Shrubs and Herbaceous Plants*. Often grown as an exotic in the antebellum South for its curious foliage and interesting shape, the paper mulberry has become widely naturalized in many areas of the lower and middle South and today is generally regarded as a weed tree with little ornamental value.

*Broussonetia papyrifera* (paper mulberry)

### Thomas Jefferson's Garden Book, 1776–1824

๛ William Hamilton to Jefferson—The Woodlands, February 5, 1808

I have prepared for you plants of *Broussonetia papyrifera*, or paper mulberry, . . . and Mimosa julibrisin. They were all designed to come last year, but no suitable opportunity offered. I hope I will be more lucky this year. . . .

### The Southern Agriculturist, 1834

๛ This is a deciduous tree—the male only having been known here till very recently. The female tree has been introduced only within a few years past. The fruit is not very palatable, being of an insipid sweet taste, but poultry is very fond of it, and the tree in full fruit has a very pretty appearance, and would be preferable as an ornamental shade tree, to the male tree, which as yet is the only one that has made its appearance in the streets of our city [Charleston, South Carolina]. The tree multiplies so rapidly from the roots as to have in some places become a nuisance.

John D. Legare, Editor

### The New American Orchardist, 1833

William Kenrick

↝ Japan Paper Mulberry

*Broussonetia papyrifera*

The tree rises to a large size, with a round head, the leaves are rough, either cordate, entire or divided into two or three lobes. It is a native of China or Japan, and from the inner bark, paper is made in these countries. The fruit is round and curious. The trees are male and female; they are of rapid growth and ornamental.

*A Treatise on the Theory and Practice of Landscape Gardening,* **1841**

Andrew Jackson Downing

↝ *Broussonetia papyrifera*

The value of the Paper mulberry, in ornamental plantations, arises from its exotic look, as compared with other trees, from the singular diversity of its foliage, the beauty of its reddish berries. . . . It is deficient in hardiness for a colder climate than that of New York; but further south it is considerably esteemed as a shade-tree for lining the side-walks in cities. In winter its light fawn or ash-colored bark, mottled with patches of a darker gray, contrasts agreeably with other trees. It has little picturesque beauty, and should never be planted in quantities, but only in scattered specimens, to give interest to a walk in the lawn or shrubbery.

*The American Handbook of Ornamental Trees,* **1853**

Thomas Meehan

↝ *Broussonetia Papyrifera*

Paper Mulberry

This tree was formerly in much request for shade. Its wide-spreading branches adapt it well for that purpose. In other respects, it possesses no beauty, and as it throws out many troublesome suckers, it is not much sought after. It is very apt to be killed by severe winters. . . . There are no very large specimens at Bartram's, the original trees having been rooted out.

## Buxus sempervirens

Common Box, American Box

Native to Europe, North Africa, and western Asia, *Buxus sempervirens* derives its scientific name from the Latin *buxus*, meaning box, and *sempervirens*, signifying "always green." A bushy shrub with a compact, oval form, common box has been grown as an ornamental for its handsome evergreen foliage since ancient times. The plant's small, lustrous, lance-shaped leaves are dark green above and light green below. Because of common box's natural dense growth, it is well adapted as a clipped hedge and for creating a variety of architectural forms. As an

*Buxus sempervirens* (common box)

eighteenth-century French writer noted, "Box has the advantage of taking any form that may be wished under the hands of the gardener." A hardy, long-lived shrub, common box (when left unclipped) can reach heights of fifteen to twenty feet. Wood of this evergreen shrub has been used for centuries for making musical and mathematical instruments, as well as combs, spoons, buttons, and cabinets.

The first planting of *Buxus sempervirens* in North America is credited to Nathaniel Sylvester on Long Island in 1652. An old favorite in American gardens for its elegant, refined, and beautiful evergreen foliage, common box was used during colonial times to create hedges, borders, topiary, and specimen plants. The use of common box is generally confined to the upper and middle South because of its intolerance of heat and high humidity. This treasured garden shrub is particularly well represented in historic gardens of Virginia and Maryland. Common box was first offered for sale in Bartram's *1807 Catalogue of Trees, Shrubs and Herbaceous Plants*, with Bernard M'Mahon advertising seeds three years earlier in his 1804 *Catalog of Garden, Herb, Flower, Tree, Shrub, and Grass Seeds*. Common box remained popular during the antebellum period, along with dwarf box (*Buxus sempervirens suffruticosa*), a smaller, slower growing species that was particularly useful as edging material for parterre gardens.

### A Treatise on the Cultivation of Ornamental Flowers, 1828
Roland Green

ᴔ Box (*Buxus sempervirens*) is a small delicate shrub, which may be pruned to any shape, to please the fancy. It is an evergreen, hardy, and is proper to trim beds. It appears well in a border. It is propagated by cuttings, or by dividing the roots. If a plant be placed deep in the earth, and the soil be brought in close contact with the small branches, (being spread as much as possible) they will send out roots, and afford a great number of plants. The small branches are used by the ladies to trim cake &c.

### The Practical Florist, 1833
A Compilation from the Best Authors

ᴔ BUXUS SEMPERVIRENS. *Common Box.* An evergreen hardy shrub; native of Europe, and abounding in some parts of Asia and America. Flowers yellow green, appearing in April. It may be propagated by suckers. The box is principally used, in gardening, to divide the beds from the walks.

### A Dictionary of Modern Gardening, 1847
George William Johnson

ᴔ Box (*Buxus sempervirens*), is noticed by the gardener chiefly as a plant suitable for edgings. For this purpose it is neat, and certainly the best article used. In some gardens it is suffered to attain too great bulk, and then becomes rather a defect than ornament. . . . It should not be allowed to rise higher than six or eight inches, and as much in breadth—if necessary to restrain the growth, transplant. The best seasons for planting box is at mid-summer, and early in the spring. . . . The best month for clipping box is June, and it should be done in showery weather.

### Report of the Commissioner of Patents, 1854
Charles Mason

ᴔ Trees and Shrubs Usually Employed for Hedges—The Evergreen Box (*Buxus sempervirens*). The tree appears to have been much employed in verdant sculpture, and close-clipped hedges in the gardens of Roman villas in the Augustinian age. Pliny describes his Tusculan villa as having a lawn adorned with figures of animals cut out in box-trees. . . . In another part of the same villa, the box is mentioned as being cut into a variety of shapes and letters; some expressing the name of the master. . . . The box may be propagated by layers, either in spring or autumn, both of the young and old wood. When the plants have obtained a sufficient size, they may be planted in the hedge-rows in double, alternate lines from 10 to 12 inches apart. They may be clipped at almost any season except mid-winter. . . . Next to the holly, a box hedge has the most beautiful appearance in winter, more especially when the ground is covered with snow.

## Buxus sempervirens suffruticosa

(*Buxus humilis*)

Dwarf Box, Edging Box, Dutch Box, English Box, Box

A native of Europe, Africa, and Asia, dwarf box is a slow-growing evergreen shrub with dark green, oval leaves that emit a distinctive fragrance that is pleasing to some and objectionable to others. Valued for centuries for use in formal gardens, this treasured ornamental can be kept a few inches high, with persistent clipping, to form neat edgings for parterres, flower beds, walks, and borders.

Of all its uses, dwarf box is unsurpassed for laying out "parterres of embroidery," which require an evergreen shrub that can be clipped into intricate designs and kept small for an indefinite period of time. Gardening instructions on the care and culture of box in parterres was provided as early as the seventeenth century when one authority advised that box used for borders should be clipped "three times per annum, in April,

*Buxus sempervirens suffruticosa* (dwarf box)

June, and August, remembering to cut their roots at the inside every second year." When left unclipped, dwarf box develops into a mounding, billowing shrub that can reach an ultimate height of five to six feet.

Introduced into North America during colonial times, dwarf box was available to southern gardeners as early as 1767 when it was advertised in the *South Carolina Gazette* as "a fresh assortment of very good garden seeds and flower roots . . . with flowering shrubs and box for edging beds." This popular edging plant first appeared in the *1807 Catalogue* of William Booth, a nurseryman located outside Baltimore, Maryland. Because dwarf box could be kept to a height of ten inches or less, it was a popular edging material for parterre gardens of the antebellum South. The plant's slow growth, tolerance of both sun and shade, resistance to leaf minors, and ease of propagation by cuttings made dwarf box a perennial favorite in gardens of the upper and middle South.

### The American Gardener's Calendar, 1806
Bernard M'Mahon

⁓ Planting Box Edging

Box of all plants, makes the neatest and most beautiful edgings . . . particularly in the middle states. . . . Where there are any gaps in the former planted edgings, let them now be made good; for when ragged and uneven they have a disagreeable appearance.

Or where any old edgings of several years standing have been permitted to run up rude and spreading, nothing in a garden looks more unsightly; and should be taken up, slipped, trimmed, and replanted in a new regular order.

### A Short Treatise on Horticulture, 1828
William Prince

⁓ *Dwarf Box:*—This is the low growing variety, generally used for edging of garden walks and flower beds. Its growth is slow, but at very advanced age it attains to a shrub of from six to eight feet high. It is this variety which is so widely spread and well known throughout the country.

### The Southern Cultivator, 1856
Daniel Lee and Dennis Redmond, Editors

⁓ *Buxus* (Boxwood).—Every person is familiar with this old customer of our gardens. The two principal species are: *Tree Box*, which grows 8 to 10 feet high, and *Dwarf Box*, from 1 to 2 feet; the latter is mostly employed for edging beds. Of both species, varieties are known with silver and gold edges. The boxwood does not thrive well on sandy soil, but on strong clay, or rich alluvial soil it succeeds admirably. Propagated by layers, cuttings, and dividing the roots.

Robert Nelson, Macon, Georgia

### The Amateur's Guide and Flower Garden Directory, 1856
John T. C. Clark

⁓ BOX EDGING, has a beautiful appearance if kept neatly trimmed and regular, especially in winter, and adds much to the beauty of the garden. The dwarf variety (BUXUS SUFFRUTICOSA) is generally employed for this purpose, and may be readily propagated from cuttings or slips, early in the spring or October.

# Calycanthus floridus

Carolina Allspice, Sweet Shrub, Sweet Scented Shrub

Native to the southeastern United States from Virginia to Florida, sweet shrub or Carolina allspice, as it is frequently called, is a deciduous shrub, six to eight feet tall, with aromatic leaves, bark, roots, and flowers. Sweet shrub leaves are dark green on top, gray green underneath and in fall, turn a bright golden yellow. Small, inconspicuous reddish brown flowers measuring two inches across appear in late April and May, producing a spicy fragrance that resembles ripe strawberries when the flowers first open.

Mark Catesby, the English naturalist, introduced the plant into England in 1726 from specimens collected outside Charleston, South Carolina. He noted, "These trees grow in the remote and hilly parts of Carolina, but no where among the inhabitants." Sweet shrub remained somewhat rare in British gardens until around 1759 when Peter Collinson, a prosperous woolen merchant, imported additional plants from Charleston, where by that time the plant had become a popular ornamental. George Washington and Thomas Jefferson both grew sweet shrub, and it was first offered for sale by an American nursery in 1783 when listed in *Bartram's Catalogue of American Trees, Shrubs and Herbaceous Plants*. Sweet shrub was consistently listed in both northern and southern nursery catalogues through the middle of the nineteenth century, confirming its continued popularity as one of the most prized native shrubs in American gardens.

*Calycanthus floridus* (Carolina allspice)

### *The American Gardener's Calendar*, 1806
Bernard M'Mahon

❧ The *Calycanthus floridus*, or Carolina Allspice, commonly called the sweet-scented shrub, is deserving of a place in every pleasure-garden, on account of the delightful odour of its flowers. It is easily propagated by layers or suckers; the most eligible time of layering it, is in autumn, and by the spring following twelve months, they may be taken off, and planted with good success.

### *The Horticulturist*, 1847/1848
Andrew Jackson Downing, Editor

❧ The Best Hardy Shrubs
Sweet Scented Shrub (*Calycanthus floridus*)
Remarkable for its brown flowers (a color rather rare among flowers) and for the delicious pine-apple perfume which they give out; a few plants scenting a whole garden, May and June.

### *The Flower Garden*, 1851
Joseph Breck

❧ *Calycanthus:* All this genus are natives of North America. They are very easy of culture, growing freely in peat or loam, or both, mixed. The flowers are a dark-brown color, and very fragrant, resembling the odor of ripe melons. The wood is also very fragrant.

*Calycanthus florida:* Carolina Allspice—This well-known species, from three to five feet high, flowering from June to August. There are also a number of other species, but all nearly resemble the last, except in height and the style of the leaves. *C. fertalis* has glaucous leaves; *C. laevigatua* smooth leaves; both about three feet high; all easily propagated from suckers or layers.

### *The Young Gardener's Assistant,* 1829
Thomas Bridgeman

↣ *Calicanthus floridus,* Allspice, or sweet-scented shrub, a native of the Southern states; the flowers are of a very dark chocolate colour, and the fragrance very much resembles ripe strawberries; easily kept when once introduced. This shrub generally grows about five feet high in gardens, and blossoms from May to August.

---

## Camellia japonica

Camellia, Japonica, Japan Rose

Native to China, Japan, and Korea, the camellia was named for George Kamel or Camellus (1661–1706), a Jesuit priest, naturalist, and world traveler. A large, upright shrub with an oval form, the camellia is prized for its waxy, evergreen foliage, and brightly colored flowers, which can be single, semidouble, or double in form. Depending on the selected variety, flowers of the camellia bloom from late fall to early spring. Camellias were cultivated and treasured in the Orient for thousands of years before being introduced into Europe in the eighteenth century. While James Cunningham, a Scottish scientist, sent dried specimens of the camellia to England in 1701, the first live plants did not arrive until 1739, when introduced by Robert James.

*Camellia japonica* (camellia)

Although introduction of the camellia into North America is generally credited to John Stevens, Esq., of Hoboken, New Jersey, in 1797, it is believed that André Michaux, the French botanist, brought specimens of the camellia to Charleston, South Carolina, several years earlier. According to tradition, gifts of the camellia were made to Henry Middleton shortly after Michaux established his botanic garden outside Charleston in 1786. While neither Michaux's nor Middleton's records have survived to authenticate this claim, the diary of Charles Drayton (1743–1820) of Drayton Hall, (located several miles south of Middleton Plantation) reveals that Mr. Drayton obtained cuttings from camellia plants being grown at Middleton Place in 1814, adding credence to the belief that camellias were being grown in Charleston before the end of the eighteenth century. (One of the original camellias that Michaux is purported to have given to Henry Middleton, Reine des Fleurs, still grows on the grounds.)

*Camellia japonica* was first offered for sale by an American nursery in 1807, appearing in Bartram's *1807 Catalogue of Trees, Shrubs and Herbaceous Plants.* Northern nurseries initially sold camellias as greenhouse plants, but it was soon discovered that in the lower and middle South these somewhat tender ornamentals could be safely grown outdoors. Southern gardeners often obtained camellias from northern growers through local agents or advertisements in newspapers and agricultural journals or, in some instances, they were imported directly from Europe. By the mid-nineteenth century, camellias had become one of the most popular ornamentals in the antebellum South.

### Charles Drayton Diaries

~ March 1817

Stumbled among rubbish—bruised and strained a wrist & bruised a shin. Brought from M. [Michaux] place a plant of Camellia & Olea fragrans.

### A Short Treatise on Horticulture, 1828

William Prince

~ GREEN-HOUSE TREES, SHRUBS, AND PLANTS

*Camellia japonica, or Japan Rose.*—Much as we are indebted to Japan and China for elegant plants, still we are more peculiarly so for the different species and varieties of the Camellias, which, for the many beauties it concentrates, may emphatically be called the "Queen of Flowers." The different varieties of this plant form the most brilliant display of the Green-house from December to May, and the splendor of their flowers, and richness of their foliage, are surpassed by no others.

### Gardening Magazine, 1832

John Claudius Loudon

~ The last few years have wonderfully changed the features of gardening in Charleston. . . . The only nurseryman is M. Noisette, brother to the celebrated nurseryman of that name at Paris. But for me to describe the beautiful specimens his grounds contain would occupy a whole magazine. *Camellias* 16 to 20 feet height, and 20 feet in circumference. . . . This garden must be seen to be duly appreciated.

Alexander Gordon

### The Southern Agriculturist, 1843

John Legare, Editor

~ The garden of Mr. James Nicholson. . . . His Camellias are the largest and finest cultivated in the open air in this neighborhood, and this successful experiment will it is hoped, be the precursor of their more general cultivation in Charleston. In common with all the Japan plants, they will bear the winter of our climate without shelter.

### The Southern Cultivator, 1851

Daniel Lee and Dennis Redmond, Editors

~ This is the climax of all winter blooming shrubs, and equal to the rose in beauty. It is a native of Japan, and perfectly hardy in this latitude. It will, in fact, stand our winters better than our summers. The single red camellia is the hardiest, but even the double ones have stood the last winters here uninjured, though the thermometer was down to 9°. I have seen Camellias (Lady Hume's Blush) here in the South 10 feet high, and covered with about 2000 flowers.

Robert Nelson, Macon, Georgia

## Camellia sinensis

(*Thea sinensis*)

Tea

According to legend, leaves of *Camellia sinenis* were used to create a refreshing beverage known as "tea" as early as 2737 B.C. Over time, this practice spread from China to Japan and other Far Eastern countries. Enterprising sea merchants introduced tea into Europe around 1600. It soon won wide appeal, and by 1650, was being imported into the American colonies. The tea plant, native to China and India, is comprised of several varieties. Two of the most common are *bohea* (black tea) and *verdis* (green tea). Black tea is characterized by light green, laurel-like leaves, while green tea has dark green leaves that are much smaller in size. Both varieties produce small, white, sweet-scented flowers that occur from September to November.

*Camellia sinensis* (tea)

Arriving in North America as early as 1735, seeds of the tea plant were first cultivated in Savannah's Trustees Garden, where they were given great care but failed to survive. America's first successful cultivation of *Camellia sinensis* appears to have occurred in 1760 at Bethabara, a Moravian settlement located in what is now Winston Salem, North Carolina. According to tradition, André Michaux, the French botanist, brought tea plants to Charleston, South Carolina, in 1786, providing the impetus for several successful tea plantations in the Carolina lowcountry. An American nursery first offered both varieties of tea, *bohea* and *verdis*, for sale when they were listed in Bartram's *1807 Catalogue of Trees, Shrubs and Herbaceous Plants.* Efforts during the first half of the nineteenth century to promote commercial tea operations in the South failed because of Asian competition and the destructive effects of the Civil War. The tea plant was generally grown for its economic value, but it was also used during the antebellum period as an ornamental in the lower and middle South, either as a specimen shrub or clipped hedge.

### *A Short Treatise on Horticulture,* 1828

William Prince

✺ *Green and Bohea Tea*—These are very hardy greenhouse plants, and would no doubt withstand the winters of the Union south of Wilmington, South Carolina. The leaves of the Greet Tea are more than double the size of the Bohea, and both produce fine flowers in abundance during the autumn and winter, and are cultivated with as much ease as any of our most common trees. It is said that all the finer teas are perfumed by the Chinese with the delightful flowers of the Olea fragrans, or Fragrant Chinese Olive.

### *The Southern Agriculturalist,* 1828

J. D. Legare, Editor

✺ *Thea Sinensis*

On inquiry, I find that the tea tree grows perfectly well in the open air near Charleston, where it has been raised for the last fifteen years, at Mons. Noisette's

Nursery. . . . Besides, as we know that the smell and flavour of tea are not natural to the plant, but given to it artificially, for the purpose of commerce, we might in Charleston raise a sufficiency of the Olea fragrans and one of the Camellias (which Kaempfer asserts is used in Japan to give the tea a high flavour) to form a very profitable kind of culture. The Philadelphia, Boston, and Salem Tea-merchants would willingly purchase all that could be raised of these flavours to flavour their teas, which would benefit their sale in Europe as well as in the United States.

### The Southern Cultivator, 1856

Daniel Lee and Dennis Redmond, Editors

☞ *Thea bohea and Thea virdis* (*Tea Plant*), belong to the Camellia tribe, to which it bears a great resemblance. It forms a nice little bush, not exceeding four feet. The white, single flowers are produced in January and February.

Robert Nelson, Macon, Georgia

### Ladies' Southern Florist, 1860

Mary Rion

☞ TEA PLANT

This plant is a half-hardy evergreen shrub, thickly branched, with dark green foliage, like the Camellia japonica. The bloom is white. It grows from four to six feet high, when cultivated for tea-making, but will obtain a height of ten feet when not dwarfed by this process.

## Campsis radicans

(*Bignonia radicans*, *Tecoma radicans*)
Trumpet Vine, Trumpet Creeper, Cow-Itch Vine

Native to the southeastern United States, trumpet vine is a rampant climber with opposite, compound leaves divided into numerous leaflets. Originally know as *Bignonia radicans*, this deciduous vine is best known for its showy clusters of bright orange, trumpet-shaped flowers that occur from June to September. Cigar-shaped seed pods appear in late summer and remain on the plant until the following spring. This long-lived vine can reach a height of twenty to thirty feet. Trumpet vine was sometimes known as cow-itch vine because of its propensity to cause skin irritation. Mark Catesby illustrated trumpet vine in his *Natural History of Carolina, Florida and the Bahama Islands* (1731–1743) and noted that hummingbirds delighted in feeding on the plant's colorful flowers.

*Campsis radicans* (trumpet vine)

This American native was introduced into England as a prized ornamental as early as 1640 and was frequently grown in British gardens. In the United States, *Campsis radicans* was first offered for sale in Bartram's *1783 Catalogue of American Trees, Shrubs and Herbaceous Plants*. Trumpet vine was grown in antebellum gardens as an ornamental to cover walls and fences. This popular native vine was consistently listed in both northern and southern nursery catalogues through the middle of the nineteenth century.

### The American Flower Garden Directory, 1839

Robert Buist

✍ *Bignonia radicans* . . . is a native plant. When in flower it is highly ornamental, but it requires great attention to keep it in regular order, being of a strong rough nature; in bloom from June to August.

### The Flower Garden, 1851

Joseph Breck

✍ *Bignonia radicans*—Scarlet trumpet Flower—This is a magnificent climbing plant, producing large, trumpet-shaped, orange-scarlet flowers, of great beauty, from July to October. They are produced in clusters; handsome in bud, as well as when fully expanded, which, when contrasted with the elegant, glossy, pinnate foliage, presents a most splendid sight when trained to a pillar or trellis.

### The Magazine of Horticulture, 1855

C. M. Hovey, Editor

✍ VINES AND CLIMBING PLANTS

THE TRUMPET FLOWER, (*Bignonia radicans*). A well known and remarkably showy climber, with clusters of large orange red flowers, which are conspicuous among its luxuriant pinnate foliage. It attains a great height, grows rapidly, and except in very bleak situations, is quite hardy. . . . It attaches itself by little rootlets to whatever supports it, and cannot be easily detached. It flowers late in the season, and its large trumpet-shaped corols in profuse clusters, are at that period exceedingly ornamental.

### The North American Sylva, 1857

Thomas Nuttall

✍ This beautiful climber is indigenous to all the states south of New York and westward to the borders of the Mississippi. . . . About mid summer, it sends out from its elevated summit . . . clusters of large brilliant red flowers . . . to which are continually attracted flocks of young humming-birds. As a hardy, ornamental . . . few plants deserve better to cultivated along walls and trellises.

---

## Catalpa bignonioides

(*Catalpa syringifolia, Catalpa catalpa*)
Southern Catalpa, Indian Bean Tree, Catawbaw Tree

Native to Georgia, western Florida, Alabama, and Mississippi, *Catalpa bignonioides* is a handsome deciduous tree with a rounded, spreading canopy that can reach a height of forty or fifty feet. It is distinguished by large coarse-textured leaves and white, trumpet-shaped flowers marked inside with yellow stripes and lavender spots. There are few native American trees that present a more splendid display than a catalpa in bloom. Flowers occur in late May and June, followed in autumn by long cigarlike, cylindrical pods containing papery, winged seeds.

Mark Catesby, the English naturalist best known for his beautifully illustrated work entitled *The Natural History of Carolina, Florida and the Bahama Islands* (1731–1743), is credited with introducing *Catalpa bignonioides* into England in 1726. Catesby collected seeds of this stately tree while traveling in Carolina in "remote parts of the country."

Catalpa's value as an ornamental during the colonial period is noted in a letter written by Eliza Lucas in 1743, describing William Middleton's renowned garden at Crowfield (located outside Charleston, South Carolina) as containing a large bowling green "with a walk quite round bordered by a double row of fine flowering Laurel [*Magnolia grandiflora*] and *Catalpa*—which afford both shade and beauty." *Catalpa bignonioides* was first offered by an American nursery when listed in William Prince's *1771 Broadside*. The catalpa was a popular ornamental during the antebellum period. By the end of the nineteenth century, however, use of this handsome indigenous species had greatly declined. Seldom grown today as an ornamental, the catalpa remains one of the South's finest native trees, still admired for its fine foliage, showy flowers, and decorative seed.

### *The North American Sylva,* 1819
François André Michaux

➳ Bignonia catalpa

In the Carolinas and in Georgia the Catalpa is called Catawbaw Tree, after the name of the Indian tribe that formerly inhabited a large part of these states, and from whose territory the tree was probably first procured: the name of Catalpa, adopted in the Middle *Section* of the United States and in Europe, is perhaps a corruption of this original. . . . The Catalpa has long been cultivated with success in Europe. . . . Its rapid growth, the remarkable size of its leaves, and the beauty of its numerous bunches of flowers entitle the Catalpa to a distinguished place among ornamental trees; but it has ceased to be rare, and is less highly esteemed than while it was less common.

### *A Short Treatise on Horticulture,* 1828
William Prince

➳ *Catalpa, or Bignonia Catalpa*—This is considered a fine commercial tree; it grows to the height of from 30 to 35 feet in this latitude, and further south doubtless to a much larger size. It should be planted at a distance from other trees, so as to allow its branches to expand, which they will do to a considerable length on all sides; the leaves are very large and cordate; the flowers are borne in numerous clusters, are white, spotted with purple, and striped on the inside . . . and being interspersed in abundance among the fine foliage, render the tree very attractive; the flowers are succeeded by long pods, which continue on during autumn and winter, and shed their seeds in the spring.

### *A Treatise on the Theory and Practice of Landscape Gardening,* 1841
Andrew Jackson Downing

➳ The Catalpa Tree

In Carolina it is called the Catawba tree, after the Catawba Indians, a tribe that formerly inhabited that country; and it is probably that the softer epithet now generally bestowed upon it in the north, is only a corruption of that original name. . . . In ornamental plantations it is much valued on account of its superb and showy flowers, and is therefore deserving a place in every lawn. It is generally seen to best advantage when standing alone, but it may be mingled with other large round-leaved trees . . . where it produces a very pleasing aspect.

*Catalpa bignonioides* (southern catalpa)

## Celtis occidentalis

Hackberry, Sugarberry, American Nettle Tree

Native to the southeastern United States, *Celtis occidentalis* or hackberry is a fast-growing, long-lived, deciduous tree that reaches a height of 80 to 100 feet. Characterized by a rounded or umbrellalike canopy, hackberry is best known for its beautiful, smooth silvery gray bark, similar to that of the native beech (*Fagus grandifolia*). A fine-textured tree with pendulous branches, the hackberry's foliage is olive gold in spring, light green in summer, and a clear yellow in fall. Inconspicuous flowers develop in spring, followed in autumn by small, purplish black berries with a sweet, saccharine taste, giving rise to the common name, sugarberry, by which the plant is sometimes known.

Early naturalists originally classified hackberry as the "unknown tree" because of difficulty in identifying the plant's nettle-like leaves. The tree's wood was often used for making hoops, whipstocks, ramrods, and other useful products. *Celtis occidentalis* was introduced into England in 1656 by John Tradescant the Younger (1608–1662), the famous English gardener and plant collector who visited Virginia in 1642, and again in 1654.

*Celtis occidentalis* was first offered in an American nursery catalogue when listed in Bartram's *1783 Catalogue of American Trees, Shrubs and Herbaceous Plants*. Hackberry was frequently collected from southern forests and planted for shade in antebellum gardens and groves. In the nineteenth century, this hardy, drought-resistant tree was often planted as a street tree in many southern cities including Charleston, South Carolina, Savannah, Georgia, and Nashville, Tennessee. The hackberry, while seldom used today, remains notable for its handsome bark, beautiful foliage, and tolerance of urban conditions.

*Celtis occidentalis* (hackberry)

### *Abrustrum Americanum: The American Grove,* 1785
Humphry Marshall

᠁ CELTIS occidentalis. American Yellow-fruited Nettle tree

This grows naturally in many parts of North America. It delights in a rich, moist soil, in which it becomes a large tree, rising with a straight stem, the bark of which, in young trees, is sometimes smooth and of a dark colour, but as they advance becomes rougher and of a lighter colour. . . . The branches are set thick on every side, and garnished with oblique oval leaves. . . . The flowers come out opposite to the leaves. . . . They are small and make but little appearance, and are succeeded by round, hard berries . . . of a yellow colour and sweet when ripe.

### *The North American Sylva,* 1819
François André Michaux

᠁ CELTIS OCCIDENTALIS

The American Nettle Tree, if not rare, is little multiplied in comparison with the Oaks, the Walnuts, and the Maples. As it is scattered singly through the forest, it is difficult to fix the point at which it ceases toward the North, but I believe it is not found beyond the river Connecticut. In the Middle, Western, and Southern states it bears the name which I have adopted and among the French of Illinois, that of *Bois inconnu*, Unknown Wood. The Nettle tree prefers a cool and shady situation, with a deep and fertile soil. I have observed the largest stocks on the banks of the Savannah, some which were sixty to seventy feet high and eighteen or twenty inches in diameter. . . . The flowers open early in spring, and are small, white, single, and auxiliary: the fruit also, is small and single, of a round form, and of a dull red color.

## *A Sketch of the Botany of South Carolina and Georgia,* vol. 2, 1824

Stephen Elliott

### ❧ CELTIS OCCIDENTALIS

A tree which sometimes on the sea-islands obtains a height of sixty to seventy feet, with a diameter of two to four feet; branches erect and expanding, bark united but corrugate. . . . Around Beaufort (South Carolina) formerly this tree was very common, and several of them in the town had obtained the size I have mentioned. The wood, however, appears not to be strong; the branches are easily broken from the stem by high winds, and in the frequent gales to which the sea-coast of Carolina and Georgia has been exposed during the last twenty or twenty-five years, the finest of these trees have literally been torn to pieces. Along the margins of the sea-islands this tree, perhaps, occurs more frequently than any other situation.

## Cercis canadensis

(*Siliquastrum cordatum*)
Redbud, Judas Tree

Occurring from Ontario, Canada, southward to Florida and westward to Texas and Mexico, *Cercis canadensis*, commonly known as redbud, is one of North America's finest, small-flowering trees. Reaching a height of twenty to thirty feet, this handsome native develops an oval to rounded form with smooth, heart-shaped leaves that turn a clear, bright yellow in fall. Redbud is best known for its small, stemless clusters of rosy pink flowers that develop on leafless branches in early spring, generally at the same time that the flowering dogwood is in bloom. Numerous flattened seed pods, two to three inches long, develop in late summer and fall, persisting on branches late into winter.

Mark Catesby described *Cercis canadensis* in *Natural History of the Carolinians, Florida and the Bahama Islands* (1734–1743), and according to John Claudius Loudon, a well-known English garden writer and author, the flowers of the redbud were "used by French Canadians in salads and pickles, and the young branches to dye wool of a nankeen color." Thomas Jefferson considered redbud an ornamental and mentioned it in his 1771 *Account Book* as being planted at Monticello. *Cercis canadensis* was introduced into England in 1730 but was never extensively planted in British gardens because of its intolerance of the cool, damp conditions of the English climate. An American nursery first offered redbud for sale in Bartram's *1807 Catalogue of Trees, Shrubs and Herbaceous Plants*. This showy, American native was often collected from southern forests and planted as an ornamental in the gardens and groves of the antebellum South, where it was greatly admired for its early spring flowers and good fall color.

*Cercis canadensis* (redbud)

### Arbustrum Americanum: The American Grove, 1785

Humphry Marshall

꩜ CERCIS canadensis. *Red-bud, or Judas Tree*

This grows naturally in several parts of North America, rising to the height of ten or fifteen feet, with a pretty strong trunk covered with a darkish coloured bark; dividing upwards into several irregular branches, furnished with heart-shaped leaves, smooth upon their upper surfaces and edges, but a little downy underneath. . . . The flowers come out upon the branches upon all sides, many arising from the same point. . . . They are of a fine red colour and coming out before the leaves, make a beautiful appearance. There is said to be a variety of this in Carolina, with small flowers.

### The Flower Garden, 1851

Joseph Breck

꩜ *Cercis canadensis*—Judas Tree—Red Bud—This is a curious shrub, or low tree, indigenous to the southern part of the United States; often seen in large collections of plants, in gardens in New England. It is curious, from being covered with bunches of flowers, of a rose color, before the leaves begin to appear. They give a brilliant appearance to the whole tree, except at the extremities of the branches. The Red Bud is beautiful in the spring, and not without interest, in full foliage, in the summer.

### The American Handbook of Ornamental Trees, 1853

Thomas Meehan

꩜ *Cercis canadensis*

Nothing can be more beautiful in April and May, than a large round-headed, "red-bud," twenty or thirty feet high, covered with the beautiful flowers before the bursting of a single leaf. The silvery under-surface of the leaves gives the tree a very bright hue. I have seen some fine specimens of this in Mr. Pierce's fine avenue. The best Bartram specimen is thirty-five feet high.

175

↬ Ornamental Trees and Shrubs for the South

*Cercis canadensis,* "*Redbud*"—a well known tree in our woods. There is a variety of the European "Redbud" with white flowers, which forms a fine contrast. Both are only fit for large gardens.

## Chaenomeles speciosa

(*Chaenomeles lagenaria, Pyrus japonica, Cydonia japonica, Pyrus speciosa*)
Flowering Quince, Japan Quince

*Chaenomeles speciosa* or flowering quince, as it is commonly known, is a native of China, Tibet, and Burma but not Japan, as originally believed. A large, deciduous shrub with an upright, mounding form, flowering quince reaches a height of eight to ten feet. This hardy shrub has dark green, ovate to oblong leaves and numerous irregular branches with formidable spines. A popular ornamental, it is best known for its scarlet, applelike blossoms that appear on leafless stems in late winter, making it one of the most valuable of the early flowering shrubs. Yellow, pear-shaped fruit develop in autumn, emitting a spicy fragrance as they ripen and fall.

Flowering quince was introduced into England from China in 1796 by Sir Joseph Banks (1743–1820), a naturalist, explorer, and president for more than forty years of the Royal Society, Britain's oldest scientific institution. Flowering quince was originally known as *Pyrus japonica,* a name first given to a similar species found in Japan and described in 1784 by the Swedish botanist, Carl Thunberg. In 1818, the mistake in nomenclature was corrected, and while *Pyrus japonica* was renamed *Pyrus speciosa,* the species name, *japonica,* is frequently used even today. Additional changes in nomenclature included *Cydonia japonica* and its current scientific name, *Chaenomeles speciosa.* In the nineteenth century, this much-loved garden shrub was in such demand that by 1869 one French nursery was offering over forty varieties to European gardeners.

Flowering quince arrived in North America early in the nineteenth century, first being offered by an American nursery when listed in Bartram's *1814 Catalogue of Trees, Shrubs and Herbaceous Plants.* A glorious display of late winter blooms, decorative fruit, and the ability to withstand both heat and cold made flowering quince a favorite in antebellum gardens both as a specimen plant and an ornamental hedge.

*Chaenomeles speciosa* (flowering quince)

### *A Short Treatise On Horticulture,* 1828

William Prince

↬ Japan Quince, or *Cydonia Japonica*—This was formerly called *Pyrus japonica,* and it is not till latterly that its title has been changed, after the discovery that its fruit, when well ripened, is of a good size and nearly equal to the favorite quinces usually cultivated in our gardens; there are two varieties, one with scarlet and the other pale blush coloured blossoms, which are very ornamental; the fruit of the two varies also as well as the blossoms. A third variety, with semi-double flowers, is now cultivated, but is still rare.

### *The Horticulturist,* 1847/1848
Andrew Jackson Downing

ᕽ Japan Quince (*Cydonia Japonica*)—This is one of the finest of early shrubs. The original species (commonly known as *Pyrus Japonica*) has a profusion of flowers of such a brilliant red that it is called "Fairies' Fire" in some parts of England. They appear early in April or early in May. The white Japan Quince has, properly, blush-colored flowers, quite like those of the apple tree.

### *The Southern Cultivator,* 1857
Daniel Lee and Dennis Redmond, Editors

ᕽ *Cydonia japonica* or *Prunus japonica* (Japan Quince)—Though a deciduous shrub, nothing can be more strikingly ornamental than a hedge of this kind during its season of blooming. . . . Its quality of blooming very early in the season (in March) when the garden is rather dreary-looking makes it so much more desirable. Besides it will answer perfectly for an outside hedge, as, when properly kept, it is very protective. Such a hedge may easily be trained from three to four feet high.

Robert Nelson, Fruitland Nurseries, Augusta, Georgia

### *The Flower Garden,* 1851
Joseph Breck

ᕽ *Cydonia japonica,* formerly *Pyrus japonica,* is indigenous to Japan, and embraces two varieties, the scarlet and variegated flowering. When in bloom, there is no plant that equals it in splendor. The *Cydonia* may be seen budding and bursting into bloom in April. The flowers are in aggregated clusters, and the branches, interspersed with the young leaves. The hue of the scarlet color is most brilliant, and no artist can find a tint that will convey an adequate idea of its splendor. . . . The perfect hardiness of the shrub, and the brilliance of the flowers, must ever render it an agreeable appendage to the shrubbery, lawn, or flower-garden.

---

## Chionanthus virginicus

(*Chionanthus virginia*)
Fringe Tree, Grancy Gray Beard, Flowering Ash

Fringe tree is native to North America with a range extending from New Jersey to Florida and westward to Texas. It can take the form of a multi-stemmed shrub or a small tree that reaches a height of thirty feet. One of the most distinguished of America's native deciduous shrubs, fringe tree derives its name from the Greek word *chion,* meaning snow, and *anthos,* meaning flower; the species name, *virginicus,* refers to the region where early botanists first identified the plant. Pure white, slightly fragrant flowers appear in late April and May before the leaves are fully extended, giving the plant a striking appearance in both woodland and garden settings. Flowers are followed in late summer by clusters of dark purple, olive-shaped berries.

Peter Collinson introduced fringe tree into England in 1736, and it was first illustrated by Mark Catesby in *Natural History of Carolina, Florida and the Bahama Islands* (1731–1743). The plant has a long history in American folk medicine, as the bark of its roots has been used since colonial days as a tonic, diuretic, and for the treatment of "intermittent fever." It first appeared for sale in America in the late-eighteenth century, appearing in Bartram's *1783 Catalogue of American Trees, Shrubs and Herbaceous Plants.* Early nursery catalogues frequently offered the plant as two distinct varieties: broad leaf (*latifolia*) and narrow leaf (*angustifolia*). A favorite in antebellum gardens, the fringe tree was enjoyed for its fleecy white floral display in late spring and early summer, a time when few flowering shrubs were in bloom.

### The Horticulturist, 1847/1848

Andrew Jackson Downing, Editor

ℋ The Best Hardy Shrubs

Virginia Fringe Tree, (*Chionanthus virginica*)

Among the most refined and attractive of flowering shrubs are the White Fringe trees of Virginia and Carolina, which are quite hardy farther north than New York. The flowers which appear early in June, in great profusion all over the branches, look like tissue paper fringe, most exquisitely cut, and contrast, in their snowy whiteness, admirable with the dark green foliage. There are two sorts; the *broad* and the *narrow leaved.*

### The Flower Garden, 1851

Joseph Breck

ℋ *Chionanthys virginica*, or Fringe Tree—This is a fine deciduous shrub, or small tree, sometimes growing twenty feet or more high, but flowering when six or eight feet high. It has large leaves, six or eight inches long, and from two to three inches wide; the flowers white, in numerous long bunches, and have a fringe-like appearance. It is a native of North America, and found growing upon the mountains at the South, and is very hardy. A light loam suits it well, but propagation is difficult. It succeeds when budded or grafted on the ash.

*Chionanthus virginicus* (fringe tree)

### The North American Sylva, 1857

Thomas Nuttall

ℋ When in flower, which is here about the commencement of June, few objects can be seen more singular and elegant; the panicles of pendant flowers with which it is then clad give it the appearance of a mass of snow-white fringe, and when the flowers fade, the ground seems covered with a carpet of white shreds. It is also highly ornamental when in fruit. . . . Mr. Elliott mentions a variety in a garden near Charleston (that of Mr. Champhrey) in which the panicles of flowers were so long and numerous that they appear cylindrical. . . . In the fine old garden of the Bartrams', at Kingsessing, there is a tree of this species which has been growing nearly a century.

*Ladies' Southern Florist,* 1860

Mary Rion

↬ Fringe Tree or Weeping Ash

"Daddy Graybeard," is a native, deciduous shrub, which grows twelve feet high. It is difficult to transplant, and does best when grafted on the common ash. Light loam is most congenial to this shrub.

## Clematis flammula

Sweet Scented Clematis, Fragrant Virgin's Bower, Creeping Climber

Native to southern Europe, sweet scented clematis is a semiwoody, deciduous vine with dark green leaves composed of individual leaflets. A vigorous climber, sweet scented clematis, or fragrant virgin's bower as it is sometimes called, is best known for its great profusion of small, white, star-shaped flowers, which produce a wonderful almond-scented fragrance in late summer. Flowers are followed by decorative, silvery-gray seeds in the fall.

Introduced into England in 1590, sweet scented clematis is an ancient garden plant whose flowers Philip Miller described in *The Gardener's Dictionary* (1731) as "of an exceedingly sweet smell, much like the fragrance of hawthorn flowers." Miller noted that if a leaf from the plant was cropped in the summer season, bruised, and then placed under the nostrils, it would cause a small pain like a "flame," from which the species name, *flammula*, was derived. According to Henry Phillips in *Sylva Florifera* (1823), *Clematis flammula* was grown in parterres in the royal gardens of Paris, noting that "it was very ornamental, being covered with white blossoms, and at the same time throwing its fragrance over the whole garden."

*Clematis flammula* was first offered for sale by an American nursery in 1815 when listed in William Prince's *Supplementary Catalogue, Containing Rare Trees, Flowering Shrubs and Plants, Principally Exotics, Newly Introduced*. It was a popular vine with southern gardeners, and American nurseries consistently offered it through the end of the nineteenth century. Rarely seen in gardens today, this once popular fragrant ornamental vine has been supplanted by *Clematis paniculata*, an Asian native similar in flower and fragrance to *Clematis flammula* but more tolerant of the summer heat and high humidity of the southern climate.

*Clematis flammula* (sweet scented clematis)

*Flora Carolinaeenis,* 1806

John L. E. Shecut

↬ Clematis flammula, *Creeping Climber,* or *Flammula,* a native of Spain and Portugal; it will rise to the height of 20 feet, the stalks are slender, and numerous, and the leaves are singular; the lower ones being pinnated, with their edges jagged, the upper ones grow singly, are of a lanceolate figure, with their edges entire; the flowers come out in June, July and August, and are of a white colour.

William Prince

⚘ Clematis flammula, or Sweetest Virgin's Bower—This is of rapid growth, but its shoots are more delicate than many other; it will mount by assistance, to 15 or 20 feet in height; the leaves are ternate, the flowers white, and yielding the most delightful fragrance imaginable; they are also so numerous as almost to totally cover the plant and are produced in June, July, and August.

### The American Flower Garden Directory, 1839

Robert Buist

⚘ *Clematis flammula*, sweet-scented virgin's bower, is of very rapid growth. Established plants will grow from twenty to forty feet in one season, producing at the axils of the young shoots, large panules of small white flowers of exquisite fragrance, the leaves are compound pinnate; in bloom from July to November, but in August, September, and October, the flowers are in great profusion, perfuming the whole garden. This is one of the best climbing plants, and ought to have a situation in every garden.

### The Magazine of Horticulture, 1855

C. M. Hovey, Editor

⚘ The Clematises (Clematis flammula, &c.) All who have seen the common Virgin's bower of our woods, know how pretty a thing it is especially when surmounting some large shrub or evergreen tree, with whose lively foliage its white flowers contrast so finely. Though common it is always beautiful. But the best of this family is the C. flammula, which in its flowers resembles the virginiana, though its foliage is very different. The flowers are white, in the greatest profusion, and exhale a most delightful odor. It dies down to the ground every year, but springs up with astonishing rapidity, and soon covers a large space.

## Clematis virginiana

(*Clematis virginicus, Clematis virginicum*)

Virgin's Bower, Virginian Virgin's Bower, Traveller's Joy

Native to eastern North America from Canada to Florida, virgin's bower is a semideciduous vine that grows in areas bordering streams and rivers, sending its long climbing stems over shrubs and small trees. The genus, *Clematis*, belongs to the buttercup family, Ranunculaceae, and was named by Dioscorides, an ancient physician of Asia Minor. The species, *virginiana*, denotes the location in North America where the plant was first collected, although it is indigenous to a much larger area.

A hardy, woody vine with stems from eight to fifteen feet in length, virgin's bower produces leaves consisting of three leaflets that are ovate or rounded at the base. Small, creamy-white, fragrant flowers are produced in great profusion in August and September. Seed clusters with long feathery tails succeed the flowers in autumn, adding to the plant's ornamental value.

*Clematis virginiana* (virgin's bower)

Philip Miller (1691–1771) first cultivated virgin's bower in England in 1767 at the Chelsea Physic Garden, but because of the plant's limited ornamental value (when compared to other clematis species) it was never extensively grown in English gardens. Virgin's bower was first offered for sale by an American nursery when listed in Bernard M'Mahon's 1804 *Catalog of Garden, Herb, Flower, Tree, Shrub, and Grass Seeds*. In antebellum times, it was used to cover arbors and to create shady bowers. Travelers making their way along the rural roads and byways of the American South frequently referenced virgin's bower in their travel accounts. In the past, virgin's bower was generally known as traveller's joy, a name that reflects the pleasure it gave to weary travelers who enjoyed its small, fragrant flowers.

### *A Short Treatise on Horticulture,* 1828

William Prince

ᐁ *Clematis virginica,* or Virginian Virgin's Bower—This is of most rapid growth, and produces, in June and August, a great abundance of white flowers, which are very fragrant; it is well calculated to cover arbours and bowers.

### *The Flower Garden,* 1851

Joseph Breck

ᐁ *Clematis virginicum* is a native plant, well known as a great climber, growing profusely upon the banks of our rivers and wet places; taking possession and covering all the shrubs in its neighborhood, to which it attaches itself by the petioles, which are given off at intervals, in pairs, twining round objects for support, and serving the purpose of tendrils. The flowers are white, borne upon cymes, and make a handsome appearance the beginning of August. The most remarkable appearance of this plant is when in fruit; the long feathery tails of seed separating like tufts of wool. It grows twenty feet or more in a season, most of which perishes, leaving but a small portion shrubby. It makes an appropriate covering for an arbor or wall; for, whether in flower or seed, it is ornamental.

### *The Southern Cultivator,* 1875

W. L. Jones, Editor

ᐁ Walks in the Flower Garden

The chief attraction, this morning, is our lovely arbor of *Clematis virginiana,* commonly called White Virgin's Bower. I wish it was in the power of all my readers to see this beautiful vine when in full bloom. . . . Its large panicles of pure white flowers now cover every portion of it; its branches resembling, in the early moonlight, a beautiful bride adorned for the bridal. To fully appreciate its merits, it should be seen, for my pen is inadequate to describe its beauty and airy lightness. I most highly recommend it, however, to all lovers of flowers, and assure them that they will never regret the trouble required to remove it from its natural wilds to their cultivated gardens.

## Cornus florida

Flowering Dogwood, Dog Wood, Virginian Dogwood

Native to North America from Maine to Florida and westward to Texas, *Cornus florida* or flowering Dogwood is one of the finest ornamental trees found in American forests.

Obtaining an average height of twenty to thirty feet, flowering dogwood has an upright, oval form, horizontal branches, and elliptical to oval-shaped leaves that turn crimson red in fall. It is widely known for the springtime showy appearance of a profusion of small, greenish white flowers, encircled by large, white, petal-like bracts. Dogwood flowers are followed in late summer and fall by clusters of bright red berries that persist well into winter. Historically the wood of the flowering dogwood was used for making handles for tools, while its bark was used for medicinal purposes as an antiseptic and for the treatment of "intermittent fevers."

*Cornus florida* was cultivated in England as early as 1730 and was described by Mark Catesby in his *Natural History of Carolina, Florida and the Bahama Islands* (1731–1743). Numerous historical records document the beauty of this native ornamental. In his travels through the South in 1776, William Bartram, the American botanist and naturalist, wrote: "We have now entered a very remarkable grove of Dogwood Trees, which continued nine or ten miles unaltered, except here and there a towering Magnolia grandiflora. . . . These trees were about twelve feet high, spreading horizontally, their limbs meeting and interlocking with each other, forming

*Cornus florida* (flowering dogwood)

one vast, shady, cool grove, so vast as to exclude the sun-beams." Flowering dogwood was first offered for sale by an American nursery when listed in William Prince's *1771 Broadside*. It was frequently collected from southern forests and planted as an ornamental in antebellum gardens, where it was greatly admired for its beautiful spring flowers, fine autumn color, and winter display of bright red berries.

### A Treatise on the Theory and Practice of Landscape Gardening, 1841
Andrew Jackson Downing

❧ The Dogwood Tree. Cornus Florida

   The Dogwood is quite a picturesque small tree, and owes its interest chiefly to the beauty of its numerous blossoms and fruit. The leaves are oval, about three inches long, dark green above and paler below. In the beginning of May, while the foliage is beginning to expand rapidly, and before the tree is in full leaf, the flowers unfold, and present a beautiful spectacle, often covering the whole tree with their snowy garniture. . . . The berries which succeed these blossoms become quite red and brilliant in autumn; and, as they are plentifully borne in little clusters, they make quite a display. . . . The foliage in autumn is also highly beautiful, and must be considered as contributing to the charms of this tree. . . . Taking into consideration all these ornamental qualities, and also the fact that it is every day becoming scarcer in our native woods, we think the Dogwood Tree should fairly come under the protection of the picturesque planter, and well deserves a place in the pleasure ground and shrubbery.

### The Horticulturist, 1847/1848
Andrew Jackson Downing

✋ The Best of Hardy Shrubs

*Cornus Florida*

Though this is plentifully seen in our woods, it well deserves to be more frequently introduced into shrubberies. Its flowers and foliage are both excellent; and the effect of its rich, purplish, autumnal leaf tint, among other shrubs, is very striking in autumn.

### The American Handbook of Ornamental Trees, 1853

Thomas Meehan

✋ *Cornus Florida*

One of the most beautiful of our native flowering small trees, the flowers appearing in April, and presenting a brilliant appearance. . . . It will thrive in the deepest shade, loves moisture, but does not do well in dry or exposed situations. The flowers are succeeded by beautiful red berries, and the leaves turn reddish in the fall. The branches grow very horizontal and give it an interest in winter.

## Cotinus coggygria

(*Rhus continus*)

Smoke Tree, Venetian Sumac, Wig Tree, Juniper's Beard, Purple Fringe Tree

*Cotinus coggygria* (smoke tree)

Native to southern Europe, central China, and the Himalayas, *Continus coggygria* has been known over the years by numerous descriptive names, including purple fringe tree, juniper's beard, wig tree, Venetian sumac, and smoke tree, the name most commonly used today. A small, deciduous tree with a rounded, bushy form, *Cotinus coggygria* generally reaches an average height of ten to fifteen feet. Its smooth, oval leaves turn a bright yellow or golden orange in fall. Smoke tree is distinguished by its plumy masses of pink to purplish panicles, which create a smoke-like effect for several weeks in late May and June. Tiny, inconsequential flowers of a purplish color develop at the end of branches, succeeded by a sparse number of tiny, kidney-shaped seeds.

*Cotinus coggygria* has been cultivated in Europe for centuries. In Greece and Russia, the plant was used for tanning and dying leather, wool, and silk. First grown in England in 1656, smoke tree was described by John Gerard, author of the *Herball* or *History of Plants* (1597), as "an excellent and beautiful plant" and by John Claudius Loudon as deserving "a place in every garden." This treasured garden shrub arrived in North America before the end of the eighteenth century, first being offered by an American nursery when listed in Prince's *1790 Broadside* as fringe tree or Venetian sumac. In antebellum gardens, the smoke tree was frequently grown in the upper and middle South as a prized ornamental.

### *A Short Treatise on Horticulture,* 1828
William Prince

ᴐ *Rhus continus* or *Venetian Sumac*—This is also well known by the name of Purple Fringe Tree. It generally forms a large shrub of nine or ten feet, but a tree of it, which had grown for a long course of years in the ancient garden of the author, and which had been planted by his father, attained the height of 18 or 20 feet. . . . The flowers are produced at the ends of branches during the month of July, and continues for a long period: they are of most singular formation, being produced in large hair-like bunches, of a fine russet color, which afterwards change to brown: these are so numerous, as almost to cover the tree, and give it that most singular and unique appearance which renders it so unusually admired. . . . It is a tree of the most easy culture, accommodating itself to almost any soil.

### *A Treatise on the Cultivation of Ornamental Flowers,* 1828
Roland Green

ᴐ Venetian Sumac, or Fringe Tree (*Rhus cotinus*) is a very singular and beautiful tree, which is loaded "during summer with tufts of russet colored down, and forms the most singular ornament of the garden." It has been called *smoke tree.* Propagated by layers and by suckers.

### *The Horticulturist,* 1847/1848
Andrew Jackson Downing, Editor

ᴐ Venetian Fringe Tree (*Rhus continus*)

This popular shrub has a dozen names, one of the most expressive of which, is that of the French—*arbre á perruki,* (Wig Tree). From July to October it is covered with the purplish or brown abortive seed plumes, which render it a highly interesting object in the shrubbery. It is very hardy and grows in all soils.

### *The Southern Cultivator,* 1853
Daniel Lee and Dennis Redmond, Editors

ᴐ *The Purple Fringe,* or *Venetian Sumac*—is a popular shrub, remarkable for its curious brown fringe or hair-like flowers, that cover the whole plant in July, giving it the appearance of a smoke tree, Juniper's beard, etc. Propagated by layers.

## Deutzia scabra

*(Deutzia scabra crenata, Deutzia crenata)*
Garland Deutzia, Rough-Leaved Deutzia

Native to China and Japan, *Deutzia scabra* is a large, deciduous shrub that reaches a height of eight to ten feet. It is principally known for its showy spring flowers and distinctive graceful form. Carl Thunberg, a Swedish physician and plant collector who traveled to Japan with the Dutch India Company, named *Deutzia scabra* in honor of Johann von der Deutz of Amsterdam, a patron of botany and one of the promoters of Thunberg's Japanese voyage. It has elegant arching branches with exfoliating bark and lanceolate to ovate leaves that are covered with short rough hairs from which the species name, *scabra*, is derived. Japanese cabinetmakers of the past used the plant's coarse-textured foliage for smoothing and polishing wood. Clusters of single, white (sometimes tinged purple on the outside), bell-shaped flowers occur in late spring, at a time when most other flowering shrubs have already bloomed. The flowers are the plant's main attraction for it has neither fruit nor good fall color.

*Deutzia scabra* (garland deutzia)

John Reeves, a tea broker with the East India Company, introduced *Deutzia scabra* into England from Canton, China, in 1822. This attractive, free-flowering shrub proved popular in English gardens and soon became the parent of many new hybrids. *Deutzia scabra* was offered to American gardeners as early as 1841, when Asa Rowe of Monroe County, New York offered it in his *1841/1842 Annual Catalogue*. It was listed as a greenhouse plant and described as "snow drop flowered deutzia." *Deutzia scabra* became a prized addition to antebellum gardens of the middle and upper South, where it was grown for its beautiful spring flowers and its ability to tolerate the heat and drought of southern summers.

### The Horticulturist, 1846/1847

Andrew Jackson Downing, Editor

꙳ The Rough-Leaved Deutzia

*Deutzia scabra*

This is one of the greatest acquisitions of the last ten years, to our list of fine hardy shrubs. It is a native of Japan, and like most plants from that country, bears our northern winters without the slightest protection. The Deutzia belongs to the same natural order as the Syringa (Philadephaceae) and considerably resembles that old favorite of the gardens; but it is a far more refined and delicate looking shrub in its blossoms, and its habit of growth. The blossoms are pure white, and are produced in the month of May in the greatest profusion, in a kind of garland-like cluster, at the end of every branch. The shrub grows about six feet high, and forms a neat bushy head, of dark green foliage. . . . We advise those who do not possess it, to obtain it immediately. It grows in any tolerable soil.

### The Horticulturist, 1847/1848

Andrew Jackson Downing, Editor

꙳ Selection of the Best Hardy Shrubs

Garland Deutzia (*Deutzia scabra*)—Unquestionably one of the best of all the new shrubs. Its numerous white flowers are not unlike those of the orange, though the general habit of the plant is that of the Syringa, to which it is related. Everybody should cultivate it; and it grows so freely from cuttings that they may easily do so.

### The Southern Cultivator, 1857

Daniel Lee and Dennis Redmond, Editors

*Deutzia scabra*

From Japan, with beautiful white bell-shaped flowers in elongated clusters, and produced in great abundance in April and May. Four to six feet high. *Deutzia gracilis*, from East India, resembles the former but is smaller.

Robert Nelson, Fruitland Nurseries, Augusta, Georgia

## Eriobotrya japonica

(*Mespilus japonica*)

Loquat, Medlar, Japanese Plum, Japan Plum

Native to China and Japan, loquat is an attractive, broadleaf evergreen with a rounded shape and a lush, tropical appearance. This exotic ornamental develops into a large shrub or small tree and reaches a height of twenty to thirty feet. Its large, leathery leaves are dark green on top with a brown, feltlike covering below. Clusters of creamy-white, fragrant flowers emerge in late fall. These are followed by small, orange, pear-shaped fruit (on plants grown in the lower South), which can be eaten raw, steamed, or used in preserves.

Sir Joseph Banks introduced the loquat into England in 1787, but it was never hardy enough to become widely cultivated except in sheltered locations. Loquat was first offered in an American nursery catalog when listed by David and Cuthbert Landreth of Philadelphia in their *1824 Catalogue of Garden Seeds* as *Mespilus japonica*. Grown in antebellum gardens of the lower and middle South, loquat remains a popular ornamental. It is highly prized for its handsome foliage, fragrant flowers, and decorative fruit.

### A Short Treatise on Horticulture, 1828
William Prince

*Eriobotrya japonica.*—This tree, whose foliage is very attractive, was formerly called *Mespilus japonica*. The Horticultural Society of London remarks, that "of all the tropical fruits, it is probable this which will be the soonest brought into use in England." The plants are pretty hardy, and with a little protection will bear the severest winters of that country against a south wall. In the south of France, and at Malta it has already become a garden fruit. It is well calculated to succeed in the southern states, and has been mentioned by the Agricultural Society of South Carolina in their Desiderata. It requires only the simplest attention in its culture, and will no doubt before long be naturalized even to middle states.

*Eriobotrya japonica* (loquat)

### The American Flower Garden Directory, 1839
Robert Buist

*Eriobotrya japonica*, Loquat, or *Mespilus japonica*, is a fine plant, with large lanceolate, distinctively serrated leaves, white underneath; small white flowers on a racemose spike, and produces a fruit about the size of a walnut, of a fine yellow blush colour, and of tartish flavour. If it flowers in the autumn, it will require the heat of a hot-house to ripen the fruit. It is of a very easy culture, and its noble aspect is never passed unobserved. It is perfectly hardy in the Southern States, and forms a handsome evergreen.

### *The American Cotton Planter,* 1855

N. B. Cloud, Editor

❧ [From the *Natchez Daily Courier,* October 28, 1954]

The Japan Plum—*Eriobotrya* (*mespilus*) *japonica*—Whether as a mere ornamental evergreen, for which it is second to few others, or for the fragrance of its flowers, or delicious fruit, is deserving of infinitely more attention that it has received. It has hitherto been somewhat scarce. . . . The Japan Plum has ripened its fruit repeatedly in this country, and a very delicious fruit it is. It is now abundant in the markets of New Orleans in April.

Thomas Affleck

### *The Southern Cultivator,* 1856

Daniel Lee and Dennis Redmond, Editors

❧ Evergreens for the South

*Eriobotrya japonica,* also called *Mespilus japonica,* (Loquat, in Japan). Though it grows up to a lofty tree in its native country, Japan, still, with us it only forms a large and wide bush with large, wrinkled leaves, dark green on the surface, and downy underneath. The yellowish-white and fragrant flowers appear in November and December, followed by an apricot-like, very palatable fruit, of the size of a plum. The fruit, however, will not come to any perfection in this latitude, always being destroyed by the frost. At Montpelier, Monroe County, Georgia, a tree of this kind is planted in the border of a green-house, where it always produces fine fruit, ripe in April. About New Orleans and Mobile, it ripens in the open gardens.

Robert Nelson, Macon, Georgia

## Euonymus japonica

(*Euonymus japonicus*)

Evergreen Euonymus, Evergreen Spindle-Tree

*Euonymus japonica* is native to southern Japan and widely cultivated in China and Korea. It is an attractive evergreen shrub with shiny, dark green leaves, two to three inches long. Commonly known as evergreen euonymus, this handsome ornamental has an upright, compact form, often obtaining a height of eight to ten feet when grown under ideal conditions. *Euonymus japonica* produces small, bright green flowers in June and July, followed in autumn by round, green fruit containing decorative seeds. Evergreen euonymus is ideally suited to coastal areas, as it is tolerant of both salty and windy conditions.

Carl Thunberg first described *Euonymus japonica* in *Flora Japonica* (1784), a monumental work containing descriptions of over 300 previously unknown Japanese plants. Introduced into England from Japan in 1804, *Euonymus japonica* became a popular shrub in British gardens along with several variegated forms, including a gold and white striped variety. In addition to its use as a specimen plant, this versatile plant was often clipped to form a beautiful hedge.

*Euonymus japonica* arrived in North America around the middle of the nineteenth century, first being offered for sale by an American nursery when listed in Prince's *1844 Catalogue of Trees, Shrubs and Herbaceous Plants*. It proved particularly valuable in antebellum gardens both as a specimen plant and as a fine evergreen hedge.

### The Horticulturist, 1855

P. Barry and J. Jay Smith

‍ *Euonymus japonicus*—This is a splendid evergreen when planted in well-drained soil, otherwise the points of the young shoots will be destroyed during winter. The golden and silver variegated forms are equally hardy, and may be rendered very effective in composition.

### The Southern Cultivator, 1856

Daniel Lee and Dennis Redmond, Editors

‍ *Euonymus japonica*

This fine evergreen deserves to be quite extremely cultivated in our gardens. Its up-right growth, bright green, glossy foliage, and easy culture, recommends it as an indispensable shrub, and its beauty still more increased in the autumn by means of its scarlet berries. While much has been said in favor of the Holly for ornamental hedges, the Euonymus is far superior to it in every aspect. . . . There are varieties of it with variegated leaves, but the color looks always dull and dingy, and whenever they are planted on rich ground and grow luxuriantly, it will change to the original color.

Robert Nelson, Fruitland Nurseries, Augusta, Georgia

### The Southern Cultivator, 1857

Daniel Lee and Dennis Redmond, Editors

‍ Ornamental Edgings and Hedges, for the South
*Euonymus japonica*

This shrub, rather too tender for the north, will unquestionably long become one of the most desirable plants for a southern ornamental hedge. As yet, it is only seen in solitary specimens as a brush, but whenever propagated in abundance, its dense compact form, beautiful glossy green color, and its quality of thriving well in any soil, will soon make it indispensable in every southern garden. It needs but very little trimming, as its natural form is somewhat tapering, and it will, if desired, form a hedge or screen, ten feet high. For the latter purpose, the plant may be set two feet apart; for smaller hedges one foot apart.

Robert Nelson, Fruitland Nurseries, Augusta, Georgia

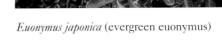

*Euonymus japonica* (evergreen euonymus)

### Ladies' Southern Florist, 1860

Mary Rion

‍ *Euonymus*

The foliage is a deep, shining green, of rapid growth, and suitable for hedges. The single plants require close and frequent pruning. The silver-edged is much the handsomer. It grows well from cuttings. No necessity for small plants to have roots, as they will grow without. Height, ten to fifteen feet. Seedlings change very much in character from the parent plant.

## Ficus carica

Common Fig

A native of the Mediterranean region, *Ficus carica* or common fig is a large deciduous shrub or small tree reaching a height of fifteen to twenty feet. The fig is characterized by

*Ficus carica* (common fig)

a broad, spreading form with multiple stems and deeply lobed leaves that are rough on the top and pubescent below. *Ficus carica* produces pear-shaped fruit both in late spring and in summer. The fruit ranges in color from green to shades of brown or maroon and can be eaten fresh, cooked, or dried. The fig is a long-lived plant, and although often killed to the ground during cold winters, its roots survive.

The Greeks and Romans were great cultivators of figs, and legend has it that the Athenians were so fond of the fruit that they forbade their exportation to other countries. According to tradition, the first fig tree was introduced into England in 1525. The earliest account of figs being grown in North America is found in the colonial records of Spanish Florida, which indicate that on April 2, 1579, Pedro Menendez, upon visiting Saint Augustine, observed, "There are beginning to be many fruits of Spain such as figs, pomegranates, oranges and grapes in great quantity." Figs were reported to have been grown in Virginia as early as 1621, when John Smith noted that figs "prospered exceedingly" after being introduced into Jamestown from Bermuda. Thomas Jefferson was an avid grower of figs often recording their dates of harvest along with information on his favorite varieties.

Figs were first offered for sale by an American nursery when listed in William Prince's *1771 Broadside*. By the early part of the nineteenth century, figs had become a popular garden fruit, and in 1833 William Kenrick, author of *The New American Orchardist*, described over twenty varieties of figs suitable for American gardens. Because of their somewhat tender nature, figs were generally grown close to a house or outbuilding for winter protection. Figs planted during the antebellum period often have survived in the gardens and grounds of the lower and middle South.

### *The American Cotton Planter,* 1854

N. B. Cloud, Editor

↬ The Fig

The fig (*Ficus carica*) should be generally cultivated throughout the Southern or Planting States, on account of its healthy and magnificent dessert fruit. . . . The few isolated varieties now in cultivation with Americanized names, induces me to furnish you with a correct description of a few of the rarest and most approved varieties of the fig. . . . Apropos—the Fig Tree delights in a light, rich soil, which is supplied with water within the reach of the roots. Its nature is to produce two crops in the year. The first crop, which is produced on the points of the shoots of last year; the second crop is produced on the shoots of the current year. Among the best varieties grown are the following: Brown Ischia . . . Black Genoa . . . Early White . . . Genoa, Large White . . . Black Ischia . . . Malta . . . Murray or Brown Naples . . . Blue or Purple . . . Naples, Large Black . . . Italian, Brown Naples, Brown Turkey, Brown Italian . . . Green Ischia . . . Brunswick, Hanover or Madonna . . . Marseilles, White Marseilles . . . Gentile . . . Lee's Perpetual . . . Ischia Small Brown . . . Ischia Yellow, Cyprus . . . Nerii . . . Pregussata . . . Small Brown Ischia.

## *The Magazine of Horticulture,* 1855

C. M. Hovey, Editor

ᔐ Figs—This is the fruit of the South which we are certain of having one crop per annum; and if the spring is mild, the first crop matures in June, the second a reliable crop in August and September; as an extra hit of fructification they bear a third crop, but like the first, seldom mature, being cut off by early frost.

Andrew Gray, Savannah, Georgia

## *The Farmer and Planter,* 1860

William Summer, Editor

ᔐ THE FIG AT THE SOUTH—Of all the fruits cultivated in the South, the fig requires the least care, and is one of the most productive and useful. South of the latitude of 32 degrees, the fig tree produces three crops a year, commencing in May and bearing until November, but in central Georgia we generally gather but two crops a year, unless the season is peculiarly favorable, the first or early crop being often killed by spring frosts. The figs are mostly eaten directly from the tree, as soon as ripe, and may be found in abundance upon the breakfast table of all lovers of fine fruit. The fig tree grows freely from cuttings planted early in the spring, and will sometimes bear the first year, generally the second. It has been a source of surprise to us that the fig is not extensively cultivated and turned to more profitable account; but this is not the only instance in which the prodigal and generous gifts of nature are lavished upon men in vain.

## Firmiana simplex

(*Sterculea platanfolia*)
Chinese Parasol Tree, Varnish Tree, Maple Leaved Sterculia

*Firmiana simplex,* previously know as *Sterculea platanfolia,* was named in honor of Karl Joseph von Firmiana (1718–1782), an early governor of Lombardy, Italy. Native to China and widely grown in Japan, it is a fast growing deciduous tree with a tall erect trunk and smooth, gray green bark. *Firmiana simplex* is commonly known as Chinese parasol tree because of its large palmate leaves (measuring ten to twelve inches across) and rounded, umbrellalike canopy. Small petal-like flowers develop in spring, followed in late summer by decorative seed pods that usually contain only two or three seeds.

Introduced into England in 1757, Chinese parasol tree was originally grown as a greenhouse plant but later was found to be hardy out-of-doors in protected locations. André Michaux, the French botanist who established a botanical garden in Charleston, South Carolina, in 1787, introduced this Asian native to North America sometime before the end of the eighteenth century. François Michaux, upon visiting his father's nursery garden outside Charleston, noted in 1802 in his *Travels* of finding "a good number of trees belonging to the old continent, that my father had planted, some of which were in the most flourishing state . . . including several *Sterculia platanfolia*, which had yielded seed upward of six years."

*Firmiana simplex* (Chinese parasol tree)

Chinese parasol tree was first offered to American gardeners when listed in Bernard M'Mahon's 1804 *Catalogue of Garden, Herb, Flower, Tree, Shrub, and Grass Seeds*. Grown as a prized exotic throughout the antebellum period, this somewhat invasive plant often escaped cultivation and has become naturalized in many areas of the lower and middle South.

### The American Cotton Planter, 1855
N. B. Cloud, Editor

☞ [From the *Natchez Daily Courier*, October 28, 1854]

The Varnish Tree (*Stericula platynifolia*) is so called from its beautiful glossy bark, and large rich colored leaves, which seem all to have been recently coated with green varnish. It is, altogether, a pretty and desirable ornamental shade tree.

Thomas Affleck

### The Southern Cultivator, 1857
Daniel Lee and Dennis Redmond, Editors

☞ Ornamental Trees and Shrubs for the South

*Sterculia platanfolia*, (Varnish Tree) from China.—Perhaps one of our best shade trees in the South. Grows very rapidly, with a straight stem and sleek green bark forms a symmetrical head with very large leaves. It has a tremendous tap-root, and will, therefore, not, like the China Tree, get blown out of the ground. It never gives suckers, and no insect ever troubles it. Thirty feet high. Propagated by seed.

Robert Nelson, Fruitland Nurseries, Augusta, Georgia

## Forsythia virdissima

Greenstem Forsythia, Golden Bell, Deep-green Forsythia

Native to China, greenstem forsythia was named in honor of William Forsyth (1737–1804), an eighteenth-century Scottish gardener, writer, and successor of Philip Miller, the first director of the Chelsea Physic Garden. Greenstem forsythia is an upright, compact deciduous shrub with arching, olive green branches. One of its most striking features is its early springtime flowers, which are bright yellow and pendulous in nature. It also produces attractive purplish red foliage in autumn.

Robert Fortune (1813–1880), a Scottish plant collector who was sent to China by the Horticulture Society of London at the end of the Opium Wars, introduced greenstem forsythia into England in 1844. Mr. Fortune described greenstem forsythia as "growing 8 to 10 feet high in gardens of northern China, forming a compact shrub, with long, opposite leaves, which emit a slight balsamic odor." American horticulturists first learned of greenstem forsythia from British journals, and in 1848 were able to purchase this newly introduced ornamental from Highland Nurseries in Newburgh, New York.

### *The Horticulturist,* 1848/1849

Andrew Jackson Downing, Editor

↬ The Dark Green Forsythia—(*Forsythia virdissima*). This fine new hardy shrub is one of the novelties brought from China to England, by Mr. Fortune. . . . It was introduced into this country last season (1848), and has flowered finely this spring. The following is Mr. Fortune's account of it: "This is a deciduous shrub, with very dark green leaves, which are prettily serrated at the margins. It grows about eight to ten feet high in the north of China, and sheds its leaves in autumn. . . . Early in spring, buds . . . gradually unfold themselves, and present a profusion of bright yellow blossoms all over the shrub, which is highly ornamental."

*The Horticulturist,* 1850

↬ FORSYTHIA VIRIDISSIMA will prove to be an evergreen in southern latitudes. It has not yet flowered . . . and will be an ornamental evergreen south of Virginia

R. Buist, Philadelphia, 1849

### *The Horticulturist,* 1851

Andrew Jackson Downing, Editor

↬ The Golden Bell Shrub—The new hardy shrub from China, Forsythia virdissima, is too gay and ornamental, and will become too popular to be commonly known by its hard botanical name and we propose to call it Golden Bell. . . . It forms the brightest embellishment of the shrubbery in early spring and its hardiness and easy culture, will soon give it a place in every garden.

### *The Southern Cultivator,* 1857

Daniel Lee and Dennis Redmond, Editors

↬ This beautiful shrub, of recent introduction, was first discovered by Mr. Robert Fortune, in China. Very early in the spring, say in February, it is loaded with bright yellow bell-shaped flowers, gracefully drooping and blooming before the leaves have appeared. Easily propagated by cuttings. Grows 4 to 5 feet high.

Robert Nelson, Fruitland, Augusta, Georgia

*Forsythia virdissima* (greenstem forsythia)

## Gardenia jasminoides

(*Gardenia florida*)
Gardenia, Cape Jasmine, Cape Jessamine

Originally thought to be a native of South Africa, the gardenia or cape jasmine, as it was originally known, was later found to be indigenous to China. An evergreen shrub with dark green, leathery leaves, the gardenia will grow to a height of four to six feet and ultimately develop into a large shrub with a rounded or oval form. It is best known for its handsome, waxy white flowers that bloom in late spring and throughout the summer, perfuming the air with its delicate fragrance.

Introduced into England in 1754, Philip Miller, author of the famous *Gardener's Dictionary* (1731), originally classified the gardenia as a jasmine. Early in 1758, John Ellis, an English merchant and naturalist, became interested in the plant and sent a specimen to his friend Carolus Linnaeus, the famous Swedish botanist. With encouragement from Ellis, Linnaeus named this new plant gardenia in honor of Dr. Alexander Garden (1728–1791), a noted physician in Charleston, South Carolina.

The first gardenia plants to arrive in North America were sent to Dr. Garden in February 1762. Unfortunately, only one of the plants arrived alive, and, even after careful nurturing, it too failed to survive. The gardenia was first offered for sale to American gardeners when listed in Bartram's *1807 Catalogue of Trees, Shrubs and Herbaceous Plants*. A popular ornamental in antebellum gardens of the lower and middle South, the gardenia was grown as a specimen plant or sometimes as a hedge. It remains a treasured ornamental in southern gardens, where it is prized for its fine evergreen foliage and fragrant flowers.

### A Short Treatise on Horticulture, 1828
William Prince

&#8667; *Gardenia*—Of this there are a number of species, many of which produce flowers of great beauty and fragrance. . . . *Gardenia florida*, or *Cape Jasmine*—This is the best known; the foliage is very beautiful, and it produces white flowers of a delicate fragrance. There are three varieties, viz., the common one, with large double flowers and broad leaves, another with smaller flowers and narrow leaves, and a third with single flowers.

### The Southern Cultivator, 1850
Daniel Lee and Dennis Redmond, Editors

&#8667; *Gardenia florida* (Cape Jasmine), is too well known to need any description. Formerly the single species was cultivated, but it is now superseded by the double variety. It thrives best in rich clay, though it will grow almost anywhere. . . . A new, and highly puffed variety, *G. fortunei*, has recently been introduced, but it is too tender for our winters, and its flowers are but little larger than those of our common double variety.

*Gardenia jasminoides* (gardenia)

N. B. Cloud, Editor

᠅ [From the *Natchez Daily Courier,* October 28, 1854]

The *Gardenias*—Cape Jessamine is the most common—are of course indispensable. The dwarf kind (*Gardenia radicans*) is a lovely little plant. Fortune's new Chinese (*G. Fortunii*) was lauded so highly that I feared a disappointment. But it proved to be all he represented—the foliage larger and richer, and the blossoms fully double the size and more perfect in form; and though fragrant, not so oppressively so as the old sort.

Thomas Affleck

## *Ladies' Southern Florist,* 1860

Mary Rion

᠅ Cape Jessamine

This handsome evergreen has beautiful dark green leaves, with a rich camellia-like flower, of delicious fragrance. It grows ten feet high, and may be propagated by layers or cuttings. They can also be grown in water, in glass, until rootlets appear, and the glass then filled with sand. The Cape Jessamine is handsome in single plants or hedges.

## Gelsemium sempervirens

(*Gelsemium nitidum, Bignonia sempervirens*)
Carolina Jessamine, Yellow Jasmine, Yellow Jessamine

*Gelsemium sempervirens* (Carolina jessamine)

Carolina jessamine is a native evergreen vine found growing from Virginia to Texas. It presents a dramatic display in early spring when its yellow, trumpet-shaped flowers adorn the swamps, riverbanks, sandhills, and pine forests of the lower and middle South. Dark green leaves, two to four inches long, emerge from wiry stems that often grow twenty feet in length, entangling themselves in shrubs and trees in a graceful and delicate fashion. Even when not in bloom, the glossy evergreen foliage of this twining woody vine has made it a favorite in southern gardens since colonial times. The Latin name *Gelsemium* is an adaptation of *gelsemno,* Italian for true jasmine (of which it has no relation) and *sempervirens,* meaning "always green."

Introduced into England as early as 1640, Carolina jessamine was originally grown as a greenhouse plant but soon was found to survive outside conservatory walls. One of the earliest illustrations of Carolina jessamine can be found in Mark Catesby's *Natural History of Carolina, Florida and the Bahama Islands* (1734–1743). Thomas Jefferson referred to it as *Bignonia sempervirens* in his *Notes on the State of Virginia* and indicated that he planned to landscape and beautify his grounds by thinning out trees and covering the ground with grass, interspersed with Carolina jessamine and other ornamentals. In the antebellum South, roots of the plant were found to be useful in the treatment of rheumatism, fever, and nervous disorders. Carolina jessamine was first offered for sale by an American nursery when listed as yellow jasmin in *Bartram's Catalogue of American Trees, Shrubs and Herbaceous Plants* (1783).

### A Sketch of the Botany of South Carolina and Georgia, vol. 1, 1821
Stephen Elliott

ᴦ *Gelsemium sempervirens*

This beautiful plant flourishes in almost every soil in the maritime districts of Carolina and Georgia, though it prefers moist and rich lands. It abounds along the roads, covering the shrubbery with its rich foliage and flowers, and perfuming the air with its delightful fragrance. Flowers—February–March; sometimes October–November.

### A Short Treatise on Horticulture, 1828
William Prince

ᴦ *Caroline yellow jasmine*, or *gelsemium nitidum*. This is justly celebrated as one of the most beautiful climbers; the shoots are small and delicate, but if trained against a wall, or any other support, they will mount to a great height by their twining stalks; the leaves are single, lanceolate, and ornamental; but it is the fine bright yellow flowers of a trumpet form, and exhaling the most delightful fragrance, that give such value to this plant. In our more southern states, where it is found wild twining around the trees of the forest, it perfumes the air for a considerable distance around during the season of its bloom.

### The American Flower Garden Directory, 1839
Robert Buist

ᴦ *Gelsemium nitidum*, Carolina jasmine, a most beautiful climbing evergreen, flowering shrub. In the months of April and May, it produces many large yellow trumpet-like blossoms of delicious fragrance. If much encouraged in growth, it will not flower so freely.

### Ladies' Southern Florist, 1860
Mary Rion

ᴦ Jessamine

The *Yellow Jessamine* is native, and will live if the plants are taken from the uplands. It is evergreen, and gorgeous in flowering. The perfume is delicious. The leaf and flower are poisonous and hence it should never be planted within the reach of children.

---

## Ginkgo biloba

(*Salisburia adiantifolia*)
Ginkgo, Maidenhair Tree

A native of China, the ginkgo tree is often described as a living fossil, as its history dates to prehistoric times. One of the most distinctive and beautiful of all deciduous trees, the gingko, or maidenhair tree as it is sometimes called, is best known for its fan-shaped leaves, which turn a brilliant, golden yellow in autumn. A slow-growing, long-lived tree with a pyramidal to irregular form, the ginkgo is classified as dioecious. Male and female flowers are borne on separate plants with only the female tree bearing fruit. Fruit of the

*Ginkgo biloba* (ginkgo)

female ginkgo is covered with a fleshy pulp that emits a strong, disagreeable odor, making it less desirable than the male tree for use as an ornamental.

Kempher, a physician with the Dutch East India Company in 1690, first observed the ginkgo in Japan. It arrived in England in 1754 where it gained instant attention as a prized ornamental. William Hamilton imported the ginkgo from England to North America in 1784, planting it on the grounds of his country estate, The Woodlands, located outside Philadelphia on the Schuylkill River. Several years later, André Michaux, the French botanist, introduced additional specimens of this ornamental tree into Charleston, South Carolina. The ginkgo was first offered for sale by an American nursery when listed in David and Cuthbert Landreth's *1811 Catalogue* as *Salisburia adiantifolia*, Japanese maidenhair tree. The ginkgo was a popular ornamental in the antebellum South, prized for its unusual foliage and brilliant fall color.

### *Travels to the West of the Alleghany Mountains*, 1805
François André Michaux

As soon as I recovered from my illness I left Charleston, and went to reside in a small plantation about ten miles from the town, where my father had formed a botanic garden. . . . I found in this garden a superb collection of trees and plants that had survived almost total neglect . . . some of which were in the most flourishing state. I principally remarked two *ginkgo biloba*, that had been planted about seven years, and which were then upward of thirty feet in height.

### *A Treatise on the Theory and Practice of Landscape Gardening*, 1841
Andrew Jackson Downing

The Salisburia, or Gingko Tree

This fine exotic tree, which appears to be perfectly hardy in this climate, is one of the most singular in its foliage that has ever come under our observations. . . . The Ginkgo is so great a botanical curiosity, and is so singularly beautiful when clad with its fern-like foliage, that it is strikingly adapted to add ornament and interest to the pleasure ground. . . . We would recommend that it be planted near the house, where its unique character can be readily seen and appreciated.

### *The Horticulturist*, 1853
P. Barry, Editor

SALISBURIA ADIANTIFOLIA—The *Ginkgo* or *Maidenhair* tree is well known in this country, where it grows more rapidly and thriftily than in any part of Britain. This is probably owing to our fine warm summers, which are like those of its native land. Here it is one among the many plants which prove that the plants of Northern China will be more at home and do better with us than in England. Whoever plants only a few trees should include this among them. The lamented Mr. Downing had a handsome specimen in his lawn. Native of Northern China and Japan.

### *The American Cotton Planter*, 1855
N. B. Cloud, Editor

[From the *Natchez Daily Courier*, October 28, 1854]

The Ginkgo (*Salisburia*) or Maiden-Hair Tree is pretty and quite ornamental. The leaves are very curious.

Thomas Affleck

---

## Halesia tetraptera

(*Halesia carolina, Mohrodendron carolinum*)
Carolina Silverbell, Snowdrop Tree, Four Winged Halesia

Native to the eastern United States, Dr. Alexander Garden named *Halesia tetraptera* in honor of Reverend Stephen Hale (1677–1761), an English botanist and author of *Vegetable Statistics*, one of the most important eighteenth-century contributions to the anatomy of plants. The species name, *tetraptera*, refers to the plant's four-winged appendages. *Halesia tetraptera* or Carolina silverbell, is best known for its beautiful clusters of pure white, pendulous flowers that occur in midspring. Reaching a height of thirty to forty feet, this native ornamental is characterized by a broad, oval form with irregular branches and large oval leaves. The bell-shaped flowers of Carolina silverbell are produced in great abundance both before and after new foliage appears. Blossoms are followed by distinctive four-winged seeds that ripen in late summer and fall.

*Halesia tetraptera* (Carolina silverbell)

Mark Catesby first described *Halesia tetratera* in *Natural History of Carolina, Florida and the Bahama Islands* (1731–1743). It arrived in England in 1756 when Dr. Alexander Garden, a noted physician of Charleston, South Carolina, sent seeds to John Ellis. *Halesia tetraptera* was considered one of the finest North American plants introduced into British gardens. It was initially offered for sale by an American nursery when listed in William Prince's *1790 Broadside* as snow-drop tree. In antebellum gardens and groves of the middle and upper South, Carolina silverbell was often collected from southern forests and grown as an ornamental for its splendid display of early springtime flowers.

### *The American Gardener's Calender,* 1806
Bernard M'Mahon

꙳ The *Halesia tetraptera*, or snowdrop tree, is exceeded by very few shrubs, for the beauty of its numerous white pendant flowers. It may be propagated by suckers or layers, or by sowing the seeds in November when ripe, or in March, and covering them near an inch deep, with light rich mold.

### *The Horticulturist,* 1846
Andrew Jackson Downing, Editor

꙳ The Common Halesia, or Silver Bell Tree, (*H. Tetraptera*), is one of the prettiest ornaments of our shrubberies, well known in the spring, by its pendant, pale, bell-like blossoms, and in summer, by its four-winged seeds.

The . . . species (*H. diptera*) is a much rarer one, its native country is Georgia and Carolina . . . and is well entitled to a prominent place in the pleasure grounds. It differs strongly from the common species (*H. tetraptera*), in both the large size, and the purer white of its flowers, and also in the foliage, which is twice as broad as that of the four-winged sort. The seeds have, as the name indicates, only two-winged appendages.

### *The Flower Garden,* 1851
Joseph Breck

꙳ *Halesia tetraptera*—Four-winged Halesia—A native of Carolina, where it is found growing on the banks of rivers. It is an ornamental shrub, five or six feet high, valuable for its early flowering in May. The flowers hang in small bunches all along the branches, each bud producing from four to eight or nine flowers; they appear before the leaves, and are of a snowy whiteness, and last for two or three weeks.

***The Southern Cultivator,* 1857**

Daniel Lee and Dennis Redmond, Editors

*Halesia diptera* and *Halesia tetraptera,* (Silver Bell)

These plants are indigenous to our swamps, but well worthy of a place in our gardens and parks. The former with a large, flat, two-winged seed is the prettiest. The numerous, white, bell-shaped, drooping flowers, like snow drops, are highly ornamental during the month of April. Ten to fifteen feet high.

Robert Nelson, Fruitland Nurseries, Augusta, Georgia

---

## Hedera helix

English Ivy, Common Ivy, European Ivy

English ivy is native to western Europe and has a long history both as a mythological and garden plant. Greeks and Romans grew it as a symbol of friendship, virtue, and prosperity. It is an evergreen climber that derives its scientific name, *Hedera,* from the Celtic word, hedrin or cord, and *helix,* the Greek word for spiral, a reference to the plant's growth habit. A hardy, woody vine best known for its three to five lobed lustrous, evergreen leaves, English ivy has been used for centuries as an ornamental to cover walls, arbors, and colonnades or to train on frames and latticework to create architectural shapes and forms. This aggressive vine climbs by means of aerial roots and can reach heights of fifteen to twenty feet when allowed to grow freely against walls or the trunks of trees. All parts of the plant are aromatic, and its fragrant resin, known as hederine (obtained from old stems), was used in the past for medicinal purposes.

*Hedera helix* (English ivy)

It was introduced from Europe to North America during colonial times. Peter Kalm, in his *Travels of North America* (1748–1751), observed near Philadelphia that "Hedera helix, planted against the wall of a stone building. . . . It was doubtless brought over from Europe for I have never perceived it anywhere else in my travels through North America." Noted in George Washington's diary and grown by Thomas Jefferson at Monticello, English ivy was first offered for sale in an American nursery when listed in Bartram's *1807 Catalogue of Trees, Shrubs and Herbaceous Plants. Hedera helix* was grown during the antebellum period and remained a popular evergreen vine throughout the nineteenth century for covering walls and fences. The use of English ivy as an evergreen ground cover is a recent horticultural practice that developed in the twentieth century.

***A Treatise on the Theory and Practice of Landscape Gardening,* 1841**

Andrew Jackson Downing

☙ The European Ivy (Hedera Helix) is certainly one of the finest, if not the very finest climbing plant (or more properly, creeping vine, for by means of its little fibres or rootlets on the stems, it will attach itself to trees, walks, or any other substance), with which we are acquainted. It possesses not only very fine dark green palmated foliage in great abundance, but the foliage has that agreeable property of being evergreen— which, while it enhances its value tenfold, is at the same time so rare among vines. . . . It never thrives well if suffered to ramble along the ground, but needs the support of a tree, a frame, or a wall, to which it attaches itself firmly, and grows with vigorous shoots."

## The Horticulturist, 1847/1848

Andrew Jackson Downing, Editor

☙ *Hedera Helix*

Certainly the finest of all . . . climbers is the European Ivy. Such rich masses of glossy, deep green foliage, such fine contrasts of light and shade, and such a wealth of associations, is possessed by no other plant; the Ivy, to which the ghost of all the storied past alone tells the tale of departed greatness, the confidant of old ruined castles and abbeys. . . .

The Ivy is the finest of climbers, too, because it is so perfectly evergreen. North of New York it is a little tender. . . . But all over the middle states it should be planted and cherished, wherever there is a wall for it to cling to.

## The Flower Garden, 1851

Joseph Breck

☙ *Hedera helix*—Common Ivy

In this country [America] it is not common, but it appears to succeed well in shady locations. There are some fine specimens in the city of Boston, which flourish finely upon the rough granite or brick walls of buildings. It is easily propagated by cuttings or layers. There are a number of varieties of this, of which all are desirable, growing to a great height, and attaching itself firmly to whatever it grows upon, without any assistance.

## The Southern Cultivator, 1856

Daniel Lee and Dennis Redmond, Editors

☙ *Hedera helix*. A beautiful evergreen climber for covering walls, particularly brick walls. It thrives best on the north side of buildings, where it is not exposed to the sun. There are varieties with silvery, as well as with golden edged leaves. Propagates itself spontaneously by layers.

Robert Nelson, Macon, Georgia

## Hibiscus syriacus

(*Althea frutex*)
Althaea, Althea, Rose of Sharon

Althaea, or rose of Sharon, is a large, deciduous shrub or small tree reaching an average height of eight to ten feet. Althaea develops a slender, upright form that becomes more rounded with age. The plant's medium-textured, dark green foliage provides a striking background to its showy, hollyhock-like flowers that bloom continuously from June until frost. Althaea's popularity as a treasured ornamental can be attributed to its hardy nature, rapid growth, resistance to disease, ability to tolerate a variety of soils and growing conditions, and its profusion of flowers that occur throughout summer and fall when few other shrubs are in bloom.

Introduced into England in 1596 from Syria, hence the species name *syriacus*, although it is, in fact, native to India and China. In China, leaves of the althaea were used for making tea, and its flowers were served as a culinary delicacy. This showy ornamental was documented in George Washington's diary and recorded in Thomas Jefferson's *Garden Book* as being planted at Monticello on April 4, 1767. Althaea was first offered for sale by an American nursery when listed in William Prince's *1793 Broadside of Fruit Trees and Shrubs* as *Althea frutex*, both blue and white. Its great profusion of flowers during the summer months as well as its tolerance of heat and drought made althaea a popular ornamental in southern gardens during the antebellum period.

### A Short Treatise on Horticulture, 1828
William Prince

↘ This shrub grows generally to the height of 10 to 12 feet. . . . It forms a fine conical shaped head, and the different varieties continue blooming from the latter part of the summer to the end of autumn. The single flowered ones commence earliest in the season and when they are nearly past, the double ones commence, and continue till frost prevents further expansion of their flowers. There are a number of varieties, among which are two new double ones, originated from seed within the last few years.

*Hibiscus syriacus* (althaea)

### The Horticulturist, 1848
Andrew Jackson Downing, Editor

↘ Altheas (*Hybiscus syriacus*). In mid-summer, when most shrubs are done blooming, the altheas are in full beauty; and they then give a gay appearance to pleasure grounds for a long time. The sort with double variegated flowers is, perhaps, the finest, though there are a great number of various shades worthy of cultivation. All seem quite hardy, and grow with great ease in all soils, except the *double white*, which is usually quite tender north of New York. August and September.

### The Flower Garden, 1851
Joseph Breck

↘ *Hibiscus syriacus*—The Althea is a well-known ornamental shrub, of easy cultivation; but a little tender in some situations, particularly the double white variety. They grow freely from cuttings, from which the double varieties are multiplied; or very easily from seed, for single varieties. We think some of the single varieties are equally handsome as the double, and generally more hardy. There is the double white, red, blue and white, with stripes, or blotches, and others.

P. Barry, Editor

ᴂ Althaea (Rose of Sharon)

There are many varieties of these—purple, violet, painted, variegated, etc. They are neat compact-growing shrubs, most of them attaining a height of eight or ten feet, and bloom profusely late in autumn, on which account they are particularly desirable. Indeed the smallest assortment of shrubs should include one or more althaeas.

## Hydrangea macrophylla

(*Hydrangea hortensia, Hydrangea hortensis*)

Common Hydranger, Chinese Guelder-Rose, French Hydrangea

*Hydrangea macrophylla* is a deciduous, woody shrub that is indigenous to China and Japan. For centuries, it was grown in Asian gardens as a prized ornamental. Generally known as common hydrangea, this treasured garden shrub is characterized by a mounding form with thick, coarse-textured, yellow green leaves, six to eight inches long. Common hydrangea has the unique habit of producing blue or pink flower clusters, depending on the acidity or alkalinity of the soil. Alkaline soils with a high lime content produce pink flowers, while acid soils containing aluminum sulfite or iron produce flowers with a blue color. The showy blossoms of common hydrangea are produced in sun or shade during the summer and remain on the plant for several months, eventually turning a warm golden brown. Florists often grow common hydrangea in greenhouses to obtain early spring blooms.

*Hydrangea macrophylla* (Common Hydranger)

Sir Joseph Banks introduced *Hydrangea macrophylla* into England from China in 1788. It was originally known as *Hydrangea hortensis*, then *Hydrangea hortensia*, and finally *Hydrangea macrophylla*, the name by which it is known today. This showy ornamental soon became popular throughout Europe, particularly in France, where numerous hybrids were developed, giving rise to one of the plant's common names, French hydrangea. An American nursery first offered it for sale when it was listed in Bartram's *1807 Catalogue of Trees, Shrubs and Herbaceous Plants.* Common hydrangea was a popular garden shrub that was grown in the antebellum gardens of the middle and lower South either as a specimen or as a pot plant for decorating piazzas or porches. During winter, potted plants often were placed in a cold frame, plant pit, or greenhouse.

*A Short Treatise on Horticulture,* **1828**

William Prince

‿ *Hydrangea hortensis*, or *Changeable Chinese*—This is well known for its extremely showy flowers, which during their development and decline, present a variety of shades and colours. It has also been found that *soil* has a singular effect in this respect; and it is remarked, that when planted in a sandy or indifferent soil, the flowers are of a rose colour—but when black swamp mould is used, the blue is found to prevail. . . . When it was first introduced into Europe, it was nursed as a very tender plant, but it is found now to withstand perfectly the winters of Long Island; and with the protection of some slight covering in winter, would doubtless succeed much further north.

### The American Flower Garden Directory, 1839
Robert Buist

‿ *Hydrangea hortensia* is a well-known plant, and much esteemed for its great profusion of very elegant, though monstrous, flowers. They are naturally of a pink colour, but under certain circumstances of culture they become blue. If grown in brown loam with a little sand, they will preserve their original colour; but if grown in swamp earth with a little mulch of decayed leaves, they will become blue. . . . It must have a very plentiful supply of water when in flower, which is produced on the shoots of the previous year. . . . Being tolerably hardy, when the winters are mild, by a little protection in the open air, they will flower profusely; the flowers will be very large, and in bloom from June to October. They are deciduous, soft wooded shrubs.

### Ladies' Southern Florist, 1860
Mary Rion

‿ HYDRANGEA

This is a deciduous shrub, and being tolerably hardy, will grow in the open air where the winters are not too severe. They require shade to grow or bloom well, and when in flower need profuse watering. The pink variety is most unusual, but the color can be changed to *blue*, by mixing a large portion of decayed leaves and swamp earth. If the plant is very thick, the oldest branches may be thinned out, never cutting out any of the *young* shoots, as these bear the flowers. Propagate by offshoots or cuttings.

## Hydrangea quercifolia

Oakleaf Hydrangea, Oak-Leafed Hydrangea

Oakleaf hydrangea is a medium-sized, deciduous shrub with a mounding form. This handsome plant is native to the southeastern United States from Georgia to Florida and westward to Louisiana. It is distinguished by large ovate leaves with numerous lobes, similar in character to many North American oaks, from which it derives its common name, oakleaf. During winter, the plant's interesting branching structure, upright stems, and exfoliating bark gives it a unique and distinctive appearance. Large clusters of creamy-white flowers, eight to ten inches long, appear in late May and June. Flowers turn a tannish brown over summer and remain on the plant until late winter and into spring. In fall, the foliage changes from a dark green to colors ranging from scarlet to bronzy red.

In 1776, William Bartram discovered oakleaf hydrangea in Crawford County, Georgia, during his travels through the southern states. William Hamilton introduced oakleaf hydrangea into England in 1803, and it was figured in Curtis's *Botanical Magazine* in 1806, in which it was noted that being a native of the Deep South, it might best be grown as a greenhouse plant. While seeds were commercially available to American gardeners from the American seedsman, Bernard M'Mahon, as early as 1804, plants were unavailable until several years later when listed in Bartram's *1807 Catalogue of Trees, Shrubs and Herbaceous Plants.* Frequently grown in gardens of the antebellum South, oakleaf hydrangea remains one of the South's finest native plants. Its ability to grow in sun and shade, its beautiful foliage, interesting branching habit, showy flowers, and brilliant fall color make it an ideal plant for southern gardens.

### *Travels Through North and South Carolina, Georgia, East and West Florida,* 1791
William Bartram

〜 I observed here [south central Georgia] a very singular and beautiful shrub, which I suppose is a species of Hydrangea [*H. quercifolia*]. It grows in coppices or clumps near or on the banks of rivers or creeks; many stems usually arise from a root, spreading itself greatly on all sides by suckers or offsets; the stems grown five or six feet high. . . . The leaves which clothe the plants are very large, pinnatifed or palmated, and serrated or toothed, very much resembling the leaves of some of our Oaks; they set opposite, supported by slender petioles, and are of a fine green colour.

### *A Sketch of the Botany of South Carolina and Georgia,* vol. 1, 1821
Stephen Elliott

〜 *Hydrangea quercifolia*

A handsome shrub, 4–5 feet high. Leaves variously sinuate, though generally 5 lobed; when young very tomentose, with the veins marked with a ferruginous colour. Flowers in long panicles . . . sterile florets numerous, at first of an obscure white color, changing afterward to pink. First discovered by Bartram, in his travels through the southern states. Grows near Milledgeville, Georgia. Flowers May–June.

### *Arboretum et Fruticetum Britannicum,* 1838
John Claudius Loudon

〜 Hydrangea quercifolia. The Oak-Leaved Hydrangea

A native of Florida, growing from 4 feet to 6 feet high. It was introduced in 1803, and flowers from June to September. This is by far the most interesting of the North American hydrangeas, from its large, deeply lobed, and sinuated leaves; and its fine, large, nearly white corymbs of flowers, which are sterile, and appear from June till they are destroyed by frosts.

*Hydrangea quercifolia* (oakleaf hydrangea)

### *The Horticulturist,* 1847/1848
Andrew Jackson Downing, Editor

〜 Oak-Leaved Hydrangea (*Hydrangea quercifolia*)

One of the handsomest of all small shrubs, both in foliage and flower. The blossoms are white, and remain in bloom for two months. The leaves are large, and in figure, are like those of the oak. This plant is, I think, from Florida; yet it bears a northern winter of 10° below zero without injury.

## Ilex opaca

American Holly

American Holly is native to the eastern United States and is best known for its glossy evergreen foliage and bright red berries, which have been used for centuries in holiday wreaths and Christmas decorations. It attracted the attention of early European voyagers, first being recorded in 1564 by a party of French explorers who landed at the mouth of Florida's Saint Johns River. A large, long-lived, slow-growing shrub, American Holly is characterized by stiff, spiny leaves and a distinctive pyramidal form. Small inconspicuous flowers develop in May and June, followed by showy red berries that remain on the plant all winter long.

The Duke of Argyle first cultivated American holly in England in 1774, but it never proved popular in British gardens because of its close similarity to the common European holly (*Ilex aquifolia*). In the United States, however, both George Washington and Thomas Jefferson planted it as an ornamental. As it proved difficult to transplant from the forest, it was generally grown from seed. This attractive evergreen was frequently used in antebellum gardens, where it was prized for its formal elegance as a specimen, a topiary plant, or a clipped evergreen hedge. It was first offered for sale by an American nursery in 1783 when included in *Bartram's Catalogue of American Trees, Shrubs and Herbaceous Plants*. American Holly remains one of the most striking and handsome of America's native evergreen plants.

*Ilex opaca* (American holly)

### *The American Gardener's Calendar,* 1806
Bernard M'Mahon

ॐ Holly Hedges

Of all other plants, there is none that makes a more durable, close, and beautiful hedge, than the *Holly*, nor one that agrees better with the shears: it may be clipped and dressed to any form; the seeds do not vegetate till the second spring. . . . They must remain two years in the seed-bed, and then should be planted either in the face of ditches, or into nursery rows, if intended for ground hedges; for which there is no equal, as to beauty, shelter and closeness. The latter of April is the best season to plant them: they never thrive well when taken out of the woods, but are very prosperous when cultivated by seeds, though not of rapid growth for a few years.

### *A Sketch of the Botany of South Carolina and Georgia,* vol. 2, 1824
Stephen Elliott

ॐ *Ilex Opaca*

A very beautiful tree, growing in rich soils 30–40 feet in height and 1–2 feet in diameter, with a compact, dense, generally oblong head. . . . This is one of our most ornamental trees; its bright deep green, perennial leaves, and the brilliant colour of its berries, which are on their pedicels generally until February, render it in the depths of our winter very conspicuous in our forest scenery. The wood is fine-grained, compact, hard, and is used by Cabinet-Makers and Turners in many of their fabrications.

## *The Horticulturist,* 1855

P. Barry and J. Jay Smith, Editors

❧ THE HOLLY (*Ilex opaca*). Among the neglected evergreens of our country, the American Holly stands conspicuous, both for its beauty at all seasons, its patience of the shears, and the red berry, valuable as it is for the eye, and acceptable to the winter birds. It is somewhat difficult to propagate from seed, but a little observation of its habit would overcome this.

## *Ladies' Southern Florist,* 1860

Mary Rion

❧ Holly

We have a fine native species, which is of slow growth, but is lovely even as a shrub. It is extremely difficult to transplant and establish. The best time to remove the plants from the woods is just before the buds begin to shoot. The smaller the plant the better the success in transplanting. . . . The native holly grows from twenty to forty feet high, and if not trimmed the lower limbs rest upon the ground, and the whole tree forms a beautiful symmetrical cone. In the fall it is covered with red berry fruit, which remain all winter.

---

## Ilex vomitoria

Yaupon Holly, Cassena Holly, South Sea Tea, Southern Tea Plant

Native to the eastern coastal plains from southeastern Virginia to Florida and westward to Texas, yaupon holly (often referenced incorrectly in historical accounts as cassena holly) is a large, multi-stemmed, evergreen shrub or small tree with an upright, oval form. Reaching a height of twenty-five to thirty feet, yaupon holly is characterized by smooth gray bark and small, white, inconspicuous flowers that appear in late spring, followed by shiny red berries in fall. American Indians used the plant's dark, blue green leaves (which contain more caffeine than any other North American plant) to prepare a strong brew that was used during ceremonial rituals to cause regurgitation, thus giving rise to the plant's species name, *vomitoria*. Early settlers also used leaves of the plant to make a mild drink called yaupon tea.

Yaupon holly was first introduced into England in 1700. While its leaves were exported from Carolina to Britain in the eighteenth century, the practice was discontinued because of the growing competition that resulted from the importation of Asian tea. American colonists discovered that yaupon holly was a good hedge plant that could be used as a substitute for boxwood. Dr. Alexander Garden (1728–1791) of Charleston, South Carolina, observed that yaupon "makes a very good and most beautiful hedge and may be kept as short and neat as Box." Yaupon holly was first offered for sale by an American nursery when listed in the 1783 edition of *Bartram's Catalogue of American Trees, Shrubs and Herbaceous Plants.* This native holly proved to be a popular plant in antebellum gardens of the lower and middle South, where it was used for formal hedges, topiary, or as a specimen plant.

*Ilex vomitoria* (yaupon holly)

### *A New Voyage to Carolina*, 1709
John Lawson

ᔰ Last of Bushes . . . is the famous *Yapon*, of which I find two sorts, if not three. I shall
speak first of the Nature of this Plant, and afterwards account for the different Sorts.
This *Yapon*, call'd by the South–*Carolina Indians*, *Cassena*, is a Bush, that grows chiefly
on the Sand-Banks and Islands, bordering on the Sea of Carolina; on the Coast it is
plentifully found. . . . It grows the most like Box, of any Vegetable [plant] that I know,
being very like it in Leaf, only dented exactly like Tea, but the Leaf somewhat fat-
ter. I cannot say, whether it bears any Flower, but a Berry it does, about the Bigness
of a Grain of Pepper, being first red, then brown when ripe, which is in December;
Some of the bushes grow to be twelve Foot high, others are three or four. . . .

The third Sort has the same kind of Leaf, but never grows a Foot high, and is
found both in rich, low Land, and on the Sand-Hills. I don't know that ever I found
any Seed, or Berries on the dwarfish Sort.

### *A Sketch of the Botany of South Carolina and Georgia*, vol. 2, 1824
Stephen Elliott

ᔰ Ilex vomitoria (*Cassena*)

This is a handsome shrub, although its flowers are not conspicuous. It forms neat
hedges, but not sufficiently strong to resist hogs and cattle, they are therefore used
as ornamentals along the borders of gardens.

Grows in loose soils, very abundantly near the ocean. A strong decoction of this
plant is used by the tribes of the Creek Indians at the opening of their councils.
They send annually to the sea-coast for a supply of the leaves. It acts as a mild emetic,

hence its name, given it in the Hortus Kewensis (vomitoria). It is universally known in this country as the Cassena, its old and appropriate name.

### The Southern Cultivator, 1856

Daniel Lee and Dennis Redmond, Editors

〜 The Yaupon, or Southern Tea Plant

Leaves of the Yaupon, when collected in August or September, carefully dried in the shade, and put up in air-tight canisters, are, when made into tea of proper strength for table use, not inferior to the tea we fine in market. Some people like it better, and certainly it exerts a less deleterious influence on the vital forces. . . . In Florida, New Orleans, Mobile, and many other points along the Southern Coast, it has been long known and esteemed by the Indians and poor people as the best remedy for yellow fever.

### The American Cotton Planter, 1855

N. B. Cloud, Editor

〜 [From the *Natchez Daily Courier*, October 28, 1854]

There is another Holly, a native of the South, and an evergreen, that is very generally overlooked. It is more commonly planted about Mobile than anywhere else. This is the *Ilex vomitoria*. The growth is slender, leaves small and numerous, and in winter the plant is covered with bright scarlet berries.

Thomas Affleck

---

## Illicum parviflorum

Yellow Anise, Yellow Anise Tree, Starry Anise

*Illicum parviflorum*, or yellow anise is native to southern Georgia and northern Florida. It is a large, evergreen shrub with an upright, pyramidal form and reaches an average height of eight to ten feet. Yellow anise is well known for its large, olive green, lanceolate leaves that emit a pleasant anise-like fragrance when crushed or bruised. Small inconspicuous, yellow green flowers (no larger than half an inch wide) appear in May and June, followed in late summer by small capsules containing tiny seed arranged in a pinwheel fashion.

William Bartram first discovered *Illicum parviflorum* in Florida while accompanying his father on a plant expedition in 1766. On January 24, 1766, John Bartram noted in his diary: "Near here [Jackson Spring] my son found a lovely sweet tree, with leaves like the Sweet Bay, which smelled like sassafras, and produces a very strange kind of seed-pod, but the seed was all shed, the severe frost had not hurt it; some of them grew 20 feet high, a charming bright evergreen aromatic." André Michaux, the noted French botanist, later found *Illicum parviflorum* in the same location in 1788. Michaux provided a description of the plant in *Flora Boreali-Americana* (1803), the first comprehensive guide to the flora of North America. Michaux likely distributed seeds and

*Illicium parviflorum* (yellow anise)

plants of this handsome evergreen from his botanic garden in Charleston, South Carolina, for Stephen Elliott noted in 1824 in his *Sketch of the Botany of South Carolina and Georgia* that "this plant, originally, I believe, from the banks of St. John's East, Florida, is now common in our gardens, and is almost naturalized."

*Illicum parviflorum* first arrived in Europe in 1789 when Michaux sent seeds to France where it was cultivated in the Jardin des Plantes. A year later in 1790, *Illicum* was introduced into England. This native shrub was first offered for sale by an American nursery when listed in Bartram's *1823 Catalogue of Trees, Shrubs and Herbaceous Plants. Illicum parviflorum* found wide appeal as an ornamental in antebellum gardens of the lower and middle South, where it was highly prized for its evergreen foliage, aromatic leaves, vigorous growth, tolerance of heat and drought, and ability to thrive in both sun and shade.

### A Sketch of the Botany of South Carolina and Georgia, vol. 2, 1824
Stephen Elliott

⁓ *Illicum parviflorum*—A handsome shrub, growing sometimes 6–10 feet high, remarkable for its bright, smooth, perennial leaves. . . . This plant, originally, I believe, from the branch of St. John's East-Florida, is now common in our gardens, and is almost naturalized. Flowers May–June.

### Arboretum Et Fruticetum Britannicum, 1838
John Claudius Loudon

⁓ *Illicum parviflorum*—The small-flowered Illicum . . . is a low evergreen shrub, or rather bush, highly aromatic in every part when in a growing state, but the scent soon evaporates from every part of the plant after it is gathered, except from the fruit, the scent of which becomes even more fragrant, and more penetrating, when it is dry. . . . In Florida it forms a compact evergreen bush from 8 feet to 10 feet high. . . . The bark has exactly the flavor of the sassafras root, and the dried fruit is used for scenting linens.

### The American Flower Garden Directory, 1839
Robert Buist

⁓ *Illicums*, Anise-seed Tree, three species. *I. floridanum* has very sweet-scented, double purple flowers, and the plant grows freely and systematically if properly treated, and deserves special attention. *I. parviflorum* has small yellow flowers; *I. anisatum* is so very like *I. parviflorum* in every respect to make us conclude they are the same, were *I. anisatum* not a native of China, and the other two natives of Florida. When the leaves and capsules of either of them are rubbed, they have a very strong smell; they grow very freely.

### Botany of the Southern States, 1856
John Darby, A. M.

⁓ *Illicium parviflorum*. In this country, the Illicums are used only as ornamentals, but they are used in other countries as aromatics, stimulants, and carminatives. In China they are burnt in the temples. In Europe they are used in giving a peculiar flavor to certain liquors. They are easily propagated by layers.

## Jasminum nudiflorum

Winter Jasmine, January Jasmine

Native to China, *Jasminum nudiflorum* is commonly known as winter jasmine. It is a deciduous shrub with a low, mounding form distinguished by small ovate leaflets on long, arching branches. A somewhat nondescript shrub during most of the year, it is the plant's brilliant, yellow flowers, which occur during the cold, gray days of winter, that make winter jasmine a treasured addition to the garden.

First discovered in China by Dr. Alexander von Bunge in 1830, *Jasminum nudiflorum* went unnoticed until Robert Fortune introduced it into England in 1844 from the nurseries and gardens of Shanghai. Fortune described this new exotic as "a very ornamental dwarf shrub . . . perfectly hardy in this country. It is deciduous; the leaves falling off in its native country early in autumn, and leaving a number of prominent flower buds, which expand in early spring, often when the snow is on the ground." Winter jasmine soon became a popular ornamental in English gardens, not only as a specimen shrub but also as a wall plant.

Winter jasmine arrived in North America in the middle of the nineteenth century, and was first offered for sale by an American nursery when listed in Prince's *1855 Select Catalogue of Fruit and Ornamental Trees and Plants*. Although winter jasmine arrived late in the antebellum period, it soon became a favorite in southern gardens where it was highly prized for its interesting evergreen branches and bright yellow flowers in late winter and early spring.

*Jasminum nudiflorum* (winter jasmine)

### *The American Flower Garden Directory,* 1839
Robert Buist

ᔓ *Jasminum nudiflorum*, flowers large, bright golden yellow, a new and desirable species from Japan, flowers very early in spring.

### *The Southern Cultivator,* 1856
Daniel Lee and Dennis Redmond, Editors

ᔓ *Jasminum nudiflorum*, the very earliest blooming shrub in our latitude. Even pretty severe frosts do not hurt the bright yellow flowers which appear in February. It is a climbing shrub.

Robert Nelson, Macon, Georgia

### *The Horticulturist,* 1859
J. Smith, Editor

ᔓ *Jasminum nudiflorum*

This out-door, winter blooming plant makes a sensation wherever it is introduced. No garden should be without it. . . . It is a shrub with angular deep green trailing branches. Its leaves are shining deep green, and each consists of three sessile leaflets of an ovate form, which fall off early in the autumn, and are succeeded by large yellow scentless flowers. . . . It was considered at the time of its introduction that it would be an excellent addition to the greenhouse, by reason of its being a winter bloomer, and continuing in flower for a length of time. . . . It is, however, as an open-air that we waved direct attention to its merits. . . . Whether as growing in the common garden soil, trained on a trellis in front of the mansion, or in that part of a colonnade with a considerable roof protection, or rambling at will, the effect produced has been of the most charming and beautiful kind; the flowers, too, have been most useful in bouquets. . . . The time is not too distant, when not only every garden, but the sunny side of every cottage, will be enlivened and beautiful, during the dull months of winter, with the golden flowers of this charming plant.

## Juniperus virginiana

Red Cedar, Eastern Red Cedar

Native to the eastern and central United States, red cedar is the most widely distributed coniferous tree in North America. Red cedar, not a cedar at all in the botanical sense but a juniper, can reach a height of 100 feet or more. This long-lived evergreen exhibits a

*Juniperus virginiana* (eastern red cedar)

diversity in growth habit and landscape form. In its early stages of development, red cedar is characterized by a compact, pyramidal form, while at maturity it develops a broad, irregular shape with a graceful crown. In addition to a variety of landscape uses during the antebellum period, red cedar was also prized for its aromatic and durable wood, which was used in making pencils, fence posts, water pipes, and furniture.

Red cedar was imported to England from North America in 1664, and was first offered for sale by a North American nursery when listed in William Prince's *1771 Broadside*. Thereafter, it was consistently listed in American nursery catalogues through the first half of the nineteenth century. As a landscape plant, it was used as a specimen in ornamental groves, clipped into formal hedges, or frequently planted as an avenue tree. Red cedar's extensive use as an avenue tree was based on its strong vertical character which replicated the formal effect of the Italian cypress that many southerners observed and admired when making the grand tour of Europe.

### *The American Cotton Planter,* 1855

N. B. Cloud, Editor

☞ [From the *Natchez (Miss.) Daily Courier,* October 28, 1854]

The Junipers, headed by our own beautiful native, the so-called Red Cedar, (*J. virginiana*) are indispensable. In the "Red Cedar" there is a great diversity of foliage and habit of growth; some being open and loose in habit, others upright and compact. The latter I have always selected from the seed-bed. They should have room to grow, and be allowed to sweep the ground with their branches; not pruned up into the likeness of a giant broom!

Thomas Affleck

*A Journey in the Seaboard Slave States,* **1856**

Frederick Law Olmsted

ॐ Public Grounds—The Red Cedar

The Grounds about the Capitol [Washington] are naturally admirable, and have lately been improved with neatness and taste. . . . Near the town, I saw a group of exceedingly beautiful trees, having the lovely green and all the lightness, gracefulness and beauty of foliage, in the Winter, of the finest deciduous trees. I could not believe until I came near them, that they were what I found them to be—our common *red cedar* (Juniperus virginiana) flattened at the top like the Cedar of Lebanon, and with a light and slightly drooping spray, deliciously delicate and graceful.

*The Southern Cultivator,* **1856**

Daniel Lee and Dennis Redmond, Editors

ॐ *Juniperus virginiana,* (red cedar).—Common all over America, and nevertheless, a common favorite. A hedge of Red Cedar is always admired, and when grown into trees, they form excellent and elegant shade trees.

Robert Nelson, Macon, Georgia

*Garden and Forest,* **1895**

C. S. Sargent

ॐ The Red Cedar

The Red Cedar can be made to take the place in formal gardens of the Cypress, to which the gardens of Southern Europe owe so much of their charm, and which cannot be grown in our severe climate. If it is desirable to produce certain effects in a garden by the use of trees that are formal in outline, the Red Cedar will produce this effect better than any other. . . . The Red Cedar is a long-lived and hardy tree, and if any man has a fancy to plant for posterity or to preserve his memory in a tree, there are few trees that he can plant with greater assurance of obtaining the object of his ambition.

## Kalmia latifolia

Mountain Laurel, Calico Bush, Spoon-Wood

*Kalmia latifolia,* commonly known as mountain laurel, is native to the eastern United States. Its scientific name was given by Linnaeus to honor Peter Kalm, who on behalf of the Swedish government, explored eastern North America from 1748 to 1751. This handsome evergreen shrub is characterized by glossy, lustrous leaves and clusters of bell-shaped flowers that bloom in May and June. Mountain laurel flowers are white to pink with purple markings, similar to calico prints, giving rise to one of the plant's common names, calico bush. While normally reaching an average height of four to five feet, older specimens often become treelike in appearance with irregular shaped branches and an interesting picturesque form. American Indians used the wood of the mountain laurel to fashion spoons and other domestic utensils.

Peter Collinson introduced mountain laurel into England in 1734. It became one of the most popular American shrubs grown in British gardens. George Washington grew mountain laurel as an ornamental, and Thomas Jefferson requested this American native from John Bartram "as a gift for a friend in Paris." Mountain laurel was first offered for sale by an American nursery in 1783 when listed in *Bartram's Catalogue of American Trees, Shrubs and Herbaceous Plants*. Greatly admired for its handsome foliage and beautiful flowers, mountain laurel was grown as a prized ornamental in antebellum gardens of the middle and upper South, though it was difficult to transplant and required many years to bloom when grown from seed.

*Kalmia latifolia* (mountain laurel)

### The North American Sylva, 1819
François André Michaux

❧ *Kalmia latifolia*—Mountain Laurel
I have no where seen it more profusely multiplied, nor of a greater height and more luxuriant vegetation, than in North Carolina, on the loftiest part of the Alleghenies. . . . The flowers are distinct of odor . . . in general they are of a beautiful rose colour and sometimes of a pure white. They are always numerous, and their brilliant effort is heightened by their richness of the surrounding foliage, hence the shrub is in great request for embellishment of gardens.

### A Sketch of the Botany of South Carolina and Georgia, vol. 1, 1821
Stephen Elliott

❧ *Kalmia latifolia*
A shrub 4–12 feet high, with branches very crooked and irregular. . . . This is probably the most ornamental shrub in the forests of North America. The foliage is handsome and perennial, and its flowers, which are produced in great profusion are no less elegant in their form than beautiful in their color. They possess however no fragrance, and the leaves are said to be deleterious to animals. Flowers April.

### The Flower Garden, 1851
Joseph Breck

❧ *Kalmia latifolia*—Mountain Laurel, Spoon Wood &c.—Among the shrubs that embellish the scenery of the interior of the country, this may be considered one of the most elegant. . . . The leaves are about three or four inches long, evergreen, giving much life to the forest in the winter, by their deep shining-green. The flowers are disposed in large corymbs, at the extremity of the branches; numerous, of a pure white, blush, or a beautiful rose-color, and more rarely a deep red. . . . There is no shrub, foreign or native, that will exceed this in splendor, when well grown.

### *The Southern Cultivator,* 1856

Daniel Lee and Dennis Redmond, Editors

↬ *Kalmia latifolia* (Calico Bush, Poison Ivy Bush)

No wonder Linnaeus, the great botanist, fell into ecstasy on beholding the first specimen of this flower, sent to him from America, for surely it was one of nature's masterpieces. The splendid pinkish white flowers possess an elegance which art has in vain tried to imitate; they are plentifully produced among foliage of the deepest, richest green.

Robert Nelson, Macon, Georgia

## Kerria japonica pleniflora

(*Corchorus japonicus, Corchorus japonica, Rubus japonicus*)
Kerria, Japanese Globe Flower, Double-Flowered Kerria

Native to China and Japan, *Kerria japonica pleniflora* was named in honor of William Kerr, an eighteenth-century plant collector for Kew Gardens. This attractive ornamental is a medium-sized, deciduous shrub with an upright, spreading form, with oval leaves that have serrated edges and distinctive veins throughout. *Kerria japonica pleniflora* is best known for its small, golden yellow flowers and multiple, reedlike stems, which remain green year-around.

Double-flowering Kerria was introduced from China into England in 1804. By 1830, according to John Claudius Loudon, it "was so common as to be found [in London] in the gardens of even labourer's cottages." It was not until 1834 that the single-flowering variety (*Kerria japonica*) made its way into England when introduced by John Reeves, a tea inspector for the East India Company and an agent for the London Horticultural Society.

*Kerria japonica pleniflora* was first offered for sale by an American nursery when listed in Bartram's *1814 Catalogue of Trees, Shrubs and Herbaceous Plants.* Some thirty years later, the single-flowering species was listed in Prince's *1844 Descriptive Catalogue of Fruit and Ornamental Trees, Shrubbery, Vines, and Plants.* In antebellum gardens of the middle and upper South, double-flowering kerria proved a popular ornamental, being highly prized for its glorious display of golden, springtime flowers and interesting branches that remained green throughout winter months.

*Kerria japonica pleniflora* (Kerria)

### *A Short Treatise on Horticulture,* 1828

William Prince

↬ *Japan Globe Flower,* or *Corchorus japonicus.*—This elegant shrub, which is one of the most hardy ever introduced into this country, was first treated as a tender plant. It will attain to the height of seven or eight feet, forming numerous slender shoots from the ground, with delicate branches near their summit; the shoals are green even in the depth of winter, and at the first of spring numerous flowers spring out at every joint, forming each of these long slender shoots into a wreath of bloom; these flowers are bright yellow and double, each resembling a double yellow rose, and it may be ranked among the most beautiful and highly ornamental shrubs that have ever been seen in our country. After the profuse flowering which takes place early in spring, occasional scattered ones will be produced during summer, towards the conclusion of which there will be a considerable show of flowers, but far less abundant than in the spring. This shrub is of the most easy culture, and will thrive in any common garden soil without care after being once planted, and will throw up numerous young plants from roots.

### The Southern Cultivator, 1857
Daniel Lee and Dennis Redmond, Editors

᠍ Ornamental Trees and Shrubs for the South

*Kerria japonica*, also called *Corchrus japonicus*, from Japan. Though quite common, still it is very ornamental in the early spring when loaded with its bright yellow flowers, beautifully contrasting with the dark, glossy green stems and foliage. As the young shoots bloom better than old ones, the shrub should be pruned often and severely. Six feet high. Propagated by suckers.

Robert Nelson, Fruitland Nurseries, Augusta, Georgia

### The Flower Garden, 1851
Joseph Breck

᠍ *Kerria japonica*, formerly *Corchorus japonica.*—Japan Globe Flower. This is an elegant shrub, growing three or four feet high, producing a profusion of double yellow globular flowers, from June to September. The branches are bright deep-green; the foliage handsome. It is a little tender in some locations, the tops being frequently killed down; but it sends up fresh shoots, which flower the same season. It is easily propagated by suckers.

---

## Lagerstroemia indica

(*Lagerstroemia chinensis*)
Crape Myrtle, Indian Lilac

Native to China, *Lagerstroemia indica* occurs as a large shrub or as a small, multi-stemmed tree with an upright form, rounded canopy, and ovate, privetlike leaves. Carolus Linnaeus, the Swedish botanist, named the genus, *Lagerstroemia*, in honor of Magnus von Lagerstroem (1696–1759), a fellow naturalist and director of the Swedish East India Trading Company. The species name, *indica*, refers to the plant's place of origin at a time when the Orient and all of eastern Asia were referenced as India or the East Indies. Reaching a height of fifteen to twenty feet, this handsome ornamental is best known for its sculptured stems, exfoliating bark, and showy clusters of brightly colored blossoms, which range in colors from white, pink, and purple to watermelon red. The plant's showy flower clusters occur throughout summer, followed by brown seed pods that persist throughout the winter months.

*Lagerstroemia indica* was introduced into England in 1759, but never proved popular because of its failure to bloom freely in the English climate. It is believed that the crape myrtle arrived in North America by way of France when André Michaux, the French botanist, introduced this Asian native into Charleston, South Carolina, around 1786. Historical records indicate that in 1799, George Washington received crape myrtle seeds from the East Indies, making him one of the earliest American gardeners to cultivate this exotic ornamental. The crape myrtle was first offered for sale by an American nursery when listed in Bartram's *1807 Catalogue of Trees, Shrubs and Herbaceous Plants. Lagerstroemia indica* was grown extensively in gardens of the antebellum South. It was highly prized for its profusion of summer flowers and tolerance of heat and summer drought. Today, the crape myrtle remains one of the showiest and most popular summer ornamentals in the southern states.

### *A Treatise on the Cultivation of Ornamental Flowers,* 1828
Roland Green

↝ Lagerstroemia indica—A flowering shrub, which endures the Winters of the Middle and Southern States —in Massachusetts it must be treated like the hydrangea, but its beauty will repay the attention.

### *The Magazine of Horticulture,* 1855
C. M. Hovey, Editor

↝ The Hardy Shrubs of the South
*Lagerstroemia indica* is the finest, and stands our winters well; indeed, it is hardy several degrees north of this; grows almost to a tree, flowering very freely in May, June, and July.
Andrew Gray, Savannah, Georgia

### *The Southern Cultivator,* 1857
Daniel Lee and Dennis Redmond, Editors

↝ Ornamental Trees and Shrubs for the South
*Lagerstroemia indica.* When this tree was first introduced from East India to Europe, nearly a hundred years ago, it created quite a sensation among horticulturists, and even now it is highly appreciated in the north. Notwithstanding it is one of the most ornamental trees, still it is so common, as hardly to be valued. A white variety is much looked for, and would be quite an acquisition, but has not yet been discovered.
Robert Nelson, Fruitland Nurseries,
Augusta, Georgia

*Lagerstroemia indica* (crape myrtle)

### *Ladies' Southern Florist,* 1860
Mary Rion

↝ Lagerstroemia, or Crape Myrtle
This may be readily grown by cuttings or suckers. No particular pains are necessary in the culture. It is improved by close winter pruning, and should be pruned only in the winter. Cut away the wood of last year to within two or three eyes of the

wood of the preceding year. By this plan you will secure the finest and largest spikes of flowers.

## Laurus nobilis

Roman Laurel, Bay Laurel, Poet's Laurel

Native to the Mediterranean region, *Laurus nobilis* is an ancient garden shrub that has been revered throughout history. During Greek and Roman times, boughs of laurel were used to make crowns for the heads of heroes, and in the middle ages, laurel branches were fashioned into wreaths to honor distinguished poets, hence the expression, poet laureate. For centuries, the plant's aromatic leaves have been used for medicinal purposes and for culinary seasoning.

*Laurus nobilis* (Roman laurel)

A large, slow-growing, evergreen shrub with an upright, irregular form, Roman laurel reaches an average height of ten to fifteen feet. The plant's handsome, evergreen foliage is its primary asset. It is bright green in color, highly aromatic, and easily clipped or sheared into formal shapes or hedges. Roman laurel produces inconspicuous yellowish flowers that are followed by small succulent fruit, dark blue in color.

It is believed that Roman laurel arrived in England around 1548 and, shortly thereafter, became a popular topiary plant for tubs and containers or was grown as a formal, evergreen hedge. Roman laurel was first offered for sale by an American nursery when David and Cuthbert Landreth of Philadelphia listed this treasured ornamental in the firm's *1811 Catalogue* as a greenhouse plant. Roman laurel was frequently grown in antebellum gardens of the lower and middle South, where it was highly prized for its beautiful, evergreen foliage and aromatic leaves.

***A Treatise on the Cultivation of Ornamental Flowers,* 1828**
  Roland Green

  ✧ Sweet Bay (*Laurus nobilis*) is a very pretty evergreen shrub—well calculated to stand (in a large pot) in the parlor during winter. Propagated by suckers.

***Arboretum et Fruiticetum Britannicum,* 1838**
  John Claudius Loudon

✧ An evergreen tree, or rather enormous shrub . . . displaying a tendency to throw up suckers. The leaves are evergreen, and a firm texture, they have an agreeable smell and an aromatic . . . slightly bitter taste. . . . In the age of Roman greatness, this tree was considered as the emblem of victory—the victorious generals were crowned with it in their triumphant processions.

***The Southern Cultivator,* 1850**
  Daniel Lee and Dennis Redmond, Editors

*↬ Laurus nobilis* (Sweet Bay, Sweet Laurel)

    The only evergreen species to be recommended for our gardens. The flowers are yellowish white, rather indifferent, but the foliage has an aromatic fragrance. The dried leaves are quite an article of commerce in Europe, being used for seasoning meat, to which they impart a very pleasant flavor. The Sweet Laurel grows finely on a gravelly clay soil, and gives many suckers, by which, as well as by layers, it is propagated. 10 to 12 feet high.

### Report of the Commissioner of Patents, 1854

    Charles Mason, Commissioner

*↬* Trees and Shrubs Usually Employed for Hedges

    Laurel or Sweet Bay (*Laurus nobilis*)

    An evergreen shrub, native of the south of Europe, always displaying a tendency to throw up suckers, and rarely, if ever, assuming a tree-like character, without the aid of art. As it forms a dense conical bush, when not trained to a single stem, it is well adapted for an ornamental hedge. It is so tenacious of life that a root or stump of it will often send up suckers two years after it has appeared to be dead. It is too tender for the Northern and perhaps for the Middle portions of the Union.

## Ligustrum vulgare

Common Privet, European Privet, Prim

*Ligustrum vulgare* (common privet)

Native to Europe, North Africa, and western Asia, common privet is a deciduous to semievergreen shrub that has an upright, irregular shape and numerous arching branches. This hardy shrub is characterized by dark green leaves and creamy-white flowers that occur in late May and June. Flowers of common privet produce a strong aroma that many consider unpleasant. Black berries appear in late September and remain on the plant until early spring. Although not highly prized as an ornamental today, common privet has long been used for hedges because of its compact growth, dark green color, and small leaves, which are not disfigured by clipping.

    Arriving in North America from Europe during the colonial period, common privet became naturalized in many eastern seaboard states by the end of the eighteenth century. So prevalent was this invasive shrub that André Michaux, the French botanist, mistook it as being native to America and included it in his monumental work, *Flora Borlei Americana* (1803), the first comprehensive guide to North American flora.

    Common privet was first offered by an American nursery when listed in Bartram's *1807 Catalogue of Trees, Shrubs and Herbaceous Plants*. Early nurseries sold many varieties, including plants with variations in leaf size, berry color, and growth habit. Catalogue listings included evergreen, myrtle-leaved, and box-leaved varieties. Common privet was sometimes used as an edging material in parterre gardens of the antebellum South when summer heat and humidity prohibited the use of box.

### A Short Treatise on Horticulture, 1828
William Prince

❧ *Privet*, or *Prim-Ligustrum vulgare*—This shrub is generally known, and was formerly greatly cultivated for hedges in this country, and is still so in many parts of Europe. The hedges formed of it are beautiful in the extreme, arising from its myrtle-like foliage, and its abundant clusters of berries in autumn and winter. . . . When planted separately, as ornamental shrubs, they have an interesting appearance, and it is only their being common which causes them to be less often used for this purpose. . . . The Privet will thrive even beneath the shade and drip of trees, and amid the smoke and confinement of cities. . . . It has been wrongly considered by some as a native of this country, to which it was long since introduced from Europe.

### The New American Orchardist, 1833
William Kenrick

❧ PRIM or PRIVET. *Ligustrum vulgare*
   A sub-evergreen, rising eight or ten feet; the leaves are lanceolate of a very dark green like the myrtle; the flowers are white; the berries black, in large clusters. The plant forms a beautiful hedge. Variegated Leaved Privet (*L. variegatum*). The leaves of this variety late in autumn are botched with a bright gold color. *Chinese Privet* (*L. sinensis*). A variety with leaves of the same dark green as the preceding, but of much larger size.

### The Young Gardener's Assistance, 1837
Thomas Bridgeman

❧ *Ligustrum vulgare, virens.* Large European Privet, a very handsome evergreen shrub, flowering in great profusion, producing bunches of black round berries. It bears clipping well, and is therefore well calculated for hedges, or to enclose ornamental plantations. It grows quickly, and is well adapted to our climate, and when planted in a hedge-row, and kept clipped, it makes a beautiful hedge, and ought to be in more general use.

### The Horticulturist, 1847/1848
Andrew Jackson Downing, Editor

❧ Privet. (*Ligustrum vulgare*). Common as the privet is, still it is one of the most valuable things for general shrubbery planting. Its white flowers are pretty, and its foliage, which hangs on till December, is thick and of a good color. It will grow in any situation, open, or under trees, etc. It will, therefore, be found valuable for thickening up shrubby plantations, concealing unsightly banks, and many other purposes. No plant is more easily grown from cuttings.

## Lonicera fragrantissima
### Winter Honeysuckle, Breath of Spring

Native to China, winter honeysuckle is a deciduous to semievergreen mounding shrub that grows six to eight feet in height. The genus *Lonicera* commemorates Adam Lonicer, a German botanist who died in 1596, and the species name *fragrantissima* is Latin for fragrant, a reference to the plant's highly scented flowers. The plant is characterized by stiff, leathery leaves, blue green in color, which are arranged in pairs along slender arching branches. Small creamy-white flowers bloom in late winter before new foliage appears. Tiny red berries, which appear in late May and early June, are eagerly devoured by birds. The true glory of winter honeysuckle is its wonderfully fragrant flowers, which begin to open in late January, heralding the promise of spring. Its blossoms are extremely fragrant, and a small spray brought indoors will perfume an entire room.

Although Robert Fortune introduced winter honeysuckle into England in 1845, it was several years before this Asian native made its way into North American gardens. The first listing of winter honeysuckle in an American nursery catalogue apparently was in Prince's *1860 Catalogue of Fruit Trees and Ornamental Trees and Shrubs.* Although winter honeysuckle arrived late in the antebellum period, it soon became widely distributed throughout the South, and it has remained a perennial favorite in southern gardens.

### The Horticulturist, 1853

P. Barry, Editor

ॐ Foreign Notices. *Lonicera fragrantissima*

A sub-evergreen hardy shrub. Flowers whitish, very sweet scented. Native of China, . . . this is one of the plants obtained from China by Mr. Fortune, while in the service of the Horticultural Society. . . . In January last it blossomed in the garden of the Marquis of Salisbury at Hatfield [England], whence Mr. William Ingram, the gardener there, sent us specimens, with the following note, . . . "The plant which affords me these flowers has been in bloom since January. . . . The flowers appear with the earliest development of the leaves, and although not large, compensate for any deficiency by their exceeding fragrance, combining the richness of the perfume of orange blossoms with the delicious sweetness of the honeysuckle."

*Lonicera fragrantissima* (winter honeysuckle)

## Lonicera japonica

(*Nintova japonica, Nintova longifolia, Lonicera japonica, Flexuosa*)
Japanese Honeysuckle

Native to eastern Asia and widely naturalized in the United States from New England to Florida and westward to Texas, Japanese honeysuckle is a vigorous, woody climber with leaves that remain green all winter long. Japanese honeysuckle is best known for its highly fragrant flowers, which are produced in great profusion in May and June and intermittently through summer and fall. The flowers of *Lonicera japonica* are white in color, sometimes tinged with pink or purple, becoming yellow or golden with age, a characteristic that prompted the Chinese to name it the "plant with golden and silver flowers." Small lustrous black berries are produced in late summer, except on plants growing in extreme shade.

William Kerr introduced Japanese honeysuckle into England in 1806. It was adaptable to the English climate, but Japanese honeysuckle was never grown extensively in British gardens. First offered for sale by an American nursery when listed in William Prince's *1823 Catalogue of Fruit and Ornamental Trees and Plants*, this woody vine soon became popular in gardens of the antebellum South. With its evergreen foliage and highly scented flowers, Japanese honeysuckle was often used to adorn porches, fences, and walls. Seldom grown in southern gardens today because of its vigorous and uncontrolled nature, this rampant climber remains an integral part of the southern landscape—each spring filling the fields and forests with its unforgettable fragrance.

### *The American Flower Garden Directory,* 1839
Robert Buist

*Lonicera japonica* (Japanese honeysuckle)

ℑ *Lonicera japonica.* There is a plant in our collections known by that name which is now *Nintova longiflora;* flowers of a straw-colour, but come out white. It has been known to withstand the winter, but does not flower, and is much esteemed in the South for its fragrance.

### *The Horticulturist,* 1848/1849
Andrew Jackson Downing, Editor

ℑ There are two very favorite climbers that belong properly to the middle states, as they are a little tender, and need protection to the north or east. One of them is the Japan Honeysuckle (*Lonicera japonica, flexuosa*), the species with very dark, half ever-green leaves, and a profusion of lovely delicate white and fawn coloured blossoms. Itis the queen of all honeysuckles for cottage walls, or veranda pillars; its foliage is always so rich; it is entirely free from the white aphis (which is the pest of the old sorts), and it blooms (as soon as the plant gets strong) nearly the whole summer—affording a perpetual feast of beauty and fragrance.

### *The Florist's Guide,* 1850
Thomas Bridgeman

ℑ *Lonicera japonica,* or Japanese Honeysuckle. This bears flowers in great profusion, which are white, afterwards becoming of a light yellow. It is not so hardy as the Chinese, and requires a little protection in the Winter.

### *The Southern Cultivator,* 1856
Daniel Lee and Dennis Redmond, Editors

ℑ *Lonicera japonica,* also called Nintova japonica (Japan Honeysuckle).—A rampant climber, whose foliage retains its lively green color during the whole winter, consequently far preferred to the well known Chinese Honeysuckle (*Lonicera flexuosa*) which turns dark brown. The very fragrant white flowers are produced in profusion.

## Maclura pomifera

(*Maclura aurantiaca*)
Osage Orange, Hedge Apple, Bow Wood

*Maclura pomifera* is a large deciduous tree native to Texas, Oklahoma, Arkansas and parts of Louisiana, named in honor of William Maclure (1763–1840), a noted American geologist.

*Maclura pomifera* can reach a height of sixty feet or more. This American native is distinguished by a rounded canopy, large ovate leaves, spiny branches, and a short trunk with deeply furrowed bark. *Maclura pomifera* has been known by numerous common names, the most widely used is Osage orange, which is a reference to the plant's large, orange-like fruit that are generally four to five inches in diameter. The Osage Indians used the wood of the tree for making bows and its inner bark and sapwood to produce a yellow dye. American pioneers employed the curious fruit of the Osage orange as an effective repellent against cockroaches and other household pests.

Osage orange was first cultivated in the eastern United States when seeds were brought back from the Lewis and Clark Expedition (1803–1805) and distributed to Bernard M'Mahon and David Landreth, well known Philadelphia nurserymen. In the early part of the nineteenth century, the Osage orange was promoted as a fine hedge plant because of its stout thorns, ease of propagation, rapid growth, and tolerance of wind, heat, and drought. Hedges of Osage orange required annual pruning and were generally maintained about four-feet high. Osage orange was first offered for sale by an American nursery when listed in David and Cuthbert Landreth's *1824 Catalogue* as "Maclura aurantiaca—A splendid forest tree, the leaves of a beautiful shining green, and the fruit of a most singular appearance." In addition to being grown as a hedge plant, Osage orange was often planted during the antebellum period as a shade tree or as an ornamental for its decorative fruit.

### A Treatise on the Theory and Practice of Landscape Gardening, 1841

Andrew Jackson Downing

☞ The Osage Orange Tree—*Maclura*

As an ornamental tree, the Osage Orange is rather too loose in the disposition of its wide-spreading branches, to be called beautiful in this form. But the bright glossy hue of its foliage, and especially the unique appearance of a good-sized tree when covered with the large, orange-like fruit, render it one of the most interesting of our native trees. . . . On a small lawn, where but few trees are needed, and where it is desirable that the species employed should all be as distinct as possible, to give the whole as much variety as can be obtained in a limited space, such trees should be selected as well not only ornamental, but combine some other charm, association, or interest. Among such trees, we would by all means give the Osage Orange a foremost place. It has the additional recommendation of being a fine shade tree and of producing an excellent and durable wood.

*Maclura pomifera* (Osage orange)

*The Southern Cultivator,* 1852

Daniel Lee and Dennis Redmond, Editors

꙳ The Osage Orange

The trees are rapid growers, and their long limbs bend over, so as to bring their ends towards the ground, giving them much of a weeping habit. The foliage is glossy and dark and not unlike that of the Orange. On the lawn the trees are beautiful objects, contrasting finely with many erect growing varieties. . . .

It is impossible to conceive of a better material for a live fence than is this tree. Evergreens would be more beautiful, but we have none adapted to such a great variety of soil and climate, nor have we any which afford as perfect a defense against all intruders. While the wood is exceedingly hard, it is of rapid growth, and is thickly armed with thorns which are stout, sharp, and strong.

*The Horticulturist,* 1855

P. Barry and J. Jay Smith, Editors

꙳ Hedges

The Osage Orange (*Maclura aurantiaca*)—This plant has some very good qualities for the purpose, but it requires great attention—more, it has often been found, than the generality of busy farmers can afford to give to it; if neglected, it runs wild, loses its lower branches, which at the best must be interlaced after the first cuttings, or they will admit smaller animals. Another disadvantage is that it is a "greedy feeder," extends its roots far and wide. . . . The roots are also of an extraordinary size, frequently as large and thick as the wood above ground, where there is a determination to have it as a hedge and give it the proper yearly attentions it may do very well, but it is open to some objection.

## Magnolia denudata

(*Magnolia conspicua, Magnolia heptapeta*)
Yulan Magnolia, Chinese White Magnolia, Lily Tree

Native to central China, *Magnolia denudata* or yulan magnolia is a large deciduous shrub or small tree with an upright, spreading form, and large elliptical leaves. Reaching a height of thirty to forty feet, yulan magnolia is best known for its creamy-white, chalice-shaped flowers, which bloom in early spring—at a time when they are frequently damaged by a late freeze or frost.

Sir Joseph Banks introduced *Magnolia denudata* into England from China in 1789. In 1791, Engelbert Kaempfer (1651–1728), a physician with the Dutch East India Company, produced a series of early drawings that incorrectly portrayed *Magnolia denudata* as having purple flowers instead of white, a mistake that for many years led to confusion in its nomenclature. Following its introduction into Britain, the yulan magnolia was neglected as a garden plant, due to the mistaken belief that it could only be grown as a greenhouse plant. *Magnolia denudata* has the distinction of being one of the parents of the well-known hybrid, *Magnolia* × *soulangiana*, which Chevalier Soulange-Bodin developed in Paris in 1820 by crossing *Magnolia denudata* and *Magnolia liliflora*.

*Magnolia denudata* was first offered to American gardeners when listed in Bartram's *1814 Catalogue of Trees, Shrubs and Herbaceous Plants* as *Magnolia conspicua*. The yulan magnolia was grown in both northern and southern gardens during the antebellum period but never proved as popular as its more colorful counterpart, *Magnolia liliflora*.

### *A Short Treatise on Horticulture,* 1828
William Prince

↬ *Magnolia conspicua–Chandelier Magnolia,* or *Yulan*—This has very large flowers of a pure white colour, very splendid in appearance, and shaped like a chandelier. In the house it flowers in March, but will support our winters unprotected. A tree is mentioned by the London Horticultural Society as growing at the seat of Sir Abraham Hume, in England, which is 14 feet high, 15½ feet broad, and which produced 956 flowers in one season.

### *The Horticulturist,* 1847/1848
Andrew Jackson Downing, Editor

↬ Chinese White Magnolia. (*M. conspicua*) No doubt this must be admitted to be the most superb of all the large shrubs of our gardens. It is perfectly hardy; and a full grown plant will produce thousands of large, pure white, and fragrant flowers. As it blooms very early in the season, it should be planted near the house, with a few evergreens to back it.

### *Rural Essays,* 1853
Andrew Jackson Downing, Editor

↬ The Chinese white magnolia (*M. conspicua*) is, in the effect of its blossoms, the most charming of all magnolias. The flowers, in color a pure creamy white, are produced in such abundance that the tree, when pretty large, may be seen at a great distance. The Chinese name, Yulan, literally *lily tree*, is an apt and impressive one, as the blossoms are not much unlike those of the white lily in size and shape, when fully expanded. Among the Chinese poets, they are considered the emblem of candor and beauty.

### *The American Handbook of Ornamental Trees,* 1853
Thomas Meehan

↬ M. conspicua

Chinese magnolia; Yulan—Flowering in April. It is a native of China, where it is said to have been in cultivation over one thousand years; and well it deserves to be. Flowering in the greatest profusion, and at a season when there is nothing else in bloom, and the flowers, too, combining the fragrance of the lily with the beauty of the rose—what can be more desirable?

*Magnolia denudata* (yulan magnolia)

## Magnolia grandiflora
(*Magnolia foetida, Magnolia altissima*)
Southern Magnolia, Bull Bay, Laurel Bay, Big Laurel

Indigenous to the southeastern United States from North Carolina to Florida and westward to Texas, southern magnolia is considered one of the finest of American trees. Growing to a height of ninety to one hundred feet in its native environment, this stately evergreen has long been revered for its imposing size and outstanding beauty. A coarse-textured plant with large, glossy leaves (green on top and velvety brown beneath), the southern magnolia produces white, saucerlike flowers that occur in late May and June, filling the air with a delicate perfume. The genus *Magnolia* was named for Pierre Magnol, a French botanist, who was administrator of the Montpellier Botanic Garden from 1638 to 1715.

*Magnolia grandiflora* (southern magnolia)

Introduced into England in 1734 "from Carolina," the southern magnolia was originally known as big laurel or bull bay. Dr. Alexander Garden (1728–1791) of Charleston, South Carolina, recognized this outstanding tree for its natural beauty and ornamental value, referring to it in 1757 as "the finest and most superb ever-green that the earth produced." George Washington is known to have planted the southern magnolia at Mount Vernon, and Thomas Jefferson wrote to a friend in Charleston, South Carolina, in 1786 requesting plants of *Magnolia grandiflora* for someone he was "very desirous of obliging." Southern magnolia was first offered for sale by an American nursery when listed in the 1783 edition of *Bartram's Catalogue of American Trees, Shrubs and Herbaceous Plants*. The southern magnolia was frequently planted in the gardens and groves of the antebellum South.

### The North American Sylva, 1819
François André Michaux

ॐ Of all the trees of North America, east of the Mississippi, the Big Laurel is the most remarkable for the majesty of its form, the magnificence of its foliage, and the beauty of its flowers. . . . The flowers of the Big Laurel are white, of an agreeable odor, and 7 or 8 inches broad. . . . Blooming in the midst of rich foliage, they produce so fine an effect, that those who have seen the tree on its native soil agree in considering it as one of the most beautiful productions of the vegetable kingdom.

### A Sketch of the Botany of South Carolina and Georgia, vol. 2, 1824
Stephen Elliott

ॐ This magnificent tree is almost too well known to need description. It rises sometimes 60, 70, or 80 feet in height, with a naked smooth columnar stem, and the head when not injured by accident is always regularly pyramidal, or semi-elliptical. From May to August in favorable situations it is almost always covered with its brilliant white flowers, terminating the young branches. The petals are large, oval, or obovate, abruptly narrowed at the base . . . of a brilliant white, but become instantly ferruginous, when scratched or bruised.

Andrew Jackson Downing

↜ The Large Evergreen Magnolia (M. Grandiflora) or Big Laurel, as it is sometimes
called, is peculiarly indigenous to that portion of our country south of North Carolina. . . . The leaves are evergreen, and somewhat resemble those of the laurel in
form, are generally six or eight inches in length. . . . The highly fragrant flowers are
composed of about six petals, opening in a wide cup-like form, of the most striking
whiteness of color. . . . At the nurseries of the Messrs. Landreth and at the Bartram
Botanic Garden of Col. Carr., near that city [Philadelphia], some good specimens of
the Magnolia and its varieties are growing thriftily.

### *The Southern Cultivator,* 1856

Daniel Lee and Dennis Redmond, Editors

↜ *Magnolia grandiflora*—The finest and most majestic evergreen tree of the South. It
often attains a height of 60 to 80 feet, its large white flowers of the size of a saucer,
filling the woods with delightful fragrance.

Robert Nelson, Macon, Georgia

## Magnolia liliflora

(*Magnolia purpurea, Magnolia obovata, Magnolia discolor, Magnolia quinquepeta*)
Lily-Flowered Magnolia, Purple Chinese Magnolia, Two Coloured Magnolia

Native to central China and widely grown in Japan, lily-flowered magnolia is a medium
to large deciduous shrub or small tree with a spreading and somewhat irregular shape.
Reaching a height of ten to twelve feet at maturity, *Magnolia liliflora* has dark green,
ovate leaves, four to eight inches long that when immature are downy on the underside.
This Asian native is best known for its colorful, lily-shaped blossoms that are dark purple

*Magnolia liliflora* (lily-flowered magnolia)

on the outside and white within. The plant's slightly fragrant flowers occur over a long time period, beginning in mid-March and continuing through spring.

A physician with the Dutch East India Company, Engelbert Kaempfer (1651–1728), first described *Magnolia liliflora* in 1712 and Carl Peter Thunberg (1775–1828) introduced it into England from Japan in 1790. Following its introduction, it quickly became a popular ornamental in British gardens. The lily-flowered magnolia not only has the distinction of being the first Asian species of magnolia with colored flowers to arrive in Europe, but it was also one of the parents of the hybrid species *Magnolia × soulangiana*, which the distinguished French horticulturist Chevalier Soulange-Bodin developed in Paris in 1820

Known by numerous botanical names throughout its history, lily-flowered magnolia was first offered for sale by an American nursery when listed in Bartram's *1807 Catalogue of Trees, Shrubs and Herbaceous Plants* as *Magnolia obovata*. This attractive ornamental proved hardy in northern and southern gardens of the antebellum period, during which time it was highly prized for its purple flowers and exotic character. *Magnolia liliflora* remained popular through the nineteenth century, but over time it was supplanted by many new hybrids with showier blossoms and more prolific flowers.

### *A Short Treatise on Horticulture,* 1828
William Prince

&#8667; *Magnolia obovata, or Chinese Purple Flowering Magnolia.*—This is esteemed for the uncommon richness and beauty of its flowers, which, in the house, are produced in March. They are bell shaped, of a delicate violet purple outside, and white within, from which circumstance it is sometimes called the Two Coloured Magnolia. It supports our winters unprotected in the vicinity of New York, and perhaps may do so further north.

### *Rural Essays,* 1853
Andrew Jackson Downing

&#8667; The Chinese magnolia—January, 1850

The purple Chinese Magnolia (*M. purpurea*) . . . is properly a shrub, some six or eight feet in its growth in this latitude. . . . Its flowers begin to open early in May, and on an old plant they continue blooming for six weeks, and indeed in a shaded situation, often for a considerable part of the summer. These blossoms are white within, of a fine, dark lilac or purple on the outside, and quite fragrant. . . . This is the oldest Chinese magnolia known here, having been brought from China to Europe in 1790—and it is now quite frequently seen in our gardens.

### *The Southern Cultivator,* 1857
Daniel Lee and Dennis Redmond, Editors

&#8667; *Magnolia*—Of all the deciduous species of this beautiful family, the M. conspicua, with large white, and M. obovata, with large purple flowers, are very ornamental in our gardens in March, when flowers are scarce. They are propagated by layers and suckers.

### *Ladies' Southern Florist,* 1860
Mary Rion

&#8667; Chinese Magnolia

This is a much more hardy species, and soon attains its full height, of six or eight feet. The flowers are lily-shaped, smaller than the Florida (*Magnolia grandiflora*) and of two colors, the white and the purple. When full grown it loses its lower branches, and assumes the appearance of an immense umbrella.

## Magnolia × soulangiana

Saucer Magnolia, Tulip Tree, Soulange's Magnolia

*Magnolia × soulangiana* is one of the most beautiful and well known of all deciduous magnolias. Chevalier Soulange-Bodin, a distinguished French horticulturist and founder of the National Horticultural Society of France, created this distinguished hybrid in 1820 by crossing *Magnolia yulan* with *Magnolia liliflora*. The event was documented in the 1827 transactions of the Linnaean Society of Paris: "By crossing of a Magnolia yulan (*Magnolia denudata*), grown from seed with the pollen of Magnolia discolor (*Magnolia liliflora*), the Fremont gardens have witnessed the birth, growth and establishment . . . of a new

hybrid which is remarkable for its tree-like habit, its handsome foliage and above all its widespread brilliant flowers. . . . My worthy colleagues have named this beautiful species *Magnolia soulangiana*."

A large, multi-stemmed, deciduous shrub or small tree with an upright, oval form and broadly elliptical leaves, *Magnolia × soulangiana* is greatly revered for its large, tulip-shaped flowers, which appear on leafless stems in late winter and early spring. Flowers of this spectacular ornamental are purplish or rose colored on the outside and white to pale-pink inside. As a result of its early blooming period, flowers of this exotic ornamental are frequently damaged by late frosts and freezes.

*Magnolia × soulangiana* was introduced into England around 1828 and arrived in North America shortly thereafter, first being offered by an American nursery when listed in Prince's *1831 Annual Catalogue of Fruit and Ornamental Trees and Plants*. Highly prized in gardens of the antebellum South, the popularity of *Magnolia × soulangiana* continued through the nineteenth century, attesting to the beauty and brilliant display of its springtime flowers.

### *A Treatise on the Theory and Practice of Landscape Gardening*, 1841

Andrew Jackson Downing

*Magnolia × soulangiana* (Saucer magnolia)

The foreign sorts introduced into our gardens from China, are the Chinese purple (*M. purpurea*), which produces an abundance of large delicate purple blossoms early in the season; the Yulan or Chinese White Magnolia (*M. conspicua*), a most abundant bloomer, bearing beautiful white, fragrant flowers in April, before the leaves appear; and the Soulange's Magnolia (*M. soulangiana*), a hybrid between the two foregoing, with large flowers delicately tinted with white and purple. These succeed well in sheltered situations, in our pleasure-grounds, and add greatly to their beauty early in the season.

## *The Horticulturist,* 1848

Andrew Jackson Downing, Editor

❧ Soulange's Magnolia (*M. soulangiana*). Flowers larger than the above (Chinese White Magnolia, M. conspicua), opening at ten days later, and equally beautiful, though of a pale purple without, and white within. It is also quite hardy; and both sorts should be found in every collection. They grow freely in any good soil but should be transplanted quite small. May.

## *Rural Essays,* 1853

Andrew Jackson Downing

❧ The next most ornamental Chinese magnolia is Soulange's purple (*M. Soulangiana*). This is a hybrid seedling. . . . The habit of the tree is closely similar to that of the Conspicua; its blossoms, equally numerous, are rather large, but the outside of the petals is finely tinged with purple. It partakes of the character of both its parents—having the growth of *Magnolia conspicua* [yulan magnolia], and the color of *Magnolia purpurea* [lily-flowered magnolia] (or indeed a lighter shade of purple). In terms of blooming is also midway between that of these two species, being about a week later than that of the white or Yulan Magnolia. It is also perfectly hardy in this latitude.

---

## Magnolia virginiana

*(Magnolia glauca)*
Sweetbay, Swamp Magnolia, White Bay

*Magnolia virginiana* (sweetbay)

Native to the coastal regions of the United States from Massachusetts to Florida and westward to Texas, sweetbay is a small, multi-stem tree growing to an average height of twenty to thirty feet. Sweetbay, or swamp magnolia as it is sometimes called, has smooth, gray bark and glossy, semievergreen foliage that is green on top and silvery gray beneath. When blown by the wind, the leaves create an interesting effect as they sparkle and glitter in the breeze. A member of the magnolia family, sweetbay is best known for its small, white, fragrant flowers, which are produced in late spring and early summer. Sweetbay's flowers are so highly scented that Peter Kalm, the Swedish naturalist, noted that when the wind was favorable, the fragrance of the flowers could be detected as far away as "three-quarters of an English mile."

John Bannister, an English missionary, introduced sweetbay into England in 1688. It has the distinction of being the first North American magnolia to arrive in the British Isles, and it became well known throughout Europe, long before other magnolia species arrived. William Cobbett, author of *The English Gardener,* described the flowers of sweetbay as "the most delightful that can be conceived, far exceeding that of the rose, in strength equaling the jasmine or tuberose, but far more delightful." An

American nursery first offered sweetbay (often referred to as white bay) for sale in 1783, when it was listed in *Bartram's Catalogue of American Trees, Shrubs and Herbaceous Plants.* A favorite in antebellum gardens, sweetbay has remained a popular ornamental in southern gardens, prized for its beautiful foliage and fragrant flowers.

### *Abrustrum Americanum: The American Grove,* 1785
Humphry Marshall

✺ MAGNOLIA glauca. *Small Magnolia or Swamp Sassafras.*

This grows naturally in low, moist, or swampy ground often to the height of fifteen or twenty feet; covered with a whitish smooth bark, and dividing into several branches; furnished with entire, oblong, oval leaves, of dark green on their upper surface, but whitish and a little hairy underneath. The flowers are produced at the ends of the branches, composed of six concave, white petals, of an agreeable smell; and are succeeded by oval, or somewhat conical seed-vessels . . . composed of many capsules, which open and discharge their seeds when ripe. . . . The seeds and bark have been used with some success in the cure of rheumatism.

### *The North American Sylva,* 1819
François André Michaux

✺ In the southern states it is generally called *White Bay* or *Sweet Bay.* . . . Near Charleston, S.C., the tree blossoms in May, and a month later in the neighborhood of Philadelphia and New York, where the women and children penetrate into the swamps and gather the sweet-scented flowers to sell in the markets. . . . Of all indigenous and exotic trees capable of enduring an equal degree of cold, there is none which rivals it in the beauty of its foliage and of its flowers. It is deservedly in great request among the amateurs of gardening, for the establishment of their country residences, cannot be too warmly recommended.

### *A Sketch of the Botany of South Carolina and Georgia,* vol. 2, 1824
Stephen Elliott

✺ *Magnolia Glauca*

A shrub frequently becoming a small tree, remarkable for its white or somewhat glaucous bark. . . . This is probably the most fragrant plant in our forest. It grows in great profusion along the margins of the rich swamps which border our rivers, and in the morning and evening during the period of its flowering, the atmosphere of our streams is often literally perfumed with its fragrance.

## Melia azedarach

Chinaberry, China Tree, Bead Tree, Pride-of-India, Pride-of-China

Native to Asia, chinaberry is a fast-growing, deciduous tree that can reach a height of thirty or forty feet. This exotic-looking tree is characterized by a rounded, umbrellalike canopy and is composed of large pinnate leaves that are subdivided into several leaflets. Graceful, purple flowers are borne in early spring, emitting a delicate fragrance similar to that of the lilac. Flowers are followed by clusters of rounded, yellow berries, which remain decorative through fall and winter. Chinaberry was commonly known in Europe as the "bead tree" because monks and religious orders used the seeds in making rosaries.

The bark of the roots was used for medicinal purposes, and the fruit pulp was employed as an insect repellant.

While John Tradescant the Younger (1608–1662), an English gardener and plant collector, was known to have cultivated the chinaberry in England in 1656, some authorities believe that it arrived in Britain before the end of the sixteenth century, making its way from the Orient by way of Asia Minor. Arriving in North America during colonial time, the chinaberry was first offered for sale by an American nursery when listed in William Prince's *1790 Broadside of Fruit Trees and Shrubs* as "pride of China." This fast-growing tree was often grown around dwellings for shade or was frequently used as a street tree in towns and cities of the middle and lower South. James Silk Buckingham, an English journalist and traveler, documented the use of the chinaberry in Savannah as a street tree in 1839, stating that "every principal street is lined on each side with rows of trees, and some of the broader streets have an avenue of trees running down their center. These trees are called by some, the pride of India, and by others the pride of China."

Well adapted to the hot, dry summers of the South, the chinaberry remained a popular shade tree through the antebellum period, after which its use and popularity rapidly declined. The chinaberry has become widely naturalized in many of the southern states and can be found growing in great abundance around old home sites and along the roads and byways of the rural South.

### A Short Treatise on Horticulture, 1828

William Prince

⌇ *Pride of India, or Melia azedarach.*—This tree is well known for its fine deep green pinnated foliage; the leaves are long, and particularly beautiful, being of a shining green on the upper surface; the flowers are produced in July from the sides of the branches in long clusters; they are of a bluish lilac color, and very fragrant. These are succeeded by yellow berries . . . and in great numbers. It is not sufficiently naturalized to withstand our severest winters without practician, and is often killed to the ground. . . . Further south, however, it is extensively planted for ornament, and the streets of Savannah, and other southern cities, are ornamented with it. The growth is very rapid and almost any soil will suit it.

*Melia azedarach* (chinaberry)

### The Southern Cultivator, 1857

Daniel Lee, M.C. and D. Redmond, Editors

⌇ The Value of the China Tree

This beautiful shade tree, under whose wide-spreading branches the Southern People spend so much of their leisure time in the hot summer, is (says the Port Gibson *Herald*) truly to them one of the greatest blessings of Providence. There is an inviting and welcome look about the refreshing shade, and we hold that man is a misanthrope indeed who loves not the China Tree. . . . Truly the China Tree is a great tree—the pride of the south, as well as of China.

Daniel Lee and D. Redmond, Editors

ॐ A Plea for the Chinas

Editors Southern Cultivator—Startle not, dear readers, . . . but I propose to say a few words in the defense of the much abused Pride of India, or "China Tree," (*Melia azedarach*). . . . I am apprised that this tree does not rank as highly as it formerly did, as an ornament for the grove. . . The great objection waged against this tree is its filthiness. If this is indeed an objection, I cannot see why it does not apply with equal force to all trees, for all must shed their leaves, and while others drop theirs gradually, the China is sooner through, and hence your cleaning up sooner done. . . . Let the matter be well considered, and I feel well-satisfied this once popular tree will again find its way around our dwellings.

V. L. Near Augusta

---

## Michelia figo

(*Magnolia fuscata*)

Banana Shrub

Native to China, *Michelia figo*, or banana shrub as it is commonly known, was named in honor of Pietro Antonio Micheli (1679–1737), a noted Florentine botanist. Banana shrub is a large, freely branched evergreen shrub that obtains a height of ten to fifteen feet and has dark green leaves and a dense, compact form. Flowers of this fragrant ornamental are generally one-half to one inches across, yellow brown in color, and edged in maroon. Depending on the location, banana shrub flowers usually bloom in early or midspring, filling the garden with a distinctive banana-scented perfume.

Sir Joseph Banks introduced banana shrub into England in 1789, where it gained instant popularity and soon became one of the choicest of greenhouse plants. Arriving in North America nearly twenty years later, banana shrub was first offered for sale by an American nursery when listed by David and Cuthbert Landreth of Philadelphia in their *1811 Catalogue of Greenhouse Plants, Hardy Trees, Evergreen Shrubs, Flowering Shrubs, Bulbous Rooted, and Herbaceous Plants.*

Grown in the north as a greenhouse plant, banana shrub was found to be a hardy outdoor plant in the lower South, where it was treasured for its fine evergreen foliage and highly fragrant flowers. In the antebellum South, tradition prevails that southern ladies warmed flowers of the banana shrub in their handkerchiefs to capture their fruity perfume. It is a favorite in southern gardens and is treasured as one of the finest and most fragrant of ornamental shrubs.

### *A Short Treatise on Horticulture,* 1828

William Prince

ॐ *Magnolia fuscata or Olive Coloured Magnolia*—This is an evergreen, with fine glossy foliage, and produces small brownish or olive coloured flowers of extreme fragrance. It does not form so large a plant as the three preceding (*Magnolia obovata, M. conspicua, and M. gracilis*), but becomes a compact and beautiful bush of moderate size, and is closely clad with its shining leaves. It produces its flowers during summer.

### *The American Flower Garden Directory,* 1839

Robert Buist

*Michelia figo* (banana shrub)

૪૭ *Magnolias.* There are four species that require the protection of our green-houses; all the others are hardy. *M. fuscata* and *M. annopaefolia*, are very similar in foliage and flower: the young branches and leaves of *M. fuscata* are covered with a brown, rusty-like down; the other by some is considered merely a variety; flowers small and very sweet scented. *M. pumila* is very dwarf growing; leaves large and netted; flowers semi-double, white, pendant, and exceedingly fragrant. They are natives of China.

**The Magazine of Horticulture, 1855**
C. M. Hovey, Editor

*Magnolia fuscata* is a most magnificent shrub, perfectly hardy and grows rapidly: we have it eight ft. high and as much in diameter at the base, forming a sort of pyramid. In March and April it bears a profusion of flowers close on the young wood, and consequently do not appear above the foliage, but emit an agreeable odor resembling the smell of the fruit of the banana. In fact it is here known by its lady admirers as the Banana shrub.

Andrew Gray, Savannah, Georgia

### *The Southern Cultivator,* 1856

Daniel Lee and Dennis Redmond, Editors

꒰꒰ *Magnolia fuscata* (Banana Shrub), from China

The leaves elliptic, leathery, dark green, smooth; the young twigs downy and brownish. Flowers pale straw color; each petal edged with carmine, about two inches in diameter and exquisitely fragrant; like a ripe banana, whence its name. Propagated by seed and layers. As yet quite rare. . . .

Robert Nelson, Macon, Georgia

## Morus rubra

Red Mulberry, American Mulberry

*Morus rubra* or red mulberry is native to the eastern United States. It is a large, fast-growing, deciduous tree that can obtain a height of forty to sixty feet and is characterized by a short trunk and a rounded, spreading form with broad, ovate leaves that are occasionally lobed. The leaves of *Morus rubra* are dark green during spring and summer, turning a golden yellow in fall. This distinctive American native is best known for its large clusters of edible fruit, which are from one inch to one and a half inches long. Fruit of the red mulberry develop in early summer, first turning red, then a dark purple when mature.

Throughout history, there have been many references to red mulberry, with the earliest account telling of the American Indians' fondness of the plant's large, juicy fruit.

Records of De Soto's travels in North America (1539–1543) indicate that at the Indian town of Cassasaqua, Georgia, the Spanish explorer "was met by twenty men from the village, each bearing a basket of mulberries." William Strachey, an English visitor who arrived in Virginia in 1610, found growing by the houses of the inhabitants "great mulberry trees and in some parts of the country are found naturally in pretty groves."

*Morus rubra* was introduced into England in the seventeenth century and was described in Parkinson's *Paradisi in Sole Paradisus Terrestris* in 1629. The red mulberry was first offered for sale by an American nursery in 1783 when listed in *Bartram's*

*Morus rubra* (red mulberry)

*Catalogue of American Trees, Shrubs and Herbaceous Plants. Morus rubra* was planted occasionally in orchards of the southern states, but generally it was regarded as undesirable for horticultural purposes. Because of its interesting shape, hardiness, and rapid growth, red mulberry was frequently planted as a shade tree or ornamental in the groves and grounds of the antebellum South.

### *A Sketch of the Botany of South Carolina and Georgia,* vol. 1, 1821
Stephen Elliott

∽ *Morus rubra*

A tree in favorable situations, is said by Michaux to attain the height of sixty to seventy feet, and a diameter of eighteen to twenty-four inches . . . [with] cylindrical fruit composed of many one seeded berries. Grows in rich alluvial soils, along the margins of rivers and swamps, not uncommon though rarely becoming a large tree in the low country. The timber is durable and is generally preferred in building boats, or for the light timbers of vessels to any wood excepting the red cedar. Flowers March.

### *The New American Orchardist,* 1833
William Kenrick

∽ MULBERRY (*Morus*)

RED MULBERRY. Morus rubra. A native of America. The tree rises to the height from thirty to forty feet; the leaves are large, dark green, rugged. The fruit is of a very deep red color, and excellent. This variety is esteemed superior to the Black Mulberry as a fruit, and the tree is more hardy.

### *A Treatise on the Theory and Practice of Landscape Gardening,* 1841
Andrew Jackson Downing

∽ THE MULBERRY TREE. *Morus*

The three principal species of the mulberry are the common Red American, the European Black, and the White mulberries. None of them are truly handsome in scenery; and the two latter are generally low spreading trees, valued entirely for the excellency of the fruit, or the suitableness of the foliage for feeding silk worms. Our common mulberry, however, in free, open situations forms a large, wide-spreading, horizontally branched, and not an inelegant tree: the rough heart-shaped leaves with which it is thickly clothed, afford a deep shade; and it groups well with the lime, the Catalpa, and many other round-headed trees. We consider it therefore duly entitled to a place in all extensive plantations; while the pleasant flavor of the slightly acid, dark red fruit, will recommend it to those who wish to add the delicacies of the dessert.

## Myrica cerifera

Southern Wax Myrtle, Bay Berry, Candle Berry Tree, Candleberry Myrtle

Native to the eastern United States from New Jersey to Florida and westward to Texas, southern wax myrtle is best known for its glossy, aromatic leaves and small gray berries, which occur in late summer and fall. When young, it is a large, evergreen shrub, but ultimately it develops into a small, multi-stem, irregular-shaped tree, which obtains a height of twelve to fifteen-feet high at maturity. Berries of southern wax myrtle are covered with a white, waxy coating, which was used during colonial and antebellum times for making candles. Peter Kalm, the Swedish naturalist, observed that candles made from these berries burned better and more slowly than ordinary tallow and when extinguished gave forth a pleasant aroma.

Southern wax myrtle was first introduced into England in 1699, and during the eighteenth century, John Bartram sent seeds of this American native to his British patrons. *Myrica cerifera* was first offered for sale by an American nursery when listed in William Prince's *1771 Broadside* as "candle berry myrtle." Frequently referenced in the literature of the antebellum period as a source of wax for soap and candles, southern wax myrtle was also grown as a useful ornamental or evergreen hedge in the lower and middle South.

### *Abrustrum Americanum: The American Grove,* 1785
Humphry Marshall

〜 MYRICA cerifera. Candleberry Myrtle.

This grows naturally upon low boggy lands, rising with many strong shrubby stalks, to the height of six or eight feet; sending out several branches, which are furnished with stiff spear-shaped leaves, a little sawed towards their extremities, of a yellowish lucid green on their upper surfaces, but paler underneath. . . . The female flowers come out on the sides of the branches in long bunches, and are succeeded by small roundish berries, covered with a mealy substance, and affording a kind of green wax, which is sometimes used in making candles.

### *A Sketch of the Botany of South Carolina and Georgia,* vol. 2, 1824
Stephen Elliott

〜 *Myrica Cerifera*

A small tree 10–18 feet high, diffusely branching, the small branches crowded near the summit of the larger ones. . . . This tree bears its small fruit in great profusion. These little drupes appear to the eye dry and juiceless, but by boiling, a wax of a very pleasant flavour is extracted from them, which is used in the manufacture of soap and candles. Grown in almost all soils, preferring those which are wet and swampy. Flowers in March and April.

*Myrica cerifera* (southern wax myrtle)

### *Arboretum et Fruticetum Britannicum,* 1838
John Claudius Loudon

〜 The principal, if not the only, use made of the Candleberry myrtle, in America is collecting from it of its resinous wax. This substance . . . was formerly procured by gathering the berries carefully with the stalk attached, and boiling them till they burst, when the oily matter which they contained, rose to the surface, . . . candles formed of this wax burn long, and yield a grateful smell; and they are said to have the advantage of producing an agreeable aromatic fragrance when they are blow out, or otherwise extinguished.

### *Resources of the Southern Field and Forest,* 1863
Francis Peyre Procher

〜 *Myrica cerifera*—Wax Myrtle

I have repeatedly seen the wax produced from the myrtle in large amounts. The berries are boiled, and the wax rises in the surface of the water. The boiling should be continued a long time, and the berries stirred and bruised. The wax may be remelted to purify it. Four pounds of this will make forty pounds of soap. The candles made of it are dark green in color. Candles and soap were made in considerable amounts by ladies in the low country of South Carolina during the autumn of 1861.

## Nandina domestica

Nandina, Heavenly Bamboo, Chinese Sacred Bamboo

Native to China, nandina or heavenly bamboo has been grown for centuries in Asian gardens as a prized ornamental. An upright evergreen shrub with long, bamboo-like stems, nandina has graceful, fine-textured foliage that is red when unfolding, light green when mature, and crimson during fall and winter. Clusters of small, white flowers with bright yellow stamens develop in great profusion in late spring, followed by waxy red berries in autumn, which remain on the plant all winter long. Robert Fortune, the Scottish plant collector, provided one of the earliest descriptions of this decorative plant on a visit to Shanghai, China, in the winter of 1843:

> In the winter season at Shanghai, a plant with red berries is seen in the gardens, which takes the place of our English holly. The Chinese call it *Sacred Bamboo*. Large quantities of its branches are brought at this time from the country and hawked about the streets. Each of these branches is crowned with a large bunch of red berries, not very unlike those of the common holly, and when contrasted with the dark, shining leaves, are singularly ornamental.

*Nandina domestica* (nandina)

Nandina arrived in England in 1804 from Canton, China, but was never grown extensively in British gardens as it failed to produce an abundance of fruit. This exotic ornamental was first offered for sale by an American nursery when listed in Bartram's *1814 Catalogue of Trees, Shrubs and Herbaceous Plants* as a greenhouse plant. Grown in gardens of the antebellum South as a prized ornamental, nandina has remained popular in southern gardens for its handsome evergreen foliage and attractive red berries.

### *A Short Treatise on Horticulture,* 1828
William Prince

&#10;  *Nandina domestica,* a Chinese garden shrub, said to produce fruit. It grows in loam and peat, and young cuttings root in sand under a bell-glass.

### *The American Flower Garden Directory,* 1839
Robert Buist

&#10;  *Nandina domestica,* the only species, and a popular shrub in the gardens of Japan, where it is called Nandin. It has supradecompound leaves, with entire lanceolate leaflets, a kind of foliage that is very rare; the flowers are small, whitish green, in panicles, succeeded by berries of the size of a pea.

### *The Florist's Guide,* 1840
Thomas Bridgeman

☞ *Nandina domestica*, Japan Nandina. A half-hardy evergreen shrub; leaves supra-compound, with entire lanceolate leaflets; a kind of foliage that is very rare.

## Nerium oleander

Oleander, Rose Bay, Rose Laurel

Native to the Mediterranean region, oleander is an evergreen shrub with an upright, rounded form characterized by canelike multi-stems and dark green, leathery leaves. A showy ornamental, the oleander produces clusters of fragrant flowers throughout the summer in colors ranging from white and yellow to pink and red. The only drawback to this handsome and versatile shrub is that all parts of the plant are poisonous, including its leaves, stems, and flowers.

John Gerard, author of *The Herball or Historie of Plants*, introduced oleander into England in 1596. In Britain, it was grown as a greenhouse or conservatory plant. By the middle of the eighteenth century, numerous varieties of this beautiful shrub were being cultivated in both single and double forms. The oleander arrived in North America during colonial times and was first offered by an American nursery when listed in William Prince's *1790 Broadside of Fruit Trees and Shrubs* as "oleander with red flowers."

Both George Washington and Thomas Jefferson grew oleander as a greenhouse plant. During the first half of the nineteenth century, oleander was a fashionable outdoor plant in the gardens of the lower South. In the upper and middle South, it was generally grown outdoors in pots or containers during the summer and moved to a plant pit or hothouse for protection during the winter months.

### *The American Flower Garden Directory,* 1839

Robert Buist

*Nerium oleander* (oleander)

☞ *Nerium* (Oleander) is a genus of a beautiful erect growing evergreen shrub, of the earliest culture, and abundant in flower. *N. oleander* is the commonest rose-coloured single flowering species, from which many varieties have originated. At present the most popular is *N. oleander splendens*, which has a double rose-coloured flower, *N. oleander striata fl. pl.*, has double striped flowers. . . . N. *oleander elegantissimum*, a most beautiful plant, with deep silver-edged foliage; and the young wood is striped white and green. There are likewise single yellow, single white and single blotched varieties of *N. oleander.*

### *The Soil of the South,* 1852

James A. Chambers and Charles A. Peabody, Editors

ↄ⟩ The Oleander is fast becoming acclimated to our soil, many having withstood the last severe winter, they with the Camellia Japonica, will, in a few years, be as common in our open grounds as the Cape Jasmine. The Oleander is easily propagated by cuttings, and we hope yet to prove the Camellia Japonica as easily propagated.

### *The Southern Cultivator,* 1856

Daniel Lee and Dennis Redmond, Editors

ↄ⟩ *Nerium Oleander*—From the South of Europe, where it grows near rivers, particularly in Sicily and Candia. The single species is the hardiest, but the double varieties produce the most splendid flowers. The single white, however, is much finer than the double white. They require a rich black sod, plenty of water, and slight protection during the winter in this latitude. Easily propagated by layers and cuttings. 6 to 8 feet high.

Robert Nelson, Macon, Georgia

### *Ladies' Southern Florist,* 1860

Mary Rion

ↄ⟩ Oleander

This is a beautiful, erect-growing shrub, of easy culture. . . . The single is not so handsome as the double rose, which is exceedingly tender. Oleanders grow eight feet high. When they become sluggish, and do not bloom well, they should be cut down to the ground. They require some protection in the winter. The roots have wonderful vitality. Indeed, many evergreens have the same vitality, and often, when apparently dead for a year, will suddenly put forth new and vigorous. We have known an oleander root longer than this in a dormant condition, to send forth fine healthy shoots.

---

## Osmanthus fragrans

### (*Olea fragrans*)
Tea Olive, Sweet Olive, Sweet Scented Olive

Native to China and Japan, tea olive is a large evergreen shrub with broad, shiny leaves and an upright, oval form. Originally known as *Olea fragrans*, the tea olive is best known for its small, sweet-scented flowers, which the Chinese have used for centuries for flavoring tea. The plant's genus name, *Osmanthus*, is derived from the Greek words *osme,* meaning fragrance, and *anthos*, signifying flowers. The highly scented flowers of the tea olive are produced in clusters in spring and fall.

Introduced into England in 1771, the tea olive was generally grown indoors. According to horticultural authorities of the time, only a few of the plant's tiny, white flowers were needed to fill an entire greenhouse or conservatory with a heavenly perfume. The tea olive arrived in North America by way of France when André Michaux, the French botanist, brought specimens of this fragrant ornamental to Charleston, South Carolina, around 1786.

The tea olive was first offered for sale by an American nursery when listed in the *1810 Catalogue* of William Booth, a well-known seedsman and nursery owner in Baltimore, Maryland. The tea olive proved to be a popular ornamental during the antebellum period in gardens of the middle and lower South. It was greatly treasured for its fine evergreen foliage and delicately scented flowers.

*Charles Drayton's Diaries,* 1784–1819

᪣ Visit to Michaux's Botanic Garden—March 9, 1805

 Went to botanic garden. It is neglected, and nearly ruined. Plants found growing included: Paveia . . . Pincknea, Kalmia, three species of vines . . . Papaw . . . *Olea fragrans* . . . lily seeds . . ."

### The American Flower Garden Directory, 1839
Robert Buist

᪣ *Olea fragrans* blooms in winter; foliage and blossoms are both highly odoriferous; the plant is much esteemed in China, and is said to be used to adulterate and flavour teas. Leaves are elliptic, lanceolate, and a little serrated; flowers white in lateral bunches. It is subject to the small white scaly insect, and ought to be kept from them by washing.

### The Southern Cultivator, 1856
Daniel Lee and Dennis Redmond, Editors

᪣ Olea fragrans (Tea olive, fragrant olive), from China. Though perfectly adapted to our climate, still it is but seldom to be met with in our gardens, it being considered a green-house plant. A tree of this kind in my vicinity (middle Georgia) is over ten feet high, perfuming the whole garden with its delightful fragrance of its little white flowers.

 Robert Nelson, Macon, Georgia

*Osmanthus fragrans* (tea olive)

### Ladies' Southern Florist, 1860
Mary Rion

᪣ The *fragrant olive* is a native of China and Japan. . . . The flowers are white, growing in bunches, and highly fragrant, and are used by the Chinese for perfuming their teas. This species requires the same treatment as the European olive, and is of very slow growth.

---

## Parthenocissus quinquefolia

 (*Hedera quinquefolia, Ampelopsis quinquefolia, Ampelopsis hederacea*)
 Virginia Creeper, American Woodbine, Virginia Vine

Native to the eastern United States, Virginia creeper is a hardy, deciduous vine characterized by large leaves that are composed of five individual leaflets. This handsome vine derives its genus name from the Greek words *parthenocissus*, meaning "virgin ivy," and its species name, *quinquefolia*, signifying five-leaved. Originally known as Virginia vine and classified as an ivy (*Hedera*), this tenacious climber is able to reach heights of thirty to fifty feet. It is able to attach to wood, stone, or tree trunks by means of tendrils equipped with small, adhesive discs. Leaves of Virginia creeper are purple when they open in spring, become dark green in summer, and turn a brilliant crimson red in fall.

Small, inconspicuous flowers are produced in summer, followed by clusters of bluish black berries in autumn.

Introduced into England in 1629, Virginia creeper proved tolerant of city conditions. In 1722, a British observer noted: "There was hardly a street, court or ally in London where Virginia Creeper could not be found growing." Virginia creeper was first offered for sale by an American nursery in 1783 when listed in *Bartram's Catalogue of American Trees, Shrubs and Herbaceous Plants.* This attractive ornamental vine was popular in the nineteenth century for softening walls and fences and covering outbuildings and utilitarian structures. Still grown today for its hardy nature and brilliant fall color, Virginia creeper remains one of America's finest native vines.

### *A Treatise on the Theory and Practice of Landscape Gardening,* 1841
#### Andrew Jackson Downing

ॐ The Virginia Creeper is a most luxuriant grower, and we have seen it climbing to the extremities of trees 70 or 80 feet in height. Like the Ivy, it attaches itself to whatever it can lay hold of, by the little rootlets which spring out of the branches and its foliage, when it clothes thickly a high wall, or folds itself in clustering wreaths around the trunk and branches of an open tree, is extremely handsome and showy. Although the leaves are not evergreen like those of the ivy, yet in autumn they far surpass those of the plant in the rich and gorgeous coloring which they assume.

*Parthenocissus quinquefolia* (Virginia creeper)

### *The Flower Garden,* 1851
#### Joseph Breck

ॐ Ampelopsis quinquefolia—American Woodbine—This is the most ornamental of its genus. It recommends itself by its hardiness, the rapidity of its growth, and the luxuriance and beauty of the foliage. It is a native of our woods and climbs rocks and trees to a great height. In cultivation it is often made to cover walls of houses, forty to fifty feet high, clinging by rootlets which proceed from its tendrils. The flower is of a reddish-brown, and not showy, which is succeeded by clusters of dark-blue, nearly black, berries when mature.

### *The Magazine of Horticulture,* 1855
#### C. M. Hovey, Editor

ॐ The Woodbine, or Virginia Creeper (Ampelopsis). For a rapid growing vine, with handsome deep green and much divided foliage, none excel the Virginia Creeper. It runs with great luxuriance, and for covering a wall or fence, or for clothing some disagreeable object with rich verdure, nothing can compare with this vine. In the autumn, with the first frosts, its leaves begin to assume the richest tints, dying off a brilliant crimson scarlet. Against a brick or stone wall it flourishes finely, inserting its little tendrils into the crevices and clinging to it without any other support.

### *The Horticulturist,* 1860

Peter B. Mead, Editor

↪ The Ampelopsis or Virginia Creeper—What a magnificent plant this is! I do think that it is one of the most beautiful things in the country, although its flowers are of little or no account. . . . Its culture is the most simple: when young it should have a moderately rich and light soil in which to establish itself. . . . The young shoots should be trained with some care to the surface which they are to occupy, whether of wood, stone or brick.

---

## Paulownia tomentosa

(*Paulownia imperialis*)
Empress Tree, Princess Tree, Royal Paulownia

*Paulownia tomentosa* (empress tree)

Native to China and widely grown in Japan, *Paulownia tomentosa*, commonly known as the empress tree, was named in honor of Anna Paulowna, daughter of Tsar Paul I of Russia and princess of the Netherlands. In 1834 Dr. von Siebold, a German medical doctor and naturalist, introduced the empress tree into Europe, where it aroused great attention in horticultural circles and was highly regarded as a prized and exotic ornamental.

A fast-growing, deciduous tree with an upright, oval form, the empress tree is characterized by broad leaves and striking trumpet-shaped flowers that are pale violet with dark spots and yellow stripes within, similar in appearance to flowers of the catalpa. Flowers of the empress tree are followed by distinctive seed pods that remain on the tree throughout the winter season.

Introduced into North American about 1840, the empress tree was first offered for sale by an American nursery when included in William Prince's *1844 Descriptive Catalogue*, in which the plant was described as "a new ornamental tree of great beauty, splendid foliage, resembling the Catalpa, and a profusion of beautiful purplish bell-shaped flowers." The empress tree remained a popular ornamental through the end of the nineteenth century, at which time it began to lose its appeal. Widely naturalized throughout the eastern United States, this once prized exotic is today considered a second-class tree and is rarely planted in American gardens.

### *A Treatise on The Theory and Practice of Landscape Gardening,* 1841

Andrew Jackson Downing

↪ The Paulownia Tree

The Paulownia is an entirely new ornamental tree, very lately introduced into our gardens and pleasure-grounds from Japan, and is likely to prove hardy here, wherever the Ailanthus stands the winter, being naturally from the same soil and climate as that tree. . . . Should the Paulownia prove as hardy as we confidently anticipate, it will be worthy of a prominent place in every arrangement of choice ornamental trees.

### *The Horticulturist,* 1849/1850

Andrew Jackson Downing, Editor

ᖭ Domestic Notices

Paulownia imperialis—Dear Sir: There are some who have doubted the merit of this tree. I have cultivated it for five years, and think more highly of it every year. In general aspect, it strongly resembles the Catalpa, both in foliage and growth, but it has several advantages over the latter tree. It is much more hardy. . . . It is of a very rapid growth, and the blossoms are of a beautiful pale lilac or French gray, with a delicate scent, not unlike violets.

Manhattan, New York, July 1849

### *The Flower Garden,* 1851

Joseph Breck

ᖭ *Paulownia imperialis.*—This is a magnificent tree, of recent introduction. To all appearances, it will not grow to a very large size in our climate. As it is perfectly hardy it will be a rich addition to our collection for the shrubbery or lawn.

### *The American Cotton Planter,* 1855

N. B. Cloud, Editor

ᖭ [From the *Natchez Daily Courier,* October 28, 1854]

The Imperial Paulownia, with its immense leaves and numberless spikes of blue bell-like blossoms, has been introduced some ten or dozen years, and is quite an acquisition. It blooms here, abundantly, both spring and fall.

Thomas Affleck

---

## Philadelphus coronarius

### (*Syringa*)

Mock Orange, English Dogwood, Syringa

Native to southern Europe and southwest Asia, *Philadelphus coronarius* is a venerable garden shrub that for centuries was grown for its orange-scented flowers, which gave rise to its common name, mock orange. A large deciduous, multi-stemmed shrub with an upright, arching form, mock orange generally reaches a height of ten to twelve feet. Leaves of this showy ornamental are dark green, oval in shape, glabrous above and slightly pubescent below. The single, dogwood-like flowers of mock orange are creamy white with bright yellow stamens. Flowers occur in great profusion in mid to late spring.

*Philadelphus coronarius*, initially called *Syringa*, was introduced into Europe along with the lilac in 1562. The lilac was also known as *Syringa*, leading to confusion in nomenclature that prevails even today. This treasured garden shrub was first cultivated in England around 1596, where it was grown as a specimen or as an unclipped hedge. The plant's flowers have an orangelike fragrance, which is pleasing to some but objectionable to others. John Gerard, author of the *Herball* (1597), registered an objection to flowers of the mock orange by noting, "They have a pleasant scent, but in my judgment, troubling and molesting the head in a very strong manner." Mock orange arrived in North America during colonial times and was first offered by an American nursery when listed in William Prince's *1771 Catalogue of Trees, Shrubs, and Herbaceous Plants* as *Philadelphus coronarius*. Mock orange was grown extensively in middle and upper South antebellum gardens for its ease of cultivation, resistance to heat and drought, and beautiful display of fragrant, springtime flowers.

### A Short Treatise on Horticulture, 1828
William Prince

ᘔ *Philadelphus coronarius or European Fragrant.*—This is the most common; it forms in time a very large compact shrub, and its white blossoms impart a most agreeable odour. Of this there are three other varieties, viz.—the Semidouble Flowering, producing single flowers and semidouble ones on the same plant; the Dwarf, which forms a low shrub, only from a foot and a half to two feet in height; and the Variegated Leafed Dwarf, similar to the preceding, except that its leaves are beautifully variegated.

### The New American Orchardist, 1833
William Kenrick

ᘔ SYRINGA. *Philadelphus coronaris.* A very ornamental shrub, producing a profusion of white flowers very early in spring, of a sweet fragrance. The variegated leaved is a curious species.

*Philadelphus coronarius* (mock orange)

### The Flower Garden, 1851
Joseph Breck

ᘔ Philadelphus. *Syringa*

The Syringa is a most delicious shrub: the foliage is luxuriant, the blossoms beautiful and abundant, white as the purest Lily, and the most fragrant scent. In a room, indeed, this perfume is too powerful, and in the air it is remarkably agreeable. There is a variety which has no scent and also a dwarf variety which does not usually exceed three feet high. The flowers sweet and some double.

*P. coronarius*—or Common Syringa—... grows about five feet high, and is delightfully fragrant when in bloom. Flowers in June and July.

### The Southern Cultivator, 1852
Daniel Lee and Dennis Redmond, Editors

ᘔ Ornamental Shrubs for the Millions

Among shrubs employed in the embellishment of ornamental grounds, there are a certain number which recommend themselves under nearly all circumstances. . . .

*The Syringas*—The common fragrant one (*Coronarius*) is well known. The flowers have the fragrance of the orange blossom. The *pubescens* has large foliage and large white flowers without odor. There are also a double flowering variety and a very dwarf one; both fragrant. Propagated by layers. Blossoms in June.

# Pittosporum tobira

(*Pittosporum chinensis, Euonymus tobira*)
Pittosporum, Japanese Pittosporum

Native to China and Japan, pittosporum is a beautiful, long-lived, evergreen shrub with a spreading, horizontal form. Most plants reach an average height of six to ten feet, but older specimens often develop into a small, multi-stem tree, reaching a height of twenty feet or more. This Asian native is highly prized for its lustrous, dark green leaves that form handsome, rosettelike clusters at the end of individual branches. Tiny, creamy-white flowers that emit a delicate scent, similar to that of orange blossoms, appear in mid-spring. Growing both in sun and shade, this highly versatile plant is tolerant of heat, drought, and salt, making it ideal for use in coastal gardens. It is useful either as a specimen or hedge plant.

Pittosporum was introduced into England in 1804 from Canton, China, by William Kerr, a botanical collector for Kew Gardens. Originally grown in Britain as a greenhouse plant, this somewhat tender ornamental soon found its way into southern Europe where it became a popular outdoor plant. Pittosporum was first offered for sale by an American nursery when listed by David and Cuthbert Landreth of Philadelphia in their *1811 Catalogue*. This handsome evergreen shrub was grown in antebellum gardens of the lower South, especially in coastal cities and towns including Charleston, Savannah, Mobile, and New Orleans.

*Pittosporum tobira* (pittosporum)

### The American Flower Garden Directory, 1839

Robert Buist

 *Pittosporums*, about nine species, with handsome foliage, and small white flowers in clusters, which are fragrant. *P. tobira* is a native of China, and nearly hardy; leaves lucid, ovate, obtuse, and smooth: there is a beautiful variegated variety of it.

### The Magazine of Horticulture, 1855

C. M. Hovey, Editor

 The Hardy Shrubs of the South

*Pittosporum tobira*, a well known denizen of the greenhouse and conservatory; stands our severest winters with perfect impunity; growing almost to a tree. Its fine dark green foliage renders it a very desirable plant for the south, and is admirably adapted for hedges and for forming groves, as it stands cutting in well, and is also of a spreading habit.

Andrew Gray, Savannah, Georgia

### The Southern Cultivator, 1856

Daniel Lee and Dennis Redmond, Editors

 *Pittosporum tobira*, a well-known, very spreading bush, quite common in many gardens. The yellowish-white and very fragrant flowers are produced in April and May. There is a variety with variegated leaves, but not so fine-looking as the green species. Propagated from layers and cuttings of the young wood in July. 6 to 8 feet high.

Robert Nelson, Macon, Georgia

Mary Rion

↬ Pittosporum

This evergreen is a native of China, and quite hardy with us, growing to a height of fifteen feet. The foliage is very handsome, and is dark green. It bears clusters of small white flowers, of fine fragrance. There is also a variegated variety of the Pittosporum. This ornamental evergreen will grow with the most simple treatment. It is easily propagated by cuttings.

## Prunus caroliniana

(*Laurocerasus caroliniana, Cerasus caroliniensis/caroliniana*)
Cherry Laurel, Carolina Bird Cherry, Lauri Mundi, Wild Olive/Orange, Mock Orange

Cherry laurel is a native shrub or small tree that ranges from North Carolina to Florida and westward to Texas. Varying in height from twenty to thirty feet with a dense, upright habit of growth, this handsome evergreen has dark, glossy leaves and small, white flowers that appear in early spring. Flowers are followed by inconspicuous shiny black berries that remain on the plant throughout the winter months. Francois Michaux in *The North American Sylva* (1819) described cherry laurel as one of the finest native plants in the southern states and noted that inhabitants frequently planted it near their homes, both as an ornamental and to provide shade.

Philip Miller cultivated this American native at the Chelsea Physic Garden in England as early as 1759, but it was never extensively grown in British gardens because of its tender nature. Cherry laurel was first offered in an American nursery catalog when William Prince listed it in his *1771 Broadside* as "Carolina bird cherry." This attractive plant was extensively used during the antebellum period as an ornamental, especially for hedges. Its beautiful foliage, rapid of growth, and ability to withstand the effects of pruning continue to make it a popular ornamental in southern gardens for hedges, topiary, and as a specimen plant.

*Prunus caroliniana* (cherry laurel)

### *The North American Sylva,* 1819

François André Michaux

↬ Cerasus caroliniana

The Wild Orange Tree may be considered as one of the most beautiful vegetable productions of this part of the United States, and it is selected with the more reason by the inhabitants to plant about their houses, as it grows with rapidity and affords an impenetrable shade.

### *The Southern Cultivator,* 1856

Daniel Lee and Dennis Redmond, Editors

↬ *Prunus caroliniana* (Mock Orange; also, though erroneously, called Wild Olive), is correctly speaking, the wild Evergreen Cherry, a native of the South, where it is often found near rivers and swamps, growing to the height of 30 feet. This is a most beautiful tree in the yard, as well as the street, forming a dense and compact head of a shining, lively green hue. It bears the shears well, and forms a beautiful ornamental hedge or screen.

Robert Nelson, Macon, Georgia

### *The American Cotton Planter,* 1858
N. B. Cloud, Editor

❧ Shade and Ornamental Trees

There are some beautiful evergreens being introduced from abroad, but not one that we have ever seen, that will compare for beauty with the wild olive. It is beautiful as an evergreen, with its dense glossy foliage and graceful form. It is beautiful in flower, showing the myriads of white blossoms among the glittering foliage. It is beautiful when in fruit, producing thousands of bright black berries, which clustering among the green foliage gives Winter the air of Summer.

### *Ladies' Southern Florist,* 1860
Mary Rion

❧ Wild orange, elsewhere known as the Carolina cherry, is one of the most beautiful vegetable productions of the South. The foliage is a dark, shining green, handsome at all seasons. It has a small white bloom, succeeded by black berries. Its growth is extraordinarily vigorous and rapid. It is universally used for hedges; and forms, when trimmed, solid walls of verdure, from ten to twenty feet high. The hedges require trimming twice in the year, in spring and in fall after it has completed its growth for the season. Single trees can be trimmed into any shape desired.

*Pyracantha coccinea* (pyracantha)

## Pyracantha coccinea

(*Mespilus coccinea, Crataegus coccinea, Crategus pyracantha*)
Pyracantha, Firethorn, Evergreen Thorn

Native to southern Europe and eastern Asia, pyracantha is an upright, spreading, evergreen shrub with a distinctive vinelike character, making it especially adaptable for use on walls and fences. Its ability to tolerate pruning coupled with its sharp, thorny branches has lead to its use throughout history as an ideal hedge plant. Pyracantha is best known for its small, fragrant flowers that appear in late May and June, which are followed by showy clusters of bright red berries.

Cultivated in Britain as early as 1629, John Parkinson (1567–1650) the noted English horticulturist and herbalist, referred to the pyracantha as the "evergreen Hawthorne" and considered it a fine ornamental. Originally classified as *Mespilus* and later as *Crataegus*, pyracantha was a favorite wall plant in English gardens, where its colorful berries were displayed to the greatest advantage. Pyracantha was first offered for sale by an American nursery when listed in Bartram's *1792 Catalogue of Trees, Shrubs and Herbaceous Plants.* It was touted during the antebellum period as a fine hedge plant, surpassed in usefulness only by the Osage orange and Cherokee rose. Pyracantha has remained a popular ornamental in southern gardens, as it is highly prized for its brilliant red berries that remain decorative all winter long.

### *A Short Treatise on Horticulture,* 1828
William Prince

↷ *Mespilus pyracantha or Evergreen Thorn*—This has very dense foliage; the leaves are small, and of a fine dark green; it produces an abundance of white flowers, which are delicate, and much admired. . . . It is its fruit which gives it the greatest claim to beauty. . . . They are of a fiery red, and are produced in the greatest abundance and retain their beauty during the autumnal and part of the winter months, and serve to decorate this shrub at a season when nature most needs their aid. Being a sub-evergreen, and retaining a large proportion of its foliage during winter, gives it another claim as an appendage to the shrubbery. It is now considerably planted for hedges, for which purpose, uniting beauty with usefulness, it does not appear to be surpassed by any other.

### *The Southern Cultivator,* 1855
Daniel Lee and Dennis Redmond, Editors

↷ *Crataegus pyracantha*, or Evergreen Thorn, for Hedging

It is an evergreen, with foliage rich and dark, and very dense; as is its habit of growth, which is horizontal to a much greater degree than is common even among Hawthornes. . . . In the spring it is covered with its very beautiful white blossoms, and all through the fall and winter, with a mass of bright scarlet berries. In four or five years, on fair soil and under good management, it forms a perfect fence. . . . As an evergreen, the *Crataegus* (or *Mespilus pyracantha*) undoubtedly possesses some advantages over the Osage Orange, especially for ornamental hedges surrounding flower gardens, lawns, etc. As a plantation or orchard hedge, however, we still adhere to the Osage Orange, on account of its vigorous growth, formidable thorns, close grain toughness, and great tenacity of life.

### *The Southern Cultivator,* 1855
Daniel Lee and Dennis Redmond, Editors

↷ Hedges—Osage Orange, Cherokee Rose, *Crataegus pyracantha*, etc.

I have the Crataegus pyracantha, growing finely, five years old last spring, and it is a very perfect hedge in every sense of the word, and is strong and tough, protected with thorns. . . . Its delicate white flowers in spring and scarlet berries in autumn and green leaves in winter, render it always attractive, while it is the receptacle of all the eggs on the plantation—the Turkeys, Guineas, and Shanghalis, all resorting to it. I have about 400 yards of this hedge and will recommend it as a good hedge for any enclosure, plantation, or garden.

Jenkins, Montgomery, Alabama

## Quercus virginiana

(*Quercus sempervirens, Quercus virens*)
Live Oak, Southern Live Oak

Live oak is a magnificent, long-lived evergreen tree that is native to the south Atlantic states from Virginia to Florida and westward to the Rio Grande River. Growing to an

*Quercus virginiana* (live oak)

average height of fifty to sixty feet, live oak (*Quercus virginiana*, originally known as *Quercus virens*) is characterized by a short trunk, horizontal branches, and a broad-spreading form. Leaves of this stately evergreen tree are two to three inches long, dark green and lustrous on top and pale green and pubescent below. Early naturalists established the tree's common name, live oak, around 1610. Mark Catesby in his *Natural History of Carolina, Florida and the Bahama Islands* (1731–1743) described the live oak as a pyramidal tree and noted that its acorns "are the sweetest of all others, of which the Indians lay up store to thicken their venison-soup. . . . They likewise draw an oil, very pleasant and wholesome, little inferior to that of almonds." In coastal areas of the lower South, Spanish moss festoons the branches of the live oak, adding to its beauty and character.

The live oak was introduced into England in 1739, but it was never extensively planted in British gardens due to the shorter growing season and colder climate. In North America, wood of the live oak was highly esteemed for shipbuilding and for making wagon wheels and handles for a variety of tools. This handsome native tree was first offered for sale by an American nursery when listed in Bartram's *1783 Catalogue of American Trees, Shrubs and Herbaceous Plants.* As an ornamental, live oak was used in the lower South as an avenue tree, as a specimen to enhance groves and grounds, and as a reliable street tree in coastal cities, including Charleston, Savannah, Mobile, and New Orleans.

### *The North American Sylva,* 1819
François André Michaux

༄ Quercus virens

> This species, which is confined to the maritime parts of the Southern States, the Floridas and Louisiana, is known only by the name of Live Oak. . . . The Live Oak is commonly 40 or 45 feet in height and 1 to 2 feet in diameter; but it is sometimes

much larger. . . . Besides the Live Oak timber exported to England, great quantities are used in ship-building in the United States, particularly Boston, New York, Philadelphia, and Baltimore. The consumption has become threefold within twenty years, in consequence of the immense development of American commerce. . . . The clearing of the islands for the culture of cotton, which they yield of a superior quantity, has contributed greatly to its destruction.

### *A Sketch of the Botany of South Carolina and Georgia,* vol. 2, 1824
Stephen Elliott

✣ It is much to be regretted, that residents on the Sea-Islands do not plant avenues of this noble tree along the roads leading up to their houses, as a means not only of preserving and eventually increasing the supply of timber, but of adding embellishments to situations. . . all, however, who have seen the fine avenues of Live Oak near Dorchester (South Carolina), will acknowledge that they would add magnificence to any landscape.

### *Arboretum et Fruticetum Britannicum,* 1838
John Claudius Loudon

✣ A modern traveler, Mr. Stuart, in his *Three Years in North America,* published in 1833, thus speaks of the live oak, while describing his journey from Georgetown to Charleston: "On this day's journey, I first saw and in great numbers, the most valuable of American trees, the Quercus virens, the most durable of oaks. . . . The object of the American government being to provide for the establishment and maintenance of a powerful navy, the cultivation of the live oak, which is almost the only oak they have suitable for ship timbers, is an object of natural importance.

### *A Treatise on the Theory and Practice of Landscape Gardening,* 1841
Andrew Jackson Downing

✣ The Live Oak (Quercus virens)
   This fine species will not thrive north of Virginia. Its imperishable timber is the most valuable in our forests; and, at the south it is a fine park tree, when cultivated, growing about 40 feet high, with . . . a rather wide and low head. The thick oval leaves are evergreen, and it is much to be regretted that this noble tree will not bear our northern winters.

---

## Rosa laevigata

### (*Rosa sinica*)
### Cherokee Rose, Nondescript Rose

Native to China, the Cherokee rose is a vigorous evergreen rose with shiny, dark green foliage that is produced on stout arching stems armed with formidable thorns. When trained as a climber, Cherokee rose grows fifteen or more feet, but when left unsupported, it develops into a mounding shrub. The Cherokee rose produces large single flowers, two to three inches across, with bright yellow stamens. Its delicately fragrant flowers are borne in late March, followed in fall by oblong to rounded hips that add seasonal interest.

Introduced into England from China in 1759 as *Rosa sinica,* the Cherokee rose was first grown by Philip Miller at the Chelsea Physic Garden. Although no records survive to

*Rosa laevigata* (Cherokee rose)

prove how or when the Cherokee rose arrived in North America, by the end of the eighteenth century, it had become so widely naturalized in several of the southern states that André Michaux, the French botanist, identified it as an American native and included it in his *Flora Boreali-Americana* or *North American Flora* (1803) as *Rosa laevigata.* The southern botanist, Stephen Elliott (1771–1830) spoke of *Rosa laevigata* in his *Sketch of the Botany of South Carolina and Georgia,* volume 2 (1824) as having been "cultivated in the gardens of Georgia for upwards of 40 years." The plant's common name, Cherokee, was derived from its association with the Cherokee Indians, who inhabited the upper reaches of present-day Georgia and North and South Carolina before being forced to move westward to Oklahoma in 1838 in the tragic saga known as the Trail of Tears.

Thomas Jefferson grew Cherokee rose from seeds he received in 1804 from Governor Milledge of Georgia. It was first offered by an American nursery when listed in Bartram's *1814 Catalogue of Trees, Shrubs and Herbaceous Plants.* In addition to its use as an ornamental, the Cherokee rose was also highly praised in nineteenth-century agricultural journals and in horticulture literature as an excellent hedge for protecting crops and as a livestock enclosure. Travel accounts of the antebellum era frequently describe hedges of the Cherokee rose lining roads and farmland throughout the lower and middle South.

### The Southern Agriculturist, 1831

John D. Legare, Editor

୬ Cherokee Rose

The history of this plant is obscure. . . . It was cultivated before the revolution by the late Nathaniel Hall, Esq., at his plantation near the Savannah River . . . under the name of the "Cherokee Rose," it is probable that it was originally brought down from our mountains by some of the Indian traders. Michaux met with it in the gardens of Georgia, and perceiving that it was an undescribed plant, he introduced it into the gardens near Charleston as a Nondescript Rose. Hence it has obtained in that neighborhood the popular name of the "Nondescript." In Georgia, it has always retained the name of Cherokee Rose. . . . (*From the proceedings of the Horticulture Society of Charleston, based on observations . . . from the unpublished manuscript of the late Stephen Elliott.*)

### *Report of the Commissioner of Patents,* 1854

Charles Mason, Commissioner

↬ Trees and Shrubs Usually Employed for Hedges

Rose, Cherokee (*Rosa laevigata*)

This plant, though known by the name of "Cherokee Rose," is believed to be a native of China, and has been adapted as a hedge-plant in the Southern States, as far north as latitude 34°, for at least sixty years. It is noted for its long, flexible branches, large, white flowers, bright-green foliage, and long, straggling and rapid growth. . . . If properly trimmed, a hedge of this sort will afford a sufficient barrier against all stock in four years. If left unpruned, the shoots are liable to extend in all directions from 10 to 20 feet. The cost per mile has been estimated at $15.

### *The Southern Cultivator,* 1855

Daniel Lee M. D. and Dennis Redmond, Editors

↬ Cherokee Rose

I am astonished that one of your taste in rural matters should prefer the Osage Orange to all other plants for a hedge. For my part, I much prefer the Cherokee Rose to the Osage Orange. I have seen hedges 12 feet high of the latter in Texas, growing in the wild unimproved state, and they present an uncouth, jagged, naked appearance, not at all "a thing of beauty," though a very effective barrier to any kind of depredators. But so is the Cherokee Rose formidable to stock, which with its evergreen leaves and flowers of snow, it is gloriously beautiful.

Montgomery, Alabama

---

## Smilax lanceolata

(*Smilax non spinosa, Smilax smallii*)

Southern Smilax, Wedding Vine, Jackson Vine, Florida Smilax, Spearshaped Smilax

The genus *Smilax*, which includes more than twenty-five native North American species, has largely been ignored for use in ornamental plantings, with the exception of *Smilax lanceolata*, generally known as southern smilax or wedding vine. Native to the southeastern United States from Virginia to Texas, *Smilax lanceolata* was first illustrated by Mark Catesby in his *Natural History of Carolina, Florida and the Bahama Islands* (1731–1743). Best known for its lustrous, evergreen foliage, this handsome vine is found growing in southern forests along riverbanks, streams, and low-lying areas. Southern smilax is characterized by waxy, lanceolate leaves, three to four inches long, that develop on long, spineless stems. Inconspicuous flowers occur in late summer followed by small, dull red fruit, which (if not eaten by birds) turn black when fully mature. This hardy vine develops from an underground tuber, similar in appearance to a large potato.

Growing in both sun and shade, southern smilax is often found cascading over balconies, doorways, fences, and garden walls in old gardens and historic landscapes. Used for generations in the South for Christmas and wedding decorations, southern smilax has the ability to retain its dark green luster and freshness when brought indoors and is able to produce an abundance of new growth each spring. William Young introduced *Smilax lanceolata* into England in 1785, and it was first offered for sale by an American nursery when listed in Bernard M'Mahon's 1804 *Catalog of Garden, Herb, Flower, Tree, Shrub, and Grass Seeds.* While southern smilax is seldom available from nurseries today, it can be collected easily from its native habitats throughout the southern states, with vines that have the smallest leaflets being considered the finest and most desirable for landscape use.

### The History of Carolina, 1709
John Lawson

*Smilax lanceolata* (southern smilax)

↝ A famous evergreen I must now mention. It is in leaf like a Jessamine, but larger, and of a harder nature. It grows up to a large vine, and twists itself around trees it grows near, making a very fine shade. I never saw anything of that nature out do it. It is an ornamental plant, and worth transplanting. The seed is a black berry.

### Abrustrum Americanum: The American Grove, 1785
Humphry Marshall

↝ SMILAX lanceolata. *Red Berried Virginian Smilax*
The stalks of this are smooth and round. The leaves are without spines and lance-shaped. The berries are red colored.

### Arboretum et Fruticetum Britannicum, 1838
John Claudius Loudon

↝ Smilax lanceolata. The Lanceolate-Leaved Smilax.
A climbing shrub, with a short, very branching stem, and smooth, entire . . . leaves, and red berries. Catesby found this species in Carolina, hanging from the branches of loftytrees, to which it had attached itself. The leaves are long, narrowed at both ends, thick, stiff, and shining with a very conspicuous rib down the middle. They are alternate at very considerable distances. The flowers, which are of a greenish white, are produced at the ends of the branches, in small tufts; and are succeeded by globular . . . red berries, each continuing one very hard round stone.

### Flora of the Southern United States, 1860
A. W. Chapman

↝ Smilax lanceolata—Stem tall, mostly unarmed . . . leaves evergreen, rather thin, varying from lanceolate to oblong-ovate, acute at each end, 5–ribbed, paler beneath. . . . Rich woods and margins of swamps, Florida to North Carolina—Stem sometimes 20" to 30" long. Root-stock tuberous. Leaves 4"–3" long. Berries black.

---

## Spiraea prunifolia plena

(*Spiraea prunifolia flora pleno*)
Bridal Wreath Spiraea, Double-Flowered Plum Leaved Spiraea

Native to China and widely cultivated in both Chinese and Japanese gardens, *Spiraea prunifolia plena* or bridal wreath spiraea is a long-lived, deciduous shrub with an upright, graceful, form. Reaching a height of four to six feet, bridal wreath spiraea is distinguished by small, glossily green leaves, which turn brilliant red or crimson in fall. This popular ornamental is best known for its pure white, double flowers, which occur in clusters along leafless stems in early spring. Each flower is a perfect rosette of many petals, giving the appearance of a miniature rose.

Robert Fortune introduced *Spiraea prunifolia plena* into England from China in 1844. It was described at the time as being "a very valuable acquisition, . . . with deciduous leaves and long slender branches. . . . The flowers, very regular and very ornamental." The single-flowered species, *Spiraea prunifolia flora simplex*, which is less ornamental than the double-flowering form, never proved popular in British gardens. Arriving in North America around 1847, bridal wreath spiraea was first offered to American gardeners by the Highland Nursery of Newburgh, New York, in the firm's *1848 Catalogue of Fruit and Ornamental Trees and Plants*. At the time of the advertisement, the Highland Nursery was under the management of A. Saul and Company, although several years earlier Andrew Jackson Downing had owned it. *Spiraea prunifolia plena* was a popular ornamental in antebellum gardens, where it was greatly admired for its great profusion of small, rosettelike flowers and colorful foliage in fall.

### The Horticulturist, 1847/1848

Andrew Jackson Downing, Editor

ᔧ *Spiraea prunifolia*, with double flowers.

This charming shrub . . . deserves the attention of all amateurs, as well for its hardiness as its elegant habit and beautiful flowers. It is a shrub of from 6 to 9 feet high and has upright, close, bushy, slender branches. . . . The leaves are oval, or ovate-elliptic, rounded at their base. The flowers, which grow by threes or sixes, cover the whole length of the branches, are as white as snow, and very double.

### The Soil of the South, 1852

James A. Chambers and Charles A. Peabody, Editors

ᔧ New Flowering Shrubs

Among the many beautiful plants, introduced by Mr. Fortune, from China, we have seen nothing more pure and beautiful than the Spiraea prunifolia (flora pleno). We have a bush of it, now in bloom, some five feet high, covered with pure double white blooms. So minute, double and snowy white are the blossoms, and com-

*Spiraea prunifolia plena* (bridal wreath spiraea)

ing out before any of its kindred shrubbery, that it looks in the flower gardens like a pure spirit, from another world. This spiraea is perfectly hardy, and when once it is known, will grace the grounds of every lover of the beautiful.

## The Southern Cultivator, 1857

Robert Nelson

☞ Ornamental Edgings and Hedges, for the South

*Spirea prunifolia* forms a beautiful ornamental hedge, blooming very early in the spring, when it produces a most charming contrast to the fiery red *Cydonia japonica*. Should be pruned by midsummer in order to produce a close hedge that will bloom well. From four to five feet high . . .

## The Southern Cultivator, 1858

Daniel Lee and Dennis Redmond, Editors

☞ *Spiraea prunifolia* (*flora pleno*) created a good deal of excitement among horticulturists, when first it was introduced from Japan to the United States, where it bloomed for the first time in 1847. Much had previously been said in its favor, and still it surpassed all expectations. Beginning to bloom, as it does, about the first of March, it opens the season for the Spiraeas. The flowers are pure white and double, like daisies. But they are very small, each of them not more than a quarter of an inch in diameter, and appear before the leaves. These may, to many persons, seem great deficiencies, but the flowers are crowded on the branches in such a profusion, and the whole bush looks like being covered with snow, that the beholder cannot help forgetting the deficiencies, and must admire this beautiful forerunner of spring.

---

## Spiraea reevesiana

(*Spiraea cantoniensis, Spiraea reevesi, Spiraea lanceolata*)
Reeve's Spiraea

*Spiraea reevesiana* or Reeve's spiraea, is native to China and Japan, and was named in honor of John Reeves Jr., an English naturalist, plant collector, and for many years the "tea-taster" for the East India Company. A deciduous shrub with blue green, lanceolate leaves, one to two inches long, Reeve's spiraea has graceful, arching stems and a mounding form. Obtaining a height of four to five feet, this handsome garden shrub was highly prized during the first half of the nineteenth century for its beautiful clusters of single, white flowers that develop in mid to late spring.

*Spiraea reevesiana* (Reeve's spiraea)

Introduced into England in 1824, *Spiraea reevesiana* never proved as popular in British gardens as the double-flowering form, *Spiraea reevesiana flora plena*. In 1862, M. Billard, a French nurseryman, crossed *Spiraea reevesiana* with *Spiraea tribolata* to produce *Spiraea vanhouttei*, a beautiful hybrid that has perhaps been planted more extensively in American gardens than any other ornamental shrub. *Spiraea reevesiana* arrived in North America around the middle of the nineteenth century, first being offered by an American nursery when listed in Prince's *1844 Descriptive Catalogue of Fruit and Ornamental Trees*. The double-flowering form, *Spiraea reevesiana flora plena*, arrived ten years later, in 1855. While Reeve's spiraea was frequently planted in antebellum gardens, *Spiraea vanhouttei* overshadowed its popularity during the second half of the nineteenth century.

### *The Southern Cultivator,* 1858

Daniel Lee and Dennis Redmond, Editors

❧ The Twelve Best Spiraeas for the South

*Spiraea Reevesi* or *lanceolata*—A very graceful shrub when in bloom. The numerous, pure white flowers, in large bunches, are beautifully interspersed with the dark green foliage in long wreaths of a drooping habit. The shrub itself is very hardy, but the flower buds are sometimes nipped by late frosts. It is a native of China. Grows 4 to 5 feet high. There is a variety with double flowers, very beautiful, but, as yet quite scarce. Its blooming season is the last week of March or beginning of April.

Robert Nelson

### *The Flower Garden,* 1851

Joseph Breck

❧ *Spiraea reevesii.*—Mr. Reeve's Spiraea—We consider this one of the most elegant and desirable species of the whole family. The flowers are of a snowy whiteness, produced in clusters, the whole length of its graceful, arching stems, which, intermingled with the handsome foliage, produces a pleasing effect. The shrub is delicate in its growth, about four feet high, and flowers in June. It is propagated by cuttings, layers, and suckers.

## Syringa laciniata

(*Syringa persica var laciniata*)
Cut Leaf Lilac, Cut Leaf Persian Lilac

Native to China, *Syringa laciniata* is a beautiful ornamental shrub with fine textured foliage and delicate clusters of purple violet flowers. Originally believed to be a variety of the familiar Persian lilac (*Syringa persica*), it was discovered that *Syringa laciniata* was a separate species, with its own defining physical characteristics. It also was learned that *Syringa persica* was a hybrid resulting from a cross between *Syringa laciniata* and an unidentified species (probably *Syringa vulgaris* or *Syringa oblata*).

*Syringa laciniata* (cut leaf lilac)

*Syringa lacinata*'s finely textured leaves, having one to three lobes, easily distinguishes it from other lilacs. In late March and early April, numerous arching branches of *Syringa laciniata* are covered with small purple buds, which develop into showy clusters of light purple blooms that emit a delicate scent similar to other lilac species.

John Tradescant cultivated *Syringa laciniata* in England before 1640, and Philip Miller in *The Gardener's Dictionary* described it as differing from other lilacs "in having many of its leaves deeply cut with several segments; the flowers are also of a brighter purple color, and make a fine appearance." *Syringa laciniata* was first offered by an American nursery when listed in David and Cuthbert Landreth's *1811 Catalogue of Greenhouse Plants, Hardy Trees, Evergreen Shrubs, Flowering Shrubs, Bulbous Rooted, and Herbaceous Plants.* While seldom seen in southern gardens today, this treasured garden shrub was a favorite during the antebellum period because of its ease of cultivation, tolerance of summer heat, and freedom from insects and diseases.

### A Short Treatise on Horticulture, 1828

William Prince

↣ *Syringa persica*, or *Persian*—This fine shrub does not rise higher than from five to six feet, the branches are long, slender, and covered with a smooth brownish bark, with a bluish tinge. The leaves grow opposite, and are of a fine green; the flowers are delicate, and are produced in panicles, in the same manner as the Common Lilac, but of much smaller size. . . . In the Cut Leaved variety, however, the foliage is very different, each leave being finely divided into a number of segments, which gives them a delicate and interesting appearance, and renders this variety greatly admired. The flowers of this kind are exactly similar to those of the Purple variety.

### The Young Gardener's Assistant, 1837

Thomas Bridgeman

↣ The *Chinese* cut-leaf Lilac is very curious and the leaves are cut like parsley, the flowers growing in longer racemes than the former (Syringa persica).

### Arboretum et Fruticetum Britannicum, 1838

John Claudius Loudon

↣ Syringa *persica laciniata. The Cut-Leaved Persian Lilac.* This variety has some of its leaves pinnatidly cut and nearly all of them cut in some manner.

### The Horticulturist, 1848

Andrew Jackson Downing, Editor

↣ Persian Lilacs (*Syringa persica*). Far more delicate and pretty than the Common lilacs, both in leaf and blossom. The bunches of flowers are frequently a foot long and weigh down the terminal shoots so as to give the plant a very graceful appearance. The white and purple—both beautiful. *The Cut-Leaved Lilac* has interesting and delicate foliage.

---

## Syringa vulgaris

Common Lilac, Pipe Tree

*Syringa vulgaris* is native to the mountainous regions of southeastern Europe and has been grown as an ornamental for over 500 years. A large, deciduous shrub or small tree that reaches a height of fifteen to twenty feet, *Syringa vulgaris*, or common lilac as it is generally known, has upright branches and a broad, oval form. Generally considered the finest of all the lilac species, generations of gardeners have loved and cherished the common lilac for its delicate fragrance and showy clusters of purple flowers, which occur in great profusion from mid to late spring.

*Syringa vulgaris* arrived in Europe from Turkey in the sixteenth century. In addition to its ornamental value, the plant's hollow, pithy wood was used for centuries for making pipes, from which the common name, pipe tree, was derived. By 1597, both blue and white lilacs were being grown in England. Today, this venerable garden shrub has become so prevalent in British gardens that it is as common as many of the country's native plants.

*Syringa vulgaris* was one of the earliest of European shrubs to arrive in North America; it was first recorded as growing in a garden in New Amsterdam (New York state) in 1655. John Custis, a well-known colonial gardener and plant collector, had a fine collection of lilacs in his garden at Williamsburg, Virginia. By the middle of the eighteenth century, lilacs had become so widespread that John Bartram discouraged Peter Collinson, his English patron, from sending him a shipment of plants containing lilacs, exclaiming that "[lilacs] are already too numerous, as roots brought by the early settlers have spread enormously." *Syringa vulgaris* was first offered for sale by a North American nursery when listed in William Prince's *1771 Broadside*. Its intolerance of both heat and humidity limited the use of the common lilac in antebellum gardens of the middle and upper South.

### *A Treatise on the Cultivation of Ornamental Flowers,* 1828
Roland Green

⏴ LILAC (*Syringa vulgaris*)—This is a large shrub, very hardy, and much admired when in bloom. It has large bunches of flowers which possess considerable fragrance. The white and the purple may be easily grafted, or inoculated into each other, and when the shrub, with a handsome head, is thus managed, some bushes producing purple and other white flowers, it makes a beautiful appearance. It is propagated from suckers, of which it sends out too many, and from which it should be kept as clear as possible. The Persian lilac (*Syringa persica*) is a neat shrub, loaded, when in bloom, with very delicate flowers. It is propagated by suckers.

### *The Southern Cultivator,* 1857
Daniel Lee and Dennis Redmond, Editors

⏴ Ornamental Trees and Shrubs for the South

*Syringa vulgaris* (Lilac)—Like so many of our ornamental shrubs, we obtained this from Asia. They are too well know to need any description. The finest are the pure-white, and the Chinese, the latter is pale purple, and blooms twice in the season, viz., in April and in September. Both require rich moist soil, and are propagated by suckers.

Robert Nelson, Fruitland Nurseries, Augusta, Georgia

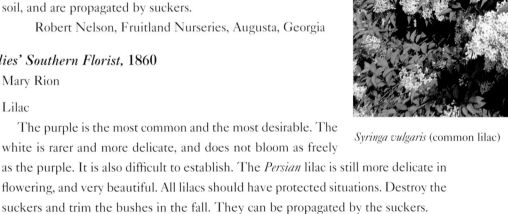

*Syringa vulgaris* (common lilac)

### *Ladies' Southern Florist,* 1860
Mary Rion

⏴ Lilac

The purple is the most common and the most desirable. The white is rarer and more delicate, and does not bloom as freely as the purple. It is also difficult to establish. The *Persian* lilac is still more delicate in flowering, and very beautiful. All lilacs should have protected situations. Destroy the suckers and trim the bushes in the fall. They can be propagated by the suckers.

## Viburnum tinus

(*Laurel tinus, Tinus laruifolius*)
Laurustinus, Laurestinus

*Viburnum tinus* is indigenous to southern Europe and the Mediterranean region. It is an ancient garden shrub that has been grown for centuries for its fine, evergreen foliage and beautiful clusters of white to pinkish flowers that develop in late winter and early spring. Reaching a height of eight to ten feet, this handsome ornamental has an upright, oval form with dark green, lustrous leaves, two to three inches long.

John Gerard, the author of the *Herball* published in 1597, first cultivated *Viburnum tinus* in England in 1596. Laurustinus proved a popular ornamental in British gardens, and J. C. Loudon, a noted English garden writer, encouraged its use in urban settings "for varying the iron palisades, poles or brick walls, which separate the front gardens of streets and suburban houses." Loudon warned, as did other authorities, that the fallen leaves of the laurustinus should be removed from paths and from below windows as they emit "an unpleasant odor." *Viburnum tinus* was first offered for sale by an American nursery when listed in Bernard M'Mahon's 1804 *Catalogue of Garden, Herb, Flower, Tree, Shrub, and Grass Seeds.* Laurustinus was a favorite in antebellum gardens of the lower and middle South, where it was grown for its elegant foliage and beautiful display of late-winter flowers either as a specimen plant or as an informal hedge.

*Viburnum tinus* (laurustinus)

### *The American Flower Garden Directory,* 1839
Robert Buist

ᘏ *Viburnums*—A few of these are very ornamental evergreen shrubs, and almost hardy. *V. tinus* is the well-known Laurestine (or what is commonly called Laurestinus), is of the easiest culture; flowers small, white and in large flattened panicles; blooming from February to May, and universally esteemed. It will stand the winter by a little protection, but the flower-buds being formed in the fall, the intense frost destroys them; consequently, it will not flower freely, except if protected from severe frost.

### *Report of the Commissioner of Patents,* 1854
Charles Mason, Commissioner

ᘏ Trees and Shrubs Usually Employed for Hedges
Laurestinus (*Viburnum tinus*)

The laurestinus is a beautiful evergreen shrub, with shining leaves and showy white flowers, which appear during the winter months. It is a native of the south of France and Northern Africa, in the region of the olive; and hence is suited to the climate of our Southern States. Like the laurel, it shoots so luxuriantly as to render it somewhat difficult to keep the hedges which are planted with it, in tolerable shape; besides, the leaves being very large, if the hedge is clipped with shears, they will be cut through, which would give them an unsightly appearance; and as one of the greatest beauties of the plant is in its blossoms, when the plants are sheared, the flowers are generally cut off, by which, much of their beauty is lost. Nor can this be avoided where the hedge is to be kept in close order. Therefore, the plant is not so proper for this purpose; but, in such places, where walls or other fences are designed to be hidden, there is no shrub better adapted than this, as the branches are slender and pliable, and may be trained close to the wall, whereby it may be entirely concealed.

Daniel Lee and Dennis Redmond, Editors

↪ *Viburnum tinus,* also called *Laurustinus,* from Spain, is a well known winter blooming shrub, always forming a neat little bush. The flowers, at first pink, and when finally open, pure white, are produced abundantly and in clusters very early in the spring. Requires rich soil. Propagated by cuttings and layers.

Robert Nelson, Macon, Georgia

## Vitex agnus-castus

Chaste Tree, Spikenard, Hemp Tree

Chaste tree is a large deciduous shrub or small tree with an upright to rounded form that is native to southern Europe and western Asia. Chaste tree's leaves are compound with individual leaflets that are dark green above and a silvery gray below. This showy ornamental is best known for its beautiful spikes of light blue to purple flowers that reach their peak in July and August, a time when few ornamentals are in bloom. Blossoms are followed by clusters of dark-colored, somewhat nondescript berries in late summer and fall. The plant's scientific name, *Vitex agnus-castus,* is derived from the Latin, *vitex,* meaning to plat or weave (a reference to the plant's use throughout history for making baskets) and *agnus-castus,* meaning pure or chaste. In ancient Greece it was believed that if leaves of the chaste tree were placed under a wife's pillow during her husband's absence, chastity would prevail.

Introduced into England from Sicily in 1570, chaste tree arrived in North America during colonial times, generally only being grown in the southern colonies because of its tender nature. On April 11, 1807, Thomas Jefferson recorded planting seeds of chaste tree at Monticello. This decorative ornamental was first offered for sale by an American nursery when listed in Bartram's *1814 Catalogue of Trees, Shrubs and Herbaceous Plants.* Chaste tree was a popular ornamental in gardens of the antebellum South, where it was highly prized for its attractive foliage and showy flowers.

### *The Gardener's Dictionary,* 1752

Philip Miller

↪ *Vitex agnus-castus*

Common in most English gardens where a variety of hardy trees are preferred. . . . These plants are all very hardy, and may be propagated by planting their cuttings in the spring. . . . If they are placed

*Vitex agnus-castus* (chaste tree)

in a warm situation and have a kindly light soil, they will grow to be eight or ten feet high, and produce their spikes of flowers at the extremity of every strong shoot. . . . Coming late in the year, and having an odd appearance, together with the variety of their leaves, renders them worthy of a place . . . amongst other shrubs.

### *Arboretum et Fruticetum Britannicum,* 1838
John Claudius Loudon

ॐ VITEX AGNUS CASTUS. The *official,* or *true,* Chaste Tree

A shrub, of the height of 5 ft. or 6 ft., which produces white, bluish white, and sometimes reddish white flowers. . . . It is a native of Sicily, Naples, the north of Africa, and Egypt, and has been in cultivation since 1570. . . . The flowers are produced in spikes at the extremities of the branches from 7 in. to 15 in. in length. . . . Its flowers have an agreeable odour, but the leaves have an unpleasant smell, although aromatic.

### *The Young Gardener's Assistant,* 1855
Thomas Bridgeman

ॐ *Vitex agnes castus,* or Chaste Tree, a pretty and singular shrub, flowering the most part of summer.

### *The Southern Cultivator,* 1857
Daniel Lee and Dennis Redmond, Editors

ॐ *Vitex agnus-castus* (Chaste Tree) from the south of Europe, produce numerous heads of neat blue flowers, and can be kept in bloom nearly all the summer, by constantly cutting off the flowers. The foliage has an odor like lavender. Ten feet high. Best propagated from seed.

Robert Nelson, Fruitland Nurseries, Augusta, Georgia

---

## Weigela florida

(*Weigela rosea, Weigela amablis, Weigela japonica, Diervilla japonica*)
Weigela, Rose Colored Weigela

Native to China and Korea, *Weigela florida* is a large, deciduous shrub that was named in honor of E. Weigel, a well-known German botanist. This handsome garden shrub was formerly classified under the genus name *Diervilla,* a name some gardeners and nurserymen still use. Reaching a height of six to eight feet, *Weigela florida* is characterized by an upright, spreading form with ascending branches and dark green, ovate leaves that are smooth on top and slightly pubescent below. This treasured garden shrub is best known for its long, tubular flowers that are purplish rose on the outside and a pale pink inside. Flowers occur in groups of threes or fours on short lateral branches in May and June.

In 1843, Robert Fortune discovered this showy ornamental in northern China. He found it "growing in a Mandarin's garden, on the island of Chuson." Fortune described the plant as "literally loaded with its fine rose-colored flowers, which hung in graceful bunches from the orbits of the leaves, and the ends of the branches. . . . Everyone saw and admired the beautiful *Weigela.* . . . It forms a neat bush, not unlike a syringa [*Philadelphus*] in habit, deciduous in winter, and flowering in the months of April and May."

*Weigela florida* was enthusiastically received in England around 1845. Three years later this elegant garden shrub was available to American gardeners when offered by the

### The Horticulturist, 1848

Andrew Jackson Downing

ᔕᖇ Weigela rosea. *The Rose-Colored Weigela.* This exquisite shrub is one of Mr. Fortune's prizes from the Mandarin's garden. We are very desirous to prove it in the United States, as we are confident, from its growing in the north of China, that it will prove quite hardy here.

### The Horticulturist, 1850

Andrew Jackson Downing, Editor

ᔕᖇ New Hardy Plants

The following plants recently introduced from China into the Horticultural Society's Gardens of London, have proven perfectly hardy with me the past winter:

> *Weigela rosea*, a strong growing shrub with a profusion of flowers in clusters from 2 to 5, of a delicate blush colour changing to deep rose; plants from 6 inches high to 1–1/2 feet, stood out fully exposed in my nursery, without protection and proves more hardy than Deutzia scabra or the common Althaea. It is also admirably adapted for forcing into bloom for bouquets.
>
> R. Buist, Philadelphia, 1849

### The Horticulturist, 1850

Andrew Jackson Downing, Editor

ᔕᖇ Among the new things to be had in the nurseries, no one can be disappointed with the *Weigela rosea*, the new shrub from China with a profusion of large flowers expanding of a delicate apple-blossom colour, and changing to a deep rose.

*Weigelia florida* (weigela)

### The Flower Garden, 1851

Joseph Breck

ᔕᖇ Weigela

> *Weigela rosea*—The Rose-Colored Weigela. This is another new shrub, introduced by Mr. Fortune into England from China, first noticed here by Mr. Downing.

---

## Wisteria frutescens

(*Glycine frutescens, Glycine fruticosa*)
American Wisteria, Shrubby Glycine, Carolina Kidney Bean

Native to the southeastern United States from Virginia to Florida and westward to Texas, American wisteria is a deciduous, woody vine that can obtain a height of twenty to thirty feet. American wisteria was known as *Glycine fruitescens* until 1818 when Thomas Nuttall renamed it *Wisteria frutescens* in honor of Dr. Caspar Wistar, a Philadelphia physician and professor of anatomy. The species name, *frutescens*, refers to the plant's shrubby habit of growth when allowed to grow unsupported. American wisteria has compound leaves that are divided into multiple leaflets, one to two inches long. This native climber is best known for its pendulous clusters of light purple flowers that, unlike the Asian varieties, bloom after the leaves unfold. American wisteria produces seeds that resemble kidney beans, thus giving rise to one of its earlier common names, Carolina kidney bean tree.

Mark Catesby introduced American wisteria into England in 1724, but it never proved popular in British gardens because of its failure to flower due to the English climate. Frequently planted in American gardens during the colonial era, this native vine was first offered for sale by an American nursery in 1783 when listed in *Bartram's Catalogue of American Trees, Shrubs and Herbaceous Plants*. American wisteria remained a favorite ornamental during the antebellum period for covering walls and fences.

### A Short Treatise on Horticulture, 1828
William Prince

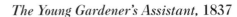

↶ *Glycine frutescens*, or *American Shrubby Glycine*

This has a very strong and vigorous growth, and will run to a great length, often forming shoots from 20 to 50 feet in a season. It will speedily cover an extensive bower or arbour, for which purpose no vine is better adapted. . . . Even in the southern states, where this plant is common, and a native, it is deemed one of the most magnificent climbers. In the vicinity of Charleston, I have noticed that it is erroneously called BARTONIA VINE.

### The Young Gardener's Assistant, 1837
Thomas Bridgeman

↶ *American glycine frutescens*, or *Wisteria frutescens*

This beautiful brother of the Chinese kind is a native of our southern states, grows in much the same ways as the others, and perhaps not inferior. Although this fine creeper has been long known in England, we have not heard much about it by English writers; the conclusion seems to be, that it does not flower well in England. . . . The American Wisteria should be planted in every garden with other creepers, or to run up the trees or shrubberies, according to its natural position.

### The Horticulturist, 1858
J. Jay Smith, Editor

↶ *Wisteria Frutescens*

More than a hundred years before the introduction of the Chinese, Europe possessed the North American Glycina, now called Wisteria Frutescens. However, as frequently happens in such cases, the new-comer has supplanted its predecessor, which it surpasses in the great development of its stems, in the astonishing profusion of its flowers, and in the size of its azure-colored clusters. To these advantages of its rival, the United States species can boast on its side of flowering on branches previously supplied with leaves, as well as of exhaling in the autumn an agreeable perfume. In other respects the resemblance is seen in the harmony of the general appearance, in the general drooping of the clusters, which are of a rich velvet color.

*Wisteria frutescens* (American wisteria)

# Wisteria sinensis

(*Glycine sinensis, Glycine chinensis*)
Chinese Wisteria

*Wisteria sinensis*, or Chinese wisteria as it is more generally known, is a vigorous, deciduous climber that is native to northern and central China. Thomas Nuttall named the genus, *Wisteria*, in honor of Dr. Caspar Wistar (1761–1818), a noted physician and professor of anatomy at the University of Pennsylvania. Nuttall's original spelling of *Wisteria*, with an *e* instead of the *a* as is used in the spelling of "Wistar," has remained unchanged because of established rules of scientific nomenclature. Chinese wisteria is a fast-growing, woody vine that can reach heights of 100 feet or more. This popular climber has compound leaves that are divided into numerous leaflets. Chinese wisteria's true glory is in early spring when it is covered with long, pendulous clusters of fragrant, blue violet flowers that bloom before the leaves unfurl. Long, flat, velvet-covered, light brown seed pods develop in late summer, remaining on the plant well into fall.

*Wisteria sinensis* (Chinese wisteria)

*Wisteria sinensis* was introduced into England from Canton, China, in 1816 and soon became a favorite in British gardens. This popular ornamental arrived in North American around 1824 when it was introduced by William Prince Jr. (1766–1842) of the famous Prince Nursery on Long Island, New York. Prince first offered this newly introduced vine for sale to American gardens in the firm's *1831 Annual Catalogue of Fruit and Ornamental Trees and Plants*. Because of its hardy nature and incomparable display of springtime flowers, Chinese wisteria soon became a popular ornamental vine in antebellum gardens throughout the southern states.

## *A Short Treatise on Horticulture*, 1828
William Prince

༄ *Glycine sinensis, or Chinese*—This species, yet very rare even in Europe, was introduced to this country by the author about four years since. From every appearance it will form a vine nearly or quite as vigorous as the preceding (*Glycine frutescens, or American Shrubby Glycine*). It has not yet flowered here that I am aware of, but has produced flowers in England, and they are described in several of the European publications of the past year as extremely beautiful, and the plant is represented as one of the most desirable on that account.

## *The Flower Garden*, 1851
Joseph Breck

༄ *Wistaria sinensis*—The Chinese Wisteria—This is one of the most magnificent climbing shrubby plants in cultivation. It was formerly treated, in the North, as a tender plant, and might be seen trained to the rafters of the green-house, in full flower, in March, with its thousands of rich clusters, or pendulous racemes of delicate pale-purple blossoms, so numerous that the whole space it occupied seemed to be covered with them. Each raceme is from ten to twelve inches long, and densely filled with its delicate and richly perfumed flowers. . . . The flowers make their appearance before the foliage starts, the last of May in the open ground. The foliage is abundant, and its color is a lively, pleasant hue of green.

***The Southern Cultivator,* 1857**

Daniel Lee and Dennis Redmond, Editors

*Glycine chinensis,* also called *Wisteria.* Of the rampant climbers, this, which was introduced from China in 1818, produces the most gorgeous clusters of pea-flower shaped blossoms, of a beautiful pale lilac color. Its growth is so strong, that I have known the vine to grow six inches in twenty-four hours. In rich moist soil, and fully exposed to the sun, it will cover a trellis in a very short time. A crimson as well as a pure white variety have recently sprung from seeds in Europe, both of which, however, are quite rare in America.

Robert Nelson, Fruitland Nurseries, Augusta, Georgia

## Yucca filamentosa

(*Yucca virginiana*)

Adam's Needle, Adam's Thread, Bear Grass, Spoonleaf Yucca

Native to the southeastern United States, *Yucca filamentosa* or Adam's needle is a low-growing, evergreen shrub characterized by stemless rosettes of radiating, swordlike leaves that are one to two feet long. The plant's gray green, lanceolate foliage has small, thread-like filaments along the margins of the leaves, giving rise to the species name, *filamentosa.* White, fragrant, cup-shaped flowers occur in June and July on erect spikes, five to six feet tall. Flowers are followed by fleshy seed pods, which turn brown in fall. American Indians used the threads of *Yucca filamentosa* for sewing moccasins, and in the southern states the plant's leaves were twisted and used for making cordage and ropes for a variety of domestic uses.

*Yucca filamentosa* (Adam's needle)

This American native was introduced into England as early as 1675 and proved perfectly hardy in British gardens. In 1794, Thomas Jefferson included *Yucca filamentosa* in his list of trees and shrubs to be planted at Monticello. This showy ornamental was first offered by an American nursery when listed in Bernard M'Mahon's 1804 *Catalog of Garden, Herb, Flower, Tree, Shrub, and Grass Seeds.* Because of its hardy nature and ability to tolerate both heat and drought, *Yucca filamentosa* was frequently grown in antebellum gardens throughout the southern states.

***A Short Treatise on Horticulture,* 1828**

William Prince

*Yucca.* Of this very curious genus there are several species which are already cultivated as hardy ornamentals in our gardens, and doubtless some others will equally with-stand the rigors of winter.

*Yucca filamentosa or Adam's Needle*—This in our vicinity is the most common, it has long lanceolate leaves, pointed at the ends, with numerous threads on both edges and which attain to a considerable degree of strength; the leaves are spread near the ground in a radiate manner, and remain during the winter. In summer the plant throws up a flower stem to the height of six to eight feet, which branches somewhat at its summit, and is garnished with numerous tulip shaped flowers, which give to the plant a striking appearance. . . . There is a most beautiful variety with variegated leaves.

## *Arboretum et Fruticetum Britannicum,* 1838
John Claudius Loudon

∽ YUCCA FIILAMENTOSA The filamentosa Yucca, or *Thready Adam's Needle.*
The stalk and leaves are like those of Y. gloriosa; but the leaves are obtuse, and have no spines. The flower-stalk rises 5 ft. or 6 ft. high, and is generally covered with flowers for most of its length. The flowers are larger and whiter than those of Y. gloriosa, and sit close to the stalk. One side of the leaves are long threads, which hang down.

## *The Horticulturist,* 1852
Andrew Jackson Downing, Editor

∽ *Yucca filamentosa or Adam's Thread*
This variety differs mainly from the former (*Yucca gloriosa*) in having no spines at the ends of the leaves, but instead, the foliage is irregularly serrated, and edged with long threads, which hang down two to three inches long. . . . It is a native of Virginia . . . both the foliage and flowers are quite ornamental, it is worthy of a place in every garden.

## *Resources of the Southern Fields and Forests,* 1863
Francis Peyre Porcher

∽ Yucca filamentosa
A tincture of the roots is much employed in rheumatism. The "Cherokee doctors" use it in the form of a poultice of the roots, or a salve, or a local application in allaying inflammation. The fiber is uncommonly strong, and is used for various purposes in our plantations . . . for making thongs for hanging up the heaviest hams, bacon, etc.

# Trees, Shrubs, and Vines Available to Southern Gardeners before 1861

| Botanical Name | Common Name/Names | Place of Origin | Date Introduced or First Cultivated in England | Date First Offered in an American Nursery/Seed Catalogue* |
|---|---|---|---|---|
| *Acacia farnesiana* | Sweet Acacia, Opopanax | Santo Domingo | 1656 | 1804 (M) |
| *Aesculus pavia* | Red Buckeye | Southeast U.S. | 1771 | 1783 (B) |
| *Ailanthus altissima* | Tree of Heaven, Tanners Sumac | China | 1751 | 1823 (P) |
| *Akebia quinata* | Five Leaf Akebia | China and Japan | 1855 | 1860 (P) |
| *Albizia julibrissin* | Mimosa, Silk Tree | Persia and China | 1745 | 1807 (B) |
| *Amerlanchier canadensis* | Serviceberry, Shadblow | Eastern and Central U.S. | 1623 | 1783 (B) |
| *Aucuba japonica variegata* | Aucuba, Gold Dust Plant | Japan | 1783 | 1807 (B) |
| *Azalea calendulaceum* | Flame Azalea | Mideastern and Central U.S. | 1800 | 1811 (L) |
| *Azalea indica* | Chinese Azalea, Indian Azalea | China | 1808 | 1814 (B) |
| *Azalea maximum* | Great Laurel, Rosebay | Eastern U.S. | 1734 | 1783 (B) |
| *Azalea nudiflorum* | Bush Azalea | Eastern U.S. | 1734 | 1804 (M) |
| *Azalea viscosa* | Swamp Azalea | Eastern U.S. | 1731 | 1783 (B) |
| *Bignonia capreolata* | Cross Vine | Southeast U.S. | 1710 | 1783 (B) |
| *Broussonetia papyrifera* | Paper Mulberry | Eastern Asia | 1751 | 1807 (B) |
| *Buxus sempervirens* | Common Box, American Box | Europe, North Africa and West Asia | Ancient Times | 1807 (B) |
| *Buxus sempervirens arborescens* | Tree Box | Europe, Africa and Asia | Ancient Times | 1811 (L) |
| *Buxus sempervirens suffruticosa* | Dwarf Box, Edging Box | Europe, Africa and Asia | Ancient Times | 1807 (WB) |
| *Callicarpa americana* | French Mulberry, American Beauty Berry | Southeastern and Central U.S. | 1724 | 1783 (B) |
| *Calycanthus floridus* | Carolina Allspice, Sweet Shrub | Southeast U.S. | 1726 | 1783 (B) |
| *Camellia japonica* | Camellia, Japonica, Japan Rose | China and Japan | 1739 | 1807 (B) |
| *Camellia sasanqua* | Sasanqua | China and Japan | 1811 | 1823 (P) |
| *Camellia sinensis (virdis & bohea)* | Tea Plant | China | 1768 | 1807 (B) |
| *Campsis radicans* | Trumpet Vine, Trumpet Creeper | Southeast U.S. | 1640 | 1783 (B) |
| *Catalpa bignonioides* | Indian Bean Tree, Southern Catalpa | Eastern U.S. | 1726 | 1771 (P) |
| *Cedrus argentea atlantica* | Atlas Cedar | North Africa | 1840 | 1852 (TH) |
| *Cedrus deodara* | Deodar Cedar | Himalayas | 1831 | 1844 (P) |
| *Cedrus libani* | Cedar of Lebanon | Lebanon and Taurus Mountains | 1683 | 1815 (P) |
| *Celtis occidentalis* | Hackberry, American Nettle Tree | Eastern U.S. | 1656 | 1783 (B) |
| *Cercis canadensis* | Redbud, Judas Tree | Eastern and Central U.S. | 1730 | 1783 (B) |
| *Chaenomeles speciosa* | Flowering Quince | China | 1796 | 1814 (B) |
| *Chimonanthus praecox* | Wintersweet, Japan Allspice | China and Japan | 1766 | 1811 (L) |
| *Chionanthus virginicus* | Fringe Tree, Grancy Gray Beard | Eastern U.S. | 1736 | 1783 (B) |
| *Clematis flammula* | Sweet Scented Clematis | Southern Europe | 1590 | 1815 (P) |
| *Clematis virginiana* | Virgin's Bower | North America | 1767 | 1804 (M) |
| *Cornus florida* | Flowering Dogwood | Eastern U.S. | 1730 | 1771 (P) |
| *Cotinus coggygria* | Smoke Tree, Venetian Sumac | Central and Southern Europe | ca. 1656 | 1790 (P) |
| *Cryptomeria japonica* | Japan Cedar | China and Japan | 1842 | 1849 (TH) |

* See Nursery Reference Key at End of Section.

Trees, Shrubs, and Vines Available to Southern Gardeners before 1861 (*continued*)

| Botanical Name | Common Name | Place of Origin | Date Introduced or First Cultivated in England | Date First Offered in an American Nursery/Seed Catalogue* |
|---|---|---|---|---|
| *Cunninghammia lanceolata* | Chinese Fir | China | 1804 | 1853 (P) |
| *Daphne odora* | Sweet Scented Daphne | China | 1771 | 1810 (WB) |
| *Deutzia gracilis* | Graceful Deutzia | Japan | ca.1840 | 1850 (HO) |
| *Deutzia scabra* | Rough-Leaved Deutzia | China | ca.1822 | 1841 (MO) |
| *Elaegnus angustifolia* | Oleaster | Southern Europe | 1633 | 1835 (P) |
| *Eriobotrya japonica* | Loquat, Medlar | China and Japan | 1787 | 1824 (L) |
| *Euonymus americanus* | Strawberry Bush | Eastern U.S. | 1683 | 1783 (B) |
| *Euonymus japonica* | Evergreen Euonymus | Japan | 1804 | 1844 (P) |
| *Fagus grandifloia* | American Beech | Eastern U.S. | 1766 | 1783 (B) |
| *Ficus carica* | Common Fig | Southern Europe | 1525 | 1771 (P) |
| *Firmiana simplex* | Varnish Tree, Chinese Parasol Tree | China and Japan | 1757 | 1804 (M) |
| *Forsythia suspensa* | Drooping Forsythia | Japan | 1850 | 1859 (BU) |
| *Forsythia viridissima* | Greenstem Forsythia, Golden Bell | China | 1844 | 1848 (H) |
| *Franklinia alatamaha* | (Extinct)Franklin Tree | Georgia | 1774 | 1783 (B) |
| *Gardenia jasminoides* | Cape Jasmine, Gardenia | China and Japan | 1754 | 1807 (B) |
| *Gardenia radicans* | Rooting Gardenia | China | 1804 | 1814 (B) |
| *Gardenia thunbergia* | Starry Gardenia | China | 1773 | 1814 (B) |
| *Gelsemium sempervirens* | Carolina Jessamine | Southeast U.S. | 1640 | 1783 (B) |
| *Ginkgo biloba* | Maidenhair Tree, Ginkgo | China | 1754 | 1811 (L) |
| *Gordonia lasianthus* | Loblolly Bay | Southeast U.S. | 1768 | 1804 (M) |
| *Halesia tetraptera* | Carolina Silverbell, Snowdrop Tree | Southeast U.S. | 1756 | 1790 (P) |
| *Hedera helix* | English Ivy | Europe | Ancient Times | 1807 (B) |
| *Hibiscus syriacus* | Althea, Rose of Sharon | India and China | 1596 | 1793 (P) |
| *Hydrangea macrophylla* | French Hydrangea, Common Hydranger | China | 1788 | 1807 (B) |
| *Hydrangea quercifolia* | Oakleaf Hydrangea | Southeast U.S. | 1803 | 1804 (M) |
| *Ilex glabra* | Inkberry, Gallberry | Eastern U.S. | 1759 | 1783 (B) |
| *Ilex opaca* | American Holly | Eastern U.S. | 1774 | 1783 (B) |
| *Ilex verticillata* | Winterberry | Eastern U.S. | 1736 | 1783 (B) |
| *Ilex vomitoria* | Yaupon Holly | Southeast U.S. | 1700 | 1783 (B) |
| *Illicium anisatum* | Japanese Anise | Japan | 1790 | 1811 (L) |
| *Illicium floridanum* | Florida Anise | Florida, Louisiana, and Alabama | 1766 | 1807 (B) |
| *Illicium parviflorum* | Yellow Anise, Starry Anise | Florida and Georgia | 1790 | 1823 (P) |
| *Jasminum nudiflorum* | Winter Jasmine | China | 1844 | 1855 (F) |
| *Jasminum officinale* | Common or Poet's Jasmine | Persia, China, India | 1548 | 1807 (B) |
| *Juniperus virginiana* | Red Cedar | Eastern and Central U.S. | 1664 | 1771 (P) |
| *Kalmia latifolia* | Mountain Laurel, Calico Bush | Eastern U.S. | 1734 | 1783 (B) |
| *Kerria japonica* | Single-Flowered Kerria | Japan | 1834 | 1844 (P) |
| *Kerria japonica pleniflora* | Double-Flowered Kerria, Japanese Rose | Japan | 1804 | 1814 (B) |
| *Koelreuteria paniculata* | Golden Rain Tree | China | 1763 | 1790 (P) |
| *Lagerstroemia indica* | Crape Myrtle | China | 1759 | 1807 (B) |
| *Laurel nobilis* | Roman Laurel, Bay Laurel | Mediterranean Region | 1548 | 1811 (B) |
| *Ligustrum japonicum* | Japan Privet | Japan | 1845 | 1848 (H) |

* See Nursery Reference Key at End of Section.

## Trees, Shrubs, and Vines Available to Southern Gardeners before 1861 (*continued*)

| Botanical Name | Common Name | Place of Origin | Date Introduced or First Cultivated in England | Date First Offered in an American Nursery/Seed Catalogue* |
|---|---|---|---|---|
| *Ligustrum lucidum* | Wax Tree of China | China | 1797 | 1823 (P) |
| *Ligustrum vulgare* | Common Privet, Prim | Europe | Ancient Times | 1807 (B) |
| *Liquidambar styraciflua* | Sweet Gum | Eastern U.S. | 1681 | 1783 (B) |
| *Liriodendron tulipifera* | Tulip Tree, Yellow Poplar | Eastern and Central U.S. | ca.1663 | 1771 (P) |
| *Lonicera fragrantissima* | Winter Honeysuckle | China | 1845 | 1860 (P) |
| *Lonicera flexosa* | Chinese Honeysuckle | China | 1806 | 1828 (B) |
| *Lonicera japonica* | Japanese Honeysuckle | Eastern Asia | 1806 | 1823 (P) |
| *Lonicera sempervirens* | Coral Honeysuckle, Trumpet Honeysuckle | Eastern U.S. | 1656 | 1783 (B) |
| *Maclura pomifera* | Osage Orange | Central U.S. | 1811 | 1824 (L) |
| *Magnolia acuminata* | Cucumber Tree | Eastern U.S. | 1736 | 1783 (B) |
| *Magnolia acuminata cordata* | Yellow Flowered Magnolia | Southern U.S. | 1801 | 1804 (M) |
| *Magnolia denudata* | Yulan Magnolia | China | 1789 | 1814 (B) |
| *Magnolia fraseri* | Fraser Magnolia | Southern U.S. | 1787 | 1804 (M) |
| *Magnolia grandiflora* | Southern Magnolia | Southern U.S. | 1734 | 1783 (B) |
| *Magnolia liliflora* | Lily-Flowered Magnolia | China | 1790 | 1807 (B) |
| *Magnolia macrophylla* | Bigleaf Magnolia | Eastern U.S. | 1800 | 1811 (L) |
| *Magnolia × soulangiana* | Saucer Magnolia | France | 1820 | 1831 (P) |
| *Magnolia tripetala* | Umbrella Magnolia | Eastern U.S. | 1752 | 1783 (B) |
| *Magnolia virginiana* | Sweetbay | Eastern U.S. | 1688 | 1783 (B) |
| *Mahonia aquifolium* | Oregon Grape | British Columbia to Oregon | 1824 | 1824 (L) |
| *Mahonia bealei* | Leatherleaf Mahonia | China | 1845 | 1859 (BU) |
| *Mahonia japonica* | Japanese Holly-Grape | China and Japan | 1845 | 1855 (P) |
| *Melia azedarach* | Chinaberry, Bead Tree | India and China | 1656 | 1790 (P) |
| *Michelia figo* | Banana Shrub | China | 1789 | 1811 (L) |
| *Morus alba* | White Mulberry | China | 1596 | 1790 (P) |
| *Morus rubra* | Red Mulberry | Eastern U.S. | 1629 | 1783 (B) |
| *Myrica cerifera* | Candle Berry, Wax Myrtle | Southern U.S. | 1699 | 1771 (P) |
| *Myrtus communis* | Myrtle, Common Myrtle | Mediterranean Region | 1562 | 1807 (B) |
| *Nandina domistica* | Nandina, Heavenly Bamboo | China | 1804 | 1814 (B) |
| *Nerium oleander* | Oleander | Southern Europe | 1596 | 1790 (P) |
| *Ophiopogon japonicus* | Sanke's Beard | Japan | 1784 | 1807 (B) |
| *Osmanthus fragrans* | Sweet Olive, Tea Olive, Sweet Scented Olive | China and Japan | 1771 | 1810 (WB) |
| *Oxydendrum aboreum* | Sourwood, Sorrel Tree | Northeast U.S. | 1752 | 1783 (B) |
| *Parkinsonia aculeata* | Prickley Parkinsonia | West Indies | 1739 | 1804 (M) |
| *Parthenocissus quinquefolia* | Virginia Creeper | Northeast U.S. | 1629 | 1783 (B) |
| *Passiflora incarnata* | Passion Flower | America | 1629 | 1811 (L) |
| *Paulownia tomentosa* | Empress Tree, Princess Tree | China and Japan | 1834 | 1844 (P) |
| *Philadelphus coronarius* | Mock Orange, Syringa | Southern Europe | 1596 | 1771 (B) |
| *Photinia serrulata* | Chinese Serrated Leaved Photinia | China | 1804 | 1835 (P) |
| *Picea abies* | Norway Spruce | Northern and Central Europe | 1548 | 1815 (P) |
| *Pinckneya pubens* | Georgia Bark | Southern U.S. | 1786 | 1811 (L) |
| *Pinus strobus* | White Pine | Eastern U.S. | 1705 | 1771 (P) |
| *Pittosporum tobira* | Pittosporum | China and Japan | 1804 | 1811 (L) |

* See Nursery Reference Key at End of Section.

| Botanical Name | Common Name | Place of Origin | Date Introduced or First Cultivated in England | Date First Offered in an American Nursery/Seed Catalogue* |
|---|---|---|---|---|
| *Platanus occidentalis* | Sycamore | Southeast U.S. | 1634 | 1783 (B) |
| *Plumbago campensis* | Cape Plumbago | Cape of Good Hope | 1818 | 1827 (T) |
| *Populas nigra* var. *italica* | Lombardy Poplar, Italian Poplar | Italy | 1758 | 1790 (P) |
| *Prunus caroliniana* | Cherry Laurel, Carolina Bird Cherry, Laura Mundi | Southern U.S. | 1759 | 1771 (P) |
| *Prunus grandulosa* | Dwarf Flowering Almond | China and Japan | 1835 | 1844 (P) |
| *Puncia granatum* | Pomegranata | Southern Europe, North Africa | Before 1548 | 1792 (B) |
| *Pyracantha coccinea* | Pyracantha, Firethorn | Southern Europe, Near East | 1629 | 1792 (B) |
| *Quercus nigra* | Water Oak | Southern U.S. | 1723 | 1783 (B) |
| *Quercus phellos* | Willow Oak | Northeast U.S. | 1723 | 1783 (B) |
| *Quercus virginiana* | Southern Live Oak | Southern U.S. | 1739 | 1783 (B) |
| *Robinia pseudoacacia* | Black Locust, False Acacia | Eastern and Central U.S. | ca.1635 | 1783 (B) |
| *Rosa banksiae* | Lady Banksiae Rose, Lady Banks | China | 1807 | 1823 (P) |
| *Rosa laevigata* | Cherokee Rose | China | 1759 | 1814 (B) |
| *Salix babylonica* | Weeping Willow | China | 1692 | 1790 (P) |
| *Sassafras albidum* | Sassafras | Eastern and Central U.S. | 1633 | 1771 (P) |
| *Smilax lanceolata* | Southern Smilax, Spearshaped Smilax, Wedding Vine | Eastern U.S. | 1785 | 1804 (M) |
| *Sophora japonica* | Japanese Pagoda Tree | China and Japan | 1753 | 1811 (L) |
| *Spiraea prunifolia plena* | Bridal Wreath Spiraea, Double-Flowered Plum Leaved Spiraea | China | ca.1845 | 1848 (H) |
| *Spiraea reevesiana* | Reeves' Spiraea | China and Japan | 1844 | 1844 (P) |
| *Spiraea reevesiana flora plena* | Double Reeves' Spiraea | China and Japan | 1855 | 1855 (P) |
| *Stewartia malacodendron* | Stewartia | Southeast U.S. | 1742 | 1783 (B) |
| *Syringa laciniata* | Cut Leaf Lilac | China | 1650 | 1811 (L) |
| *Syringa persica* | Persian Lilac | Persia | Before 1640 | 1792 (B) |
| *Syirnga vulgaris* | Common Lilac | E. Europe | 1500 | 1771 (P) |
| *Taxus baccata* | English Yew, Common Yew | Europe, North and West Africa | Native to Britain | 1814 (B) |
| *Thuja occidentalis* | American Arborvitae, White Cedar | Eastern U.S. | 1596 | 1783 (B) |
| *Thuja orientalis* | Oriental Arborvitae | China | Before 1737 | 1792 (B) |
| *Trachelospermum jasminoides* | Star Jasmine, Confederate Jasmine | China and Japan | 1844 | 1855 (P) |
| *Tsuga canadensis* | Eastern Hemlock | Eastern U.S. | 1736 | 1771 (P) |
| *Ulmus alata* | Winged Elm | Southeast U.S. | 1820 | 1811 (L) |
| *Viburnum opulus* "sterile" | Snowball, Guelder-Rose | Netherlands | 1750 | 1771 (P) |
| *Viburnum tinus* | Laurustinus | Southern Europe | 1596 | 1804 (M) |
| *Vinca major* | Bigleaf Periwinkle | England | Native | 1807 (B) |
| *Vinca minor* | Common Periwinkle | Britain | Native | 1807 (B) |
| *Vitex agnus-castus* | Chaste Tree, Spikenard | Mediterranean Region | 1570 | 1814 (B) |
| *Weigela florida* | Weigela | China | 1845 | 1848 (H) |
| *Wisteria floribunda* | Chinese Profuse Fld. Wisteria | China | 1830 | 1844 (P) |
| *Wisteria frutescens* | American Wisteria, Shrubby Glycine | Southern U.S. | 1724 | 1783 (B) |
| *Wisteria sinensis* | Chinese Wisteria | China | 1816 | 1831 (P) |
| *Yucca aloifolia* | Spanish Bayonet | Southern U.S. | 1696 | 1804 (M) |
| *Yucca filamentosa* | Adam's Needle, Spoonleaf Yucca | Southeast U.S. | 1675 | 1804 (M) |
| *Yucca gloriosa* | Superb Adam's Needle | Southeast U.S. | 1596 | 1792 (B) |

* See Nursery Reference Key at End of Section.

**Nursery—Reference Key**

| | |
|---|---|
| B | (Bartram Nursery—Philadelphia, Pennsylvania) |
| BU | (Buist Nursery—Philadelphia, Pennsylvania) |
| F | (Fruitland Nurseries—Augusta, Georgia) |
| H | (The Highland Nursery—Newburgh, New York) |
| HO | (Hovey & Co.—Cambridge, Massachusetts) |
| K | (Kenrick Nursery—Boston, Massachusetts) |
| L | (Landreth Nursery—Philadelphia, Pennsylvania) |
| M | (M'Mahon Seedsman—Philadelphia, Pennsylvania) |
| MO | (Monroe Nursery—Rochester, New York) |
| P | (Prince Nursery—Long Island, New York) |
| T | (Thorburn Seedsmen and Florists—New York, New York) |
| TH | (Thomas Hancock Nursery—Aston, New Jersey) |
| WB | (William Booth Nursery and Seedsman—Baltimore, Maryland) |

## FLOWERS FOR THE SOUTH

Records reveal that as early as the second half of the eighteenth century numerous advertisements appeared in newspapers and periodicals offering American gardeners a wide selection of flower seeds and bulbs from various European sources. One such notice was published in the *South Carolina Gazette* in 1786, in which Peter Croswell (representing a nursery in Holland) announced the sale of an "extensive collection of the most rare and curious bulbous flowers, roots and seeds . . . including choice sorts of hyacinths, double jonquilles, polyanthus, narcissusses, tarcetts, tulips, double tuberoses, pasteouts, carnations, and a great variety of double ranunculas and anemonies." While the majority of flower seeds and bulbs grown by American gardeners were initially obtained from Europe, beginning in the nineteenth century a number of American seed merchants and nurseries began to emerge. Prominent among these were David Landreth, Bernard M'Mahon, and Robert Buist of Philadelphia, Grant Thorburn and Thomas Bridgeman of New York, and Joseph Breck and C. M. Hovey of Boston. These businesses not only supplied seeds and bulbs to northern buyers, but they also supplemented the needs of southern gardeners as well.

Although interest in the cultivation of flowers dramatically increased in the nineteenth century, it was not until 1832 that an American garden book devoted solely to the cultivation of flowers was available to American gardeners. Written by Robert Buist and Thomas Hibbert (Philadelphia seedsmen and florists), *The American Flower Garden Directory* was intended for general use, as is indicated it the introduction: "This volume owes its existence principally to the repeated requests . . . for a practical manual on Floriculture. . . . That now offered is given unaffectedly and simply as a plain and easy treatise on this increasingly interesting subject." The first American flower book to contain colored engravings of flowers was published a year later in 1833, titled, *The Florist's Manual: . . . For Cultivators of Flowers*. Other American works on flowers followed, including Edward Sayers' *Flower Garden Companion* (1838), Joseph Breck's *The Flower Garden* (1851), and John Clark's *The Amateurs' Guide and Flower Garden Directory* (1856). The first gardening book in the South to provide substantial information on flowers that were ideally suited to the southern climate was Mary Rion's *Ladies' Southern Florist*, published in Columbia, South Carolina, in 1860. Some of the more prominent flowers Mrs. Rion recommended for southern gardens included petunia, portulacea, morning glory, coxcomb, larkspur, hollyhock, sweet William, mullen pink, bachelor button, clarkia, mignonette, tassel flower, sweet pea, amaranth, feverfew, gilley flower, verbena, coreopsis, snapdragon, four-o'clocks, double rocket, columbine, forget-me-not, and dahlias.

Flowers played an important role in southern gardens during the antebellum era. They not only were cherished for their beauty, color, and fragrance, but in many cases they had sentimental appeal, perhaps invoking a childhood memory or honoring a loved one or special occasion. In addition to being grown as a "delightful and engaging employ-ment," the cultivation of flowers also served as a means of preserving and improving "both body and mind." Robert Nelson, one of the South's most respected horticulturist, prepared a comprehensive list of flowers recommended for southern gardens during the antebellum period. This authoritative source was published in *The Southern Culti-vator* in 1856 and has been reprinted in its entirety as a valuable resource in the recre-ation of period gardens.

EDITORS SOUTHERN CULTIVATOR—Though we of "The Sunny South," are blessed with a beautiful climate, still our friends from the North feel somewhat disappointed in examining our gardens. . . . I will, there-fore, here give a short list of such kinds of flowers, as will thrive in our latitude, and will at some future time make additions to this list. The seeds of them should be sown in the fall or early in the spring:

*Adonis oestivalis*, pheasant's eye, with a deep scarlet flower and feathery foliage.

*Ageratum coeuleum*, a beautiful blue an-nual, recently introduced from Mexico.

*Ameranthus tricolor*, well known under the name of Joseph's coat.

*Althea rosea*, hollyhock, a well known peren-nial, which of late has been highly im-proved.

*Althea chinensis*, Chinese hollyhock, in many double varieties, introduced from China.

*Ammobium alatum*, an everlasting little white flower from Australia.

"There are few subjects that can engage the attention and leisure hours of the intelligent observer of nature in a more satisfactory manner than the culture of flowers . . . and perhaps no flower was ever more diversified, and improved in a floricultural view, than the *Dahlia;* for within a few years we have been made acquainted with many hundreds of varieties proceeding from a few. Nor are they more remarkable for their number than for their brilliant and diversified shades and colors."

*A Treatise on the Culture of the Dahlia* (1839)
E. Sayers

*Antirrhinum Majus*, snapdragon, in a great variety of colors.

*Aster chinensis*, German asters. More than 30 double varieties of this beautiful flower are offered by florists.

*Calendula crista galli*, a well known annual.

*Callispsis bicolor*, yellow, with a dark brown centre.

*Carthamus tinctorius*, with an orange colored flower and a thistle-like appearance.

*Catanauche carulea* and

*Catanauche bicolor*, with handsome everlasting flowers, natives of Turkey.

*Celosia cristata*, cockscombe, in great variety of shades, one of our very best annuals.

*Celosia indica*, slender cockscomb, at first deep pink, changes to silvery white.

*Centaunea cyanus*, blue.

*Centaunea moschata*, sweet sultan, lilac colored.

*Centaurea svaveolens*, yellow sultan.

*Delphinium*, Larkspur, in many varieties, the hyacinth-like flowering are the finest.

*Delphinuim chinensis*, a beautiful perennial Larkspur of several colors, from China.

*Dianthus caryophyllus*, double carnations. This is an old and highly esteemed flower, still seldom to be met with in our gardens. Must be increased by layers every year, as the old plants are very apt to die out.

*Dianthus chinensis*, Chinese pink, of an almost endless diversity of shades, single as well as double.

*Dianthus imperialis plenissima*, a new and splendid variety, just introduced.

*Dracocephalum moldavicum*, blue dragons head, from Turkey.

*Double balsoms*, in many colors.

*Elicrysium lucindum*, yellow, and

*Elicrysium Macranthum*, white or pink, both very valuable flowers, from Australia. They are everlasting flowers, and will, when put in a drawer, keep fresh for many years.

*Emilea flammea*, a small scarlet annual.

*Gilia tricolor*, three colored gilia.

*Gomphrena globosa*, batchelors button, either crimson, white, or orange colored.

*Heliotropium peruvianum*, This flower, so highly esteemed for its delicious vanilla fragrance, will, when covered over in the autumn with earth, stand our winters south of latitude 33 degrees.

*Hesperis tristis*, dark rocket, and

*Hesperis matronalis*, white rocket, both biennials, are very fragrant after sunset.

*Iberis speciosa*, purple candytuft.

*Ipomoea quamoclit*, cypress vine, from Mexico, the most graceful and fairy-like climbers, when trained as an arbor or screen.

*Lavatera trimestris*, a pink flower, from the south of Europe.

*Papavea murselli*, splendid poppy.

*Papaver somniferum*, double poppy, in a great many colors.

*Pharbitis limbata*, This beautiful "morning glory," of recent introduction, has a dark purple flower, distinctly edged with pure white, in beautiful contrast.

*Phlox drummondi*, in a great variety of colors.

*Polygonum teretifolium*, an exceedingly graceful Southern perennial, described in the February number (1856) of the *Southern Cultivator*.

*Portulacca thellusoni*, Scarlet Portulacca, blooms all summer, but only in the forenoon.

*Poterium sangvisorba*, is excellent for edging flowerbeds; perennial.

*Reseda odorata*, mignonette. This very fragrant little flower, from Egypt, will continue blooming for a long time, if constantly cut off, and not suffered to produce seed.

*Rhodanthe manglessii*, from Swan River, in Australia. Of all the everlasting flowers this is certainly the most beautiful, the drooping, pink colored flowers have an exceedingly graceful appearance.

*Salpiglossis variabilis*, petunia, from Buenos Aires, in many different colors; will stand our winters under a slight protection.

*Scabiosa atropurpurea*, mourning bride, in several shades.

*Senecio elegans*, double purple jacoboa.

*Tagetes erecta*, double yellow, African marigold.

*Tagets patula*, double French marigold.

*Verbena melindris*, It is but a few years since this plant was introduced from Buenos Aires; varieties of the greatest diversity of colors have sprung from the original scarlet flower; and now it is considered indispensable in any garden.

*Viola odorata*, fragrant violet; perennial.

*Xeranthemum anunum*, a purple eternal annual.

*Zinnia elegans*, in many varieties, of which the scarlet is one of the finest.

Gillyflowers and ten weeks stock have been described in the December number of the *Southern Cultivator.*

Wallflowers, double in different shades, are biennial, and will not, therefore, bloom before the second year.

Robert Nelson
*The Southern Cultivator*
Augusta, Georgia, 1856

*Viola odorata*—Fragrant violet.

## ROSES FOR SOUTHERN GARDENS

No flower throughout history has inspired greater admiration, nor formed more endearing associations, than the rose. The rose in any language brings to mind an image of beauty and charm. Universally referred to as the "Queen of Flowers," gardeners have loved and cherished the rose since the earliest of times for its variations in form, color, fragrance, hardiness, and diversity of bloom. By the middle of the nineteenth century, the rose had become one of the most popular garden plants in America. In 1846, William Prince of the famous Linnaean Nursery of Flushing, New York, observed: "During the last ten years the acquisitions made by the Family of Roses, have been so remarkable for their splendor, fragrance and other fine qualities, that public attention has been awakened to their culture in a degree unprecedented in the annals of Floriculture." To meet this overwhelming demand, Prince offered American gardeners over 1500 different varieties of roses in his 1846 nursery catalogue.

The first American garden book on the rose, *The Rose Manual*, was written in 1844 by Robert Buist, a respected nurseryman in Philadelphia, Pennsylvania. *The Rose Manual* contained descriptions of roses grown in America during the first half of the nineteenth century, along with instructions on their propagation and care. Written in a simple and informative manner, *The Rose Manual* went through four editions in less than ten years. In 1846, William Robert Prince, of the famous Prince Nurseries, authored the *Manual of Roses*. Additional books written on the rose during the antebellum period included Samuel Parsons's *The Rose* (1847) and C. M. Sexton's *American Rose Culturist* (1856).

*Rosa Noisettiana* by Pierre-Joseph Redouté. Circa 1811, John Champneys (a Charleston rice planter) crossed *Rosa chinensis* and *Rosa moschata* to produce Champneys' pink cluster (*Rosa noisettiana*). From Champneys' pink cluster arose the class of roses known as the Noisettes.

*Ladies' Southern Florist* (1860) by Mary C. Rion provided descriptions of roses ideally suited for the South along with advice on their culture and pruning.

In *The Rose Manual*, Buist noted, "The Sunny South is the home of the rose; there it grows and blooms from January to Christmas." The rose was indeed a popular plant in southern gardens as evidenced in letters, diaries, travel accounts, and agricultural journals of the period. In a letter written on April 17, 1854, and recorded in *The Garden History of Georgia*, Mrs. Butler King of Retreat Plantation (St. Simons Island, Georgia) described the beauty of her garden, in which roses appear to have been the central theme: "I want every one to see my Garden in its beauty. I now have 92 different kinds of roses in bloom, forming I may say thousands of flowers." Another account from a visitor to Savannah, Georgia, in April 1856, appeared in *The Southern Cultivator:* "The whole city was a perfect Rosary—every wall and trellis, pillar and garden nook, being covered and glorified with all the finest varieties of the 'Queen of Flowers' and the whole air redolent as the 'spicy gale of Araby.' We thought we had never seen roses as luxuriant and perfect before."

Articles on the culture of roses often appeared in southern agricultural journals. Two of the most informative were titled "Mr. Nelson's Roses" (1855) and "Roses for the South" (1856). Because they are informative and comprehensive, both have been reprinted in their entirety, serving as a valuable source of information on roses grown in gardens of the antebellum South.

꒰꒱

We clip the following rhapsody on Roses from a late number of the Macon *Georgia Citizen*. The varieties mentioned are all noted for their beauty and fragrance, and should have a place in the collection of every amateur:

## MR. NELSON'S ROSES (1855)

꒰꒱ We have on our table before us, so gorgeous a display of those fair creations, that we cannot forgo the pleasure of a short word with them ere they go to greet the eyes of the beautiful one for whom they were gathered. In all climes and in all ages the Rose has been the most admired of flowers. Its very name has a charm in it; and though it might, by any other name, *smell* as sweet, by none other could it sound half so soft and beautiful. No where but in Persia does it bloom in greater perfection, or flourish more luxuriantly than in the "Sunny South." In vain does one look in the *Royal* of other gardens of Europe, except in Italy, for such Roses as Mr. Nelson grows at Troup Hill Nursery [Macon, Georgia]. Though the cold and drouth [*sic*] have been exceedingly unfavorable to their development, yet, in a few days, they will present a scene no lover of the beautiful should fail to witness. The heart that is not touched and softened by the contemplation of such an array of Nature's floral gems, must be hard indeed. What more fitting tribute can be offered, at the shrine of beauty and loveliness, than a boquet [*sic*] of the *Queen of Flowers*?

But we must proceed to the chat with *our* Roses, ere the fresh blush of Nature fades from their bright petals. Alas, for the briefness of Beauty in this dull, rude world! Even whilst we gaze upon it and admire, it dims and fades away!

Most conspicuous in our group is the magnificent *Souvenir de la Malmaison*, with a face as delicately beautiful and softly tinted as the full orbed moon rising through those light mists that float about the horizon of a calm summer sea. Its enormous flowers, its gorgeous buds, and its luxuriant foliage entitle it to the appellation of the *Queen of Roses*. One who has only seen this noble flower on a slight stem in a Northern green-house, about the circumference of a silver dollar, would fail to recognize the same in those mammoth productions of Troup Hill.

Next in superbness, is the beautiful *Devoniensis*, with perfume as deliciously sweet as the scented gales of Araby. Of a light pink color, tinged with buff, its petals of a soft delicate texture, and of an elegant form, few roses possess more attractions than that which honors the Earl of Devon. Its buds are unsurpassed in beauty, and its foliage is rich and luxuriant.

Somewhat resembling the last is the *Triomphe de Luxembourg*, curious for its coriaceous petals, and beautiful for its pale, rosy tints shaded with light buff.

Scattered through our cluster is the *Arch Duke Charles*, remarkable for its endless variety of shades and tints, no two roses being exactly of the same hue, nor any two parts of the same flower. Passing through all shades from the deepest crimson to the palest pink, and varigated with clouded spots and marbled veins, they would form a beautiful boquet [*sic*] by themselves.

Beautiful *Moss Rose* buds nestle sweetly in the group, and the *Duchess of Kent*, with its light pink, and cream-colored centre smiles coyly upon the *Giant of Battles*. *Queen Victoria* hugs close to *Prince Albert*, and *Comte Robinski* kisses the blushing cheeks of *Madame Desprez*. The beautiful *Hermosa* clasps tenderly the frail *Enfant d' Ajaccio*, and the *Princess Clementine* looks lovingly upon the proud *Edouard Desfosses*.

But we are falling into a tender mood. The blushing petals, and white buds of our gorgeous boquet [*sic*] are so like the beauty and the purity of another "fairer flower," that we almost fancied a pair of soft eyes peering upon us from out that group of fairy forms.

We can only mention the names of the rest. We have the *Madam Breon, the Acidalie, Lavinia, Costa Jaune Desprez, Madam Bassanquet, Abricote, Virginie, Saffrano, Solfatare, Lamarque, La Sylphide, Princesse Maria, Triomphe de la Dachere*, with its reflexed petals, and beautifully starred centre.

Mr. Nelson has over two hundred different kinds of roses embracing all the best varieties know to floriculture, and no one can look upon them in their prime, without emotions of delight. For his industry and enthusiasm in the beautiful department to which he is devoted, and for the improvements he is introducing in Horticulture, in Agriculture, and in our general taste for the beauties of the Garden and the Conservatory, he deserves much of Georgia and the South. A love for flowers begets a love for all else that is good and beautiful, and no man's life can be altogether bad, surrounded by those blooming "stars of earth." L.

ॐ

## ROSES FOR THE SOUTH (1856)

*By Robert Nelson, of Macon, Georgia*

ॐ Editors Southern Cultivator—Among all the shrubs which are cultivated in the Southern gardens, Everblooming Roses unquestionably hold the highest rank. Our climate is as congenial to them as that of Italy, and, with a little care, they may be easily raised to the highest perfection. They are too tender for cultivation in the open gardens of the North, where they, after a short summer, must be lifted in the fall, just when they have well established their roots, and would commence blooming luxuriantly; they are then potted for wintering in the house until next spring; and those left in the ground even under the best covering, are frequently killed by the frosts. In the South, it is quite different; here they are perfectly hardy, and will, with proper treatment, bloom for nine months, with a few intervals. In fact, nothing is more astonishing or interesting to Northern horticulturist than our splendid everblooming Roses. Several of the greatest nurserymen in the North, who have visited my grounds, could not recognize our gorgeous Roses which were so far superior to the best ones in the North.

The South possesses immense advantages over the North, not only in roses and other flowers, but also in fruits and vegetables. The proper cultivation of these things, however, is, in many points, different and must be studied; but a little care will be properly rewarded.

The word "everblooming" does not, of course indicate that they will bloom the whole season without interruption. They do, however, bloom so abundantly that they become exhausted and need a short period of rest. This is the moment for pruning them, after which they will soon commence blooming again, and thus keep on until arrested by frost. A supply of water or a weak solution of manure or guano, will greatly promote their blooming qualities. Many rose catalogues enumerate a thousand names, and even more, while one-tenth of that number will comprise all the finest ones. I have, therefore, made it my rule to keep a small, but superior collection on hand, not cultivating more than about 200 varieties, always getting new kinds on trial and rejecting all second-rate ones.

It is useless to try to grow anything in poor soil and in a careless way. Therefore, as a basis for all horticultural operations, I must urge the necessity of *manuring* the soil and *working* it *deeply*. This latter operation can be done either with the spade, or, where a larger space is to be cultivated, with a turning plow, followed by a sub-soil plow, burying the manure deeply. From 14 to 20 inches deep will answer for most purposes.

The everblooming roses are subdivided into five families, viz:—China, Tea, Bourbon, Noisette and Remontant or Hybrid Perpetuals. The first four classes, however, have been so much hybridized, in order to produce new varieties, that it often becomes difficult to classify them, as it would be to distinguish the different cross-breeds of dogs or chickens.

I will here enumerate some varieties, which may be considered *first-rate* ones, or which possess some peculiar or interesting qualities:

"The Sunny South in the home of the rose; there it grows and blooms from January to Christmas."

*The Rose Manual* (1844)
Robert Buist

CHINA ROSES

*Arch Duke Charles;* of very luxuriant growth, and a most prolific bloomer. The flowers are very different in color, varying from light pink to deep crimson, with all the intermediate shades, sometimes, also, marbled and spotted; grows 4 to 5 feet high.

*Camelliaflora;* light rosy purple, in very large clusters; grows about 4 feet high.

*Carmine Superbe;* flowers medium, in great profusion, of a very dark crimson hue, and of a globular form; foliage dark reddish; it forms a neat little hedge.

*Duchesse of Kent;* flowers of medium size, beautifully formed, and in great clusters; color, light pink, or nearly white, with a cream colored centre. It is almost a never-ceasing bloomer, but during the droughts, in summer, the white flowers look as if sprinkled with blood. It grows very compact and bushy—almost dwarfish.

*Madam Breon;* bright rosy crimson; very large and brilliant flowers, which, in the fall, assume a still more brilliant hue.

*Marjolin;* an immense bloomer of a brilliant dark scarlet color and velvety tint. This variety, planted close to "Duchesse of Kent," or planted promiscuously in a hedge, will form a most beautiful object.

*Lawrenciana;* also called the "Picayune" is remarkable for its very small flowers and foliage; it forms a neat edging around beds.

*Lawrenciana Viridis;* the "Green Rose," is a botanical curiosity. The flower, if it can be called so, consists of a greet tuft of leaves, or, more correctly, in a double calyx, destitute of petals. It blooms, however, in this way, from early spring until Christmas, and is almost indispensable for bouquets.

TEA ROSES

The Tea Roses (*Rosa, indica odarata*), so called on account of their fragrance, somewhat resembling the odor of fine tea. The light colors, as well as the yellow hues, are predominant in this class; no dark colored Tea Roses being known yet. Some of the best are:

*Abricote;* fawn color, tinged with pink; a very pretty rose.

*Adam;* light pink; very large and splendid flower; a good bloomer; middling growth; an improvement on Lyonnaise.

*Antherose;* white, with creamy centre; very double; fine habit; 2 feet high.

*Bon Silene;* one of the deepest colored Tea Roses; of a coppery hue and delightful fragrance; the flower often very large; 2 or 3 feet high.

*Bougerie;* a singular rosy bronze color; fine shaped flower; good bloomer; 2 or 3 feet high.

*Clara Sylvain;* white with creamy centre; rather dwarfish growth.

*Devoniensis;* who would not know this beautiful rose of a pale flesh color, tinged with buff, and exceedingly fragrant? It is of very luxuriant growth, with dark wood and strong thorns. On poor soil, however, this splendid rose grows weak, turning, also, pure white and almost single; 4 or 5 feet high.

*Gaubault;* another highly fragrant rose, resembling somewhat "Bon Silene" in color and habit; one of the earliest in the spring.

*Julie Mansars;* yellowish white; beautiful in spring and autumn, less so during the heat of the summer. Its growth is very compact, bushy and very dwarfish; 1 or 2 feet high.

*Lady Warrender;* a beautiful little rose, but of very dwarfish growth. The flower opens pale pink, but soon turns white; the petals finely imbricated.

*La Sylphide;* very light pink, often nearly white, with a buff centre and fine form. It is a fine bloomer in autumn, the flowers at that season coming to their greatest perfection; strong grower.

*Madam Desprez;* pure white, but rather small flowers; dwarfish growth.

*Marechal Bugeaud;* a very large and fine rose of a pale pink color, tinged with light buff; strong growth; 4 feet high.

*Nyphetas;* a splendid pure white rose, buds remarkably long and pointed; growth somewhat straggling; 1 or 2 feet.

*Pauline Plantier;* yellowish white; a very good bloomer; robust growth.

*Princess Maria;* beautiful rosy pink, with a creamy tint; very double, so much so, even, that it does not always come to full perfection during the drouths of summer; but in the spring, and still more so in the autumn, it is splendid.

*Saffrano;* very deep buff, a most remarkable color. It is magnificent while in bud; it does not, however, show itself to an advantage when fully open. But if a person will take the trouble of tying a little sewing cotton around the bud, it will be prevented from expanding, and keep for many days in its highest beauty; vigorous growth, the stem often measuring two inches in diameter.

*Triumph de Luxembourg;* also often called "Luxembourg Tea," is a magnificent flower, with thick leathery petals of pale rosy color, tinged with pale buff.

*Virginie;* clear pink; a beautiful shape and a great bloomer. It always forms a neat, close and round bush; about 2 feet high.

THE BOURBON ROSES

Were first discovered in the Island of Bourbon, on the east coast of Africa, whence their name. By hybridizing and cultivation they have reached a high degree of perfection. Their colors in the deep crimson shades are very brilliant; their flowers luxuriant and profuse; their growth stout and very thorny. Nearly all of them are very constant bloomers. Some of the best are:

*Acidalie;* nearly white; of a globular, regular form and a splendid waxy appearance; growth very robust; 3 or 4 feet.

*Crimson Globe;* also called "Dr. Roques;" a rather small, but very regularly imbricated flower of an exceedingly rich, vivid crimson hue. It is one of those few roses which will have to be mulched during the hottest part of the summer. It always does better when grafted than on its own roots; 1 to 2 feet high.

*Cardinal Fesh;* violet crimson; very double; a fine bloomer; of rather low growth.

*Edouard Desfosses;* dark pink; very distinct; the flower rather expanded and flat, but very regularly imbricated and star-shaped; growth, low and bushy; will do much better when mulched.

*Enfant d'Ajaccio;* also called "Souvenir de Anselme;" brilliant scarlet crimson, in large clusters; a constant bloomer, of luxuriant and slender growth, almost climbing; excellent for pillars.

*General Dubourg;* a rather insignificant pink flower, which properly does not deserve a place in a fine collection were it not for its delicious fragrance, the pure "Attar of Rose;" strong, slender growth.

*Hermosa;* pale rosy color; very fine; globular form; a great bloomer; of luxuriant growth.

*Lady Canning;* rosy lilac; in large clusters; very fine.

*Lavinia Costa;* flower of but medium size, but produced in very large clusters, and of a brilliant deep crimson color.

*Leveson Gower;* a very large and fine flower of a bright rosy color; in shape somewhat resembling "Souvenir de la Malmaison."

*Madam Angelina;* white, tinged with fawn; flower rather small.

*Madam Bossanquet;* pale cream color; of fine globose form and waxy appearance; profuse bloomer; makes a stout bush.

*Madam Desprez;* deep pink, turning rosy lilac; blooms in very large clusters; a profuse and constant bloomer, and strong grower, when grafted; on its own roots, however, it is of rather feeble growth and bloom.

*Paul Joseph;* a very rich crimson rose, but of feeble growth, and rather difficult to cultivate.

*Pourpre de Tyre;* dark purple of rather dwarfish growth.

*Princesse Clementine;* brilliant deep crimson with a velvety tint.

*Queen* or *Queen of Bourbons;* a fine rose of pinkish fawn color, of globose form; grows stout and bushy.

*Souvenir de la Malmaison;* this pale flesh colored rose, though not very fragrant, stands perhaps at the head of all roses. It is, indeed, a worthy representative of the splendid garden of "Malmaison," the celebrated garden of the Empress Josephine. The flowers are very large, often from 5 to 6 inches in diameter, and produced in clusters; growth low, say about 2 feet, but very stout and bushy.

*Sully;* flowers small, star-shaped and in large clusters; of a bright deep crimson color; a constant bloomer.

*Triumph de la Duchcre;* pale rosy blush, with deeper colored, star-shaped centre; profuse bloomer, and of luxuriant growth.

NOISETTE ROSES

*Noisette* Roses are said to have originated in Charleston, S.C., and to have taken their name after Mr. Noisette, of that city, a cousin to the celebrated French rose grower in Paris, of that same name. The characteristic is a profusion of flowers produced in large clusters. The predominant color is bright, and comprises more shades of yellow than any other class of roses. The Noisette roses may properly be subdivided into two families:—1. Those that are low and bushy. 2. Those that are climbing. Some of the best are:

*Aime Vibert;* pure white, but rather small flowers; growth quite dwarfish.

*Augusta;* so much has been said of this new yellow climber that it may not be out of place to say a few words about it. It was raised a few years ago in Ohio, and is a very fine yellow climbing rose. It resembles, however, the "Solfatara" so much that it is hardly worth while to raise both varieties. Its chief merits in preference to the "Solfatara" is, that it is perfectly hardy in the North, where the climate is entirely too severe for the "Solfatara."

*Caroline Marniesse;* this new rose, which ranks among the best roses in Europe, is, in spite of its beauty, not likely to be fully appreciated here in the South, where everybody goes for "size." In fact, "mighty big" is the description that is sure to enchant every person. It has a very peculiar appearance. True, the flower is quite small, not much more than an inch in diameter, with recurved petals; opening light pink, but soon changing to pure white. The flowers are produced in great profusion, and in large clusters, besides, it is a most constant bloomer. I hardly know a more suitable rose for a grave.

*Chromatella,* or *Cloth of Gold;* but few roses have caused such an excitement in the floral world as this. It is a climber of the most luxuriant kind; for I have seen it trained up to the very top of a chimney of a two story building; but, at the same time being one of our most tender roses, it is easily understood why all Northern horticulturists are complaining of its blooming qualities. In the South, however, it blooms well, producing a very large, cup-shaped flower of the deepest chrome yellow. In order to show itself in its highest beauty, it must be planted in very rich soil.

*Fellemberg;* this is a very strong growing, bushy, variety, producing very large clusters, of a color approaching to scarlet. It is a great bloomer; particularly showy in the fall, and at a distance.

*Jaune Desprez;* light buff, slightly tinged with pink, and deliciously fragrant. It is a climber, though not of the strongest kind.

*Lamarque;* this is another very luxuriant climber, producing splendid, pure white and large clusters of flowers. A very good bloomer.

*La Pactole;* few roses bloom so constantly and profusely as this variety, producing immense clusters of pale sulphur colored flowers; bushy; 3 feet high.

*Octavie;* one of the few dark coloured climbers, of late introduction; fine reddish purple and a good bloomer.

*Ophire;* a trailing rose of a rather awkward habit; the flower is small, but of a remarkable deep salmon color. It shows its highest beauty in the morning, the colors fading very soon.

*Smithii,* or *Smith's Yellow;* it is a beautiful yellow rose when grown in perfection; in order, however, to show its full beauty, it ought to be grafted and planted in a rich and damp situation; not a very good bloomer, and rather dwarfish.

*Solfatara;* a luxuriant climber, somewhat resembling the "Chromatella," but flowers of a more pale yellow than that variety. It is a profuse bloomer, with an exquisite fragrance.

I am now coming to the last class of everblooming roses, or the

## HYBRID PERPETUALS

They are a cross between the varieties of the old Provence and Damask roses, and the everblooming varieties of the Bourbon, Tea, and China Roses. Most of them have sprung up in France, where they are called "Remontants," or roses which will "bloom again" in the same season. They are very hardy, and, therefore, invaluable in the North, where the winters are too severe for the finer, everblooming roses, which are grown to such a perfection in our Southern gardens. Many of them are very fine; all of them of a luxuriant growth and rich colors, ranging from pure white to deep purple and crimson. Some of the best are:

*Amanda Pattenotte;* pale rose; very large and full; excellent for pillars.

*Baronne Hallez de Clapparede;* brilliant deep carmine; very double and of a most regular and imbricated form; petals a little recurved, and very thick. Very fragrant.

*Baronne Prevost;* deep, brilliant rose-color; flowers very large, often measuring 5 inches across. It is of a most luxuriant growth.

*Blanche Vibert;* this is, as yet, the only pure white rose of this class; the flowers are rather small, but produced in large clusters, and of delicious fragrance.

*Caroline Sansal;* this magnificent new rose is worthy of a place in even the smallest collection. It is very large, double, of a fine form and a delicate blush, with an exquisite satin tint.

*Comte Bobinski;* a new rose of the nearest approach to scarlet, brighter in color than the "Giant of Battles;" the most showy autumnal rose.

*Duplesis Mornais;* another new rose of high merit. It is large, expanded, with a most beautiful shaped centre; brilliant rosy scarlet; middling growth.

*Giant of Battles;* this is a splendid variety, opening deep scarlet, velvety, changing to purple; deliciously fragrant and quite distinct.

*La Reine;* deep rosy lilac; very double and fragrant. This beautiful rose, an improvement of the well known old "cabbage or hundred-leaved" is worthy of a place in any garden, and will, by good culture, bloom three or four times during the summer.

*Madam Laffay;* rosy lilac; beautiful form.

*Pius the IXth;* light crimson; very fine.

*Prince Albert;* a magnificent variety, and a great bloomer, of a rich, deep, purplish crimson color, which is particularly showy late in the fall.

*Queen Victoria* (Paul's); this rose is also called the "White La Reine," and has commanded a high price in the Northern Nurseries. It is pale blush; very double and a very fine flower.

*Rivers;* very brilliant, rosy crimson; exceedingly thorny; a fine variety, which is most showy in the fall.

*William Griffith;* superb pale rose of the most perfect globular form; worthy of a place in the most limited collection; grows very luxuriant.

Many more and fine varieties could be added to this list, but the above named ones are the most distinct.

Before concluding this schedule, I must mention a few spring roses, or such as only bloom in the spring, and are well adapted to the South, where they are great favorites.

MOSS ROSES

There is an opinion prevailing that Moss Roses will not thrive in the South, and, in fact, several of the varieties may require more attention than most persons may feel disposed to bestow upon them. Fortunately some of the finest will succeed admirably by proper treatment and very little trouble. Let it, however, be borne in mind that they always require a deeply worked and very rich soil, where moisture is within the reach of the roots. Wherever such a location can be found, or artificially prepared, a judicious pruning as well as mulching during the heat of summer are the means by which success may be insured. The most suitable for the South are:

*Princesse Adelaide;* rosy pink; in large clusters, and of very luxuriant growth. This is, perhaps, the most profuse bloomer of all the Moss roses in a Southern climate; it often will make standards, 6 feet high, on its own roots.

*Pink Moss;* this is the world renowned Moss Rose of the poets, the emblem of loveliness, and the finest of all. The flower is beautiful pale rose, with a most delicate tint, surrounded, while in bud, with a very mossy calyx of the finest texture. When well mulched, there is no difficulty in raising it in perfection.

*Scarlet Moss* or *Luxembourg Moss;* deep red, approaching to scarlet, while in bud, but of a more purple hue when fully open; calyx very mossy. It has long and slender branches.

*Perpetual White;* every person combines with a white moss rose the idea of something very beautiful; and, in fact, if the flowers were so perfect as those of the pink moss, it would excel all other roses. But it is only beautiful while in bud. Some white moss roses, as "Unique de Provence" and "Maiden of Bath," have more or less perfect flowers, but are seldom seen in their glory in our hot and dry climate. The "Perpetual White," though by no means perpetual, will stand our climate well, and bloom twice during the season. It is of vigorous growth and produces large clusters of flowers, which, however, as mentioned before, are always sure to give disappointment when fully open.

MISCELLANEOUS ROSES

*Banksia Alba;* often called the "White Multiflora," is as fragrant as the violet.

*Banksia Lutea;* yellow; is not fragrant. Both are of a most vigorously climbing habit, with long, slick and slender thornless vines, growing from ten to twenty feet in a season. What a contrast to behold this rampant climber in our "Sunny South," when a Northern horticulturalist never has seen it otherwise than a little miserable sprig in a pot! The flowers are very small, not larger than a dime, but produced in bunches and in great profusion.

*Fortune's New Yellow;* a climbing rose (from China) of late introduction. Notwithstanding all that has been said respecting the merits of this rose, together with may *beautiful* drawings presented thereof, I will try to give a true description of it, as it blooms with me. It is true, the color is remarkable, being a nankeen buff, the edges slightly tinged with pink; but the flowers are but *half* double; of short duration, and beautiful in the morning only, before fully expanded. Its blooming season is also very short.

*Persia Yellow;* this is, as yet, the deepest chrome yellow rose. The flower is below medium size, globular and often marked with a deep crimson stripe on the back of the petals. The bark is dark glossy brown; the foliage small, and of a peculiar fragrance, like the "Sweetbriar."

In order to grow these last four varieties, as well as the Moss Roses, in their perfection, and to have them to bloom abundantly they must (particularly the two last ones) be pruned severely immediately after having finished their blooming. It is the nature of these varieties to produce their flowers on the growth of the passed season, wherefore their blooming would also be prevented if the pruning was delayed till winter. The treatment will cause them to throw out many new shoots, which will produce an abundance of flowers by next spring.

It is a well known fact that nearly all roses obtained from Northern nurseries are budded, often on high, unsightly stems, and are, consequently, almost worthless.

All roses for the South should be strong, bushy plants on their own roots; though there are a few varieties which never succeed well unless they are grafted on the roots of some other strong growing kind, and this operation may be done by a practiced hand, in such a way that it will never be noticed.

# ⊹⇒APPENDIX A⇒⊹

*Biographical Sketches*

IN THE PRECEDING PAGES a number of key individuals, including naturalists, botanists, nurserymen, horticulturists, writers, travelers, and garden designers, are frequently referenced. To assist the reader, short biographical sketches are provided for some of the more important and influential of these individuals, along with references regarding important books, diaries, and nursery catalogues of the times.

AFFLECK, THOMAS (1812–1868). Born in Dumfries, Scotland, in 1812, Thomas Affleck was briefly employed in the banking business before studying science and agriculture in Edinburgh. In 1832, Affleck emigrated to America where he worked first in the East then in the Midwest prior to becoming junior editor of *The Western Farmer and Gardener* in Cincinnati in 1840, a position that initiated a life-long career as an agricultural and horticultural writer. Affleck moved to the South and in 1842 married Anna Smith of Washington, Mississippi. It was here that Affleck established his famed Southern Nurseries—one of the first and largest in the region. In addition to the nursery operation, he also published *Affleck's Southern Rural Almanac and Plantation/Garden Calendar.* Through his writing, Affleck did much for the advancement of agricultural and horticultural practices in the southern states. Affleck moved to Washington County, Texas, shortly before the Civil War and established Central Nurseries. Following the war, he traveled to England and Scotland to promote various business schemes that he hoped would utilize the vast resources of Texas. Affleck died on December 30, 1868.

AITON, WILLIAM (1731–1793). In 1755, William Aiton, a Scottish gardener, found employment at the Chelsea Physic Garden in London as an assistant to Philip Miller, the garden's director and author of the famous *Gardener's Dictionary*. In 1759 Aiton was engaged to develop a new botanic garden at Kew; it was there he would remain until his death, tending and studying the garden's expanding collection. Apart from being the first head gardener at Kew, Aiton's greatest contribution was the preparation (along with the assistance of other prominent botanists) of *Hortus Kewensis* (1773), a three-volume catalogue of over 5500 plants cultivated at Kew. In addition to providing general plant descriptions, *Hortus Kewensis* is particularly valuable to garden historians, as Aiton expended great efforts to include the date each plant was introduced into England, its country of origin, and who introduced it. Aiton's eldest son, William Townsand (1766–1849), prepared an enlarged edition of *Hortus Kewensis* between 1810 and 1813. A less expensive and more concise version, *Epitome*, was published in 1814. This one-volume publication contained three hundred additional species, as well as a selection of fruits and vegetables that were cultivated at Kew.

BARTRAM, JOHN (1699–1777). John Bartram, a Pennsylvania farmer of Quaker descent, was America's first native botanist. He developed the earliest botanical garden in America, located along the Schuylkill River several miles south of Philadelphia. Bartram also was well known for his frequent correspondence with other botanists and naturalists, both in the colonies and abroad. Linnaeus, the noted Swedish naturalist, referred to Bartram as "the greatest natural botanist in the world." John Bartram was appointed "His Majesty's Botanist for North America" under King George III of England. This position provided Bartram with a stipend that allowed him to travel from Canada to Florida and westward into the Ohio Valley to collect plants. Bartram is credited with establishing one of the first plant nurseries in America, which at his death in 1777 was carried on by his son, John Bartram Jr.

**BARTRAM, WILLIAM** (1739–1824). William Bartram was a poet, naturalist, artist, writer, and eldest son of John Bartram. William traveled with his father on botanical trips to Georgia and Florida. It was during one of these trips that they discovered the Franklinia tree (*Franklinia alatamah*) growing along the banks of the Altamaha River in southern Georgia. William described this unusual plant as "a flowering tree of the first order for beauty and fragrance of blossoms." William traveled on his own in the southeast from 1773 to 1778. The account of his travels was published in 1791 under the title *Travels Through North and South Carolina, Georgia, East and West Florida*. His vivid descriptions of nature in this work had a profound influence on the English poets Coleridge and Wordsworth. William Bartram is equally well known for his beautiful illustrations of fauna and flora, which were commissioned by John Fothergill, an English physician and naturalist. These drawings reside today in the British Museum in London.

**BERCKMANS, PROSPEROUS JULIUS** (1830–1910). P. J. Berckmans, as he was affectionately known, was born in Arschot, Belgium, where his education included courses in botany and horticulture. For political and religious reasons, Berckmans left Belgium for America in 1850. Upon arriving in the United States he settled in Plainfield, New Jersey, where with his father, also a distinguished horticulturist, he established a nursery and met many prominent figures in American horticulture. In 1857, P. J. Berckmans moved to Augusta, Georgia, and acquired Fruitland Nurseries. In addition to offering a wide variety of fruit trees and ornamentals, Fruitland Nurseries was instrumental in distributing and popularizing camellias and azaleas for outdoor culture throughout the southern states. P. J. Berckmans was active in numerous horticultural and pomological societies, having held many responsible positions. In recognition of his many professional achievements, Berckmans was awarded an honorary master of science degree from the University of Georgia in 1880.

**BREMER, FREDRIKA** (1801–1865). Born in Sweden in 1801, Fredrika Bremer was a well-known Swedish novelist, social worker, humanitarian, and traveler who was admired for her accomplishments and love of humanity. From 1841 to 1851, Fredrika Bremer traveled widely in the United States and Cuba where she was warmly welcomed and graciously received. During her travels she met Andrew Jackson Downing, Joel Poinsett, and other prominent individuals of the period. Unlike most travelers to the South who chose a southern route, Ms. Bremer traveled by the Ohio River, first visiting Cincinnati and Memphis before proceeding to New Orleans, Mobile, Savannah, and Charleston. While Fredrika Bremer's travel accounts were originally written as letters to her sister in Sweden, upon returning home she published her correspondence in a book entitled *Homes of the New World* (1853). In this publication Ms. Bremer provided an intelligent and sensitive assessment of various aspects of her visit, including descriptive accounts of gardens, local scenery, the natural environment, and the indigenous landscape.

**BUIST, ROBERT** (1805–1880). After receiving his training at the Royal Botanic Garden in Edinburgh, Scotland, Robert Buist immigrated to Philadelphia and entered into a partnership with Thomas Hibbert to develop a successful florist business. In 1832, Buist and Hibbert coauthored *The American Flower Garden Directory*, the first American garden book devoted exclusively to flowers. Following Hibbert's death, Buist expanded the business to include the sale of camellias and roses, for which he became well known throughout the country. Buist is credited with introducing the poinsettia (*Euphorbia pulcherrima*) into the nursery trade in 1833. In 1844, Buist published *The Rose Manual*, which went through four editions in just ten years. Robert Buist was recognized as one of the most prolific horticultural writers in America during the first half of the nineteenth century.

DOWNING, ANDREW JACKSON (1815–1852). Born in Newburgh, New York, in 1815, Andrew Jackson Downing was a nurseryman, landscape gardener, and author of numerous books including *A Treatise on the Theory and Practice of Landscape Gardening* (1841), as well as editor of *The Horticulturist* magazine. Downing is recognized today for his many outstanding accomplishments in the annals of American horticulture and garden design. An enthusiastic admirer of English author and horticulturist, J. C. Loudon and his views on landscape gardening, Downing included many of Loudon's principles of design in his *Treatise*, which was directed at improving taste in America and awakening a sense of beauty regarding the design and layout of gardens and grounds. While many of Downing's ideas were widely accepted and employed in the North, they were seldom followed in the South during the antebellum period, as adherence to the principles of formal design remained firmly entrenched. Downing was only thirty-eight years of age at the time of his death, which was the result of a boating accident on the Hudson River in 1852.

ELLIOTT, STEPHEN (1806–1866). Stephen Elliott, first bishop of the Episcopal Church in Georgia, was an educator, scholar, writer, gardener, and orator of the highest caliber. Born in Beaufort, South Carolina, in 1806 to Stephen Elliott Sr. (a distinguished botanist, educator, and author in his own right), Stephen Elliott Jr. studied at both Harvard and South Carolina College before being admitted to the bar in 1827. Elliott entered the ministry in 1832 and eight years later, at the age of thirty-three, was elected the first Episcopal Bishop of Georgia. His duties as bishop allowed him to travel freely about the country and to observe and discuss all aspects of agriculture, horticulture, and landscape gardening. On October 29, 1851, Bishop Elliott delivered an address on horticulture before the Central Agricultural Society of Georgia in Macon. In this address, Bishop Elliott provided an insightful look at the practice of ornamental gardening in the South at a period of time when recorded information on the subject was rare.

FORTUNE, ROBERT (1812–1880). Robert Fortune was a Scottish plant collector who worked for two years at the Royal Botanic Garden in Edinburgh before traveling to China to collect plants under the auspices of the Royal Horticultural Society. Fortune returned to England in 1846 with an extensive collection of live plants that were transported in Wardian cases—a device similar to a large terrarium that was used to transport plants over long distances. In 1848, and again in 1853, Fortune returned to China for the East India Company with the primary mission to collect the Chinese tea plant for introduction into India for commercial tea production. A fourth trip, this time independent of a sponsor, was made in 1860 to China and Japan. Following each of his visits, Fortune published a descriptive account of his travels, which provided valuable insight into various aspects of China and its culture. Fortune is credited with introducing over 190 species of plants into England, 120 of which were new species. Among the new plants introduced by Fortune that proved ideally suited to the gardens of the American South included winter jasmine (*Jasminum nudiflorum*), forsythia (*Forsythia viridissima*), winter honeysuckle (*Lonicera fragrantissmia*), and mahonia (*Mahonia beali*).

GORDON, ALEXANDER (1813–1871). Alexander Gordon was a Scottish botanist, plant collector, and noted writer who traveled throughout the United States collecting plants and seeds for George Charlwood, a British nurseryman and "Covent Garden Seedsman" in London. In 1843, Gordon accompanied Sir William Drummond Stewart on a western expedition along the Oregon Trail through the South Pass and the Wind River Mountains. Upon his return, in 1845, Gordon served as superintendent on an estate near Mobile, Alabama, using the money he earned to finance a trip to the southwest to further his collection of plants and seeds. Little is known of Gordon's botanical explorations or his later life after 1850. During his travels across the country, Gordon visited a number of important American nurseries and private gardens, which he described in an article that appeared in *Gardener's Magazine* in 1837 entitled,

"Notices of Some of the Principal Nurseries, Made During a Tour Through the Country, in the Summer of 1831; with Some Hints on Emigration." Additional observations are presented in a second article titled "Remarks on Gardening and Gardens in Louisiana," which appeared in *The Magazine of Horticulture and Botany* in 1849.

**INGRAHAM, JOSEPH HOLT** (1809–1860). A native of Portland, Maine, Joseph Ingraham moved south around 1830 to teach at Jefferson College, which was located in Washington, Mississippi, several miles north of Natchez. It was here that Ingraham experienced a social order and way of life far different from what he had known in New England. To help acquaint others with life and society in the South, Ingraham set out to write and publish a two-volume book entitled *The South-West* (1835). This informative work provides a detailed account of Ingraham's voyage from New England to the mouth of the Mississippi River, then to Baton Rouge and finally Natchez. In elaborate detail Ingraham describes images of his travels and personal observations of the region's character, with particular emphasis on New Orleans and Natchez. During his adult life, Ingraham wrote profusely, specializing first in adventure novels, then later concentrating on books with religious themes. Among his efforts, Ingraham served as editor (or perhaps used the title "editor" to disguise his authorship) of a collection of letters by a young, unnamed northern governess who set out to present an accurate portrayal of the South during antebellum times, published under the title *The Sunny South; or, The Southerner at Home* (1860).

**LANDRETH, DAVID** (1752–1836). David Landreth Sr., a native of England, immigrated to Canada in 1781. In 1786, Landreth relocated to Philadelphia where in partnership with his brother, Cuthbert, he established the first seed business in America. In 1804, David Landreth received a number of seeds and plants from the Lewis and Clark Expedition, including the Osage orange (*Maclura pomifera*). David Landreth Jr. succeeded his father as manager of the company in 1828. It was under his direction that the business grew and prospered into one of the leading seed houses in America, as well as one of the largest establishments of its kind in the world. David Landreth Jr. maintained a branch office in Charleston, South Carolina, until it closed on April 22, 1862, when the Confederate States District Court confiscated both the property and stock. The third proprietor of the business was Thomas Landreth. Under his direction the firm specialized in the sale of roses, camellias, azaleas, magnolias, and a wide assortment of greenhouse plants.

**LOUDON, JOHN CLAUDIUS** (1783–1843). Born the son of a Scottish farmer in 1783, John Loudon became a well-known horticultural and garden writer in England during the early part of the nineteenth century. Loudon's views and philosophy not only influenced European gardening practices but also had a profound impact on American landscapes and gardens through the writings and work of Andrew Jackson Downing (1815–1852). According to Downing, Loudon was "the most distinguished gardening authority of his age." A prolific writer, Loudon published numerous books, publications, and articles on gardening, horticulture, agriculture, architecture, and other related subjects. Several of Loudon's most important works include *An Encyclopedia of Gardening* (1822), *The Suburban Gardener and Villa Companion* (1836), and *Arboretum et Fruiticetum Britannicum* (1838), an ambitious eight-volume work on the trees and shrubs of Britain, including dates of introduction. He also served as editor of *The Gardener's Magazine* (1826–1834). Following a prolific career as a writer, garden designer, and advocate for social reform, Loudon died in 1843 of an incurable lung disease. Loudon was survived by his wife, Jane, who devoted her energy and talents to updating her husband's books and articles, as well as writing numerous garden books and publications of her own.

**MICHAUX, ANDRÉ** (1746–1802). A French botanist and dedicated naturalist, André Michaux conducted botanical expeditions in England, Spain, and Persia, from the Indian Ocean to the Caspian Sea. By way of a commission from Louis XVI, Michaux came to America along with his son, François, in 1785 to collect flora from North America that had potential economic value to France. After an unsuccessful attempt to set up a botanical garden in New Jersey, Michaux and his son moved to Charleston, South Carolina, in 1786. It was here that Michaux established a plant nursery known as the "French Garden," located some ten miles outside the city. Michaux collected hundreds of native American plants and seeds, which he shipped to France in exchange for a great variety of exotic species collected from all parts of the world. Michaux is credited with introducing into America the tea olive (*Osmanthus fragrans*), the crape myrtle (*Lagerstroemia indica*), the mimosa (*Albizia julibrissin*), the ginkgo (*Ginkgo biloba*), and, according to tradition, the camellia (*Camellia japonica*). He died in 1802 in Madagascar while conducting a plant expedition. Michaux is credited with two outstanding works, *History of the North American Oaks* (1801) and *Flora Boreali-Americana* (1803). The latter was the first comprehensive guide to the flora of North America.

**MICHAUX, FRANÇOIS ANDRÉ** (1770–1855). François Michaux was born on August 16, 1770, at Satory, France, a royal domain located in the vicinity of Versailles, outside of Paris. François was the only son of André Michaux and Cecile Claye. After receiving a formal education in France, François accompanied his father to North America, arriving in New York in 1785. With his father, he relocated to Charleston, South Carolina, in 1786. In Charleston, he helped his father with the management of a plant nursery located several miles outside the city and assisted him in the collection and shipment of numerous American plants and seeds to France. In 1790, François returned to France to study medicine. Following his father's death in 1802, François arranged for the sale and disposition of the Charleston nursery. He returned to the United States in 1806 and again in 1808 for the purpose of studying the trees of North America. From these efforts François published *Histoire des Arbres Forestiers de l'Amérique du Nord*, the first volume of which appeared in 1810. Augustus L. Hillhouse translated Michaux's monumental work into English. It was published in Paris in four volumes between 1817 to 1819 under the title of *North American Sylva*. Besides this comprehensive work on North American trees, he published additional material of scientific and literary importance. François Michaux died on October 23, 1855, at his home near Pontoise, France.

**M'MAHON, BERNARD** (1775–1816). Born in Ireland of good birth and fortune, Bernard M'Mahon was forced to leave the country in 1796 for political reasons. Upon arriving in America, M'Mahon enjoyed the friendship of Thomas Jefferson and other distinguished Americans. In 1804, M'Mahon established a seed and nursery business in Philadelphia and shortly thereafter was granted permission to propagate seeds and plants obtained from the Lewis and Clark Expedition. The first catalogue issued by M'Mahon in 1804 contained over a thousand varieties of seeds, many of which were native American species. M'Mahon's extensive nursery trade, especially with the southern and western states, enabled him to introduce many new species and maintain an immense collection of the finest exotics in cultivation. M'Mahon is credited with writing the first American garden book *The American Gardener's Calendar* in 1806, which according to some authorities, was one of the most comprehensive works of its kind ever written, having a profound influence on horticulture and gardening in America for over fifty years.

**NELSON, ROBERT** (1803–ca. 1860–1866). Robert Nelson (originally spelled Nielson) was a political refugee from Denmark and a well-educated, highly competent horticulturist who relocated to America in 1846, where he initially served as a gardener in Newburyport, Massachusetts. Nelson moved to Macon, Georgia, in 1848 and established Troup Hill Nursery in 1852. After being engaged in this commercial enterprise for less than a year, Nelson successfully developed a collection of fruit trees and ornamentals that rivaled many nurseries in the North. In addition to offering fruit trees and ornamentals, Nelson also began to disseminate "nontraditional" vegetables he had known in Europe. Nelson closed Troup Hill Nursery in

1857 and moved to Augusta, Georgia, where he assisted in the management of Fruitland Nurseries. In 1858, Nelson relocated to Montgomery, Alabama, to serve as horticultural editor of the *American Cotton Planter and Soil of the South* from 1859 to 1860. In June 1860, he became head of the Horticultural Department of the *Montgomery Mail* newspaper. Nelson died, presumably in Montgomery, sometime between August 1860 and 1866. Agricultural leaders throughout the South recognized and respected Robert Nelson's contributions to the field of horticulture, as well as the educational value and instructional nature of the many articles he contributed to newspapers, agricultural journals, and horticultural magazines.

**NOISETTE, PHILIPPI** (1775–1835). Philippi Noisette was a French horticulturist and nurseryman who relocated to Charleston, South Carolina, circa 1793 by way of Santo Domingo. Upon arriving in Charleston, Noisette accepted a position as superintendent of the Charleston Botanic Garden. Shortly thereafter, he purchased a large tract of property on the outskirts of the city and developed both an ornamental garden and a commercial nursery. Around 1811, John Champneys, a wealthy rice planter, developed a new rose, later to be known as Champneys's Pink Cluster. Champneys gave cuttings of the rose to Noisette who in turn sent specimens to his brother, Louis Noisette (1772–1849), a celebrated French garden writer, horticulturist, and hybridizer who owned a nursery outside Paris. Louis crossed Champneys's rose with other roses of the period to produce the class known as the Noisettes. From his Charleston nursery, Philippi Noisette supplied local gardeners with a wide selection of roses, camellias, and a variety of native and exotic plants. Among Noisette's friends and associates was Joel Poinsett, who introduced the poinsettia into Charleston from Mexico, around 1828.

**OLMSTED, FREDERICK LAW** (1822–1903). Frederick Olmsted was born in Hartford, Connecticut, in 1822. At an early age Olmsted developed an interest in wildlife, nature, travel, and people. His career included experience as a writer, engineer, farmer, and landscape architect. Notable examples of his work as "the father of the landscape architectural profession" include New York City's Central Park, along with numerous park and recreation facilities, campus plans, residential subdivisions, and large estates throughout the country. Olmsted proved to be one of the most important observers of life in the American South prior to the Civil War. He traveled extensively throughout the southern states recording and documenting his observations and experiences. Olmsted produced three travel books on the South: *A Journey in the Seaboard Slave States, with Remarks on their Economy* (1856), *A Journey Through Texas; or a Saddle-Trip on the Southwestern Frontier* (1857), and *A Journey in the Back Country in the Winter of 1853–54* (1860). In each of these works, Olmsted presented his personal observations and views on the southern landscape, along with various social and agricultural practices in the region. In spite of distinct faults and exaggerations in his writings (deliberate or unconscious), Olmsted's accounts provide valuable descriptions and observations of the antebellum South.

**PRINCE, WILLIAM** (1725–1802). William Prince Sr. founded the famous Prince Nursery in Flushing, New York, around 1770. Considered to be the first commercial nursery in America, the Prince Nursery became the center of horticulture in America, publishing the country's first nursery catalogue (broadside) in 1771. William Prince Jr. (1766–1842) succeeded his father in the management of the nursery and authored a short book entitled *Treatise on Horticulture* (1828) in which he described many new plants that had recently been introduced into the American nursery trade. William Robert Prince (1795–1869), a naturalist and botanical explorer, was the fourth proprietor of the nursery and was author of the *Manual of Roses* (1846). Throughout its history, the Prince Nursery led all others in size and the number of plants offered for sale, both in this country and abroad. The nursery remained under the ownership of the Prince family until the late 1860s.

**RION, MARY CATHERINE** (1829–1901). Mary Catherine Rion was born in Sparta, Georgia, in 1829 to northern parents who had moved South in the late 1820s. Following her marriage to James Henry Rion in 1851, the couple settled in Winnsboro, South Carolina, where James Rion developed a successful law practice. In addition to her duties as a wife and mother of nine children, Mary Catherine found time to indulge her interests in ornamental gardening. Finding little in the way of books and printed material offering advice on preparing and planting a flower garden in the South, Mary Catherine set out to combine her own knowledge of gardening with that found in garden books by northern authors to produce *Ladies' Southern Florist*. Published in 1860, on the eve of the Civil War, this small but informative work was intended to provide ladies in the South with a practical book on flower gardening. It was written in an informative and clear style and specifically addressed the unique growing conditions of the southern climate. *Ladies' Southern Florist* was important not only because it was the first garden book written specifically on ornamentals for southern gardeners, but also because it was the earliest garden book of its kind in the South written by a woman.

**SUMMER, WILLIAM** (1815–1878). Born in Newbury County, South Carolina, in 1815, William Summer developed an early interest in plants. In 1840, at age twenty-five, Summer established Pomaria Nurseries in Pomaria, South Carolina. Pomaria Nurseries quickly became one of the most well-known and successful nurseries in the region, offering many varieties of fruit trees, as well as native and exotic ornamentals. Summer took meticulous care to test each of his selections to insure their success in his patrons' gardens. In addition to managing the nursery, Summer also assisted in the publication of several agricultural journals including, *The Southern Agriculturist* and *The Farmer and Planter*. In 1865, Pomaria Nurseries was largely destroyed by General Sherman's army as it marched from Columbia northward, burning and looting all that was in its path. Pomaria was rebuilt over time, with the first post-war catalogue being published in 1872. The nursery continued to prosper for the next six years until Summer's death of pneumonia in 1878. William Summer's knowledge and expertise in all aspects of agriculture made him one of the finest horticulturist and pomologist in the South during the antebellum period.

**THUNBERG, PETER CARL** (1743–1828). The son of a Swedish clergyman, Peter Thunberg studied medicine at the University of Uppsala. His medical education included botanical training under Linnaeus, the noted Swedish botanist. Following graduation, Thunberg was awarded a travel scholarship that permitted him to further his education in Holland and France. Upon completion of his studies, Thunberg accepted a position as surgeon for the Dutch India Company, with an assignment to Japan. Before traveling to Japan, Thunberg spent three years in Cape Town, South Africa, learning Japanese and gathering specimens of local flora. After living in Japan for a year (during which time his travels were strictly monitored), Thunberg traveled to Ceylon for an extended stay before returning to Europe in 1779. Thunberg was later appointed professor of botany at the University of Uppsala, a position once held by Linnaeus. While Thunberg was unable to bring back seeds and live plants from his travels, he was successful in publishing *Flora Japonica* (1784), a comprehensive work that contained over 300 previously unknown plants that he had observed while living in Japan.

**TURNBULL, MARTHA BARROW** (1810–1896). The daughter of William Barrow III, of West Feliciana Parish, Louisiana, Martha Turnbull was one of ten children born to the Barrow household. Upon completing her education at Madam Legoin's Institute in Philadelphia, Pennsylvania, Martha married Daniel Turnbull, a descendent of another prominent southern family. The couple settled in St. Francisville, Louisiana, where Daniel developed a successful cotton plantation known as Rosedown. It was here that Martha developed an extensive ornamental garden based on travels to Europe and her passionate interest in plants. Martha tended and maintained her beloved garden for over sixty years, during which time she kept a detailed diary of her gardening activities. Martha's remarkable garden at Rosedown and her surviving diary provide a wealth of information regarding various aspects of gardening in the South before and after the Civil War.

WHITE, WILLIAM NATHANIEL (1819–1867). Horticulturist, editor, and author, William Nathaniel White was born on November 28, 1819, in Langridge, Connecticut. Shortly after his birth, White's parents moved to New York where his boyhood years were spent assisting with the care and management of his family's farm. After attending Hamilton College, White moved South hoping a warmer climate would improve his failing health. Settling in Athens, Georgia, White operated a bookstore in addition to conducting experiments with fruits, vegetables, and flowers to determine their adaptability to the southern climate. White's greatest contribution to the field of horticulture was his book *Gardening for the South*. First published in 1856, *Gardening for the South* soon became the standard gardening book in the southern states. White was equally well known for his connection with *The Southern Cultivator* for which he became assistant editor in 1862. In 1865, White became the magazine's sole owner and moved the publication from Augusta to Athens. *The Southern Cultivator* prided itself on never missing an issue during the turbulent years of the Civil War. William White died of typhoid fever on July 14, 1867, at the age of forty-eight. White is recognized today as being one of the foremost leaders in the field of southern horticulture and pomology during the antebellum period.

# ⁑APPENDIX B⁑

*Historical Resources for Documenting the Past*

A wide range of historic material, including diaries, letters, journals, travel accounts, photographs, paintings, garden plans, and nursery/seed catalogues are available to assist in the research and documentation of historic gardens and landscapes. While all referenced sources will seldom apply to a single property, one or more can often provide valuable clues regarding a site's history and its relationship to the past. The following is an overview of potential resources available to support historic landscape and garden research:

DIARIES, LETTERS, AND JOURNALS—Written material including diaries, letters, and journals often provide personal accounts of past horticultural practices, planting procedures, ornamental plants, growing conditions, as well as descriptions of some of the joys, pleasures, and disappointments associated with gardening. Much of this material resides in private collections or with family members or descendants, often making it difficult and time consuming to locate and use. An outstanding example of written material describing life in the antebellum South is contained in the published work of Francis Anne (Fanny) Kemble entitled *Journal of a Residence on a Georgia Plantation in 1838–1839*. This notable work describes Mrs. Kemble's observations of rice and cotton plantations in coastal Georgia over a ten-year period. Another notable example is *The Sixty Year Garden Diary of Martha Turnbull, Mistress of Rosedown Plantation* (1836–1896). This comprehensive work chronicles the horticultural and gardening activities of Martha Turnbull of Rosedown Plantation in St. Francisville, Louisiana, before and after the Civil War. Mrs. Turnbull's diary provides a revealing look at the day-to-day activities of one of the South's most notable gardeners.

DAGUERREOTYPES, PHOTOGRAPHS, AND OTHER VISUAL MATERIAL—Visual images captured in daguerreotypes and old photographs serve as a useful source of information on historic landscapes, even though most nineteenth-century images typically focused more on houses and people rather than on gardens and grounds. In the American South, images of the antebellum era generally reflect urban settings rather than rural sites. As most photographers of the period were located in large towns and cities, images of rural settings are rare. It should also be noted that many photographs taken before 1861 were destroyed during the Civil War. However, photographs taken between 1865 and 1900 generally reflect houses and landscapes much as they were before the Civil War, as most southerners could neither afford to modernize or change their homes nor adapt to new garden styles. A fine collection of nineteenth-century photographs of historic houses and associated landscapes can be found in New Orleans at the Williams Research Center of the Historic New Orleans Collection and at the Southeastern Architectural Archives at Tulane University. An outstanding resource for early twentieth-century images of American gardens and landscapes is located in the Archives of American Gardens, a collection in the Horticulture Services Division of the Smithsonian Institution in Washington, D.C.

PAINTINGS AND LITHOGRAPHS—Early paintings and lithographs often provide valuable insight into historic gardens and landscapes, including walls, fences, gates, decorative structures, and garden designs. While limited in number, antebellum paintings and lithographs frequently provide visual images that reflect regional garden styles and patterns. For example,

A *Charleston Sketchbook* by Charles Fraser (1782–1860) of Charleston, South Carolina, contains more than forty watercolors showing views of plantation houses, gardens, and landscapes of urban and rural scenes in the Carolina lowcountry. Fraser's keen eye and articulate style convey visual images that are remarkable in their simplicity yet intricate in their quality and attention to detail. Another nineteenth-century illustrator, Marie Adrien Persac (1823–1873), a French-born artist living in New Orleans, produced remarkable images of Louisiana cotton and sugar cane plantations prior to the Civil War. Persac's detailed paintings of plantation scenes provide excellent documentation of antebellum landscapes. Persac also worked as an architect, engineer, and cartographer, and is well known for his map showing the locations of plantations along the Mississippi River north of New Orleans, published by B. M. Norman of New Orleans in 1858 as *Norman's Chart of the Lower Mississippi River.* In addition to Persac's work, there are the little known paintings of Father Joseph Michael Paret, a parish priest in St. Charles Parish from 1848 to 1869. Paret's paintings provide detailed images of plantation layouts, building types, and garden views of the Louisiana landscape.

GARDEN PLANS—Garden plans serve as an invaluable tool in historic landscape research. Even though few plans of antebellum gardens survive, there are a number of sources available to assist in establishing a general understanding of garden styles and patterns of the period. It is interesting to note that the layout of old gardens, unlike historic houses, were seldom recorded. Even when a house plan was lost or destroyed it could be easily redrawn throughout time based on the existing structure. In the case of gardens, however, with their fragile and ephemeral nature, it is difficult or impossible to document a design or pattern once they had experienced the vicissitudes of time. Of the existing publications that provide documentation of southern gardens, none are more useful than *Homes and Gardens of Old Virginia* (1930), *Garden History of Georgia* (1931), *Gardens of Colony and State*, vol. 2 (1934), *History of Homes and Gardens of Tennessee* (1936), and *Old Kentucky Homes and Gardens* (1939). Among the publications documenting antebellum gardens of the lower and middle south, *Garden History of Georgia* and *Gardens of Colony and State*, vol. 2, are the most valuable. In addition to providing narrative descriptions and plans of gardens in the region, several of the referenced works also contain references to period plants.

TRAVEL ACCOUNTS—Travel accounts offer a valuable insight into life as it existed at a particular time in history. Of special value to the garden historian are references to and documentation of particular gardens and cultural landscapes. Northerners, as well as foreign travelers, frequently visited the antebellum South, observing and documenting the conditions at a time when the production of cotton and sugar cane created an affluent lifestyle that was unique to the American South. A comprehensive list of travel accounts of the southern states can be found in *Travels in the Old South* (1955). Compiled by a number of well-known historians and edited by Thomas D. Clark, this collection of books and journals provides descriptive accounts of gardens, landscapes, and ornamental plants, as well as personal comments and observations of individual properties and sites.

LEGAL RECORDS—A variety of legal records are available to assist with garden research. Although these documents may vary in content and value, they often provide invaluable assistance regarding a specific site or property. Legal records include wills, property descriptions, surveys, ledgers, and account books. In each case, legal records must first be located, then analyzed, researched, and interpreted in order to obtain maximum benefit. Several examples of legal records that provide documentation of early gardens and landscapes include those found in Charleston, South Carolina, and New Orleans, Louisiana. In Charleston, many plans of the city's early gardens are contained in the record books in the Register of Mesne Conveyance Office for Charleston County. Known as the *McCrady Plat Books*, these historic documents record eighteenth and nineteenth-century property transfers and provide plans of gardens and buildings, as well as property layout and boundaries. In New Orleans, documents known as the New Orleans Notarial Archives, dating from 1802 to 1918, contain illustrative drawings that provide visual documentation of property at the time of its sale as required by Louisiana Civil Law. Engineers, artists, and architects prepared the drawings contained in the Notarial Archives, including images of houses, gardens, and site plans for properties located in New Orleans as well as fifteen Louisiana parishes. Drawings in the Notarial Archives frequently include details of fences, gates, arbors, paving, and planting schemes.

THE HISTORIC AMERICAN BUILDING SURVEY (HABS)—The Historic American Building Survey, generally known as HABS, was initiated in 1933 during the Great Depression as a means to put unemployed architects, engineers, draftsmen, historians, and photographers to work and to establish an organized national effort for documenting America's historic buildings. The HABS program represents a collaborative effort between the National Park Service, the Library of Congress, and the American Institute of Architects. Today, this endeavor has resulted in the production of more than 43,000 measured drawings, 100,000 photographs, and 52,000 pages of written historical and architectural data, which are housed at the Library of Congress in Washington, D.C. This monumental collection serves as a major resource for the study of historic structures. While primarily focused on building documentation, many HABS drawings and photographs in the collection provide valuable information on gardens, walls, fences, gates, and other landscape features. The HABS continues today, a rare legacy of the New Deal. HABS records are available at the Library of Congress, Prints and Photographic Reading Room in Washington, D.C. In addition, many libraries and state preservation offices maintain duplicate or microfilm copies of HABS photographs and drawings, which are available for public use. Efforts have recently been initiated by the American Society of Landscape Architects, the Library of Congress, and the National Park Service to establish an Historic American Landscape Survey (HALS).

MAPS AND PLANS—Historic city and town maps and plans often provide graphic evidence of street and road layouts, building locations, landscape features, and, in some instances, the design of gardens dating to the eighteenth century. Early maps of Charleston, South Carolina, New Bern and Edenton, North Carolina, Savannah, Georgia, New Orleans, Louisiana, and Natchez, Mississippi are but a few that provide valuable clues as to the physical layout of historic gardens and landscapes. In addition to traditional maps and plans, early aerial views of towns and cities, both large and small, are another valuable source of information. Several comprehensive works contain early maps, plans, and aerial views of American towns and cities, including *The Making of Urban America* (1964) and *Bird's Eye Views—Historic Lithographs of North American Cities* (1998) by John Reps, professor emeritus of the Department of City and Regional Planning at Cornell University. Sanborn Maps, which date back to 1867 also, serve as another valuable information source. Designed to assist fire insurance agents in determining potential hazards associated with buildings and property, Sanborn Maps provide information on the size and shape of residential dwellings, commercial buildings, and factories, along with a variety of site information and data.

LIBRARIES AND HISTORIC COLLECTIONS—In addition to local, state, and regional facilities, a number of outstanding libraries are available to assist in the specialized research associated with southern garden history. Several of the more important of these include the Cherokee Garden Library (Center for the Study of Southern Garden History) of the Atlanta History Center, Atlanta, Georgia, the Charleston Library Society, Charleston, South Carolina, the South Carolinian Library, Columbia, South Carolina, and the Historic New Orleans Collection, New Orleans, Louisiana. Additional facilities offering invaluable resources (including original and archival copies of agricultural journals) can be found in the special collection at the following academic institutions: the University of North Carolina, Chapel Hill, North Carolina; Clemson University, Clemson, South Carolina; the University of Georgia, Athens, Georgia; Tulane University, New Orleans, Louisiana; and Louisiana State University, Baton Rouge, Louisiana. For specialized research associated with a specific site or individual the libraries of state historical societies often provide files, records, manuscripts, photographs, and other data seldom found at other facilities or institutions. For comprehensive information on plants, botanists, naturalists, and the natural sciences, several facilities offer outstanding resources. Included among these are the research libraries at the Arnold Arboretum, Cambridge, Massachusetts; the National Agricultural Library, Beltsville, Maryland; Longwood Gardens, Kennett Square, Pennsylvania; the Pennsylvania Horticultural Society, Philadelphia, Pennsylvania; and the Missouri Botanical Garden, St. Louis, Missouri.

NURSERY AND SEED CATALOGUES—Early nursery and seed catalogues serve as excellent sources of information on fruit trees, ornamentals, flowers, and bulbs that were available to gardeners at a particular location and period in time. These unique resources also provide dates as to when plants (both native and imported species) were first available to American gardeners through the nursery trade. While old nursery and seed catalogs are rare and difficult to find, there are a number of large collections available for public use. The finest and most comprehensive collection can be found in the archives of the National Agricultural Library in Beltsville, Maryland. Beginning with the earliest catalogues of the Prince and Bartram nurseries, the holdings include original and archival copies of important nursery and seed companies of the eighteenth, nineteenth, and twentieth centuries. Additional collections can be found at Cornell University, the University of Delaware, the Horticulture Branch Library of the Smithsonian Institution in Washington, D.C., Old Sturbridge Village in Massachusetts, and the Cherokee Garden Library in Atlanta, Georgia.

PLANT RESEARCH AND DATES OF INTRODUCTION—Beginning in the late eighteenth century, England began to record the dates when imported plants were first introduced into that country. Unfortunately, similar efforts were never carried out in the United States. As a result, it is extremely difficult to establish definitive dates as to when nonindigenous plants first arrived in America. However, English dates of introduction provide a good frame of reference, for once a plant arrived in England, it generally made its way from that country into the American nursery trade in five to ten years. This time was greatly reduced by the middle of the nineteenth century with improvements in the shipping industry and increased demand for exotic plants by American nurseries. The following sources provide dates when plants first arrived in England: *Hortus Kewensis* (1810–1813), *Arboretum Horticus Anglicus* (1822), *Arboretum et Fruticetum Britannicum* (1838), and *Trees and Shrubs Hardy in the British Isles* (1914). It should be noted that when American garden and horticultural books include dates of introduction, the dates provided generally indicate when the plant first arrived in England, not the United States—a fact seldom conveyed to the reader. A comprehensive review of early nursery catalogues is useful in determining when imported plants were first offered commercially to American gardeners. Old nursery catalogues also frequently provide an invaluable insight into various horticultural practices and procedures. For those who wish to conduct extensive plant research, the finest collection of historic American nursery catalogues can be found at the National Agricultural Library in Beltsville, Maryland.

# ⊹≋APPENDIX C≋⊹

## *Composite List of Pre-1861 American Nursery Catalogues*

The following pre-1861 nursery and seed catalogues (beginning with the earliest known American nursery catalogue, William Prince's 1771 catalogue, and concluding with Kames M. Thorburn and Company's 1860 catalogue) were employed to determine the approximate dates when selected plants of the antebellum period were first offered in the American nursery trade. Initially issued as large, oversized sheets known as "broadsides," these early listings of plants and seeds soon evolved into multipaged printed catalogues. Typically fruit trees were the main selections in the earliest catalogues; however, by the first quarter of the nineteenth century, a large selection of ornamentals were offered as well. Copies of the referenced catalogues were obtained from a variety of sources, but the vast majority were secured from the National Agricultural Library in Beltsville, Maryland, which houses one of the largest collection of American nursery catalogues in the country. Today, nursery and seed catalogues represent one of the most neglected and unexplored segments of America's horticultural past.

Archival copies of each of the referenced pre-1861 nursery and seed catalogues are contained in the collections of the Cherokee Garden Library (Center for the Study of Southern Garden History) of the Atlanta History Center, Atlanta, Georgia.

| Date | Nursery/Seed Catalogue | Location |
|---|---|---|
| 1771* | William Prince | Long Island, New York |
| 1783* | Bartram's Catalogue of Trees, Shrubs and Herbaceous Plants | Philadelphia, Pennsylvania |
| 1790* | Bartram's Catalogue | Philadelphia, Pennsylvania |
| 1790* | William Prince | Long Island, New York |
| 1792** | Bartram's Catalogue (George Washington) | Philadelphia, Pennsylvania |
| 1793* | William Prince | Long Island, New York |
| 1799* | William Prince | Long Island, New York |
| Pre-1804 | Bernard M'Mahon | Philadelphia, Pennsylvania |
| 1804 | Bernard M'Mahon | Philadelphia, Pennsylvania |
| 1806* | Daniel Smith and Company | Burlington, New Jersey |
| 1807 | John Bartram and Son | Philadelphia, Pennsylvania |
| 1810 | William Booth | Baltimore, Maryland |
| 1811 | David and Cuthbert Landreth | Philadelphia, Pennsylvania |
| 1814 | Bartram's Botanical Garden | Philadelphia, Pennsylvania |
| 1815 | William and Benjamin Prince | Long Island, New York |
| 1815* | William Prince | Long Island, New York |
| 1816 | Michael Floy | New York, New York |
| 1818* | William Prince | Nursery Near New York, New York |
| 1819* | William Prince | Nursery Near New York, New York |
| 1820* | Benjamin Prince | Long Island, New York |
| 1822* | William Prince | Long Island, New York |
| 1822 | William Prince | Long Island, New York |

*Broadside; **Handscribed by Bartholomew Danbridge, secretary to George Washington.

Composite List of Pre-1861 American Nursery Catalogues (*continued*)

| Date | Nursery/Seed Catalogue | Location |
|------|------------------------|----------|
| 1823 | Prince & Mills | Flushing Landing, New York |
| 1823* | William Prince | Long Island, New York |
| 1823 | William Prince | Long Island, New York |
| 1824 | David and Cuthbert Landreth | Philadelphia, Pennsylvania |
| 1824 | Stephen F. Mills (Late Prince & Mills) | Long Island, New York |
| 1825* | William Prince | Long Island, New York |
| 1825 | G. Thorburn and Son | New York, New York |
| 1826 | David and Cuthbert Landreth | Philadelphia, Pennsylvania |
| 1827 | Joshua Pierce | Washington, D.C. |
| 1827 | William Prince | Long Island, New York |
| 1827 | G. Thorburn and Son | New York, New York |
| 1828 | Bartram's Botanic Garden | Philadelphia, Pennsylvania |
| 1828 | G. Thorburn and Son | New York, New York |
| 1830 | A. M'MAHON and Co. | Philadelphia, Pennsylvania |
| 1830* | William Prince | Long Island, New York |
| 1830 | G. Thorburn and Son | New York, New York |
| 1831 | William Prince & Sons | Long Island, New York |
| 1833 | Brighton Nurseries | Boston, Massachusetts |
| 1833–1834 | William Kenrick | Boston, Massachusetts |
| 1833–1834 | William Prince & Sons | Long Island, New York |
| 1835 | William Prince & Sons | Long Island, New York |
| 1834–1835 | Hovey & Co. | Boston, Massachusetts |
| 1836 | Agricultural Warehouse and New England Seed Store | Boston, Massachusetts |
| 1836 | David Landreth & Co. | Philadelphia, Pennsylvania |
| 1836–1837 | Clairmont Nurseries | Baltimore, Maryland |
| 1839 | William Prince & Sons | Long Island, New York |
| 1841 | Linnaean Botanic Garden and Nursery | Long Island, New York |
| 1841 | Monroe Garden and Nurseries | Rochester, New York |
| 1843 | A. J. Downing (Highland Nurseries) | Newburgh, New York |
| 1843 | Parsons & Co. | Long Island, New York |
| 1844 | Hovey & Co. | Boston, Massachusetts |
| 1844 | Linnaean Botanic Garden and Nursery | Long Island, New York |
| 1844 | James M. Thorburn & Co. | New York, New York |
| 1844–1845 | R. Buist | Philadelphia, Pennsylvania |
| 1844–1845 | Linnaean Botanic Garden and Nursery | Long Island, New York |
| 1844–1845 | D. Landreth & Fulton | Philadelphia, Pennsylvania |
| 1845 | D. Landreth & Fulton | Philadelphia, Pennsylvania |
| 1845 | Linnaean Botanic Garden and Nursery | Long Island, New York |
| 1845 | Parsons & Co. | Long Island, New York |
| 1845 | Warren's Garden & Nurseries | Boston, Massachusetts |
| 1845–1846 | A. J. Downing (Highland Nurseries) | Newburgh, New York |
| 1845–1846 | Ellwanger & Barry | Rochester, New York |
| 1845–1847 | Ellwanger & Barry | Rochester, New York |

*Broadside

| Date | Nursery/Seed Catalogue | Location |
|------|------------------------|----------|
| 1846–1847 | The Lake Erie Nurseries | Cleveland, Ohio |
| 1847 | William R. Prince & Co. | Flushing, New York |
| 1847 | James M. Thorburn & Co. | New York, New York |
| 1848 | Lake Erie Nurseries | Cleveland, Ohio |
| 1848 | McIntosh & Co. | Cleveland, Ohio |
| 1849 | Thomas Hancock | Ashton, New Jersey |
| 1849 | Morris & Stokes | West Chester, Pennsylvania |
| 1850–1851 | Hovey & Co. | Boston, Massachusetts |
| 1851–1852 | The Southern Nurseries | Washington, Mississippi |
| 1852 | Thomas Dunlap | New York, New York |
| 1852 | Thomas Hancock | Ashton, New Jersey |
| 1852 | Parsons & Co. | Long Island, New York |
| 1852–1853 | Mount Nursery | Canton, Illinois |
| 1852–1853 | Thorp, Smith, Hanchett & Co. | Syracuse, New York |
| 1853 | Saco Nurseries | Saco, Maine |
| 1853–1854 | William R. Prince & Co. | Flushing, New York |
| 1855 | Hovey & Co. | Boston, Massachusetts |
| 1855 | William R. Prince & Co. | Flushing, New York |
| 1855–1856 | E. B. Coleman | Peoria, Illinois |
| 1855–1856 | Downing Hill Nursery | Atlanta, Georgia |
| 1855–1856 | William R. Prince & Co. | Flushing, New York |
| 1856 | A. Frost & Co. | Rochester, New York |
| 1856 | John Sigerson & Bro. | St. Louis, Missouri |
| 1856–1857 | Piasa Nursery | Alton, Illinois |
| 1856–1857 | William Summer (Pomaria Nurseries) | Pomaria, South Carolina |
| 1857 | Columbus Nursery | Columbus, Ohio |
| 1857 | Linnaean/Hill, Rock Creek | Near Washington, D. C. |
| 1857 | Old Colony Nursery | Plymouth, Massachusetts |
| 1857–1858 | Fruitland Nurseries | Augusta, Georgia |
| 1857–1858 | William Summer (Pomaria Nurseries) | Pomaria, South Carolina |
| 1858 | Alton Nursery | Alton, Illinois |
| 1858 | P. J. Berckmans & Co. (Fruitland Nurseries) | Augusta, Georgia |
| 1858 | Persimmon Grove Nursery | Princeton, Illinois |
| 1858 | Staunton Nurseries | Staunton, Virginia |
| 1858–1859 | William Summer (Pomaria Nurseries) | Pomaria, South Carolina |
| 1858–1859 | Vineland Nursery | Near Mobile, Alabama |
| 1859 | Ashley Nursery & Gardens | Du Quoin, Illinois |
| 1859 | Bloomington Nursery | Bloomington, Illinois |
| 1859 | DuPage Co. Nurseries | Naperville, Illinois |
| 1859 | John A. Pettingill | Binker Hill, Illinois |
| 1859 | Woodburn Nurseries | Alton, Illinois |
| 1859–1860 | P. J. Berckmans & Co. (Fruitland Nurseries) | Augusta, Georgia |
| 1859–1860 | Robert Buist (Rosedale Nurseries) | Philadelphia, Pennsylvania |
| 1859–1860 | The Cumberland Nurseries | Carlisle, Pennsylvania |
| 1859–1860 | Hopewell Nurseries | Fredericksburg, Virginia |

Composite List of Pre-1861 American Nursery Catalogues (*continued*)

| Date | Nursery/Seed Catalogue | Location |
|---|---|---|
| 1860 | Carew Sanders & Co. | St. Louis, Missouri |
| 1860 | Commercial Nursery | Bloomington, Illinois |
| 1860 | Mount Hope Nurseries | Rochester, New York |
| 1860 | Persimmon Grove Nursery | Princeton, Illinois |
| 1860 | William Summer (Pomaria Nurseries) | Pomaria, South Carolina |
| 1860 | William R. Prince & Co. | Flushing, New York |
| 1860 | James M. Thorburn & Co. | New York, New York |

# SELECTED BIBLIOGRAPHY

Affleck, Thomas. *Natchez (Mississippi) Daily Courier,* October 28, 1854.

———. *Southern Rural Almanac and Plantation/Garden Calendar, for 1860.* Washington, Mississippi: n.p., 1860.

Aiton, William Townsend. *Hortus Kewensis; or A Catalogue of the Plants Cultivated in the Royal Botanic Garden at Kew by the Late William Aiton.* 2d ed. 5 vols. London: Longman, Hurst, Rees, Orme, and Brown, 1810–1813.

Bacot, H. Parrott. *Marie Adrien Persac: Louisiana Artist.* Baton Rouge: Louisiana State University Press, 2000.

Barnard, Henry. *The South Atlantic States in 1833, as Seen by a New Englander.* Baltimore: Maryland Historical Society, 1918.

Bartram, William. *Travels Through North and South Carolina, Georgia, East and West Florida.* 1791. Reprint, New York: Macy-Masius, 1933.

Bean, William Jackson. *Trees and Shrubs Hardy in the British Isles.* London: Murray, 1914.

Bell, Laura Palmer. "The Vanishing Gardens of Savannah." *Georgia Historical Quarterly* 28, no. 3 (September 1944): 196–208.

Bernard, Duke of Saxe-Weimar Eisenach. *Travels Through North America, during the Years 1825 and 1826.* Philadelphia: Carey, Lea & Carey, 1828.

Betts, Edwin, ed. *Thomas Jefferson's Garden Book, 1766–1824.* Philadelphia: The American Philosophical Society, 1944.

Boyer, Marcel. *Plantations by the River.* Baton Rouge: Department of Geography and Anthropology, Louisiana State University, 2002.

Breck, Joseph. *The Flower Garden.* Boston: J. P. Jewett and Co., 1851.

Bremer, Fredrika. *The Homes of the New World.* Vol. 1. London: A. Hall, Virtue and Co., 1853.

Bridgeman, Thomas. *The Young Gardener's Assistant.* New York: Mitchell and Turner, 1829.

———. *The Florist's Guide.* Boston: J. Breck, 1840.

Briggs, Loutrel W. *Charleston Gardens.* Columbia: University of South Carolina Press, 1951.

Bryant, J. Advertisement. *The Charleston City Gazette,* June 6, 1795.

Bryant, William Cullen, ed. *Picturesque America.* Vol. 1. New York: D. Appleton and Company, 1874.

Buckingham, James Silk. *The Slave States of America.* London and Paris: Fisher, Son and Co., 1842.

Catesby, Mark. *The Natural History of Carolina, Florida and the Bahama Islands.* 2 vols. London: Printed at Expense of Author, 1731–1743.

Chapman, A. W. *Flora of the Southern United States.* New York: Ivison, Phinney and Co., 1860.

Clark, Thomas D. *Travels in the Old South, a Bibliography.* Norman: University of Oklahoma Press, 1956.

Clarke, Stephen Reynolds. *Hortus Anglicus; or the Modern English Garden.* London: F. C. & J. Rivington, 1822.

Coker, William Chambers. "The Garden of André Michaux." *Journal of Elisha Mitchell Scientific Society* 27 (1911): 65–72.

Cothran, James R. *Gardens of Historic Charleston.* Columbia: University of South Carolina Press, 1995.

Dezallier d'Argenville, A. J. *The Theory and Practice of Gardening.* Translated by John James. London: Printed by George James, 1712.

Douglas, Lake and Jennifer Hardy. *Gardens of New Orleans; Exquisite Excess.* SanFrancisco: San Francisco Chronicle Books, 2001.

Downing, Andrew Jackson. *A Treatise on the Theory and Practice of Landscape Gardening.* New York: Wiley and Putnam, 1841.

―――. *Rural Essays.* New York: G. P. Putnam, 1853.

Drayton, Charles. Charles Drayton's Diaries. Archives, Drayton Hall, Charleston, South Carolina.

Eaton, Clement. *A History of the Old South: The Emergence of a Reluctant Nation.* 3d ed. Prospect Heights, Illinois: Waveland Press, Inc., 1987.

Elliott, Stephan. *A Sketch of the Botany of South Carolina and Georgia.* 2 vols. Charleston: J. R. Schenk, 1821–1824.

Fish, George W. Letter to the Editor. *The Horticulturist* 2 (September 1847): 196–97.

Fraser, Charles. *Reminiscences of Charleston.* Charleston, South Carolina: John Russell, 1854.

―――. *A Charleston Sketchbook, 1796–1860.* Rutland, Vermont: C. E. Tuttle Co., 1959.

Gordon, Alexander, Letter to the Editor, H. G. Hovey. *The Magazine of Horticulture* 15 (1849): 245–49.

Gray, Andrew. "The Hardy Shrubs of the South." *The Magazine of Horticulture* 21 (1855): 190–93.

Gray, Lewis Cecil. *History of Agriculture in the Southern United States to 1860.* 2 vols. Washington: Carnegie Institution of Washington, 1933.

Green, Roland. *A Treatise on the Cultivation of Ornamental Flowers.* Boston: J. B. Russell and New York: G. Thorburn and Son, 1828.

Hall, Basil. *Travels in North America in the Years 1827 and 1828.* Vol 3. Philadelphia: Carey, Lea and Carey, 1829.

Hamlin, Talbot. *Greek Revival Architecture in America.* London: Oxford University Press, 1944.

Hardy, Jeannette and Lake Douglas. *Gardens of New Orleans: Exquisite Excess.* San Francisco: Chronicle Books, 2001.

Hedrick, U. P. *A History of Horticulture in America to 1860.* New York: Oxford University Press, 1950. Reprint, *A History of Horticulture in America to 1860 with an Addendum of Books Published 1861–1920 by Elisabeth Woodburn,* Portland, Oregon: Timber Press, 1988.

Hillier, Harold G. *Hilliers' Manual of Trees and Shrubs.* 5th ed. London: David & Charles, 1981.

Hume, Harold Hardrada. *Gardening in the Lower South.* New York: Macmillan, 1929.

Ingraham, Joseph Holt. *The South-West.* 2 vols. New York: Harper & Brothers, 1835; Reprinted as, *The South-West, by a Yankee.* Ann Arbor, Mich.: University Microfilms, 1966.

Ingraham, Joseph Holt, ed. *The Sunny South; or, The Southerner at Home.* Philadelphia: G. G. Evans, 1860. Reprint, New York: Negro Universities Press, 1968.

Jenkins, Virginia Scott. *The Lawn: A History of an American Obsession.* Washington: Smithsonian Institution Press, 1994.

Johnson, George William. *A Dictionary of Modern Gardening.* Philadelphia: Lea and Blanchard, 1847.

Jones, Katharine M. *The Plantation South.* Indianapolis, Ind.: Boggs-Merrill, 1984.

Kenrick, William. *The New American Orchardist.* Boston: Carter, Hendee, 1833.

Kern, G. M. *Practical Landscape Gardening.* Cincinnati, Ohio: Moore, Wiltach, Keys & Co., 1855.

Lane, Mills. *Architecture of the Old South: South Carolina.* Savannah: Beehive Press, 1989.

Lanman, Charles. *Adventures in the Wilds of the United States and British American Provinces.* 2 vols. Philadelphia: John W. Moore, 1856.

Latrobe, Charles Joseph. *The Rambler in North America.* London: R. B. Seeley and W. Burnside, et al., 1835.

Lawson, John. *A New Voyage to Carolina.* London: n.p., 1709. Reprinted as *A New Voyage to Carolina.* Edited with an introduction and notes by Hugh Talmage. Chapel Hill: University of North Carolina Press, 1967.

―――. *The History of Carolina.* London: Printed for T. Warner, 1718.

Leighton, Ann. *America Gardens of the Nineteenth Century*. Amherst: University of Massachusetts Press, 1987.

Lelièvre, Jacques-Felix. *Nouveau Jardinier de la Louisiane*. New Orleans: Published by the
Author, 1838.

Levasseur, A. "Lafayette's Visit to Baton Rouge, . . . from . . . *Lafayette in America*, . . . 1829."
Translated by R. W. Colomb. *Louisiana Historical Quarterly* 14 (1931): 178–79.

Linley, John. *The Georgia Catalog: Historic American Buildings Survey*. Athens: University of
Georgia Press, 1982.

———. "Architecture, Landscape Architecture, City Planning: Charleston and Savannah."
*Georgia Landscape* (1992): 7–8.

Lockwood, Alice B., ed. *Gardens of Colony and State; Gardens and Gardeners of the American
Colonies and of the Republic before 1840*. 2 vols. New York: Published for the Garden Club
of America by C. Scribner's Sons, 1931–1934.

Loudon, J. C. *Encyclopedia of Gardening*. London: Longman, Rees, Orme, Brown and Green,
1822.

———. *Arboretum et Fruticetum Britannicum*. London: Printed for the Author, 1838.

Mackay, Alexander. *The Western World; or, Travels in the United States in 1846–1847*. London:
R. Bentley, 1850.

Mackay, Charles. *Life and Liberty in America*. New York: Harper and Brothers, 1859.

Mackie, J. Milton. *From Cape Cod to Dixie and the Tropics*. New York: G. P. Putnam, 1864.

Marshall, Humphrey. *Arbustrum Americanum: The American Grove*. Philadelphia: Crukshank,
1785.

Martha Turnbull Garden Diary, 1836–1895. Manuscript in Collection of Friends of Oakley,
Oakley Plantation, St. Francisville, Louisiana.

Martineau, Harriet. *Retrospect of Western Travel*. London: Saunders and Otley, 1838.

Mason, Charles. *Report of the Commission of Patents*. Washington: United States Patent Office,
1854.

McMurran, Mary Louisa. Letter, April 7, 1851. Lemuel P. Connor Papers. In *Melrose Estate—
Cultural Landscape Report*. Boston: Ann Beha Associates, 1996.

Meehan, Thomas. *The American Handbook of Ornamental Trees*. Philadelphia: Lippincott,
Grambo and Co., 1853.

Meriwether, Margaret Babcock, ed. *The Carolinian Florist of Governor John Drayton of South
Carolina, 1766–1822*. Columbia: South Carolinian Library of the University of South
Carolina, 1943.

Michaux, André. *Flora Boreali-Americana*. Paris: n.p., 1803.

Michaux, François André. *Travels to the West of the Allegheny Mountains in the States of Ohio, Kentucky and Tennessee, and Back to Charleston by the Upper Carolinas*. 3d ed. London: B. Crosby
and J. F. Hughes, 1805.

———. *The North American Sylva*. Paris: C. D'Hautel, 1819.

Miller, Philip. *The Gardener's Dictionary*. London: Printed for author by John and James Rivington, 1731.

M'Mahon, Bernard M. *The American Gardener's Calendar*. Philadelphia: B. Graves, 1806.

Moore, Francis. *A Voyage to Georgia*. London: Printed for J. Robinson, 1744.

Murray, Amelia. *Letters from the United States, Cuba, and Canada*. New York: n.p., 1856.

Myers, Robert Manson, ed. *Children of Pride: Selected Letters of the Rev. Charles Colcock Jones*.
New Haven: Yale University Press, 1984.

National Park Service. *Melrose Estate, Natchez National Historical Park, Natchez, Mississippi Cultural Landscape Report*. Atlanta: U.S. Department of the Interior, National Park Service,
Gulf Coast System Support Office and Ann Beha Associates, 1996.

Nelson, Robert. "Trees and Shrubs Usually Employed for Hedges." *The Southern Cultivator*
14, no. 3 (1856): 91–92.

———. "*Buxus* (Boxwood)." *The Southern Cultivator* 14, no. 6 (1856): 188.

———. "*Kalmia latifolia* (Calico Bush, Poison Ivy Bush)." *The Southern Cultivator* 14, no. 6 (1856): 184.

———. "*Jasminum nudiforium.* (Winter Jasmine)." *The Southern Cultivator* 14, no. 7 (1856): 219.

———. "*Magnolia grandiflora.*" *The Southern Cultivator* 14, no. 7 (1856): 219.

———. "*Olea fragrans* (Tea Olive, Fragrant Olive)." *The Southern Cultivator* 14, no. 7 (1856): 219.

———. "*Pittosporum tobira.*" *The Southern Cultivator* 14, no. 7 (1856): 220.

———. "Roses for the South." *The Southern Cultivator* 14 (1856): 58–61.

———. "Flowers for the South." Letter to the Editor. *The Southern Cultivator* 15, no. 1 (1857): 27–28.

———. "*Vitex agnus castus.* (Chaste Tree)." *The Southern Cultivator* 15, no. 4 (1857): 126.

———. "The Golden Bell Shrub." *The Southern Cultivator* 15, no. 5 (1857): 127.

———. "Ornamental Edgings and Hedges, for the South." *The Southern Cultivator* 15, no. 5 (1857): 126.

Nuttall, Thomas. *The North American Sylva.* Philadelphia: D. Rice and A. N. Hart, 1857.

Odenwald, Neil G. and James R. Turner. *Identification, Selection and Use of Southern Plants for Landscape Design.* Baton Rouge: Claitor's Press, 1987.

Olmsted, Frederick Law. *A Journey in the Seaboard Slave States, with Remarks on Their Economy.* New York: Dix and Edwards, 1856.

———. *A Journey in the Back Country in the Winter of 1853–54.* New York: Mason Brothers, 1860.

———. *The Cotton Kingdom: A Traveller's Observations on Cotton and Slavery in the American Slave States.* New York: Mason Brothers, 1861.

Owens, Hubert B. *Georgia's Planting Prelate.* Athens: University of Georgia Press, 1945.

Paulsen, J. W. Letter to Editor, H. C. Hovey. *The Magazine of Horticulture* 12 (1846): 22–24.

Poesch, Jessie and Barbara SoRelle Bacot, eds. *Louisiana Buildings, 1720–1940: The Historic American Buildings Survey.* Baton Rouge: Louisiana State University Press, 1997.

Porcher, Francis Peyre. *Resources of the Southern Fields and Forests.* Charleston: Evans and Cogswell, 1863.

Power, Tyrone. *Impressions of America during the Year 1833, 1834, and 1835.* 2 vols. London: R. Bentley, 1836.

Prince, William. *A Short Treatise on Horticulture.* New York: T. & J. Swords, 1828.

Ramsay, David. *The History of South Carolina, from Its First Settlement in 1670 to the Year 1809.* Charleston: David Long worth, 1809.

Reader, Alfred. *Manual of Cultivated Trees and Shrubs.* New York: Macmillan, 1914.

Regales, C. Letter to the Editor. *The Horticulturist,* New Series 7 (1857): 52.

Reps, John W. *Cities of the Mississippi: Nineteenth-Century Images of Urban Development.* Columbia, Missouri: University of Missouri Press, 1994.

Richardson, Emma B. "The Hayward-Washington House Garden." *The Charleston Museum Leaflet,* no. 15. Charleston, South Carolina: The Charleston Museum, 1941.

———. "Charleston Garden Plants." *The Charleston Museum Leaflet,* no. 19. Charleston, South Carolina: The Charleston Museum, 1943.

Rijn, Mary. *Ladies' Southern Florist.* Columbia, South Carolina: P. B. Glass, 1860. Reprint, *Ladies' Southern Florist: A Facsimile of the 1860 Edition with New Introductions by James R. Cothran and Debra McCoy-Massey.* Columbia: University of South Carolina Press, 2001.

Rozier, John, ed. *The Granite Farm Letters.* Athens: University of Georgia Press, 1988.

Sargent, C. S. "The Red Cedar." *Garden and Forest* 8 (1895): 61.

Sarudy, Barbara Wells. "South Carolina Seed Merchants and Nurserymen before 1820." *Mag-

*nolia: Bulletin of the Southern Garden History Society* 8, no. 3 (winter 1992): 6–10.

Saunders, William. "Evergreen Shrubs." *The Horticulturist*, New Series 5 (1855): 165.

Schwab, Eugene L. and Jacqueline Bull, eds. *Travels in the Old South.* 2 vols. Lexington: University Press of Kentucky, 1973.

Shaffer, Edward Terry Hendrie. *Carolina Gardens.* New York: Devin-Adair Co., 1963.

Sherman, William T. *Memoirs of General William T. Sherman.* Westport, Connecticut: Greenwood Press, 1972.

Smith, Alice Ravenel Huger. *A Carolina Rice Plantation of the Fifties.* New York: William Morrow Co., 1936.

———— and D. E. Smith. *The Dwelling Houses of Charleston, South Carolina.* Philadelphia: J. B. Lippincott, 1917.

Smith, J. Calvin. *The Illustrated Hand-Book, A New Guide for Travelers Through the United States of America.* New York: Sherman & Smith, 1847.

Smith, J. Frazer. *White Pillars: Early Life and Architecture of the Lower Mississippi Valley Country.* New York: William Helburn, Inc., 1941. Reprint, *Plantation Houses and Mansions of the Old South*, New York: Dover, 1993.

Squibb, Robert. *The Gardener's Calender for South-Carolina, Georgia and North-Carolina.* Athens: University of Georgia Press, 1980.

Stoney, Samuel Gaillard. *Plantations of the Carolina Low Country.* Charleston: The Carolina Art Association, 1938.

————. "The Poinsett-Campbell Correspondence." *The South Carolina Historical and Genealogical Magazine* 42, no. 2 (April 1941): 36–37.

Stritikus, George R. "The Battle-Friedman Garden Blooms Again." *Alabama Heritage* (winter 2000): 8–15.

Stuart, James. *Three Years in North America.* Edinburgh: R. Cadell, 1830.

Taylor, Raymond L. *Plants of Colonial Days: A Guide to 160 Flowers, Shrubs, and Trees in the Gardens of Colonial Williamsburg.* Williamsburg, Virginia: Colonial Williamsburg, 1952.

Thomas Affleck Papers. Louisiana and Lower Mississippi Valley Collections (LLMVC), Louisiana State University Libraries, Baton Rouge, Louisiana.

Thornton, Phineas. *The Southern Gardener and Receipt Book.* [Camden, S.C.]: printed for the author, 1840. A 2d, improved and enlarged, edition was printed for the author in Newark, N.J., 1845; a 3d edition, revised and corrected by Mrs. Mary L. Edgeworth, was issued in 1860 by J. B. Lippincott in Philadelphia.

Thorpe, Thomas Bangs. "Our Visit to Natchez." *Southern Sportsman* 1 (1843): 68, 88.

Tidball, Eugene. "A Northern Army Officer in Antebellum Savannah: The 1849 Memoirs of Second Lieutenant John C. Tidball." *Georgia Historical Quarterly*, 84, no. 1 (spring 2000): 117.

Turner, Suzanne. *The Gardens of Louisiana; Places of Work and Wonder.* Baton Rouge: Louisiana State University Press, 1997.

Walters, John Bennett. *Merchant of Terror—General Sherman and Total War.* New York: The Bobbs-Merrill Co., 1973.

Warder, John A. *Hedges and Evergreens.* New York: Orange, Judd & Co., 1858.

Welch, William and Greg Grant. *The Southern Heirloom Garden.* Dallas: Taylor Publishing Company, 1995.

Wigginton, Brooks E. *Trees and Shrubs for the Southern Coastal Plain.* Athens: University of Georgia Press, 1957.

# ➼INDEX➼

Illustrations are indicated by page numbers in **bold**

*Acacia farnesiana*, 266

*Acacia julibrissin*. See *Albizia julibrissin*

Adam's needle, superb (*Yucca gloriosa*), 269

Adam's needle (*Yucca filamentosa*), 264–65, **264**, 269

Adam's thread. *See* Adam's needle

*Aesculus pavia*, 266

Affleck, Thomas, 142–43, 285

*Affleck's Southern Rural Almanac, Plantation and Garden Calendar* (Affleck), 142, 285

agricultural journals, 132–33

agriculture, 1–3

Aiken County, S.C., 59

*Ailanthus altissima*, 152–54, **153**, 266

*Ailanthus glandulosa*. See *Ailanthus altissima*

Aiton, William, 151, 285

*Akebia quinata*, 266

Alabama: agricultural journals, 133; Huntsville, **10**; Mobile, 27–30, **28**, 143–44; nurseries, 145; Tuscaloosa, **51**, 107–9, **108**

*Alabama Planter*, 133

*Albizia julibrissin*, 154–55, **154**, 266

*Albizzia julibrissin*. See *Albizia julibrissin*

althaea (althea) (*Hibiscus syriacus*), 199–201, **200**, 267

*Althea frutex*. See *Hibiscus syriacus*

*Amateurs' Guide and Flower Garden Directory, The* (Clark), 270

*Amelanchier canadensis*, 266

American arborvitae (*Thuja occidentalis*), 269

American beauty berry (*Callicarpa americana*), 266

American beech (*Fagus grandifolia*), **64**, 267

*American Book of Ornamental Trees, The* (Meehan), 131

American box (*Buxus sempervirens*), 47, 70, 161–63, **161**, 266

*American Cotton Planter*, **132**, 133, 290

*American Farmer, The*, 132, 133

*American Flower Garden Companion, The* (Sayers), 130, 270

*American Flower Garden Directory, The* (Buist & Hibbert), 130, 270, 286

*American Gardener, The* (Gardiner & Hepburn), 127, 129

*American Gardener's Calendar, The* (M'Mahon), 127, 129, 289

American holly (*Ilex opaca*), 70, 204–5, **204**, 267

American mulberry. *See* red mulberry

American nettle tree. *See* hackberry

*American Rose Culturist* (Sexton), 273

American wisteria (*Wisteria frutescens*), 261–62, **262**, 269

American woodbine. *See* Virginia creeper

*Ampelopsis hederacea*. See *Parthenocissus quinquefolia*

*Ampelopsis quinquefolia*. See *Parthenocissus quinquefolia*

anise. See *Illicium* spp.

annuals, 270–73

*Arboretum et Fruiticetum Britannicum* (Loudon), 151, 288

arborvitae (*Thuja*), 269

architecture, 6–8

Athens, Ga., **63**, 102–4, **103**, **104**

atlas cedar (*Cedrus argentea atlantica*), 266

*Aucuba japonica variegata*, 155–56, **156**, 266

Augusta, Ga., 27, **70**. *See also* Fruitland Nurseries

avenues, **43**, **55–58**, 55–61, 121, 210

*Azalea calendulaceum*, 266

*Azalea indica*, **150**, 157–58, **157**, 266

*Azalea maximum*, 266

*Azalea nudiflorum*, 158–59, **159**, 266

*Azalea viscosa*, 266

banana shrub (*Michelia figo*), 231–33, **232**, 268

Bartow County, Ga., 116–18

Bartram, John, 235, 285–86

Bartram Nursery, 133, 286

Bartram, William, 75–76, 202, 207, 286

Batersby-Hartridge Garden (Savannah, Ga.), **48**, 89–90

Battle, Millicent Bealle, 50, 108–9

Battle-Friedman Garden (Tuscaloosa, Ala.), **51**, 108–9, **108**

bay berry. *See* wax myrtle

bay laurel (*Laurus nobilis*), 216–17, **216**, 267

bead tree. *See* chinaberry

bear grass. *See* Adam's needle

Beaufort, S.C., **55**

beech, American (*Fagus grandifolia*), **64**

Bennett, Thomas (garden, Charleston, S.C.), 84

Berckmans, Prosperous Julius, 59, 144, **144**, 286

Bermuda grass (*Cynodon dactylon*), 78

big laurel. *See* southern magnolia

bigleaf magnolia (*Magnolia macrophylla*), 268

bigleaf periwinkle (*Vinca major*), 269

*Bignonia capreolata*, 266

*Bignonia radicans*. See *Campsis radicans*

*Bignonia sempervirens.* See *Gelsemium sempervirens*

black locust (*Robinia pseudoacacia*), 269

blotch plant. *See* gold dust plant

Bois de Fléche (St. Martins Parish, La.), **140**

Bonaventure Cemetery (Savannah, Ga.), 25, 58

*Book of Fruits* (Manning), 130

books on gardening, 126–32, 273–75

Boone Hall Plantation (Mount Pleasant, S.C.), **56–57**

Bosworth House (New Orleans, La.), **94**

Bourbon roses, 279–80

bow wood. *See* Osage orange

box. *See* common box; dwarf box; tree box

Boxwood House and Garden (Madison, Ga.), **8, 97**

Boylston Garden (Columbia, S.C.), **101**, 102

breath of spring. *See* winter honeysuckle

Breck, Joseph, 131, 270

Bremer, Fredrika, 13, 15–16, 24–25, 286

brick edging, 54

brick walks, 55

bridal wreath spiraea (*Spiraea prunifolia plena*), 252–54, **253**, 269

*Broussonetia papyrifera*, 160–61, **160**, 266

Brown, Andrew (garden, Natchez, Miss.), 110–12, **110**

Buckingham, James Silk, 7, 13, 23–24, 102–3, 230

Buist, Robert, 130, 131, 141, 270, 273, 286

bull bay. *See* southern magnolia

bush azalea. *See* pinxter bloom azalea

*Buxus humilis.* See *Buxus sempervirens suffruticosa*

*Buxus sempervirens*, 47, 70, 161–63, **161**, 266

*Buxus sempervirens arborescens*, 70, 266

*Buxus sempervirens suffruticosa*, 53, 70, 163–64, **163**, 266

Caldwell House and Gardens (Columbia, S.C.), 100–102, **101**, **102**

calico bush. *See* mountain laurel

*Callicarpa americana*, 266

*Calycanthus floridus*, 165–66, **165**, 266

Camden, S.C., **62**

*Camellia japonica*, **17**, **138**, 166–67, **166**, 266

*Camellia sasanqua*, 168–69, **168**, 266

*Camellia sinensis*, **138**, 139, 266

*Campsis radicans*, 169–70, **169**, 266

candle berry. *See* wax myrtle

cape jasmine (jessamine) (*Gardenia jasminoides*), 191–93, **192**, 267

cape plumbago (*Plumbago capensis*), 269

Carolina allspice (*Calycanthus floridus*), 165–66, **165**, 266

Carolina bird cherry. *See* cherry laurel

Carolina kidney bean. *See* American wisteria

Carolina jessamine (*Gelsemium sempervirens*), 193–94, **193**, 267

Carolina silverbell (*Halesia tetraptera*), 196–98, **197**, 267

cassena holly. *See* yaupon holly

cassine holly (*Ilex cassine*), 69

Casulon Plantation (High Shoals, Ga.), **114**

catalogues, nursery and seed, 133–34, 296, 297–300

*Catalpa bignonioides*, 170–71, **171**, 266

*Catalpa catalpa.* See *Catalpa bignonioides*

Catalpa Plantation (Coweta County, Ga.), **66**

*Catalpa syringifolia.* See *Catalpa bignonioides*

Catawbaw tree. See *Catalpa bignonioides*

Catesby, Mark, 67, 169, 170, 173, 177, 181, 193, 197, 248, 251, 262

cedar of Lebanon (*Cedrus libani*), 266

cedars. See *Cedrus* spp.; eastern red cedar; white cedar

*Cedrus argentea atlantica*, 266

*Cedrus deodara*, 266

*Cedrus libani*, 266

*Celtis occidentalis*, 172–73, **172**, 266

Center Hall (Darlington County, S.C.), **148**

*Cerasus caroliniensis.* See *Prunus caroliniana*

*Cercis canadensis*, 173–75, **174**, 266

ceremonial trees, 65

*Chaenomeles lagenaria.* See *Chaenomeles speciosa*

*Chaenomeles speciosa*, 175–76, **175**, 266

Champneys, John, 274, 290

Champneys' Pink Cluster rose (*Rosa noisettiana*), **274**, 290

*Charleston Sketchbook, A,* (Fraser), 67, 86, 294

Charleston, S.C., 13–18, **14**, **15**, 83–86; Boone Hall Plantation, **56–57**; Crowfield Plantation, **112**; Jenkins Mikell House, **84**; live oak avenues, 56–58; Lucas garden, 85; Nathaniel Russell House, 85; nurseries, 136–37, 141, 289, 290; Thomas Bennett garden, 84; William A. Hayne garden, 84–85

chaste tree (*Vitex agnus-castus*), 259–60, **259**, 269

Chelsea Plantation (Beaufort, S.C.), **55**

Cherokee rose (*Rosa laevigata*), 47, 72–73, **72**, 249–51, **250**, 269

cherry laurel (*Prunus caroliniana*), 47, 70, 72, 245–46, **245**, 269

*Chimonanthus praecox*, 266

China roses, 278

China tree. *See* chinaberry

chinaberry (*Melia azedarach*), **22**, 229–31, **230**, 268

Chinese azalea (*Azalea indica*), **150**, 157–58, **157**, 266

Chinese fir (*Cunninghamia lanceolata*), 267

Chinese guelder-rose (*Hydrangea macrophylla*), 201–2, **201**, 269

Chinese honeysuckle (*Azalea indica*). *See* Chinese azalea

Chinese honeysuckle (*Lonicera flexosa*), 268

Chinese parasol tree (*Firmiana simplex*), 189–90, **190**, 267

Chinese profuse flowered wisteria (*Wisteria floribunda*), 269

Chinese sacred bamboo. *See* heavenly bamboo

Chinese serrated leaf photinia (*Photinia serrulata*), 268

Chinese sumac (*Ailanthus altissima*), 152–54, **153**, 266

Chinese white magnolia. *See* yulan magnolia

Chinese wisteria (*Wisteria sinensis*), 263–64, **263**, 269

*Chionanthus virginia. See Chionanthus virginicus*

*Chionanthus virginicus*, 176–78, **177**, 266

Christiansburg, Va., **66**

*Citrus sinensis*, **38**, 60–61, 139

Civil War, 10–11, 86–87, 91, 98, 107–8, 118

Clark, John, 270

*Clematis flammula*, 178–79, **178**, 266

*Clematis virginiana*, 179–80, **179**, 266

*Clematis virginicus. See Clematis virginiana*

cold frames, 96, 148

Columbia, S.C., 18–20, 98–102; Boylston Garden, **101**; burning of during Civil War, 11, 98; Caldwell House and Gardens, 100–102, **101**, **102**; Hampton-Preston House and Gardens, 98–100, **99**, **100**

common box (*Buxus sempervirens*), 47, 70, 161–63, **161**, 266

Confederate jasmine (*Trachelospermum jasminoides*), 269

coral honeysuckle (*Lonicera sempervirens*), 268

*Corchorus japonicus. See Kerria japonica*

*Cornus florida*, 180–82, **181**, 266

*Cotinus coggygria*, 182–83, **182**, 266

cotton (*Gossypium vitifolium*), **2**, 139

*Cotton Kingdom, The* (Olmsted), 6, 29, **33**

cotton production, 2–3, **4**

Coweta County, Ga., **66**

cow-itch vine. *See* trumpet vine

Coxe, William, 130

crape myrtle (*Lagerstroemia indica*), 214–16, **215**, 267

*Crataegus coccinea. See Pyracantha coccinea*

*Crategus pyracantha. See Pyracantha coccinea*

creeping climber. *See* sweet scented clematis

cross vine (*Bignonia capreolata*), 266

Crowfield Plantation (Charleston, S.C.), **112**, 171

*Cryptomeria japonica*, 267

cucumber tree (*Magnolia acuminata*), 268

*Cunninghamia lanceolata*, 267

cut leaf lilac (*Syringa laciniata*), 255–56, **255**, 269

cut leaf Persian lilac. *See* cut leaf lilac

cutwork parterres, 47–48, **48**

*Cydonia japonica. See Chaenomeles speciosa*

*Cynodon dactylon*, 78

*Dahlia*, **271**

*Daphne odora*, 267

Darlington County, S.C., **148**

deep-green forsythia. *See* greenstem forsythia

deodar cedar (*Cedrus deodara*), 266

design. *See* garden design

*Deutzia crenata.* See *Deutzia scabra*

*Deutzia gracilis*, 267

*Deutzia scabra*, 183–85, **184**, 267

*Deutzia scabra crenata.* See *Deutzia scabra*

Dezallier d'Argenville, A. J., 47, 127

*Diervilla japonica.* See *Weigela florida*

*Directions for the Transplantation and Management of Young Thorn or Other Hedge Plants* (Main), 129

dogwood (*Cornus florida*), 180–82, **181**, 266

double flowered kerria (*Kerria japonica pleniflora*), 267

double flowered plum leaved spiraea. *See* bridal wreath spiraea

Downing, Andrew Jackson, **129**; biographical sketch, 287; books by, 128–29, 131; naturalistic landscape design, 51–52, 63, 67

drooping forsythia (*Forsythia suspensa*), 267

Dunleith (Natchez, Miss.), **31**

Dutch box. *See* dwarf box

dwarf box (*Buxus sempervirens suffruticosa*), 53, 70, 163–64, **163**, 266

eastern hemlock (*Tsuga canadensis*), 269

eastern red cedar (*Juniperus virginiana*), 210–11, **210**, 267; in avenues, 58–59, **58**, 121, 210; as hedge, 69, 210

Eden Hall (McCormick County, S.C.), 115–16, **115**, **116**

Edgar, La., 120–21, **120**, **121**

edging box (*Buxus sempervirens suffruticosa*), 53, 70, 163–64, **163**, 266

edging materials, 53–55

*Elaeagnus angustifolia*, 267

Elliott, Stephen, 74–75, 149, 250, 287

elm, winged (*Ulmus alata*), 269

empress tree (*Paulownia tomentosa*), 241–42, **241**, 268

*Encyclopedia of Gardening, An*, 288

English box. *See* dwarf box

English dogwood. *See* mock orange

English ivy (*Hedera helix*), 198–99, **198**, 267

English manorial model, 5, 113, 114–15

English naturalistic design, 47, 51–52, 74, **76**

English yew (*Taxus baccata*), 269

*Eriobotrya japonica*, 185–86, **185**, 267

*Euonymus americanus*, 267

*Euonymus japonica*, 53, 54, 186–88, **187**, 267

*Euonymus japonicus.* See *Euonymus japonica*

*Euonymus tobira.* See *Pittosporum tobira*

European privet. See *Ligustrum vulgare*

evergreen euonymus (*Euonymus japonica*), 53, 54, 186–88, **187**, 267

Evergreen Plantation (Edgar, La.), 120–21, **120**, **121**

evergreen spindle tree. *See* evergreen euonymus

evergreen thorn. *See* firethorn

exotic plants, 65, 124, 136–39, 146–47, 151–52

*Fagus grandifolia*, **64**, 267

false acacia (*Robinia pseudoacacia*), 269

*Family Kitchen Garden, The* (Buist), 131

*Farmer and Planter, The*, 133, 291

Faye-Webster Plantation (St. Mary's Parish, La.), **61**

Feliciana Parish, La., **44**

fence laws, 69

fences, 65–69, **66–68**, 72–74

Ferrell Gardens (LaGrange, Ga.), 105–7, **106**, **107**

Ferrell, Sarah Coleman, 105–7, **105**

*Ficus carica*, 188–89, **188**, 267

fig, common (*Ficus carica*), 188–89, **188**, 267

firethorn (*Pyracantha coccinea*), 246–47, **246**, 269

*Firmiana simplex*, 189–90, **190**, 267

five leaf akebia (*Akebia quinata*), 266

flame azalea (*Azalea calendulaceum*), 266

*Flora Boreali-Americana* (Michaux, A.), 207, 217, 250, 289

*Flora Japonica* (Thunberg), 291

Florida anise (*Illicium floridanum*), 267

Florida smilax. *See* southern smilax

*Florist's Manual: . . . For Cultivators of Flowers, The*, 270

*Flower Garden, The* (Breck), 131, 270

flowering almond, dwarf (*Prunus glandulosa*), 269

flowering ash. *See* fringe tree

flowering dogwood (*Cornus florida*), 180–82, **181**, 266

flowering quince (*Chaenomeles speciosa*), 175–76, **175**, 266

flowers (annuals and perennials), 270–73

formal gardens. *See* parterres

Forsyth Park (Savannah, Ga.), 86, **87**

*Forsythia suspensa*, 267

*Forsythia viridissima*, 190–91, **190**, 267

Fortune, Robert: biographical sketch, 287; plants introduced by, 156, 191, 209, 219, 236, 253, 260

four winged halesia. *See* Carolina silverbell

Franklin tree (*Franklinia alatamaha*), 267, 286

Fraser, Charles, 67, 86, 294

Fraser magnolia (*Magnolia fraseri*), 268

French hydrangea (*Hydrangea macrophylla*), 201–2, **201**, 267

French mulberry (*Callicarpa americana*), 266

French style of design, 47–48. *See also* parterres

fringe tree (*Chionanthus virginicus*), 176–78, **177**, 266

*From Cape Cod to Dixie and the Tropics* (Mackie), 17–18, 26, 30, 41–42, 45, 57

fruit tree cultivation, 127

Fruitland Nurseries, 134, 143, 144, 157, 286, 290

*Fruits and Fruit Trees of America, The* (Downing), 131

gallberry (*Ilex glabra*), 267

garden design: city gardens, 82; English naturalistic design, 47, 51–52, 74, **76**; French style of design, 47–48; geometric style, 9, 47–48; manor house tradition, 5, 113, 114–15; plantation gardens, 112–15; site plans, 123–24, **123**; town gardens, 96–97. *See also* parterres

garden designers, 48–51, 108

Garden District (New Orleans, La.), 93–94, **96**

Garden, Dr. Alexander, 192, 197, 205, 224

garden plans, 52–55, 294. *See also* garden design

*Gardener's Dictionary* (Miller), 127, 151, 285

*Gardeners Kalendar, The* (Logan), 126

*Gardeners Kalendar for South Carolina, The* (Squibb), 126

*Gardenia florida*. See *Gardenia jasminoides*

*Gardenia jasminoides*, 191–93, **192**, 267

*Gardenia radicans*, 267

*Gardenia thunbergia*, 267

*Gardening for the South* (White), 127, 131, 292

gardens: numbers of in South, 113–14, 124–25; overview, 8–10. *See also* garden design; plant materials

Gardiner, John, 127, 129

garland deutzia (*Deutzia scabra*), 183–85, **184**, 267

*Gelsemium nitidum*. See *Gelsemium sempervirens*

*Gelsemium sempervirens*, 193–94, **193**, 267

geometric garden design, 9, 47–48

Georgetown, S.C., 71

Georgia: agricultural journals, 133; agriculture in, 2–3; Athens, **63**, 102–4, **103**, **104**; Augusta, 27, **70**; Bartow County, 116–18, **117**; Coweta County, **66**; High Shoals, **114**; LaGrange, 104–7, **106**, **107**; Macon, 27, 143, 275, 289; Madison, **8**, **97**; Newnan, 125; nurseries, 134, 143, 144, 157, 275, 286, 289, 290; Thomasville, **147**. *See also* Savannah, Ga.

Georgia bark (*Pinckneya pubens*), 268

*Ginkgo biloba*, 194–96, **195**, 267

*Glycine chinensis*. See *Wisteria sinensis*

*Glycine frutescens*. See *Wisteria frutescens*

*Glycine fruticosa*. See *Wisteria frutescens*

*Glycine sinensis*. See *Wisteria sinensis*

gold dust plant (*Aucuba japonica variegata*), 155–56, **156**, 266

golden bell (*Forsythia viridissima*), 190–91, **191**, 267

golden rain tree (*Koelreuteria paniculata*), 267

Gordon, Alexander, 95, 287–88

*Gordonia lasianthus*, 267

*Gossypium vitifolium*, **2**, 139

graceful deutzia (*Deutzia gracilis*), 267

grancy gray beard (*Chionanthus virginicus*), 176–78, **177**, 266

grasses for lawns, 75, 77–80

Gray, Andrew, 71, 78

great laurel (*Azalea maximum*), 266

Greek revival style architecture, 6–8, **7**

Green, Rowland, 130

greenhouses, 96, 149–51

Green-Meldrin House (Savannah, Ga.), 90, **90**

greenstem forsythia (*Forsythia viridissima*), 190–91, **191**, 267

Greenwood Plantation (Feliciana Parish, La.), **44**

groves, 59, 62–65, **62**

guelder-rose, Chinese (*Hydrangea macrophylla*), 201–2, **201**, 267

guelder-rose (*Viburnum opulus* "sterile"), 269

hackberry (*Celtis occidentalis*), 172–73, **172**, 266

*Halesia carolina. See Halesia tetraptera*

*Halesia tetraptera*, 196–98, **197**, 267

Hall, Basil, 13, 14–15, 21

Hampton-Preston House and Gardens (Columbia, S.C.), 98–100, **99**, **100**

Hayne, William A. (garden, Charleston, S.C.), 84–85

Hearst, John Wardlaw, 115–16

heavenly bamboo (*Nandina domestica*), 236–37, **236**, 268

*Hedera helix*, 198–99, **198**, 267

*Hedera quinquefolia. See Parthenocissus quinquefolia*

hedge apple. *See* Osage orange

hedges, 47, 69–74, **70**; plants for, 204, 205, 210, 221, 245, 246, 251

*Hedges and Evergreens* (Warder), 69, 131

hemlock, eastern (*Tsuga canadensis*), 269

hemp tree. *See* chaste tree

Hepburn, David, 127, 129

Hermann-Grima House (New Orleans, La.), **92**, 93

Hibbert, Thomas, 130, 141, 270, 286

*Hibiscus syriacus*, 199–201, **200**, 267

High Shoals, Ga., **114**

high-style gardens, 81, 124–25

Hills and Dales (LaGrange, Ga.), 106, **107**

*Histoire des Arbres Forestiers de l'Amérique du Nord* (Michaux, F. A.), 289

Historic American Building Survey, 295

Historic American Landscape Survey, 295

*History of the North American Oaks* (Michaux, A.), 289

hollies. See *Ilex* spp.

Holmes, Francis S., 127, 131

*Homes of the New World* (Bremer), 15–16, 24–25, 286

honeysuckle. See *Lonicera* spp.

*Horticulturist, The*, 129, 287

*Hortus Kewensis*, 151, 285

hothouses, 96, **148**, 149–51

Huntsville, Ala., **10**

hybrid perpetual roses, 281–82

*Hydrangea hortensia. See Hydrangea macrophylla*

*Hydrangea macrophylla*, 201–2, **201**, 267

*Hydrangea quercifolia*, 202–4, **203**, 267

Ile Copal (Louisiana), **5**

*Ilex cassine*, 69

*Ilex glabra*, 267

*Ilex opaca*, 70, 204–5, **204**, 267

*Ilex verticillata*, 267

*Ilex vomitoria*, 47, 53–54, 69, 205–7, **206**, 267

*Illicium anisatum*, 267

*Illicium floridanum*, 267

*Illicium parviflorum*, 207–8, **207**, 267

imported plants, 65, 124, 136–39, 146–47, 151–52

Indian bean tree (*Catalpa bignonioides*), 170–71, **171**, 266

Indian lilac. *See* crape myrtle

Indica (Indian) azalea (*Azalea indica*), **150**, 157–58, **157**, 266

Ingraham, Joseph Holt, 13, 288. See also *The South-West; The Sunny South*

inkberry (*Ilex glabra*), 267

introduced plants, 65, 124, 136–39, 146–47, 151–52

introduction dates, 151–52, 266–69, 296. *See also* specific plants

Italian poplar (*Populus nigra* var. *italica*), 269

ivy, common (*Hedera helix*), 198–99, **198**, 267

Jackson vine. *See* southern smilax

James, John, 47, 127

January jasmine. *See* winter jasmine

Japan allspice (*Chimonanthus praecox*), 266

Japan cedar (*Cryptomeria japonica*), 267

Japan quince. *See* flowering quince

Japan rose (*Camellia japonica*), 166–67, **166**, 266

Japanese anise (*Illicium anisatum*), 267

Japanese aucuba (*Aucuba japonica variegata*), 155–56, **156**, 266

Japanese euonymus (*Euonymus japonica*), 54

Japanese globe flower (*Kerria japonica*), 213–14, **213**, 267

Japanese holly-grape (*Mahonia japonica*), 268

Japanese honeysuckle (*Lonicera japonica*), 219–20, **220**, 268

Japanese pagoda tree (*Sophora japonica*), 269

Japanese pittosporum. See *Pittosporum tobira*

Japanese plum. *See* loquat

Japanese privet (*Ligustrum japonicum*), 267

Japanese rose (*Kerria japonica pleniflora*), 267

Japonica (*Camellia japonica*), 166–67, **166**, 266

jasmine, cape (*Gardenia jasminoides*), 191–93, **192**, 267

jasmine, common (*Jasminum officinale*), 267

jasmine, Confederate (star) (*Trachelospermum jasminoides*), 269

jasmine, winter (*Jasminum nudiflorum*), 209–10, **209**, 267

*Jasminum nudiflorum*, 209–10, **209**, 267

*Jasminum officinale*, 267

Jenkins Mikell House (Charleston, S.C.), **84**

*Journal of a Residence on a Georgia Plantation in 1838–1839* (Kemble), 293

journals, agricultural, 132–33

*Journey in the Back Country, A* (Olmsted), 73, 290

*Journey in the Seaboard Slave States, A* (Olmsted), 26, 56–57, 290

*Journey Through Texas, A* (Olmsted), 290

Judas tree (*Cercis canadensis*), 173–75, **174**, 266

Juniper's beard. *See* smoke tree

*Juniperus virginiana. See* eastern red cedar

*Kalmia latifolia*, 211–13, **212**, 267

Kemble, Francis Anne (Fanny), 293

Kendrick, William, 130

Kentucky bluegrass (*Poa protensis*), 79

*Kentucky Farmer*, 133

*Kerria japonica*, 267

*Kerria japonica pleniflora*, 213–14, **213**, 267

kitchen gardens, 8, 127

*Koelreuteria paniculata*, 267

Kolb-Pou-Newton Place (Madison, Ga.), **8, 79**

*Ladies' Southern Florist* (Rion), 128, 131, 270, 274, 291

Lady Banks (Lady Banksiae) rose (*Rosa banksiae*), 269, 283

*Lagerstroemia chinensis. See Lagerstroemia indica*

*Lagerstroemia indica*, 214–16, **215**, 267

LaGrange, Ga., 104–7, **106, 107**

Landreth, David, 141, 221, 288

Landreth Seed Company, 133, 141

landscape traditions, 122–25

Langdon, C. C., 143–44

Langdon Nursery, 144

laurel bay. *See* southern magnolia

*Laurel tinus. See Viburnum tinus*

Laurestinus. *See* Laurustinus

lauri mundi. *See* cherry laurel

*Laurocerasus caroliniana. See Prunus caroliniana*

*Laurus nobilis*, 216–17, **216**, 267

laurustinus (*Viburnum tinus*), 71, 257–59, **258**, 269

lawns, 74–80, **75, 78**

leatherleaf mahonia (*Mahonia bealei*), 268

Leliévre, Jacques-Felix, 96, 130

*Ligustrum japonicum*, 268

*Ligustrum lucidum*, 268

*Ligustrum vulgare*, 47, 54, 69–70, 217–18, **217**, 268

lilac, common (*Syringa vulgaris*), 256–57, **257**, 269

lilac, cut leaf (*Syringa laciniata*), 255–56, **255**, 269

lilac, Persian (*Syringa persica*), 269

lily tree. *See* yulan magnolia

lily-flowered magnolia (*Magnolia liliflora*), 225–27, **225**, 268

*Liquidambar styraciflua*, 268

*Liriodendron tulipifera*, 268

live oak (*Quercus virginiana*), 62, 247–49, **248**, 269; in avenues, **43**, 55–58, **55, 56–57**, 121

loblolly bay (*Gordonia lasianthus*), 267

Logan, Martha, 126

Lombardy poplar (*Populus nigra* var. *italica*), 269

*Lonicera flexosa*, 268

*Lonicera fragrantissima*, 218–19, **219**, 268

*Lonicera japonica*, 219–20, **220**, 268

*Lonicera sempervirens*, 268

loquat (*Eriobotrya japonica*), 185–86, **185**, 267

Loudon, John Claudius, 128, 151, 287, 288

Louisiana: agriculture in, 3; Edgar, 120–21, **120, 121**; Feliciana Parish, **44**; nurseries, 95, 145; St. Charles Parish, **123**; St. Francisville, 58, 73, 118–20, **119**, 293; St. John's Parish, **53**; St. Martins Parish, **140**; St. Mary's Parish, **61**; Vacherie, **43**, 58. *See also* Mississippi River plantations; New Orleans, La.

Low House Garden (Savannah, Ga.), **54**, 90

Lucas garden (Charleston, S.C.), 85

Mackie, J. Milton, 17–18, 26, 30, 41–42, 45, 57

*Maclura aurantiaca. See Maclura pomifera*

*Maclura pomifera*, 47, 73–74, **73**, 220–22, **221**, 268

Macon, Ga., 27, 143, 275, 289

Madison, Ga., **8, 97**

*Magnolia acuminata*, 268

*Magnolia acuminata cordata*, 268

*Magnolia altissima. See Magnolia grandiflora*

*Magnolia conspicua. See Magnolia denudata*

*Magnolia denudata*, 222–23, **223**, 268

*Magnolia discolor. See Magnolia liliflora*

*Magnolia foetida. See Magnolia grandiflora*

*Magnolia fraseri*, 268

*Magnolia fuscata. See Michelia figo*

*Magnolia glauca. See Magnolia virginiana*

*Magnolia grandiflora*, **60**, 224–25, **224**, 268; in avenues, 59, 121

*Magnolia heptapeta. See Magnolia denudata*

*Magnolia liliflora*, 225–27, **225**, 268

*Magnolia macrophylla*, 268

Magnolia Nurseries, 95

*Magnolia obovata. See Magnolia liliflora*

*Magnolia purpurea. See Magnolia liliflora*

*Magnolia quinquepeta. See Magnolia liliflora*

*Magnolia tripetala*, 268

*Magnolia virginiana*, 228–29, **228**, 268

*Magnolia × soulangiana*, 227–28, **227**, 268

*Mahonia aquifolium*, 268

*Mahonia bealei*, 268

*Mahonia japonica*, 268

maidenhair tree (*Ginkgo biloba*), 194–96, **195**, 267

Main, Thomas, 129

Manning, Robert, 130

manor house tradition, 5, 113, 114–15

*Manual of Roses* (Prince, W. R.), 131, 273, 290

maple leaved sterculia. *See* Chinese parasol tree

Martineau, Harriet, 13, 35–36

McCormick County, S.C., 115–16

medlar (*Eriobotrya japonica*), 185–86, **185**, 267

Meehan, Thomas, 131

*Melia azedarach*, **22**, 229–31, **230**, 268

Melrose (Natchez, Miss.), **7**

*Mespilus coccinea*. See *Pyracantha coccinea*
*Mespilus japonica*. See *Eriobotrya japonica*
Michaux, André: biographical sketch, 288–89; Charleston nursery, 136, 289; *Flora Boreali-Americana*, 207, 217, 250, 289; plants introduced by, **17**, 136, 154, 166, 168, 190, 196, 214, 238
Michaux, François André, 245, 289
Michaux's nurseries, 136, 289
*Michelia figo*, 231–33, **232**, 268
Midway Plantation (Georgetown, S.C.), 71
Miller, Philip, 127, 151, 285
mimosa (*Albizia julibrissin*), 154–55, **154**, 256
Mississippi, 133, 134, 142, 285. *See also* Mississippi River plantations; Natchez, Miss.
*Mississippi Farmer and Mechanic*, 133
Mississippi River plantations, 39, 42–45, **43**, 58
M'Mahon, Bernard, 127, 129, 221, 289
M'Mahon nursery and seed business, 133, 289
Mobile, Ala., 27–30, **28**, 143–4
mock orange (*Philadelphus coronarius*), 242–43, **243**, 268
mock orange (*Prunus caroliniana*). *See* cherry laurel
*Mohrodendron carolinum*. See *Halesia tetraptera*
Monterey Square (Savannah, Ga.), **24**
Montgomery Place (Tarrytown, N.Y.), **75**
*Morus alba*, 139, 268
*Morus rubra*, 233–34, **233**, 268
moss roses, 282–83
Mount Pleasant, S.C., **56–57**
mountain laurel (*Kalmia latifolia*), 211–13, **212**, 267
mulberry, French (*Callicarpa americana*), 266
mulberry, paper (*Broussonetia papyrifera*), 160–61, **160**, 266
mulberry, red (*Morus rubra*), 233–34, **233**, 268
mulberry, white (*Morus alba*), 139, 268
*Myrica cerifera*, 234–36, **235**, 268
myrtle, common (*Myrtus communis*), 268
Myrtle Land (St. Charles Parish, La.), **123**
*Myrtus communis*, 268

*Nandina domestica*, 236–37, **236**, 268
Natchez, Miss., 30–35, **33**, 109–12; Andrew Brown garden, 110–12, **110**; Dunleith, **31**; groves, 62–63; Melrose, **7**; plantation gardens, 113–14; Rosalie, **110**
Nathaniel Russell House (Charleston, S.C.), 85
native plants, 62–64, 65, 124, 146–47
*Natural History of Carolina, Florida and the Bahama Islands* (Catesby), 67, 169, 170, 173, 177, 181, 193, 197, 248, 251
naturalistic design, 47, 51–52, 74, **76**
Nelson, John M., 95
Nelson, Robert, 50, 143, 271, 275–83, 289–90
*Nerium oleander*, 237–38, **237**, 268
*New American Orchardist, The* (Kendrick), 130
*New Louisiana Gardener, The* (Leliévre), 96, 130

New Orleans, La., 35–42, **36**, **41**, 90–96; Bosworth House, **94**; courtyard, **40**; Garden District, 93–94, **96**; Hermann-Grima House, **92**, 93; live oak avenues, 58; Magnolia Nurseries, 95; parterres, 54; Vieux Carré, 90–93
New Orleans Notarial Archives, 91
Newnan, Ga., 125
*Nintova japonica*. See *Lonicera japonica*
Noisette, Philippi, 136–37, 290
Noisette roses, **274**, 280–81, 290
Noisette's nursery, 290
nomenclature, 134, 151
nondescript rose. *See* Cherokee rose
*North American Sylva* (Michaux, F. A.), 245, 289
*North Carolina Planter*, 133
Norway spruce (*Picea abies*), 268
*Nouveau Jardinier de la Louisiane* (Leliévre), 96, 130
nurseries and seed businesses: influence of, 10, 133–34; northern, 133, 135–36, 139–42; southern, 134, 136–39, 142–45. *See also specific nursery names*
nursery and seed catalogues, 133–34, 296, 297–300

Oak Alley Plantation (Vacherie, La), **43**, 58
Oak Lawn (Thomasville, Ga.), **147**
oakleaf hydrangea (*Hydrangea quercifolia*), 202–4, **203**, 267
oaks. See *Quercus* spp.
*Olea fragrans*. See *Osmanthus fragrans*
oleander (*Nerium oleander*), 237–38, **237**, 268
oleaster (*Elaeagnus angustifolia*), 267
Olmsted, Frederick Law: biographical sketch, 13, 290; travel observations, 6, 26, 29, **33**, 56–57, 73
Onslow County, N.C., **68**
*Ophiopogon japonicus*, 268
opopanax (*Acacia farnesiana*), 266
orange trees (*Citrus sinensis*), **38**, 60–61, 139
Oregon grape (*Mahonia aquifolium*), 268
oriental arborvitae (*Thuja orientalis*), 269
*Ornamental Gardening in the South* (Gray), 71
Osage orange (*Maclura pomifera*), 47, 73–74, **73**, 220–22, **221**, 268
*Osmanthus fragrans*, 239–39, **239**, 268
Owens-Thomas House (Savannah, Ga.), 88–89, **89**
*Oxydendrum arboreum*, 268

pale fences, 66
Paret, Father Joseph Michael, 123, 294
*Parkinsonia aculeata*, 268
Parsons nurseries, 133
Parsons, Samuel, 131, 273
parterres, 8, 47–48, **48**, **88**, 123
*Parthenocissus quinquefolia*, 239–41, **240**, 268
*Passiflora incarnata*, 268
passion flower (*Passiflora incarnata*), 268

*Paulownia imperialis. See Paulownia tomentosa*

*Paulownia tomentosa*, 241–42, **241**, 268

perennials, 270–73

periodicals, 129, 132–33

periwinkle (*Vinca*), 269

Persac, Marie Adrien, **5**, 294

Persian cut leaf lilac (*Syringa laciniata*), 255–56, **255**, 269

Persian lilac (*Syringa persica*), 269

*Philadelphus coronarius*, 242–43, **243**, 268

*Photinia serrulata*, 268

piazzas, 7, 83

*Picea abies*, 268

picket fences, 66–67, **66**

*Pinckneya pubens*, 268

*Pinus strobus*, 268

pinxter bloom azalea (*Azalea nudiflorum*), 158–59, **159**, 266

pipe tree. *See* lilac, common

*Pittosporum chinensis. See Pittosporum tobira*

*Pittosporum tobira*, 70–71, 244–45, **244**, 268

plant materials: availability of, 82, 97; exotic plants, 65, 124, 136–39, 146–47, 151–52; native plants, 62–64, 65, 124, 146–47; sources of, 135–45. *See also names of specific plants*

plant pits, 96, 148–49

plantations, 4–6; along Mississippi River, 39, 42–45, **43**, 58; gardens of, 5, 9, 112–21; layout of grounds, 5, 112–15, 124; scarcity of gardens on, 113–14, 124–25. *See also* specific plantations

*Platanus occidentalis*, 269

pleasure gardens, 8–10

*Plumbago capensis*, 269

*Poa protensis*, 79

poet's jasmine (*Jasminum officinale*), 267

poet's laurel. *See* bay laurel

Pomaria Nurseries, 134, 142, 291

pomegranate (*Punica granatum*), 269

*Pomological Manual, The*, 130

poplar, Lombardy (*Populus nigra* var. *italica*), 269

*Populus nigra* var. *italica*, 269

post-and-rail fence, 68

prickley parkinsonia (*Parkinsonia aculeata*), 268

pride-of-India. *See* chinaberry

prim. See *Ligustrum vulgare*

Prince Nursery, 133, 139–41, 290

Prince, Robert, 139

Prince, William, 290

Prince, William Robert, 130, 131, 273, 290

*Prince's Manual of Roses* (Prince, W. R.), 131, 273, 290

princess tree (*Paulownia tomentosa*), 241–42, **241**, 268

privet, common. See *Ligustrum vulgare*

privet, Japanese (*Ligustrum japonicum*), 268

*Prunus caroliniana*, 47, 70, 72, 245–46, **245**, 269

*Prunus glandulosa*, 269

*Punica granatum*, 269

purple Chinese magnolia. *See* lily-flowered magnolia

purple fringe tree. *See* smoke tree

*Pyracantha coccinea*, 246–47, **246**, 269

*Pyrus japonica. See Chaenomeles speciosa*

*Pyrus speciosa. See Chaenomeles speciosa*

*Quercus nigra*, 269

*Quercus phellos*, 269

*Quercus sempervirens. See* live oak (*Quercus virginiana*)

*Quercus virens. See* live oak (*Quercus virginiana*)

*Quercus virginiana. See* live oak (*Quercus virginiana*)

red buckeye (*Aesculus pavia*), 266

red cedar. *See* eastern red cedar

red mulberry (*Morus rubra*), 233–34, **233**, 268

redbud (*Cercis canadensis*), 173–75, **174**, 266

Redcliffe Plantation (Aiken County, S.C.), 59

Reeve's double spiraea (*Spiraea reevesiana flora plena*), 269

Reeve's spiraea (*Spiraea reevesiana*), 254–55, **254**, 269

resources on garden history, 293–96

*Retrospect of Western Travel* (Martineau), 13, 35–36

Reynolds House (Camden, S.C.), **62**

*Rhododendron indicum. See Azalea indica*

*Rhododendron nudiflorum. See Azalea nudiflorum*

*Rhododendron periclymenoides. See Azalea nudiflorum*

*Rhus continus. See Cotinus coggygria*

rice production, 3

Rion, Mary Catherine, 128, 131, 270, 274, 291

*Robinia pseudoacacia*, 269

Roman laurel (*Laurus nobilis*), 216–17, **216**, 267

rooting gardenia (*Gardenia radicans*), 267

*Rosa banksiae*, 269, 283

*Rosa laevigata*, 47, 72–73, **72**, 249–51, **250**, 269

*Rosa noisettiana*, **274**, 290

*Rosa sinica. See Rosa laevigata*

Rosalie (Natchez, Miss.), **110**

*Rose, The* (Parsons), 131, 273

rose bay. *See* oleander

rose colored weigela. See *Weigela florida*

rose laurel. *See* oleander

*Rose Manual, The* (Buist), 131, 141, 273–74, 286

rose of Sharon (*Hibiscus syriacus*), 199–201, **200**, 267

rosebay (*Azalea maximum*), 266

Rosedown Plantation (St. Francisville, La.), 58, 118–20, **119**, 293

Rosemary (Newnan, Ga.), 125

roses: books on, 273–75; Bourbon roses, 279–80; Cherokee rose, 47, 72–73, **72**, 249–51, **250**, 269; China roses, 277–78; cultivation of, 276–77, 283; hybrid perpetual roses, 281–82; Lady Banks rose, 269, 283; moss roses,

282–83; Noisette roses, **274**, 280–81, 290; tea roses, 278–79

rough-leaved deutzia (*Deutzia scabra*), 183–85, **184**, 267

royal paulownia. See *Paulownia tomentosa*

*Rubus japonicus*. See *Kerria japonica*

*Salisburia adiantifolia*. See *Ginkgo biloba*

*Salix babylonica*, 269

San Francisco (St. John's Parish, La.), **53**

sasanqua (*Camellia sasanqua*), 168–69, **168**, 266

*Sassafras albidum*, 269

saucer magnolia (*Magnolia × soulangiana*), 227–28, **227**, 268

Savannah, Ga., 20–26, **21**, **24**, **26**, 86–90; Batersby-Hartridge Garden, **48**, 89–90; Bonaventure Cemetery, 25, 58; Forsyth Park, 86, **87**; garden descriptions, 53, 71; Green-Meldrin House, 90, **90**; live oak avenues, 58; Low House Garden, **54**, 90; Owens-Thomas House, 88–89, **89**; tiles for edging, 55; Trustee's Garden, 137–39

Sayers, Edward, 130, 270

seed businesses. See nurseries and seed businesses

seed catalogues, 133–34, 296, 297–300

serviceberry (*Amelanchier canadensis*), 266

Sexton, C. M., 273

shadblow (*Amelanchier canadensis*), 266

Sherman, William. T., 11, 86–87, 98, 100

shrubby glycine. See American wisteria

*Siliquastrum cordatum*. See *Cercis canadensis*

silk tree (*Albizia julibrissin*), 154–55, **154**, 256

single flowered kerria. See *Kerria japonica*

single houses, 83–84, **83**, 87

site plans, 5, 123–24, **123**. See also garden design

*Sixty Year Garden Diary of Martha Turnbull, The* (Turnbull), 293

*Sketch of the Botany of South Carolina and Georgia* (Elliott), 250

*Slave States of America, The* (Buckingham), 7, 23–24

*Smilax lanceolata*, 251–52, **252**, 269

*Smilax non spinosa*. See *Smilax lanceolata*

*Smilax smallii*. See *Smilax lanceolata*

smoke tree (*Cotinus coggygria*), 182–83, **182**, 266

snake's beard (*Ophiopogon japonicus*), 268

snowball (*Viburnum opulus* "sterile"), 269

snowdrop tree (*Halesia tetraptera*), 196–98, **197**, 267

*Soil of the South*, 133, 290

*Sophora japonica*, 269

sorrel tree (*Oxydendrum arboreum*), 268

Soulange's magnolia. See saucer magnolia

sourwood (*Oxydendrum arboreum*), 268

*South Atlantic States in 1833, The* (Barnard), 22, 27

South Carolina: agricultural journals, 133; agriculture in, 2–3; Aiken County, 59; Beaufort,

55; Camden, 62; Charleston County, **56–57**, **112**; Darlington County, **148**; Georgetown, 71; McCormick County, 115–16, **115**, **116**; nurseries, 134, 136–37, 142, 289, 291. See also Charleston, S.C.; Columbia, S.C.

*South Countryman*, 133

south (southern) tea plant. See yaupon holly

*Southern Agriculturist*, 133, 291

southern catalpa (*Catalpa bignonioides*), 170–71, **171**, 266

*Southern Cultivator*, 132, 133, 292

*Southern Farmer*, 133

*Southern Farmer and Market Gardener, The* (Holmes), 127, 131

*Southern Field and Forest*, 133

*Southern Gardener and Receipt Book, The* (Thornton), 127, 131

*Southern Homestead*, 133

southern live oak. See live oak

southern magnolia. See *Magnolia grandiflora*

Southern Nurseries, 134, 142, 285

*Southern Planter, The*, 133

southern smilax (*Smilax lanceolata*), 251–52, **252**, 269

*South-West, The* (Ingraham), 42–44, 61, 92–93, 113–14, 147, 288

Spanish bayonet (*Yucca aloifolia*), 269

spearshaped smilax. See southern smilax

spikenard (*Vitex agnus-castus*), 259–60, **259**, 269

*Spiraea cantoniensis*. See *Spiraea reevesiana*

*Spiraea lanceolata*. See *Spiraea reevesiana*

*Spiraea prunifolia flora plena*. See *Spiraea prunifolia plena*

*Spiraea prunifolia plena*, 252–54, **253**, 269

*Spiraea reevesi*. See *Spiraea reevesiana*

*Spiraea reevesiana*, 254–55, **254**, 269

*Spiraea reevesiana flora plena*, 269

spoonleaf yucca. See Adam's needle

spoon-wood. See mountain laurel

spruce, Norway (*Picea abies*), 268

Squibb, Robert, 126

St. Charles Parish, La., **123**

St. Francisville, La., 58, 73, 118–20, **119**, 293

St. John's Parish, La., **53**

St. Martins Parish, La., **140**

St. Mary's Parish, La., **61**

star jasmine (*Trachelospermum jasminoides*), 269

starry anise (*Illicium parviflorum*), 207–8, **207**, 267

starry gardenia (*Gardenia thunbergia*), 267

*Sterculea platanfolia*. See *Firmiana simplex*

Stevens Thomas Place (Athens, Ga.), **63**

*Stewartia malacodendron*, 269

strawberry bush (*Euonymus americanus*), 267

*Suburban Gardener and Villa Companion, The* (Loudon), 288

sugar cane production, 3

sugarberry. See hackberry

Summer, William, 142, 291

*Sunny South, The* (Ingraham), 28–29, 33–35, 41, 59, 76, 109, 288

superb Adam's needle (*Yucca gloriosa*), 269

swamp azalea (*Azalea viscosa*), 266

swamp magnolia. *See* sweetbay

sweet acacia (*Acacia farnesiana*), 266

sweet gum (*Liquidambar styraciflua*), 268

sweet olive (sweet scented olive). *See* tea olive

sweet scented clematis (*Clematis flammula*), 178–79, **178**, 266

sweet scented daphne (*Daphne odora*), 267

sweet shrub (*Calycanthus floridus*), 165–66, **165**, 266

sweetbay (*Magnolia virginiana*), 228–29, **228**, 268

swept yards, 79

sycamore (*Platanus occidentalis*), 269

syringa. *See Philadelphus coronarius*

*Syringa laciniata*, 255–56, **255**, 269

*Syringa persica*, 269

*Syringa persica* var. *laciniata. See Syringa laciniata*

*Syringa vulgaris*, 256–57, **257**, 269


tanners sumac (*Ailanthus altissima*), 152–54, **153**, 266

*tapis vert*, 74

*Taxus baccata*, 269

tea olive (*Osmanthus fragrans*), 239–39, **239**, 268

tea plant (*Camellia sinensis*), **138**, 139, 266

tea roses, 278–79

*Tecoma radicans. See Campsis radicans*

*Thea sinensis. See Camellia sinensis*

*Theory and Practice of Gardening, The* (Dezallier), 47, 127

Thomas Grant House and Garden (Athens, Ga.), 103–4, **103**, **104**

Thomasville, Ga., **147**

Thorburn, Grant, 141–42

Thorburn seed company, 133, 141–42

Thornton, Phineas, 127, 131

*Thuja occidentalis*, 269

*Thuja orientalis*, 269

Thunberg, Peter Carl, 291

tile edging, 54–55

*Tinus laurifolius. See Viburnum tinus*

town houses, **84**, 88, 92

*Trachelospermum jasminoides*, 269

traveller's joy. *See* virgin's bower

*Travels in North America* (Hall), 14–15, 21

*Travels Through North and South Carolina, Georgia, East and West Florida* (Bartram), 75–76, 286

*Treatise on Horticulture* (Prince, W. R.), 290

*Treatise on the Cultivation of Ornamental Flowers, A* (Green), 130

*Treatise on the Theory and Practice of Landscape Gardening, A* (Downing), 51–52, 63, 67, 128–29, 131, 287

*Treatise on the Vine, A* (Prince, W. R.), 130

tree box (*Buxus sempervirens arborescens*), 70, 266

tree of heaven (*Ailanthus altissima*), 152–54, **153**, 266

trees, 62–65. *See also* avenues; groves

Troup Hill Nursery, 143, 275, 289

trumpet honeysuckle (*Lonicera sempervirens*), 268

trumpet vine (trumpet creeper) (*Campsis radicans*), 169–70, **169**, 266

Trustee's Garden (Savannah, Ga.), 137–39

*Tsuga canadensis*, 269

tulip tree (*Liriodendron tulipifera*), 268

tulip tree (*Magnolia × soulangiana*), 227–28, **227**, 268

Turnbull, Martha Barrow, 118–20, 291–92, 293

Tuscaloosa, Ala., **51**, 107–9, **108**


*Ulmus alata*, 269

umbrella magnolia (*Magnolia tripetala*), 268


Vacherie, La., **43**, 58

Valley View (Bartow County, Ga.), 116–18, **117**

variegated laurel. *See* gold dust plant

varnish tree (*Firmiana simplex*), 189–90, **190**, 267

vegetable gardens, 8, 127

Venetian sumac (*Cotinus coggygria*), 182–83, **182**, 266

*Viburnum opulus* "sterile," 269

*Viburnum tinus*, 71, 257–59, **258**, 269

Vieux Carré (New Orleans, La.), 90–93

*View of the Cultivation of Fruit Trees, A* (Coxe), 130

*Vinca major*, 269

*Vinca minor*, 269

Vineland Nursery, 143–44

*Viola odorata*, **273**

Virginia creeper (*Parthenocissus quinquefolia*), 239–41, **240**, 268

Virginia rail fence, 67–68, **67**

Virginia virgin's bower. *See* virgin's bower

Virginian dogwood. *See* flowering dogwood

virgin's bower (*Clematis virginiana*), 179–80, **179**, 266

virgin's bower, fragrant (*Clematis flammula*), 178–79, **178**, 266

*Vitex agnus-castus*, 259–60, **259**, 269


walks, material for, 55

Wallace House (Onslow County, N.C.), **68**

Warder, John A., 69, 131

Washington, Miss., 285

water oak (*Quercus nigra*), 269

Watson, John, 136

wax myrtle (*Myrica cerifera*), 234–36, **235**, 268

wax tree of China (*Ligustrum lucidum*), 268

wedding vine (*Smilax lanceolata*), 251–52, **252**, 269

weeping willow (*Salix babylonica*), 269

*Weigela amablis. See Weigela florida*

*Weigela florida*, 260–61, **261**, 269

*Weigela japonica. See Weigela florida*

*Weigela rosea. See Weigela florida*

white bay. *See* sweetbay

white cedar (*Thuja occidentalis*), 269
white mulberry (*Morus alba*), 268
white pine (*Pinus strobus*), 268
White, William Nathaniel, 127, 131, 292
wig tree. *See* smoke tree
wild honeysuckle (*Azalea nudiflorum*), 158–59, **159**, 266
wild olive. *See* cherry laurel
wild orange. *See* cherry laurel
willow oak (*Quercus phellos*), 269
winged elm (*Ulmus alata*), 269
winter honeysuckle (*Lonicera fragrantissima*), 218–19, **219**, 268
winter jasmine (*Jasminum nudiflorum*), 209–10, **209**, 267
winterberry (*Ilex verticillata*), 267
wintersweet (*Chimonanthus praecox*), 266
wire fencing, 69
*Wisteria floribunda*, 269
*Wisteria frutescens*, 261–62, **262**, 269
*Wisteria sinensis*, 263–64, **263**, 269

wood edging, 55
woodbine, American. *See* Virginia creeper
worm fence, 67–68, **67**

yaupon holly (*Ilex vomitoria*), 47, 53–54, 69, 205–7, **206**, 267
yellow anise (*Illicium parviflorum*), 207–8, **207**, 267
yellow flowered magnolia (*Magnolia acuminata cordata*), 268
yellow jessamine (*Gelsemium sempervirens*), 193–94, **193**, 267
yellow poplar (*Liriodendron tulipifera*), 268
yew, common (English) (*Taxus baccata*), 269
*Yucca aloifolia*, 269
*Yucca filamentosa*, 264–65, **264**, 269
*Yucca gloriosa*, 269
yulan magnolia (*Magnolia denudata*), 222–23, **223**, 268

zigzag fence, 67–68, **67**

# ILLUSTRATION CREDITS

Pages 1 and 9. Courtesy of Georgia Department of Archives and History: P. Thornton Marye Drawings, ac 52–101.

Page 2. The LuEsther T. Mertz Library of the New York Botanical Garden, Bronx, New York.

Page 4. From Richard N. Current, T. Harry Williams, Frank Freidel, and Alan Brinkley's *American History: A Survey*, 7th ed., © 1987, Alfred A. Knopf. Reproduced with permission of The McGraw-Hill Companies, New York, New York.

Page 5. *Ile Copal* by Marie Adrien Persac. Private collection.

Page 7. Photograph from Library of Congress, Prints and Photographs Division.

Page 8. Photograph by author.

Page 10. Image from Library of Congress, Prints and Photographs Division.

Page 12. Courtesy of Georgia Department of Archives and History: P. Thornton Marye Drawings, ac 52–101.

Page 14. Courtesy of Historic Charleston Foundation, Charleston, South Carolina.

Page 15. A Garden in Charleston, from William Bryant's *Picturesque America*, vol. 2 (1874). Author's collection.

Page 17. From *Encyclopedie Artistique Documentaire de la Plante*. Courtesy of the Cherokee Garden Library, Atlanta History Center, Atlanta, Georgia.

Page 21. Author's collection.

Page 22. From François Pierre Chaumeton's *Flore médicale* (1814–1820). Courtesy of Hunt Institute of Botanical Documentation, Carnegie Mellon University, Pittsburgh, Pennsylvania.

Page 24. Private collection.

Page 28. Courtesy of The Museum of Mobile, Mobile, Alabama.

Page 29. From *Appleton's Journal of Literature, Science, and Art* (1869). Courtesy of Charleston Library Society, Charleston, South Carolina.

Page 31. Photograph from Library of Congress, Prints and Photographs Division.

Page 36. Courtesy of The Historic New Orleans Collection, accession no. 1947.20.

Page 38. From Risso and Poiteau's *Histoire naturelle des orangers* . . . (1818–1822). Courtesy of Hunt Institute for Botanical Documentation, Carnegie Mellon University, Pittsburgh, Pennsylvania.

Page 40. Photograph from Library of Congress, Prints and Photographs Division.

Page 41. Author's collection.

Page 43. Photograph by Alan Nyiri.

Page 44. Plan from Library of Congress, Prints and Photographs Division.

Pages 46 and 63. Courtesy of Georgia Department of Archives and History: P. Thornton Marye Drawings, ac 52–101.

Page 48. Photograph by author.

Page 49. Courtesy of Cherokee Garden Library, Atlanta History Center, Atlanta, Georgia.

Page 51. Prepared by author based on original sketch and documentation by George Stritikus.

Page 53. Courtesy of San Francisco Plantation, Garyville, Louisiana.

Page 54. Photograph by author.

Page 55. Courtesy of the Cherokee Garden Library, Atlanta History Center, Atlanta, Georgia.

Pages 56–7. Courtesy of Boone Hall Plantation, Mt. Pleasant, South Carolina.

Page 58. Photograph © Richard Cheek for the Garden Club of Virginia.

Page 60. Colonial Williamsburg Foundation, Williamsburg, Virginia.

Page 61. *Faye-Webster Plantation* by Marie Adrien Persac (1823–1873). From the Collection of the LSU Museum of Art, Baton Rouge, Louisiana. Donated by the Friends of the LSU Museum of Art.

Page 62. Courtesy of the South Caroliniana Library, Columbia, South Carolina.

Page 64. Photograph by author.

Page 66 (top). Courtesy of the Virginia Historical Society, Richmond, Virginia.

Page 66. Courtesy of Rod Smith.

Page 67. Photograph by author.

Page 68. Courtesy of Onslow County Museum, Richlands, North Carolina.

Page 70. Author's collection.

Page 72. Photograph by author.

Page 73. Photograph by author.

Page 75. Photograph by author.

Page 76. Collection of the author.

Page 78. Photograph by author.

Pages 81 and 104. Courtesy of the Georgia Department of Archives and History: P. Thornton Marye Drawings, ac 52–101.

Page 83. Collection of the author.

Page 84. Photograph by author.

Pages 85 and 146. From Loutrel Briggs, *Charleston Gardens* (1951). Reproduced with permission of Janet B. Tantum.

Page 87. Author's collection.

Page 88. Plans prepared by the author based on original drawings by Clermont Lee, Savannah, Georgia.

Page 89. Photograph by author.

Page 90. Author's collection.

Page 91. Courtesy of New Orleans Notarial Archives, Plan Book 64, Folio 27.

Page 92. Plan by author based on sketch by Nathan C. Curtis (1933). Photograph courtesy of Tulane University Library, Louisiana Collection, New Orleans, Louisiana.

Page 94. Photograph from Library of Congress, Prints and Photographs Division.

Page 96. Courtesy of New Orleans Notarial Archives, Plan Book 97, Folio 18.

Page 97. Photograph by Van Jones Martin.

Page 99. Photograph by author based on 1940 sketch plan.

Page 100. Courtesy of the South Caroliniana Library. Columbia, South Carolina.

Page 101. Plan prepared by author based on drawings by Robert E. Marvin and Associates.

Page 102. Photograph by author.

Page 103. Courtesy of Hargrette Rare Book and Manuscript Library, University of Georgia Libraries, Athens, Georgia.

Page 105. Courtesy of the F. C. Johnson, III, Collection, Troup County Archives, LaGrange, Georgia.

Page 106. From the Garden Club of America's *The Gardens of Colony and State*, vol. 2 (1934). Reproduced with the permission of The Garden Club of America.

Page 107. Photograph by author.

Page 108. Courtesy of the Tuscaloosa County Preservation Society, Tuscaloosa, Alabama.

Page 110 (top). Photograph from Library of Congress, Prints and Photographs Division.

Page 110. Collection of the author.

Page 111. Garden plans prepared by author.

Page 112. Plan prepared by author based on drawings by A. T. S. Stoney and Garrow and Associates, Inc.

Page 114. Photograph from Library of Congress, Prints and Photographs Division.

Page 115. Photograph by author.

Page 116. Plan prepared by author.

Page 117 (top). Photograph by author.

Pages 117 and 126. Courtesy of Georgia Department of Archives and History: P. Thornton Marye Drawings, ac 52–101.

Page 119 (top). Photograph by author.

Page 119. Plan prepared by author.

Page 120. Courtesy of The Historic New Orleans Collection, accession no. 2000.79.86.

Page 121 and 135. From J. Frazer Smith's *Plantation Houses and Mansions of the Old South* (1993). Courtesy of Dover Publications, Inc.

Pages 122 and 125. Courtesy of Georgia Department of Archives and History: P. Thornton Marye Drawings, ac 52–101.

Page 123. Courtesy of Jay Edwards and Marcel Boyer.

Page 128. University of South Carolina Press, Columbia, South Carolina.

Page 129. Courtesy of the Cherokee Garden Library, Atlanta History Center, Atlanta, Georgia.

Page 130. Courtesy of the Cherokee Garden Library, Atlanta History Center, Atlanta, Georgia.

Page 132. Courtesy of the Cherokee Garden Library, Atlanta History Center, Atlanta, Georgia.

Page 134. Courtesy the South Caroliniana Library, Columbia, South Carolina.

Page 137. Photograph by author.

Page 138. Author's collection.

Page 140. Louisiana State Museum, New Orleans, Louisiana.

Page 141. Photograph by author.

Page 142. Photograph by author.

Page 144. Courtesy of the Cherokee Garden Library, Atlanta History Center, Atlanta, Georgia.

Page 147. Thomas County Historical Society, Thomasville, Georgia.

Page 148. Courtesy of W. Reaves McCall.

Page 150. Author's collection.

Pages 153–273. Photographs by author.

Page 274. From Pierre Joseph Redouté's *Les Roses* (1817–1824). Courtesy of Hunt Institute of Botanical Documentation, Carnegie Mellon University, Pittsburgh, Pennsylvania.

Page 277. Photograph by author.